DOCUMENTS ON
THE LAWS OF WAR

I0887574

DOCUMENTS ON THE LAWS OF WAR

Edited by

ADAM ROBERTS
M.A. (Oxford)

and

RICHARD GUELFF
B.A. (Yale), M.Sc. (London),
J.D. (S. California), LL.B. (Cambridge)

CLARENDON PRESS · OXFORD
1982

Oxford University Press, Walton Street, Oxford OX2 6DP
London Glasgow New York Toronto
Delhi Bombay Calcutta Madras Karachi
Kuala Lumpur Singapore Hong Kong Tokyo
Nairobi Dar es Salaam Cape Town
Melbourne Auckland
and associate companies in
Beirut Berlin Ibadan Mexico City

Published in the United States by
Oxford University Press, New York

© Adam Roberts and Richard Guelff 1982

All rights reserved. No part of this publication may be reproduced,
stored in a retrieval system, or transmitted, in any form or by any means,
electronic, mechanical, photocopying, recording, or otherwise, without
the prior permission of Oxford University Press

British Library Cataloguing in Publication Data
Documents on the laws of war.
    1. War (International law) — History
    I. Roberts, Adam   II. Guelff, Richard
    341.6'09   JX4508
    ISBN 0–19–876117–1
    ISBN 0–19–876118–X Pbk

Library of Congress Cataloging in Publication Data
Main entry under title:
Documents on the laws of war.
    Bibliography: p.
    Includes index
    1. War (International law)   I. Roberts, Adam.
II. Guelff, Richard, 1950–
JX4505.D62   341.6   81–14212
ISBN 0–19–876117–1   AACR2
ISBN 0–19–876118–X (pbk.)

Typeset by Anne Joshua Associates (Oxford)

Printed in Great Britain
at the University Press, Oxford
by Eric Buckley
Printer to the University

For Captain Pierre Henri Guelff, SC, USN

Acknowledgements

We could not have prepared this book at all without incurring many debts of gratitude. While collaborating on this project, both of us were on the teaching staff of the London School of Economics and Political Science, where many people, especially in the departments of International Relations and Law, made it possible for us to carry out this work.

In London, we relied heavily on the excellent library of the Institute of Advanced Legal Studies; and at LSE we used extensively the international law collection in the British Library of Political and Economic Science.

In Geneva, our project received much encouragement and expert assistance from many people. First and foremost, from the International Committee of the Red Cross, whose library contains many materials not obtainable elsewhere, and whose legal department gave much help and advice: we are particularly grateful for the help given over a long period by Dr Hans-Peter Gasser, Head of the Legal Division, and by Bruno Zimmermann, Member of the Legal Division. We also received generous encouragement and advice from Dr Jiri Toman of the Institut Henry-Dunant, who himself has collaborated on an extremely useful comprehensive work in this field. We also used the resources of the libraries of the Institut Henry-Dunant, the Graduate Institute of International Studies, and the United Nations.

We received further advice from Julian Perry Robinson of the Science Policy Research Unit of the University of Sussex.

The Depositaries of the various international agreements contained in this book were particularly helpful. The foreign ministries of France, United Kingdom, the Netherlands and Switzerland, the Treaty Section of the UN, and the Office of International Standards and Legal Affairs of UNESCO, all provided very full information and answered many queries.

Our greatest debt is to those who typed the editorial material in this book, which involved a seemingly endless series of drafts and revisions: this work was done, over and above all their other tasks, mainly by Elizabeth Leslie, Anjum Orooj, Jane Harris, Sophie Ali, and Angela Kaufman.

To all those who helped, who are so many that it is impossible to name them all here, we owe deepest thanks. We take responsibility for any error.

We intend to revise and update this volume periodically, and any suggestions for such revisions may be sent to us care of the publisher.

April 1981   Adam Roberts
                                                               Richard Guelff

Contents

Principal Abbreviations

AJIL	*American Journal of International Law*
BFSP	*British and Foreign State Papers*
Cd., Cmd. & Cmnd.	Command Papers, laid by command of the Crown before UK Parliament
CTS	*Consolidated Treaty Series*, ed. Clive Parry
ICRC	International Committee of the Red Cross
LNTS	*League of Nations Treaty Series*
Martens NRG	G. F. Martens, *Nouveau Recueil Général de Traités*, published in several series
UK Misc.	UK Miscellaneous Papers
UKPP	UK *Parliamentary Papers (House of Commons and Command)*
UKTS	UK *Treaty Series*
UNTS	*United Nations Treaty Series*

Introduction by the Editors

This book is a comprehensive collection of documents and other basic factual information on the 'laws of war' — that is to say, on those aspects of international law which relate to the conduct of armed conflict and military occupations. We believe there has long been a need for such a volume in a convenient and accessible form. The need is particularly great in view of the conclusion of new agreements: the 1977 UN Environmental Convention, the two 1977 Geneva Protocols, and the 1981 UN Weapons Convention.

The focus of this book is on the laws of war as they are currently applicable. Hence, we have included three main kinds of item: (1) the texts of international agreements which are formally in force today; (2) detailed lists of the states which are parties to the various international agreements; and (3) certain texts which, while not themselves constituting formal international agreements, are none the less an authoritative exposition of the law and have clear contemporary relevance.

THE TERM 'LAWS OF WAR'

The term 'laws of war' is taken in this volume as referring only to the rules governing the actual conduct of armed conflict (*jus in bello*) and not to the rules governing the resort to armed conflict (*jus ad bellum*). For most purposes, *jus ad bellum* can legitimately be regarded as a separate question meriting separate attention. The reason for this lies in the cardinal principle that *jus in bello* applies in cases of armed conflict whether the conflict is lawful or unlawful in its inception under *jus ad bellum*.

The term 'laws of war' is a well-recognized term of art, and not one of absolute precision. The application of the laws of war does not depend upon the recognition of the existence of a formal state of 'war', but (with certain qualifications) comprehends situations of armed conflict and military occupation in general, whether formally recognized as 'war' or not. This has come to be reflected in the terminology of the most recent documents, in which the term 'war' has been superseded by 'armed conflict', 'armed hostility', or other comparable terms. Although the term 'laws of armed conflict' may therefore be more precise, the 'laws of war' is widely used and understood.[1]

THE DIFFERENT SOURCES OF THE LAW

The idea that the conduct of armed conflicts is governed by rules appears to have been found in almost all societies, without geographical limitation.[2]

The historical development of the laws of war has had an important impact on both the form and the content of the present law. While this volume focuses on the laws of war as they are currently applicable, a word about the historical background may be useful.

The regulation of armed conflict has occupied the attention of scholars, statesmen, and soldiers for thousands of years. The Greeks and Romans customarily observed certain humanitarian principles which have become fundamental rules of the contemporary laws of war.[3] During the Middle Ages, a law of arms was developed in Europe to govern discipline within armies as well as to regulate the conduct of hostilities.[4] As the body of international law began to develop in Europe, early writers (such as Legnano, Victoria, Belli, Ayala, Gentili, and Grotius)[5] gave priority to consideration of hostility in international relations. The work of Grotius, published during the Thirty Years War (1618-48), was inspired by the author's desire to ameliorate the practices witnessed during that war. It has since come to be regarded as perhaps the first systematic treatment of international law, and one in which the laws of war played a principal part. Over this period, the practice of states led to the gradual emergence of customary principles regarding

---

[1] The International Committee of the Red Cross (ICRC) has increasingly used the term 'international humanitarian law applicable in armed conflicts'. This term has found its way into some international agreements such as the 1977 *Final Act of the Diplomatic Conference on the Reaffirmation and Development of International Humanitarian Law Applicable in Armed Conflicts* in connection with 1977 Geneva Protocols I and II.

[2] For example, see S. V. Viswanatha, *International Law in Ancient India*, Longmans Green, Bombay, 1925, pp. 108-200; Emmanuel Bello, *African Customary Humanitarian Law*, Oyez, London, and ICRC, Geneva, 1980, pp. 1-62; and Majid Khadduri, *War and Peace in the Law of Islam*, Johns Hopkins Press, Baltimore, Maryland, [1955], pp. 83-137.

[3] See Coleman Phillipson, *The International Law and Custom of Ancient Greece and Rome*, Macmillan, London, 1911, vol. II, pp. 166-384.

[4] See Maurice Keen, *The Laws of War in the Late Middle Ages*, Routledge and Kegan Paul, London, 1965.

[5] Giovanni da Legnano, *De Bello, de Represaliis et de Duello*, Bologna, 1477; Franciscus de Victoria, *Relectiones Theologicae*, Lyons, 1557; Pierino Belli, *De Re Militari et Bello Tractatus*, Venice, 1563; Balthazar Ayala, *De Jure et Officiis Bellicis et Disciplina Militari*, Douay, 1582; Alberico Gentili, *Commentationes de Jure Belli*, London, 1588-9, and *De Jure Belli, libri tres*, Hanau, 1598; and Hugo Grotius, *De Jure Belli ac Pacis, libri tres*, Paris, 1625.

the conduct of armed hostilities. These principles were preserved not only in the writings of scholars but also through the contribution of soldiers and the conduct of armed forces in the field.

International Agreements

Although the foundation of the contemporary legal regime is thus very old, it was only in the second half of the nineteenth century that the customary principles began to be codified in particular binding multilateral agreements. Since that time, such international agreements have taken the form of declarations, conventions, and protocols. The major agreements are mentioned below.

The first such agreement was the 1856 Paris Declaration on maritime war. Other agreements followed: the 1864 Geneva Convention on wounded and sick, and the 1868 St. Petersburg Declaration on explosive projectiles. The 1868 Additional Articles on wounded, and the 1874 Brussels Declaration on the laws and customs of war, were signed but did not enter into force.

The process of codification accelerated at the turn of the century. The First Hague Peace Conference, held in 1899, led to the conclusion of three conventions (two of which dealt with the laws of land and maritime war) and three declarations (relating to particular means of conducting warfare). Following the First Hague Peace Conference, states adopted the 1904 Hague Convention on hospital ships and the 1906 Geneva Convention on wounded and sick. The Second Hague Peace Conference, held in 1907, led to the conclusion of thirteen conventions (ten of which dealt with the laws of land and maritime war) and one declaration (relating to a particular method of conducting warfare). While no single conference since the Second Hague Peace Conference has succeeded in formulating as many conventions concerning the laws of war, the process of codification continued, with varying degrees of success. In 1909 the London Declaration on naval war was signed, but did not enter into force.

At the conclusion of the First World War the 1919 Treaty of Versailles as well as other peace treaties expressly recognized that certain methods of conducting warfare were prohibited. In 1922 the Treaty of Washington on submarine and gas warfare was signed, but did not enter into force. The 1925 Geneva Protocol on gas and bacteriological warfare, the 1929 Geneva Convention on wounded and sick, the 1929 Geneva Convention on prisoners of war, the 1930 London Treaty on naval armaments and warfare, and the 1936 London Procès-Verbal on submarine warfare were all signed in this inter-war period, and all of these agreements entered into force.

After the Second World War additional international agreements were concluded. In 1948 the UN Genocide Convention was adopted. Particular progress in codification was made at the 1949 Geneva diplomatic conference with the adoption of the four 1949 Geneva Conventions (relating to wounded and sick; wounded, sick, and shipwrecked; prisoners of war; and civilians). Further codification continued thereafter, with the 1954 Hague Convention and Protocol on the protection of cultural property, and the 1968 UN Convention on statutory limitations regarding war crimes. The most recent codification includes the 1977 UN Convention on the hostile use of environmental modification techniques; the two 1977 Geneva Protocols on victims of armed conflicts; and the 1981 UN Convention on specific conventional weapons.

Customary Law

Despite the importance of international agreements in the contemporary development of the law, any work concerning the laws of war which is limited to international agreements runs the risk of distorting not only the form but also the substance of the law. As noted above, the present laws of war emerged as customary rules from the practice of states. The codification of rules into particular agreements which began to occur in the second half of the nineteenth century did not displace customary law. During the very process of codification it was recognized that much of the law continued to exist in the form of unwritten customary principles. This was expressly enunciated in what has come to be known as the Martens Clause, which first appeared in the Preamble to 1899 Hague Convention II:

> Until a more complete code of the laws of war is issued, the high contracting Parties think it right to declare that in cases not included in the Regulations adopted by them, populations and belligerents remain under the protection and empire of the principles of international law, as they result from the usages established between civilised nations, from the laws of humanity, and the requirements of the public conscience.[6]

The Martens Clause is not merely of historical interest. Although there has been a great deal of subsequent codification of the laws of war, a significant part of the law continues to be in the form of customary principles. A common article in each of the four 1949 Geneva Conventions borrows from the very terminology of the Martens Clause in reaffirming that even if a party denounces the Convention, this:

[6] For the version of the Martens Clause which appeared in 1907 Hague Convention IV see below, p. 45.

shall in no way impair the obligations which the Parties to the conflict shall remain bound to fulfil by virtue of the principles of the law of nations, as they result from the usages established among civilized peoples, from the laws of humanity and the dictates of the public conscience.[7]

Perhaps the most fundamental customary principle is that the right of belligerents to adopt means of injuring the enemy is not unlimited. This notion, which clearly rests at the very foundation of the laws of war, was incorporated in the 1874 Brussels Declaration and the 1880 Oxford Manual, and was formally codified in 1899 Hague Convention II and 1907 Hague Convention IV.

Three general customary principles seek to delineate legal limits on belligerent conduct: the principle of military necessity, the principle of humanity, and what is still called the principle of chivalry. The principle of military necessity provides that, strictly subject to the principles of humanity and chivalry, a belligerent is justified in applying the amount and kind of force necessary to achieve the complete submission of the enemy at the earliest possible moment and with the least expenditure of time, life, and resources. The principle of humanity prohibits the employment of any kind or degree of force not actually necessary for military purposes. The principle of chivalry denounces and forbids resort to dishonourable means, expedients, or conduct in the course of armed hostility. All three principles are integrally related and require an appropriate balance to be struck. In general, the law which has been codified is the product of such balancing; consequently, arguments of military necessity cannot be used as pretexts for evading applicable provisions of the law. In general, military necessity has been rejected as a defence for acts forbidden by the customary and conventional laws of war because such laws have, in any case, been developed with consideration for the concept of military necessity. The only exception to this arises with provisions which expressly contain the specific qualification that particular rules are only applicable if military circumstances permit. Where new law is in the process of being created, or where certain long-established general terms such as 'unnecessary suffering' are being interpreted, the balancing process continues to be applicable.

In general, customary international law is binding on all states. Principles of customary law may come to be codified in a particular agreement: in such a case, the principles remain binding on all states

---

[7] 1949 Geneva Convention I, Article 63; Convention II, Article 62; Convention III, Article 142; and Convention IV, Article 158. The same principle was reaffirmed in 1977 Geneva Protocol I, Article 1; 1977 Geneva Protocol II, Preamble; and 1981 UN Weapons Convention, Preamble.

as customary law, but those parties to the agreement are further bound through their treaty obligations. Customary law may also develop to bring the substance of pre-existing written agreements within its ambit; in such a case, the particular agreement (which is already binding upon all states which are parties to it) then becomes generally binding upon all states as customary law. Perhaps the best recognized example of this is 1907 Hague Convention IV. In its 1946 Judgment, the International Military Tribunal at Nuremberg stated that the provisions of the Convention were declaratory of the laws and customs of war.[8] In 1948 the International Military Tribunal for the Far East sitting in Tokyo expressed a similar view.[9]

Although the primary sources of the law are custom and treaties, the other areas in which evidence of the law may be found should not be ignored. They are discussed under separate headings below.

Judicial Decisions

The decisions of international and national judicial bodies, possessing the necessary jurisdiction to render legally binding decisions, have long played an important role in the clarification and development of the law. The International Military Tribunals which sat in Nuremberg and Tokyo following the Second World War are the best known, but in fact the overwhelming majority of those accused of committing crimes against international law during the Second World War were tried (during and after the war) by national courts or military courts established by occupying states. In addition, some members of armed forces were tried by their own national military courts. If attention is frequently focused on Second World War cases, it should be noted that in conflicts both before and since that time there have been very many judicial decisions relating to the laws of war. While the interpretation of the laws of war embodied in the decisions of these disparate tribunals has by no means always been consistent, the majority of such decisions have played an invaluable role in applying the law to particular circumstances, in thereby clarifying it, and in stimulating further efforts at codification. There is a particularly large number of important decisions relating to those parts of the law which govern military occupations.

---

[8] See the extract from the 1946 Nuremberg Judgment which includes this statement, below, p. 156.

[9] International Military Tribunal for the Far East, Judgment delivered 4–12 November 1948, duplicated transcript, p. 30.

National Manuals of Military Law

The most famous early example of a national manual outlining the laws of war for the use of armed forces, and one of the first attempts to codify the laws of land warfare, was the 1863 'Instructions for the Government of Armies of the United States in the Field' prepared by Dr Francis Lieber of Columbia University. This manual, which came to be known as the 'Lieber Code', was issued to the Union Army on 24 April 1863, and was applied by the forces of the United States during the American Civil War. It became the model for many other national manuals (for example, those of the Netherlands in 1871, France in 1877, Serbia in 1879, Spain in 1882, Portugal in 1890, and Italy in 1896), and it prepared the way for the calling of the 1874 Brussels Conference and the two Hague Peace Conferences of 1899 and 1907. National manuals have continued to be published to the present day and they frequently serve as the closest link which the laws of war maintain with the belligerent armed forces in the field.

Although such national manuals may also have some function in providing evidence of the law, they are in general bound to be viewed with some caution. For example, during the case of *USA* v. *Wilhelm List et al.* (the 'Hostages Case') following the Second World War, the defence attempted to counter the argument that superior orders are not a defence to an international law crime (one of the key legal bases of the Nuremberg Tribunals) by successfully showing that both the British and the American military manuals used during the Second World War had favoured obeying superior orders. The US Military Tribunal did not consider the statements in these two military manuals as conclusive on this point, and stated in its judgment:

. . . army regulations are not a competent source of international law . . . It is possible, however, that such regulations, as they bear upon a question of custom and practice in the conduct of war, might have evidentiary value, particularly if the applicable portions had been put into general practice.[10]

Writings of Publicists

The writings of distinguished legal specialists (often called 'publicists') on the subject of the laws of war have been cited frequently as evidence of where the law stands on particular issues. Traditionally, the weight such writings have been given has depended on the stature of the legal specialist as well as the quality of the reasoning.

[10] *Trials of War Criminals Before the Nuernberg Military Tribunals*, US Government Printing Office, Washington, D.C., 1950, vol. XI, p. 1237.

The general importance of such writings has not decreased despite the fact that formal codifications have increased. Indeed, the importance of such writings has perhaps increased owing to the evident need to clarify the greater number of codified provisions, to relate the provisions of the various codifications to each other and to other sources of law, and to consider other problems. The attempt to interpret the bare provisions of codified agreements without the benefit of such interpretative writings may lead to an inaccurate view of the law. None the less, legal specialists may disagree, and, particularly in areas of controversy in the law, reliance upon the writings of a single specialist (or even a limited number of specialists) may be hazardous. Various writings of publicists which interpret different aspects of the laws of war are listed in the bibliography.

The Role of Various International Bodies

Non-governmental organizations, particularly those consisting of legal specialists, have played an important role in the clarification as well as development of the laws of war. For example, the Institute of International Law prepared both the 1880 Oxford Manual of Land War and the 1913 Oxford Manual of Naval War, and in 1971 adopted a resolution on the application of the laws of war to United Nations forces. In 1923 a Commission of Jurists meeting in The Hague drafted the Hague Rules of Aerial Warfare. In 1938 the International Law Association adopted a draft convention for the protection of the civilian population in time of war. The above are only some of the better-known expositions by such bodies. Particular mention should be made of the International Committee of the Red Cross (ICRC), which was founded, at the 1863 Geneva International Conference, with the express purpose of reducing the horror of warfare. Since that time, the ICRC has distinguished itself through its involvement with various investigations, reports, draft rules, conferences of government experts, and diplomatic conferences relating to humanitarian law. The ICRC has been particularly known for its work relating to the preparation of draft texts of what later became the Geneva Conventions of 1864, 1906, 1929, and 1949, and the Geneva Protocols of 1977. In addition, in 1970 the International Institute of Humanitarian Law was founded in San Remo by legal specialists and, since that time, has organized various conferences, meetings, and seminars of specialists, and has established several commissions relating to the laws of war.

Public international organizations, such as the League of Nations and the United Nations, have also played an important role in clarifying and developing the laws of war. Certain conferences, organized under the auspices of such organizations, have led to the conclusion of agreements on the laws of war. For example, the 1925 Geneva Protocol on gas warfare was adopted at a conference held under the auspices of the League of Nations; and the 1981 Convention on specific conventional weapons was adopted at a conference convened by the UN. Such organizations have prepared various drafts of agreements on the laws of war. For example, drafts of the 1948 Genocide Convention were prepared by the UN Secretary-General and the UN Economic and Social Council; and drafts of the 1977 Environmental Convention were prepared by the Conference of the Committee on Disarmament. Such organizations have adopted various resolutions on the laws of war. For example, in 1938 the League of Nations Assembly unanimously adopted a resolution on the law of air warfare; in 1946 the UN General Assembly unanimously adopted a resolution affirming the principles of international law recognized by the Charter and Judgment of the International Military Tribunal at Nuremberg; in 1947 the UN General Assembly adopted a resolution directing the International Law Commission (a subsidiary organ of the General Assembly) to prepare a draft code relating to the Nuremberg principles; and in 1948 the UN General Assembly adopted a resolution inviting the ILC to look into the feasibility of establishing an international criminal court in which cases involving the alleged commission of war crimes could be heard. Such organizations have also prepared various reports on the laws of war. For example, in 1950 the ILC adopted a formulation of the Nuremberg principles; and in 1969 the UN Secretary-General prepared his first report on respect for human rights in armed conflict.

Although regulations, draft rules, resolutions, and reports adopted by various international bodies may not possess legally binding force *per se*, they have played, and continue to play, an important role in clarifying the content of pre-existing customary or conventional law, and in influencing the development of the law.

APPLICATION TO STATES

In analysing the application of the laws of war to states, several distinctions should be drawn.

First, a distinction exists between an agreement generally entering into force and an agreement entering into force for particular parties. An agreement generally enters into force when, according to its terms, certain conditions are fulfilled (for example, when a certain number of signatory states have ratified the agreement). Hence, until such conditions are fulfilled, the agreement is not formally in force even among states which have already ratified the agreement. Once the agreement generally enters into force, it is binding on all those states which have ratified the agreement, and becomes binding on all subsequent parties according to its terms (for example, when a signatory state deposits its instrument of ratification or when a non-signatory state deposits its instrument of accession).

Second, a distinction exists between an agreement entering into force as between parties and being applicable in a particular conflict. In general, the binding force of agreements is limited to states parties, and then only to the extent delineated by the terms of the agreement. For example, most of the earlier international agreements on the laws of war (such as the 1868 St. Petersburg Declaration, the 1899 Hague Declarations, the 1899 Hague Convention II, the 1906 Geneva Convention, and the 1907 Hague Conventions) contain a 'general participation clause', whereby the agreement is applicable only if all of the belligerents in the conflict are parties to the agreement. If one belligerent is not a party to the agreement, it is not technically applicable even though it has generally entered into force. In analysing the technical application of international agreements on the laws of war during armed hostilities, reference must therefore be made to any 'general participation clause' in conjunction with the identity of states parties and belligerents. However, reference must also be made to whether or not the agreement (or a part thereof) has come to be considered as codifying customary international law. To the extent that any international agreement (or a part thereof) embodies customary international law, it is binding upon all states whether or not it contains a 'general participation clause'. 1907 Hague Convention IV is a case in point. More recent agreements on the laws of war have avoided the 'general participation clause'. Some agreements, like the 1949 Geneva Conventions, remain binding as between parties even if one of the belligerents is a non-party. Moreover, they are applicable to any non-party which accepts and applies the provisions of the agreement.

APPLICATION TO INDIVIDUALS AS WELL AS STATES

Where the laws of war are applicable in a particular armed conflict, they are binding not only upon states as such but also upon individuals, and in particular, the individual members of armed forces. The notion that individuals bear direct responsibility for violations of the laws of war is one which arose with the development of the law. The first major attempt to punish war crimes took place following the First World War, and the legal ramifications of individual responsibility began to receive their most famous expression in the course of the Second World War, during which Allied governments issued several individual and joint declarations relating to the punishment of war criminals.

The first inter-Allied declaration was signed in London in 1942 by the representatives of several Allied European governments, and stated that the punishment of war crimes was one of the principal war aims of the Allied governments. In 1943, the Moscow Declaration stated the intention of the Allied governments to adjudicate and punish war criminals in the countries in which the crimes were committed, with the exception that major war criminals (whose offences had no particular geographical location) would be dealt with by a joint decision of the Allied governments. In the same year, the London Conference established the United Nations War Crimes Commission to investigate war crimes, and the Commission first met in 1944. In 1945, Allied governments met in London to implement the Moscow Declaration, and the result was an agreement relating to the prosecution and punishment of the major war criminals of the European Axis powers. The agreement provided for the establishment of an International Military Tribunal (eventually convened at Nuremberg) in accordance with a charter, annexed to the agreement, which set forth principles to be applied by the Tribunal in reaching its judgment. The Nuremberg Charter recognized that individual responsibility applied to 'crimes against peace' (violations of *jus ad bellum*), 'war crimes', and 'crimes against humanity' (both the latter comprehending violations of *jus in bello*). While the Charter recognized that the defence of superior orders could operate as a mitigating factor in the determination of punishment, such a plea would not remove individual responsibility. The Judgment of the Nuremberg Tribunal, delivered in 1946, pronounced its provisions relating to individual responsibility to be declaratory of customary international law.

With regard to the war in the Pacific, the 1945 Potsdam Proclamation stated the intention of the Allied governments to prosecute and punish war criminals. In 1946, the Far Eastern Commission delegated to the Supreme Allied Commander the power to appoint special international military courts for the trial of war criminals in the Far East. In the same year, the Supreme Allied Commander issued a proclamation establishing an International Military Tribunal for the Far East, and approved the Charter of the Tribunal, which was convened in Tokyo. The Tokyo Charter and the Judgment of the Tokyo Tribunal, delivered in 1948, affirmed the provisions of the Nuremberg Charter and Judgment relating to individual responsibility.

Despite the criticisms which some have raised with respect to the

International Military Tribunals, the notion that individual responsibility is a part of customary international law remains unchallenged.

APPLICATION IN NON-INTERNATIONAL CONFLICTS

The distinction between international and non-international armed conflicts, which is perhaps easier to draw in theory than in practice, has played an important role in the development and application of the law. Before the mid-twentieth century, the principal international agreements governing the laws of war applied only to armed conflict between states and had no formal bearing (according to their specific terms) on non-international armed conflicts. However, certain regional agreements (such as the 1928 Havana Convention on civil strife) related to internal conflicts. Also, customary international law provided that the laws of war might become applicable to a non-international conflict through the doctrine of 'recognition of belligerency'.

According to this doctrine, the government of a state in which an insurrection existed could recognize the belligerency of the insurgent faction, and the laws of war would thereby become applicable. A third state could also recognize the belligerency of the insurgent faction, and such state would then be subject to the rights and duties of neutrality embodied in the laws of war. The recognition of the belligerent status of insurgent forces by a third state did not imply recognition of that group as the legitimate sovereign, but only transformed the situation in terms of the application of the laws of war. Recognition of belligerency by the lawful government would not impose a legal obligation upon third states to do the same. Equally, the lawful government would not be legally bound by the decision of third states to recognize the belligerency of an insurgent faction, although such recognition by a number of third states might influence the legal government to take that action. Practical as well as legal difficulties could obviously arise when the legal government refused to recognize the belligerent status of a particular group with which it was engaged in armed conflict, even though such recognition had been granted by other states. Difficulties could also arise with the existence of contradictory points of view as to whether or not recognition of belligerency could be implied from certain acts of the legal government.

In general, the doctrine of recognition of belligerency appears to have fallen into decline. However, certain international agreements adopted since the mid-twentieth century have established a basic written regime for *jus in bello interno*, not dependent upon recognition of belligerency, which provides that certain fundamental humanitarian principles may be applicable in non-international armed conflicts. Common Article 3 of the four 1949 Geneva Conventions provides that in the case of an armed conflict not of an international character occurring in the territory of one of the parties to the Conventions, each party to the conflict shall be bound to apply, as a minimum, certain fundamental humanitarian provisions. By referring expressly to 'parties to the conflict', and not merely to states parties to the Convention, common Article 3 attempts to ensure that insurgents engaged in armed conflict against a lawful government would be bound to observe the same provisions as those which would bind the lawful government. However, common Article 3 is only applicable in cases where there is a genuine 'armed conflict' as distinct from riots, isolated or sporadic acts of violence, or other acts of a similar nature.

Article 19 of the 1954 Hague Cultural Property Convention provides for the application, in a non-international armed conflict, of at least those provisions of the Convention which relate to respect for cultural property. Again, the application of Article 19 depends upon the existence of an 'armed conflict'.

The 1977 Geneva Protocol II relating to non-international armed conflicts is intended to develop and supplement common Article 3 of the 1949 Geneva Conventions without modifying its existing conditions of application. Thus, it too depends upon the existence of an 'armed conflict'. The Protocol begins with a more extensive list of fundamental guarantees than those provided under common Article 3 of the 1949 Geneva Conventions, and proceeds thereafter to define those rights and duties, albeit in a rather rudimentary form.

In addition, insurgent forces may unilaterally declare their acceptance of at least certain aspects of the laws of war, such as the 1949 Geneva Conventions, and the laws of war may thereby be relevant to non-international armed conflicts.

PRACTICAL IMPACT OF THE LAWS OF WAR

Advocates of far-ranging proposals to secure the complete abolition of the use of armed force have often been sceptical of the apparent reformism of the approach underlying the laws of war, supporting instead a variety of ideas such as the complete legal prohibition of the use of force, the achievement of general and complete disarmament, pacifism, or a new international political order which may include world government. The underlying concept is not new in that plans for peace date from ancient times. Without addressing the value of any of these ideas, at present none of them seems likely either to abolish the numerous causes of conflict in the world, or to ensure that in all such conflicts as do occur, only non-violent methods of struggle are used. Therefore, the need to mitigate the worst effects of armed conflict, by attempting to maintain the idea that there are standards of civilization by which conduct may be judged, is likely to remain. The legal regime embodying these standards is by no means prejudicial to various proposals to limit the use of force, and may even contribute to the achievement of the broader objectives referred to above.

Those who suggest that the rules of warfare cannot be reconciled with existing fundamental rules governing the legality of the use of force (such as the 1928 Kellogg–Briand Pact and the 1945 UN Charter) neglect two important points. First, neither the Kellogg–Briand Pact nor the UN Charter embodies an absolute prohibition of the use of force. Second, and more important, the laws of war are applicable whether or not a particular armed conflict may be regarded as lawful under *jus ad bellum*. The value of the laws of war lies in the attempt to bring humanitarian considerations to bear, whatever the circumstances.

It is sometimes suggested that the laws of war make little practical difference to the conduct of armed conflicts and military occupations. Cicero's maxim *inter arma silent leges* (in war the law is silent) is often quoted. Such pessimistic views need to be taken seriously, reflecting as they do two sombre realities. First, war is by definition an exercise in violent coercion and is precisely characterized by the breakdown of certain legal norms and constraints. Second, the era in which the modern laws of war have largely developed, namely the last 100 years, has also seen extreme developments both in the conduct of war and in the types of weaponry. There have been all too many violations of the laws of war which have often involved appalling consequences, including the crippling and destruction of life and the devastation of property. It is not surprising that there is a widespread pessimism as to the role which the laws of war are able to play in governing the activities of statesmen and soldiers.

However, there is much evidence that the laws of war have exerted at least some influence on the conduct of armed hostilities. They have helped to bring about a degree of acceptance and observance of certain valuable basic ideas: for example, that prisoners of war are to have their lives spared and to be treated humanely; that a state may be entitled to be neutral *vis-à-vis* an armed conflict involving other states; that military occupation of another country's territory must be regarded as provisional, and involves duties as well as rights for the occupant; that certain places (e.g. hospitals) are not legitimate targets in warfare; that persons not taking an active part in a conflict (e.g. children) should be spared from the consequences as much as possible; and that torture is wrong.

Critics may argue that states involved in conflicts will always put their vital interests first, and the law will be violated if it clashes with those interests. But in fact the position is not nearly so simple. The law has been created by states with their general interests and the particular interests of their armed forces in mind. Thus it is not an abstract and external imposition on the international system, but rather a direct outgrowth of it.

The factors which lead states and armed forces involved in armed conflicts or occupations to comply with the law are complex. They include a need to be viewed as acting in accord with internationally agreed norms, or with ethical beliefs widely held within the state; a hope that compliance with the law will be reciprocated; and also a fear that if the law is violated, there may be adverse military consequences (such as reprisals, that is, otherwise illegal acts of retaliation carried out in response to illegal acts of warfare and intended to cause the enemy to comply with the law); adverse political consequences (such as loss of friends and allies); and also judicial consequences (trials, whether before national or international tribunals). Even if these factors do not work equally all of the time, or do not apply equally at all levels of decision-making, they are seldom wholly absent. At the very least, the law provides a standard of conduct which states need to consider in the formulation and implementation of their policies. This, in and of itself, may influence decisions in subtle but important ways.

In so far as the laws of war are complied with, this may arguably be due to the wide range of factors mentioned above rather than to the specific mechanisms for compliance which have been built into some of the international agreements contained in this volume. Yet the specific mechanisms should not be ignored. For example, the four 1949 Geneva Conventions contain extensive (albeit little used) provisions for the long-established diplomatic device of the 'protecting power' — that is, a state (or an impartial, humanitarian organization acting as a substitute) which is authorized by a belligerent state to carry out various duties in its interests in relation to an opposing state. In addition, the 1949 Geneva Conventions allow for activities (which have often included monitoring duties) by impartial, humanitarian organizations such as the International Committee of the Red Cross.

To say that the laws of war have had some practical impact is not to say that the state of the law itself is by any means satisfactory. The written laws of war contain manifest imperfections. First, the existence of different interpretations of various legal provisions may preclude a common understanding of existing law. For example, not only have states maintained different interpretations of certain provisions of the 1925 Geneva Protocol on gas warfare since the date of signature, but also some states have changed their positions over time. Second, many aspects of warfare and military occupation have been inadequately dealt with by the written law: for example, the cruelties of certain long-standing forms of hostilities, such as siege warfare. Technological developments in the methods of conducting war have increased the extent to which the written law is inadequate or absent. Although such developments have led to the codification of new law at various times, the ongoing nature of technological change may make such codification as exists vulnerable to the passage of time: for example, the principal reference in 1907 Hague Declaration (XIV) is to the use of balloons in air warfare. Even though certain general principles which have been codified (for example the prohibition of means of warfare causing unnecessary suffering) can be applied to new weapons, it has been extremely difficult to achieve any consensus in particular cases. However, the state of the law cannot be properly judged by referring to the written law alone. As noted above, the laws of war comprehend customary (as well as formally codified) law, and a significant part of the laws of war continues to be in the form of custom. Such customary law may assist in interpreting provisions of the written law, may address aspects of armed conflict and military occupation which have been inadequately dealt with by the written law, and may clarify the application of certain general principles (whether formally codified or not) to particular means of armed conflict and military occupation. Although customary law (created through state practice) may thereby strengthen the written legal regime, it should not be overlooked that state practice may also derogate from earlier written or customary law. If such state practice is widespread, the question would arise as to whether a new custom could be regarded as superseding the earlier law.

PRINCIPLES OF SELECTION IN THIS VOLUME

Documents Included

Although this volume is a collection of documents, it is not a documentary history. Emphasis is firmly placed on the laws of war which remain applicable today, and the content of the contemporary written legal regime is set forth in a relatively wide and representative variety of types of document. To facilitate easy reference, the documents are placed in chronological order.

Because of the central importance of binding international agreements in the contemporary law governing the conduct of armed conflict, we have made as complete a selection of this type of document as space permits. We have provided a complete and unabridged text of each international agreement. Any minor omissions (for example, most annexes) have been noted at the relevant point.

To ensure that attention is not focused exclusively on formally binding agreements, various other types of document are included where they may clarify some aspect of the laws of war: the 1923 Hague Rules of Air Warfare, extracts from the 1946 Judgment of the International Military Tribunal at Nuremberg, the 1971 resolution of the Institute of International Law on the application of the laws of war to UN forces, and the 1978 Red Cross fundamental rules of international humanitarian law applicable in armed conflicts. As with the international agreements, so with these documents (with the one exception of the Nuremberg Judgment) we have provided complete and unabridged texts.

Documents Omitted

Many types of document having an important bearing on the laws of war have been omitted for reasons of space. Some of the most notable types of document are referred to below.

Some multilateral agreements on the laws of war have been omitted in cases where their relevance is more historical than contemporary: for example, the 1899 and 1907 Hague Declarations on the discharge of projectiles and explosives from balloons.

Multilateral agreements on the laws of war which have been superseded by later agreements, so far as most or all of the states parties are concerned, have been omitted. For example, on the question of the laws of land warfare in general, 1907 Hague Convention IV was preceded by 1899 Hague Convention II; on the question of wounded and sick on land, 1949 Geneva Convention I was preceded by the 1864 Geneva Convention and its revisions of 1906 and 1929; on the question of wounded, sick and shipwrecked at sea, 1949 Geneva Convention II was preceded by 1899 Hague Convention III and 1907 Hague Convention X; and on the question of prisoners of war, 1949 Geneva Convention III was preceded by the 1929 Geneva Convention.

Regional agreements on the laws of war have been omitted. Such agreements include: the 1935 Roerich Pact on cultural property;

the 1937 Nyon Agreement on submarine warfare; the 1928 Havana Convention on maritime neutrality; the 1928 Havana Convention on duties and rights of states during civil strife, and its 1957 Protocol; and the 1938 Scandinavian Rules of Neutrality.

Agreements of an essentially bilateral character on the laws of war have been omitted: for example, the 1854 Washington Convention on the rights of neutrals at sea, signed by Russia and the USA.

Agreements relating to *jus ad bellum* (the law governing resort to armed conflict) have been omitted. Among the notable agreements of this type are 1899 Hague Convention I on the pacific settlement of disputes; 1907 Hague Convention I on the pacific settlement of disputes; 1907 Hague Convention II on the limitation of force in recovering contract debt; 1907 Hague Convention III on the opening of hostilities; the 1919 Covenant of the League of Nations; the 1928 General Treaty For the Renunciation of War as an Instrument of National Policy, otherwise known as the Kellogg-Briand Pact or the Pact of Paris; and the 1945 Charter of the United Nations.

Agreements relating to arms control and disarmament, including those with provisions on the demilitarization or neutralization of particular areas, have been omitted. Arms control and disarmament agreements do not expressly address the actual conduct of armed conflict; rather, they establish some controls over the production, testing, stockpiling, transfer or deployment of the weapons by which armed conflict might be conducted. For example, the 1972 Biological Weapons Convention prohibits the development, production, and stockpiling of certain weapons, rather than regulating their use in warfare *per se*. Such agreements may have considerable implications for the conduct of armed conflict, and their terms may remain applicable during situations of armed conflict and military occupation.

Agreements on general human rights have been omitted, but may be relevant to situations of armed conflict and occupation. For example, the 1966 International Covenant on Civil and Political Rights contains provisions which are expressly applicable in time of 'public emergency which threatens the life of the nation'; and the 1950 European Convention on Human Rights makes explicit reference to rights 'in time of war or other public emergency threatening the life of the nation'.

UN General Assembly resolutions relating to armed conflict have also been omitted. Among the better known are Resolution 95 (I) of 11 December 1946, 'Affirmation of the Principles of International Law Recognized by the Charter of the Nuremberg

Tribunal'; Resolution 1653 (XVI) of 24 November 1961, 'Declaration on the Prohibition of the Use of Nuclear and Thermo-nuclear Weapons'; and Resolution 2675 (XXV) of 9 December 1970, 'Basic Principles for the Protection of Civilian Populations in Armed Conflicts'.

Unilateral declarations made by states, national judicial decisions, national laws and regulations relating to the laws of war, and national manuals of military law have, despite their considerable importance, also been omitted.

FOOTNOTES

All footnotes in this volume are written by us and are not to be taken as being a formal part of the documents themselves.

THE PREFATORY NOTES

Each document in this volume is preceded by a prefatory note in which we have attempted to set forth the chain of events leading to the adoption of the document and, where relevant, other information. These prefatory notes are of an informal character, intended solely to put the documents in context. They are in no sense definitive legal commentaries.

In the case of binding international agreements, each prefatory note is followed by a list which includes the date of the original signature, the date of entry into force, the official Depositary, and the authentic (i.e. official) language or languages.

In addition, in respect of all documents we have listed the treaty collection or publication from which the document is reprinted. In cases where English is not one of the official languages of a document, we have used a translation. If there are several recognized English translations, we have compared them and have used the one which we consider to be the clearest and most faithful to the original. Finally, a partial list of other sources in which the document may be found is included: some of these contain useful further information, such as records or final acts of the conferences which adopted the document, or the texts of annexes omitted from this volume.

THE CONCLUDING NOTES

Each binding international agreement in this volume is followed by concluding notes which set forth: (i) an alphabetical list of states signing, ratifying, acceding or notifying succession to such agreement, with the respective dates; (ii) a figure for the total number of states included in the lists as having at any time become bound;

(iii) a note on entry into force for states parties; (iv) any subsequent denunciations of the agreement; and (v) any reservations, declarations, and objections. These concluding notes are based on information obtained from the official Depositaries, whether governments or international organizations. We have checked the information in various treaty series and other sources, and where any serious and unexplained discrepancy has appeared, we have raised it with the Depositary. Where a discrepancy continued to exist, we have used the information supplied by the Depositary unless compelling reasons suggested otherwise. We are grateful to the Depositaries for their painstaking responses to our numerous queries. The information in the concluding notes is up to date as of 1 January 1981. The complete texts of the concluding notes, as published here, have all been submitted to the respective Depositaries and checked by them.

Lists of States

The name of each state in these lists is in general derived from the name by which it was officially known at the time of its adherence to a particular international agreement. For example, following earlier agreements 'Siam' is listed, while following later ones 'Thailand' is listed. Thus, while we have relied heavily on the Depositaries for the information used in the lists, we have tried to resist the tendency of some of the Depositaries to modernize the names of states in their lists. In those rather few cases where we considered it useful, we have provided in parentheses some additional indentification of states: for example, 'Congo, Democratic Republic of (now Zaïre)'. However, for convenience we have used short versions of the names of many states: for example, 'Netherlands' rather than 'The Kingdom of The Netherlands'.

In the lists of states, we have included all those states which have at any time been recognized by Depositaries as signing or adhering. We have made no attempt of our own to distinguish states whose international status is unquestioned from those whose status has been or is disputed. We have also included states which have ceased to exist: we have done so not only because of historical interest, but also because in many cases adherence by states which have later ceased to exist may still have a bearing on the question of succession.

Succession

The lists of states include certain states bound by succession. The question as to which states are bound to particular international agreements through succession poses a special problem. On a theoretical level, the doctrine of state succession in international law is fraught with difficulties. In particular cases, governments may differ as to whether a state should be formally regarded as having succeeded to a particular international agreement. Hence, the attempt to list all states bound to any particular international agreement through succession is bound to be perilous. Where a specific instrument of succession has been deposited and its legal efficacy has been recognized by the Depositary, such a state has been listed. The date for succession given in the lists is the date of deposit of the instrument of succession. This is not necessarily the date on which succession was regarded as having taken effect, which in many instances is earlier — for example, the date of independence. States other than those listed may be regarded by some as being bound through succession, either if a specific instrument of succession exists which may not be formally recognized by the Depositary, or if no such specific instrument of succession exists, but succession may be implied through a general declaration or treaty regarding succession to international obligations, or through other action on the part of the state concerned.

Reservations, Declarations, and Objections

At the time of signature, ratification, accession, or succession to an international agreement, any state party may submit reservations (which purport to exclude or modify the legal effect of certain provisions of the agreement in their application to that state); or interpretative declarations (which set forth that state's understanding of certain terms of the agreement). Also, at any time, any state party may submit objections (which object to the reservations or declarations made by other states).

The manner in which reservations, declarations, and objections may operate to alter the legal effect of an international agreement merits brief comment. The question as to whether an interpretative declaration forms a part of an international agreement so as to qualify its operation is difficult. Moreover, in practice, the distinction between declarations and reservations may be hard to draw. The question of the validity of a reservation, in terms of its compatibility with the objects and purposes of the agreement, is complicated. In general, any agreement may expressly provide whether or not, or to what extent, reservations are acceptable, and, if acceptable, whether or not unanimous or majority acceptance of each reservation is required. If the agreement contains no such express provision, it is necessary to look to the number of negotiating states and the purposes and objects of the agreement to determine whether the application of the agreement in its entirety between all parties is intended, and, therefore, acceptance of any reservation by all parties is required. If it is determined that the 'unanimity principle' is unwarranted, then any reserving state becomes bound to the agreement in relation to (i) any other party accepting the reservation, (ii) any other party failing to make an objection to the reservation, and possibly (iii) any party making an objection to such reservation which fails to definitely express that, as a consequence, no treaty relationship exists. Consequently, where such reservations exist, any particular treaty may represent a series of international relationships.

Important as reservations, declarations, and objections are, reprinting their full texts, with all of their introductory and concluding diplomatic language, may get in the way of understanding their substance, and may inhibit comparative analysis. Therefore, in those cases where it is possible without sacrificing the meaning, we have provided abbreviated or summarized versions of such statements rather than the full texts. In many such cases, a full text may be found in certain other sources (e.g. treaty series), including any referred to in the concluding notes. Any translations of such statements into English are, except where otherwise noted, either from the Depositaries or from such other sources as may be referred to in the concluding notes: nevertheless, in some of these cases translations of these texts into English are unofficial. Finally, where there are statements having the character of declarations or objections, we have generally followed the practice of some Depositaries in listing such statements together with reservations: in such cases, we have put all of them under the single heading 'Reservations etc.'.

1. 1856 Paris Declaration Respecting Maritime Law

PREFATORY NOTE

In the centuries preceding the Crimean War, maritime rules adopted by various European states did not reflect a generally and continuously accepted regime relating to the treatment of enemy vessels and property as distinguished from neutral vessels and property. With the outbreak of the Crimean War in 1854, all belligerents proclaimed that they would not authorize privateering (the use of privately owned and manned ships to attack and capture enemy vessels and property). In addition, France and Great Britain, as allies, felt the need to harmonize their hitherto different rules on the capture of property at sea. To this end, France declared that neutral property aboard enemy vessels would not be liable to seizure, and Great Britain declared that enemy property aboard neutral ships would not be liable to seizure. This regime was originally only intended to govern the Crimean War. However, when the representatives of seven states assembled at the Congress of Paris from 25 February to 16 April 1856 to conclude terms of peace, they adopted, as the last act of the Congress, the Declaration of Paris.

The Declaration stated that privateering was abolished, prohibited seizure of either enemy or neutral property (except contraband) aboard neutral ships, prohibited seizure of neutral property (except contraband) aboard enemy ships, and stated that blockades must be effective in the sense of being maintained by a force capable of actually preventing access to the enemy coast.

Although the Declaration was only signed by seven states, virtually all other maritime powers acceded to it over time, and many non-parties acted in accordance with the rules, which acquired the status of customary international law. For example, the USA, which sought complete immunity for belligerent merchant ships, did not formally adhere to the Declaration, but followed its provisions and at the outbreak of the First World War considered them binding upon all belligerents.

Because the Declaration has never been formally abandoned, it may still be formally regarded as valid. However, the practical significance of the Declaration has been called into question by practices of belligerents, particularly in the two world wars. First, privateering (which the Declaration prohibits) has become a less salient issue, because the conversion of merchant ships into warships has come to play the same functional role as that formerly played by privateering. Second, the significance of the provisions relating to the exemption of goods from seizure has been reduced by the Declaration's excepting contraband — a category of goods subject to confiscation which was not defined in the Declaration and has since been widened considerably by increasingly extensive lists of items to be considered contraband. Third, the requirement that all blockades be effective is less significant because of controversy over the extent to which access must be prevented: in fact a large measure of discretion has been exercised by belligerents in interpreting this provision. Moreover, in both world wars belligerents resorted (technically as reprisals) to the so-called 'long-distance blockade'. The 'long-distance blockade', while accomplishing the same purpose as the traditional blockade, did not conform to the customary requirements for the latter, but was rather an extensive naval war zone in which ships were liable to destruction. In such circumstances certain provisions of the Declaration are of reduced significance.

Date of signature:	16 April 1856
Entry into force:	16 April 1856
Depositary:	Not specified in the text. The UK Foreign and Commonwealth Office states that the UK is Depositary. In addition, the French Ministry of Foreign Affairs states that it has received certain instruments of accession.
Authentic language:	French
Text reprinted from:	LXI *UKPP* (1856) 153
Also published in:	15 *Martens NRG, 1ère sér.* (1720–1857) 791–2 (Fr.); 46 *BFSP* (1855–1856) 26–7 (Fr.); 1 *AJIL* (1907) Supplement 89–90 (Eng.); 115 *CTS* (1856) 1–3 (Fr.)

Declaration Respecting Maritime Law

THE Plenipotentiaries who signed the Treaty of Paris of the thirtieth of March, one thousand eight hundred and fifty-six, assembled in Conference, —

Considering:

That maritime law, in time of war, has long been the subject of deplorable disputes;

That the uncertainty of the law and of the duties in such a matter, gives rise to differences of opinion between neutrals and belligerents which may occasion serious difficulties, and even conflicts;

That it is consequently advantageous to establish a uniform doctrine on so important a point;

That the Plenipotentiaries assembled in Congress at Paris cannot better respond to the intentions by which their Governments are animated, than by seeking to introduce into international relations fixed principles in this respect;

The above-mentioned Plenipotentiaries, being duly authorized, resolved to concert among themselves as to the means of attaining this object; and, having come to an agreement, have adopted the following solemn Declaration:—

1. Privateering is, and remains, abolished;
2. The neutral flag covers enemy's goods, with the exception of contraband of war;
3. Neutral goods, with the exception of contraband of war, are not liable to capture under enemy's flag;

4. Blockades, in order to be binding, must be effective, that is to say, maintained by a force sufficient really to prevent access to the coast of the enemy.

The Governments of the undersigned Plenipotentiaries engage to bring the present Declaration to the knowledge of the States which have not taken part in the Congress of Paris, and to invite them to accede to it.

Convinced that the maxims which they now proclaim cannot but be received with gratitude by the whole world, the undersigned Plenipotentiaries doubt not that the efforts of their Governments to obtain the general adoption thereof, will be crowned with full success.

The present Declaration is not and shall not be binding, except between those Powers who have acceded, or shall accede, to it.

Done at Paris, the sixteenth of April, one thousand eight hundred and fifty-six.

CONCLUDING NOTES

Signatures and Accessions[1]

State	Date of Signature[2]		Date of Accession (a)[3]	
Anhalt-Dessau-Coethen			17 June	1856 a
Argentine Republic			1 October	1856 a
Austria	16 April	1856		
Baden			30 July	1856 a
Bavaria			4 July	1856 a
Belgium			6 June	1856 a
Brazil			18 March	1858 a
Bremen			11 June	1856 a
Brunswick			7 December	1857 a
Chile			13 August	1856 a
Denmark			25 June	1856 a
Ecuador			6 December	1856 a
France	16 April	1856		
Frankfort			17 June	1856 a
Germanic Confederation			10 July	1856 a

[1] Information supplied in communications from the UK Foreign and Commonwealth Office, and the French Ministry of Foreign Affairs, between December 1979 and January 1981.

[2] The Declaration became binding upon the seven signatory states without need of ratification. Ratification is not always necessary to bring an agreement into effect. Signature alone may suffice where (as in this case) the intent is for signature to bring the document into effect, or where the document expressly states that signature is sufficient.

[3] There have not been any instruments of succession.

State	Date of Signature		Date of Accession (*a*)	
Great Britain	16 April	1856		
Greece			20 June	1856 *a*
Guatemala			30 August	1856 *a*
Haiti			17 September	1856 *a*
Hamburg			27 June	1856 *a*
Hanover			31 May	1856 *a*
Hesse-Cassel			4 June	1856 *a*
Hesse-Darmstadt			15 June	1856 *a*
Japan			30 October	1886 *a*
Lubeck			20 June	1856 *a*
Mecklenburg-Schwerin			22 July	1856 *a*
Mecklenburg-Strelitz			25 August	1856 *a*
Mexico[4]			13 February	1909 *a*
Modena			29 July	1856 *a*
Nassau			18 June	1856 *a*
Netherlands			7 June	1856 *a*
Oldenburg			9 June	1856 *a*
Parma			20 August	1856 *a*
Peru			23 November	1857 *a*
Portugal			28 July	1856 *a*
Prussia	16 April	1856		
Roman States			2 June	1856 *a*
Russia	16 April	1856		
Sardinia	16 April	1856		
Saxe-Altenburg			9 June	1856 *a*
Saxe-Coburg-Gotha			22 June	1856 *a*
Saxe-Meiningen			30 June	1856 *a*
Saxe-Weimar			22 June	1856 *a*
Saxony			16 June	1856 *a*
The Two Sicilies			31 May	1856 *a*
Spain[4]			18 January	1908 *a*
Sweden and Norway			13 June	1856 *a*
Switzerland			28 July	1856 *a*
Turkey	16 April	1856		
Tuscany			5 June	1856 *a*
Wurtemberg			25 June	1856 *a*

Total Number of Parties Listed: 51

Note A. *New Granada* and *Uruguay* assented to the entire Declaration, and *Venezuela* to the second, third, and fourth points only, but there is no record that their respective legislatures ratified the Declaration or that formal instruments of accession were deposited.

[4] Spain and Mexico formally acceded to the entire Declaration on these dates. They had, however, previously declared that they accepted the second, third, and fourth points of the Declaration.

Note B. *USA* expressed readiness to accede to the Declaration provided it were added, with reference to privateering, that the private property of subjects or citizens of belligerent nations was exempt from capture at sea by the respective naval forces.

Note on Entry into Force for States Parties

The Declaration entered into force for each state on the date of its respective signature or accession.

Denunciations

None

Reservations

None

2. 1868 St. Petersburg Declaration Renouncing the Use, in Time of War, of Explosive Projectiles Under 400 grammes Weight

PREFATORY NOTE

Attempts to prohibit the use of particular weapons in warfare have been made in various civilizations over a long period of time. For example, in ancient times, the Laws of Manu (the greatest of the ancient Hindu codes) prohibited Hindus from using poisoned arrows;.and the Greeks and Romans customarily observed a prohibition against using poison or poisoned weapons. During the Middle Ages the Lateran Council of 1132 declared that the crossbow and arbalest were 'unchristian' weapons. When the laws of war began to be codified by states in the mid-nineteenth century, the prohibition of a particular weapon was the subject of one of the first international agreements.

The 1868 St. Petersburg Declaration has been regarded as the first major international agreement prohibiting the use of a particular weapon in warfare. The prohibition followed the development of a bullet which exploded upon contact with a hard surface. In 1863 the bullet was introduced into the Imperial Russian Army to be used for blowing up ammunition wagons. In 1864 the Imperial War Minister considered it to be improper to use such a bullet against troops and its use was therefore strictly controlled. However, in 1867 a modification of the bullet was developed which enabled it to explode on contact with even a soft surface. Moreover, unlike the previous projectile, the new bullet shattered upon explosion. Understanding that such a bullet posed a greater danger to troops, the Imperial War Minister did not want it used either by the Imperial Russian Army or the armies of other states. The Imperial War Minister proposed to Tsar Alexander II that the use of all explosive bullets, or at least the bullet developed in 1867, should be renounced. Tsar Alexander II invited states to attend an International Military Commission in St. Petersburg to consider the matter.

The conference met in St. Petersburg in three sessions, on 9, 13, and 16 November 1868 (all dates are by the Western calendar), attended by the representatives of sixteen states. All of these states, with the single addition of Persia, formally signed the Declaration on 11 December.

At the conference, Prussia reiterated a request it had made earlier, that the scope of the enquiry be broadened to deal generally with the application of scientific discoveries to armed conflict and to extend the proposed prohibition to other types of projectile. British and French opposition to any general consideration of projectiles led to the Prussian suggestion being dropped. However, the Swiss suggestion that the proposed prohibition be extended to include inflammable bullets was accepted. Because none of the states objected to the use of explosives in shells, the prohibition was restricted to projectiles under 400 grammes weight.

The St. Petersburg Declaration is regarded as expressing, with respect to a particular means of warfare, the customary principle prohibiting the use of means of warfare causing unnecessary suffering. This general customary principle was later embodied in Article 23(*e*) of the Regulations annexed to 1899 Hague Convention II and 1907 Hague Convention IV. To the extent that the St. Petersburg Declaration represents customary international law, it would be binding upon all states and not merely those which are formally parties to it, and its 'general participation clause' would cease to be relevant.

The St. Petersburg Declaration led to the adoption of other declarations renouncing particular means of warfare at the First Hague Peace Conference of 1899 and the Second Hague Peace Conference of 1907.

The application of the St. Petersburg Declaration to certain weapons which were developed later raises difficult questions. With respect to incendiary weapons, such as flame-throwers and napalm, the Declaration's prohibition does relate to projectiles under 400 grammes weight containing inflammable substances, and this has been taken by some to imply, by analogy, that it is unlawful to use fire weapons. Others suggest that it is thereby only unlawful to use such fire weapons so as to cause unnecessary suffering to individuals. Still others doubt that any prohibition may be inferred by analogy. State practice has demonstrated that such incendiary weapons have been widely used. (Indeed, the use of tracer, incendiary or explosive projectiles by or against aircraft was specifically not prohibited in Article 18 of the 1923 draft Hague Air Rules.) With respect to incendiary weapons in general, reference should be made to the 1981 UN Weapons Convention, Protocol III.

Date of signature:	11 December 1868 (29 November by the Julian calendar)
Entry into force:	11 December 1868
Depositary:	None specified in the text. Presumably Russia. See footnote 1 in the concluding notes below.
Authentic language:	French
Text reprinted from:	LXIV *UKPP* (1869) 659
Also published in:	18 *Martens NRG, 1ère sér.* (1860–1873) 474–5 (Fr.);
	58 *BFSP* (1867–1868) 16–17 (Fr.);
	1 *AJIL* (1907) Supplement 95–6 (Eng.);
	138 *CTS* (1868–1869) 297–9 (Fr.)

Declaration Renouncing the Use, in Time of War, of Explosive Projectiles Under 400 grammes Weight

ON the proposition of the Imperial Cabinet of Russia, an International Military Commission having assembled at St. Petersburgh in order to examine into the expediency of forbidding the use of certain projectiles in times of war between civilized nations, and that Commission, having by common agreement fixed the technical limits at which the necessities of war ought to yield to the requirements of humanity, the Undersigned are authorized by the orders of their Governments to declare as follows:—

Considering that the progress of civilization should have the effect of alleviating as much as possible the calamities of war;

That the only legitimate object which States should endeavour to accomplish during war is to weaken the military forces of the enemy;

That for this purpose it is sufficient to disable the greatest possible number of men;

That this object would be exceeded by the employment of arms which uselessly aggravate the sufferings of disabled men, or render their death inevitable;

That the employment of such arms would, therefore, be contrary to the laws of humanity;

The Contracting Parties engage mutually to renounce, in case of war among themselves, the employment by their military or naval troops of any projectile of a weight below 400 grammes, which is either explosive or charged with fulminating or inflammable substances.

They will invite all the States which have not taken part in the deliberations of the International Military Commission assembled at St. Petersburgh, by sending Delegates thereto, to accede to the present engagement.

This engagement is obligatory only upon the Contracting or Acceding Parties thereto, in case of war between two or more of themselves: it is not applicable with regard to non-Contracting Parties, or Parties who shall not have acceded to it.

It will also cease to be obligatory from the moment when, in a war between Contracting or Acceding Parties, a non-Contracting Party or a non-Acceding Party shall join one of the belligerents.

The Contracting or Acceding Parties reserve to themselves to come hereafter to an understanding whenever a precise proposition shall be drawn up in view of future improvements which science may effect in the armament of troops, in order to maintain the principles which they have established, and to conciliate the necessities of war with the laws of humanity.

Done at St. Petersburgh, the twenty-ninth of November/eleventh of December, one thousand eight hundred and sixty-eight.

CONCLUDING NOTES

Signatures and Accessions[1]

State	Date of Signature[2]	Date of Accession (a)[3]
Austria-Hungary	11 December 1868	
Baden		11 January 1869 a
Bavaria	11 December 1868	
Belgium	11 December 1868	
Brazil		23 October 1869 a
Denmark	11 December 1868	
France	11 December 1868	
Great Britain	11 December 1868	
Greece	11 December 1868	
Italy	11 December 1868	
Netherlands	11 December 1868	
Persia	11 December 1868	
Portugal	11 December 1868	
Prussia and the North German Confederation	11 December 1868	
Russia	11 December 1868	
Sweden and Norway	11 December 1868	
Switzerland	11 December 1868	
Turkey	11 December 1868	
Wurtemberg	11 December 1868	

Total Number of Parties Listed: 19

Note on Entry into Force for States Parties

The Declaration entered into force for each state on the date of its respective signature or accession.

[1] Although no Depositary is specified in the agreement itself, the French Ministry of Foreign Affairs states that the original copy was placed in the Russian archives. However, the Ministry of Foreign Affairs of the USSR has not responded to requests for a list of states parties. In the absence of information from the Depositary, this list has been compiled from information supplied by the UK Foreign and Commonwealth Office, and the French Ministry of Foreign Affairs, between December 1979 and January 1981. This information has been checked in a variety of published sources, including those mentioned under the prefatory notes and also F. Martens, *Recueil des Traités et Conventions conclus par la Russie*, vol. IV, part 2, Devrient, St. Petersburg, 1878, pp. 953–61; and J. Basdevant, *Traités et Conventions en Vigueur entre la France et les Puissances Entrangères*, vol. III, Imprimerie Nationale, Paris, 1920, pp. 750-1. The latter alone gives the exact dates of accession of Baden and Brazil.

All dates in this table are according to the Western calendar, not the Julian one which was in use in Russia at the time.

[2] Like the 1856 Paris Declaration, the 1868 Declaration became binding on the signatory states without need of ratification.

[3] There is no evidence of any instruments of succession.

Denunciations

There is no evidence of any.

Reservations

There is no evidence of any.

3. 1899 Hague Declaration 2 Concerning Asphyxiating Gases

PREFATORY NOTE

The 1899 Hague Conventions and Declarations: General

What was to become known as the First Hague Peace Conference was convened through the personal initiative of Tsar Nicholas II of Russia, with the primary objective of limiting armaments. Among the factors which led to the calling of the conference was a concern about the impact of various technical developments on warfare. The representatives of twenty-six states met in The Hague from 18 May to 29 July 1899, and although they failed to reach any general agreement on arms limitation, they were successful in adopting three conventions (relating to the peaceful settlement of disputes, the laws and customs of war on land, and maritime warfare) and three declarations (prohibiting the launching of projectiles and explosives from balloons, the use of projectiles diffusing asphyxiating gases, and the use of expanding bullets). The three 1899 Conventions are not included in this volume. The first is not part of the laws of war; the second is discussed in the prefatory note to 1907 Hague Convention IV; and the third is discussed in the prefatory note to 1949 Geneva Convention II. Also, 1899 Hague Declaration 1 on balloons, like the 1907 Hague Declaration on balloons, is not included in this volume, but both documents are discussed in the prefatory note to the 1923 Hague Rules of Aerial Warfare.

1899 Hague Declaration 2

This agreement, prohibiting the use of projectiles whose sole object is to diffuse asphyxiating gases, was derived from the general principles of customary international law prohibiting the use of poison and materials causing unnecessary suffering. These general customary principles were embodied in Articles 23(*a*) and 23(*e*) of the Regulations annexed to 1899 Hague Convention II and 1907 Hague Convention IV.

To the extent that the specific prohibition embodied in 1899 Hague Declaration 2 may be considered a particular rule of customary international law, it would be applicable to all states and not merely those which have formally ratified or acceded to it, and the Declaration's 'general participation clause' would cease to be relevant.

During the First World War, the use of gas began with irritant gas, but escalated rapidly. After the end of the war, the prohibition of gas warfare was reaffirmed in the 1919 Treaty of Versailles, similar provisions in other World War I peace treaties, the unratified 1922 Treaty of Washington, and the 1925 Geneva Protocol: see the prefatory note to the latter.

Because 1899 Hague Declaration 2 prohibits the use of *projectiles* whose *sole* object is the diffusion of asphyxiating or deleterious gases, some suggest that the Declaration may have been overtaken by the more comprehensive prohibition in the 1925 Geneva Protocol.

Date of signature:	29 July 1899
Entry into force:	4 September 1900
Depositary:	Netherlands
Authentic language:	French
Text reprinted from:	J. B. Scott (ed.), *The Hague Conventions and Declarations of 1899 and 1907*, Oxford University Press, New York, 3rd edn., 1918, pp. 225–6. (English translation by US Department of State, with minor corrections by J. B. Scott.)
Also published in:	26 *Martens NRG*, 2ème sér. (1899) 998–1002 (Fr. Ger.);
	91 *BFSP* (1898–1899) 1014–16 (Fr.);
	UKTS 32 (1907), Cd. 3751 (Eng. Fr.);
	CXXV *UKPP* (1908) 898–900 (Eng. Fr.);
	1 *AJIL* (1907) Supplement 157–9 (Eng. Fr.);
	187 *CTS* (1898–1899) 453–5 (Fr.)

Declaration (IV, 2) Concerning Asphyxiating Gases

The undersigned, plenipotentiaries of the Powers represented at the International Peace Conference at The Hague, duly authorized to that effect by their Governments, inspired by the sentiments which found expression in the Declaration of St. Petersburg of the 29th November (11th December), 1868,

Declare as follows:

The contracting Powers agree to abstain from the use of projectiles the sole object of which is the diffusion of asphyxiating or deleterious gases.

The present Declaration is only binding on the contracting Powers in the case of a war between two or more of them.

It shall cease to be binding from the time when, in a war between the contracting Powers, one of the belligerents shall be joined by a non-contracting Power.

The present Declaration shall be ratified as soon as possible.

The ratifications shall be deposited at The Hague.

A procès-verbal shall be drawn up on the receipt of each ratification, a copy of which, duly certified, shall be sent through the diplomatic channel to all the contracting Powers.

The non-signatory Powers can adhere to the present Declaration. For this purpose they must make their adhesion known to the contracting Powers by means of a written notification adressed to the Netherland Government, and by it communicated to all the other contracting Powers.

In the event of one of the high contracting Parties denouncing the present Declaration, such denunciation shall not take effect until a year after the notification made in writing to the Government of the Netherlands, and forthwith communicated by it to all the other contracting Powers.

This denunciation shall only affect the notifying Power.

In faith of which the plenipotentiaries have signed the present Declaration, and affixed their seals thereto.

Done at The Hague, the 29th July, 1899, in a single copy, which shall be kept in the archives of the Netherland Government, and copies of which, duly certified, shall be sent by the diplomatic channel to the contracting Powers.

CONCLUDING NOTES

The concluding notes for 1899 Hague Declaration 2 are combined with those for 1899 Hague Declaration 3 and are to be found after the end of the latter document, below, p. 41.

4. 1899 Hague Declaration 3 Concerning Expanding Bullets

PREFATORY NOTE

1899 Hague Declaration 3 was adopted by the First Hague Peace Conference of 1899 in response to the introduction of a bullet (first manufactured at the British Indian arsenal of Dum-Dum, near Calcutta) which expanded and flattened in the human body. Great Britain objected to the proposed prohibition on the grounds that the dumdum bullet did not expand in such a manner as to create wounds of exceptional cruelty and that, in fact, the wounds were less severe than those produced by certain rifles which had been in use. The USA objected to the proposed declaration on three grounds: first, a prohibition based on the specification of details of construction might not be useful because of the possibility that a bullet might be made to expand in such a regular manner as to simply assume the form of a larger calibre; second, such an expanding bullet might be the most humane way of increasing the shocking power of the bullet; and third, the bullet was actually being used by the British Army, and any condemnation should follow from real evidence against its effects, rather than from implication drawn from its design. However, the objections of both Great Britain and the USA were overruled, and the Declaration was adopted.

The Declaration has been regarded as codifying one aspect of the customary rule prohibiting weapons causing unnecessary suffering. This general customary principle was embodied in Article 23(e) of the Regulations annexed to 1899 Hague Convention II and 1907 Hague Convention IV. To the extent that the Declaration reflects customary international law, it would be applicable to all states and not merely those which have formally ratified or acceded to it, and its 'general participation clause' would cease to be relevant.

Controversies about the use of expanding bullets have arisen in many wars since the Declaration was adopted. Early examples included the Boer War of 1899–1902 and the Russo-Japanese War of 1904–5.

While 1899 Hague Declaration 3 was drawn up with the dumdum bullet in mind, its impact may extend to weapons developed later. Some have suggested that high-velocity rifle ammunition, tumbling end over end on striking its target and thereby producing a large, jagged wound, has a similar effect to the dumdum bullet. Although there is no specific prohibition of high-velocity ammunition, the argument is that the weapon is prohibited by analogy to the prohibition of the dumdum bullet. Others contest the validity of any such analogy. This issue, which was discussed before and during the 1979–80 UN Weapons Conference in Geneva without resulting in agreement, remains controversial.

Date of signature: 29 July 1899
Entry into force: 4 September 1900
Depositary: Netherlands

Authentic language: French
Text reprinted from: J. B. Scott (ed.), *The Hague Conventions and Declarations of 1899 and 1907*, Oxford University Press, New York, 3rd edn., 1918, pp. 227-8. (English translation by US Department of State, with minor corrections by J. B. Scott.)
Also published in: 26 *Martens NRG, 2ème sér.* (1899) 1002-6 (Fr. Ger.);
91 *BFSP* (1898-1899) 1017-19 (Fr.);
UKTS 32 (1907), Cd. 3751 (Eng. Fr.);
CXXV *UKPP* (1908) 893-5 (Eng. Fr.);
1 *AJIL* (1907) Supplement 155-7 (Eng. Fr.);
187 *CTS* (1898-1899) 459-61 (Fr.)

Declaration (IV, 3) Concerning Expanding Bullets

The undersigned, plenipotentiaries of the Powers represented at the International Peace Conference at The Hague, duly authorized to that effect by their Governments, inspired by the sentiments which found expression in the Declaration of St. Petersburg of the 29th November (11th December), 1868.

Declare as follows:

The contracting Parties agree to abstain from the use of bullets which expand or flatten easily in the human body, such as bullets with a hard envelope which does not entirely cover the core or is pierced with incisions.

The present Declaration is only binding for the contracting Powers in the case of a war between two or more of them.

It shall cease to be binding from the time when, in a war between the contracting Powers, one of the belligerents is joined by a non-contracting Power.

The present Declaration shall be ratified as soon as possible.

The ratification shall be deposited at The Hague.

A procès-verbal shall be drawn up on the receipt of each ratification, a copy of which, duly certified, shall be sent through the diplomatic channel to all the contracting Powers.

The non-signatory Powers may adhere to the present Declaration. For this purpose they must make their adhesion known to the contracting Powers by means of a written notification addressed to the Netherland Government, and by it communicated to all the other contracting Powers.

In the event of one of the high contracting Parties denouncing the present Declaration, such denunciation shall not take effect until a year after the notification made in writing to the Netherland Government, and forthwith communicated by it to all the other contracting Powers.

This denunciation shall only affect the notifying Power.

In faith of which the plenipotentiaries have signed the present Declaration, and have affixed their seals thereto.

Done at The Hague, the 29th July, 1899, in a single copy, which shall be kept in the archives of the Netherland Government, and of which copies, duly certified, shall be sent through the diplomatic channel to the contracting Powers.

CONCLUDING NOTES
RELATING BOTH TO 1899 HAGUE DECLARATION 2,
AND TO 1899 HAGUE DECLARATION 3

Except where otherwise stated, all entries in this list apply *both* to 1899 Hague Declaration 2 relating to asphyxiating gases, *and* to 1899 Hague Declaration 3 relating to expanding bullets.

Signatures, Ratifications, Accessions, and Successions[1]

State	Date of Signature		Date of Ratification (r), Accession (a), or Succession (s)	
Austria-Hungary	29 July	1899	4 September 1900	r
Belgium	29 July	1899	4 September 1900	r
Bulgaria	29 July	1899	4 September 1900	r
Byelorussian SSR[2, 3]			4 June 1962	s
China	29 July	1899	21 November 1904	r
Denmark	29 July	1899	4 September 1900	r
Ethiopia			9 August 1935	a
Fiji[2]			2 April 1973	s
France	29 July	1899	4 September 1900	r
Germany	29 July	1899	4 September 1900	r
German Democratic Republic[2] (Decl. 3)			9 February 1959	s
Great Britain and Ireland			30 August 1907	a

[1] Information supplied in communications from the Netherlands Ministry of Foreign Affairs between December 1979 and April 1981.

[2] By letters dated 1 April 1980 and 16 March 1981 the Netherlands Ministry of Foreign Affairs confirmed that these cases constituted successions.

[3] USSR recognized the ratification by the Russian Empire of 1899 and 1907 Hague Conventions and Declarations in so far as these are not in contradiction with the UN Charter, and if they have not been changed or replaced by later international conventions to which USSR is a party, such as the 1925 Geneva Protocol and the 1949 Geneva Conventions. Byelorussia made a similar statement on notifying succession.

State	Date of Signature		Date of Ratification (*r*), Accession (*a*), or Succession (*s*)		
Greece	29 July	1899	4 April	1901	*r*
Italy	29 July	1899	4 September	1900	*r*
Japan	29 July	1899	6 October	1900	*r*
Luxembourg	29 July	1899	12 July	1901	*r*
Mexico	29 July	1899	17 April	1901	*r*
Montenegro	29 July	1899	16 October	1900	*r*
Netherlands	29 July	1899	4 September	1900	*r*
Nicaragua			11 October	1907	*a*
Norway[4]	29 July	1899	4 September	1900	*r*
Persia	29 July	1899	4 September	1900	*r*
Portugal (Decl. 2)	29 July	1899	4 September	1900	*r*
(Decl. 3)			29 August	1907	*a*
Romania	29 July	1899	4 September	1900	*r*
Russia	29 July	1899	4 September	1900	*r*
Serbia	29 July	1899	11 May	1901	*r*
Siam	29 July	1899	4 September	1900	*r*
South Africa[2]			10 March	1978	*s*
Spain	29 July	1899	4 September	1900	*r*
Sweden[4]	29 July	1899	4 September	1900	*r*
Switzerland	29 July	1899	29 December	1900	*r*
Turkey	29 July	1899	12 June	1907	*r*
USSR[2, 3]			7 March	1955	*s*
Yugoslavia[2, 5]			8 April	1969	*s*

Total Number of Parties Listed: 33 for Declaration 2; 34 for Declaration 3.

Note on Entry into Force for States Parties

Both Declaration 2 and Declaration 3 entered into force on 4 September 1900 for the states which ratified them on that day. For each of the other ratifying states, and for each of the acceding states, each Declaration formally entered into force on the date of ratification or accession.

Denunciations

None

Reservations

None

[4] Signature for Norway and Sweden was in the name of the United Kingdoms of Sweden and Norway.

[5] Yugoslavia, in a note received by the Netherlands Ministry of Foreign Affairs on 8 April 1969, confirmed that it considers itself a party to the Conventions and Declarations of The Hague of 29 July 1899, ratified by Serbia.

5. 1907 Hague Convention IV Respecting the Laws and Customs of War on Land

PREFATORY NOTE

The 1907 Hague Conventions and Declaration: General

The Final Act of the First Hague Peace Conference of 1899 proposed that a subsequent conference be held to consider matters on which agreement had not been reached. The initiative for convening the second conference was made by President Theodore Roosevelt of the USA in 1904. Russia did not take the leading role because of its involvement in the war with Japan in 1904–5. However, in 1906, after the conclusion of the Russo-Japanese War, Tsar Nicholas II invited states to attend a Second Hague Peace Conference with the primary objective of limiting armaments. This second Conference, attended by representatives of forty-four states, met from 15 June to 18 October 1907. Once again no general agreement on arms limitation was reached, but the Conference was successful in adopting thirteen conventions (three of which revised the three 1899 Conventions), and one declaration (which renewed 1899 Hague Declaration 1 on balloons, which had expired). 1907 Hague Conventions I, II, III, X, and XII and the 1907 Hague Declaration have been omitted from this volume: Conventions I, II, and III are not part of the laws of war *per se*; Convention X is discussed in the prefatory note to 1949 Geneva Convention II; and Convention XII did not enter into force.

The Final Act of the Second Hague Peace Conference proposed that a third conference be held within a period corresponding to the time elapsed since the first conference. Unfortunately, the timetable alluded to wound up being that for the outbreak of the First World War, and the Third Hague Peace Conference was never held.

1907 Hague Convention IV

Before 1899, agreements relating to the laws of land warfare had only addressed specialized areas of the law (such as wounded, and explosive projectiles); and although the 1874 Brussels Conference, convened on the initiative of Tsar Alexander II of Russia, had led to the adoption of a relatively comprehensive declaration concerning the laws of land warfare, the 1874 Brussels Declaration was never ratified and did not enter into force.

The immediate precursor of 1907 Hague Convention IV was 1899 Hague Convention II Respecting the Laws and Customs of War on Land. This had been adopted at the First Hague Peace Conference and had entered into force on 4 September 1900. The 1899 Convention was of particular importance in the development of the laws of war in that it represented the first successful effort of the international community to codify a relatively comprehensive regime governing the laws of land warfare. The provisions of 1907 Hague Convention IV represent a slight revision of those embodied in 1899 Hague Convention II.

Most articles of the Regulations annexed to the Conventions are identical, and only a few contain substantial changes. The texts of both conventions are usefully juxtaposed in J. B. Scott (ed.), *The Hague Conventions and Declarations of 1899 and 1907*.

Several points should be noted about the applicability of 1907 Hague Convention IV. It was intended to replace 1899 Hague Convention II as between states parties to both agreements. However, eighteen states parties to the 1899 Convention did not become parties to the 1907 Convention (Argentina, Bulgaria, Chile, Colombia, Ecuador, Greece, Honduras, Italy, Korea, Montenegro, Paraguay, Persia, Peru, Serbia, Spain, Turkey, Uruguay, Venezuela). They or their successor states (e.g. Yugoslavia) remain formally bound by the 1899 Convention. The application of each convention was made more complex by the inclusion of a 'general participation clause' (Article 2). However, identifying formal states parties to one convention or the other and applying the general participation clauses is only of limited importance in cases where conventions are regarded as representing customary international law, and hence binding on all states. The International Military Tribunal at Nuremberg in 1946 expressly recognized 1907 Hague Convention IV as declaratory of customary international law.

While representing a relatively comprehensive agreement on the law of land warfare, 1907 Hague Convention IV (like 1899 Hague Convention II) was not regarded as a complete code of the applicable law. What has come to be known as the Martens Clause, appearing in the Convention's Preamble, declares that cases not included in the Regulations annexed to the Convention remain governed by customary international law relating to the conduct of warfare.

Date of signature:	18 October 1907
Entry into force:	26 January 1910
Depositary:	Netherlands
Authentic language:	French
Text reprinted from:	J. B. Scott (ed.), *The Hague Conventions and Declarations of 1899 and 1907*, Oxford University Press, New York, 3rd edn., 1918, pp. 100–27. (English translation by US Department of State, with minor corrections by J. B. Scott.)
Also published in:	3 *Martens NRG*, 3ème sér. (1862–1910) 461–503 (Fr. Ger.);
	100 *BFSP* (1906–1907) 338–59 (Fr.);
	UKTS 9 (1910), Cd. 5030 (Eng. Fr.);
	CXII *UKPP* (1910) 59 (Eng. Fr.);
	2 *AJIL* (1908) Supplement 90–117 (Eng. Fr.);
	205 *CTS* (1907) 227–98 (Fr.)

Convention (IV) Respecting the Laws and Customs of War on Land

His Majesty the German Emperor, King of Prussia; [etc.] :
Seeing that, while seeking means to preserve peace and prevent

armed conflicts between nations, it is likewise necessary to bear in mind the case where the appeal to arms has been brought about by events which their care was unable to avert;

Animated by the desire to serve, even in this extreme case, the interests of humanity and the ever progressive needs of civilization;

Thinking it important, with this object, to revise the general laws and customs of war, either with a view to defining them with greater precision or to confining them within such limits as would mitigate their severity as far as possible;

Have deemed it necessary to complete and explain in certain particulars the work of the First Peace Conference, which, following on the Brussels Conference of 1874, and inspired by the ideas dictated by a wise and generous forethought, adopted provisions intended to define and govern the usages of war on land.

According to the views of the high contracting Parties, these provisions, the wording of which has been inspired by the desire to diminish the evils of war, as far as military requirements permit, are intended to serve as a general rule of conduct for the belligerents in their mutual relations and in their relations with the inhabitants.

It has not, however, been found possible at present to concert regulations covering all the circumstances which arise in practice;

On the other hand, the high contracting Parties clearly do not intend that unforeseen cases should, in the absence of a written undertaking, be left to the arbitrary judgment of military commanders.

Until a more complete code of the laws of war has been issued, the high contracting Parties deem it expedient to declare that, in cases not included in the Regulations adopted by them, the inhabitants and the belligerents remain under the protection and the rule of the principles of the law of nations, as they result from the usages established among civilized peoples, from the laws of humanity, and the dictates of the public conscience.

They declare that it is in this sense especially that Articles 1 and 2 of the Regulations adopted must be understood.

The high contracting Parties, wishing to conclude a fresh Convention to this effect, have appointed the following as their plenipotentiaries:

[Here follow the names of plenipotentiaries.]

Who, after having deposited their full powers, found in good and due form, have agreed upon the following:

Article 1

The contracting Powers shall issue instructions to their armed land forces which shall be in conformity with the Regulations respecting the laws and customs of war on land, annexed to the present Convention.

Article 2

The provisions contained in the Regulations referred to in Article 1, as well as in the present Convention, do not apply except between contracting Powers, and then only if all the belligerents are parties to the Convention.

Article 3

A belligerent party which violates the provisions of the said Regulations shall, if the case demands, be liable to pay compensation. It shall be responsible for all acts committed by persons forming part of its armed forces.

Article 4

The present Convention, duly ratified, shall as between the contracting Powers, be substituted for the Convention of the 29th July, 1899, respecting the laws and customs of war on land.

The Convention of 1899 remains in force as between the Powers which signed it, and which do not also ratify the present Convention.

Article 5

The present Convention shall be ratified as soon as possible.

The ratifications shall be deposited at The Hague.

The first deposit of ratifications shall be recorded in a procès-verbal signed by the Representatives of the Powers which take part therein and by the Netherland Minister for Foreign Affairs.

The subsequent deposits of ratifications shall be made by means of a written notification, addressed to the Netherland Government and accompanied by the instrument of ratification.

A duly certified copy of the procès-verbal relative to the first deposit of ratifications, of the notifications mentioned in the preceding paragraph, as well as of the instruments of ratification, shall be immediately sent by the Netherland Government, through the diplomatic channel, to the Powers invited to the Second Peace Conference, as well as to the other Powers which have adhered to the Convention. In the cases contemplated in the preceding paragraph the said Government shall at the same time inform them of the date on which it received the notification.

Article 6

Non-signatory Powers may adhere to the present Convention.

The Power which desires to adhere notifies in writing its intention to the Netherland Government, forwarding to it the act of adhesion, which shall be deposited in the archives of the said Government.

This Government shall at once transmit to all the other Powers a duly certified copy of the notification as well as of the act of adhesion, mentioning the date on which it received the notification.

Article 7

The present Convention shall come into force, in the case of the Powers which were a party to the first deposit of ratifications, sixty days after the date of the procès-verbal of this deposit, and, in the case of the Powers which ratify subsequently or which adhere, sixty days after the notification of their ratification or of their adhesion has been received by the Netherland Government.

Article 8

In the event of one of the contracting Powers wishing to denounce the present Convention, the denunciation shall be notified in writing to the Netherland Government, which shall at once communicate a duly certified copy of the notification to all the other Powers, informing them of the date on which it was received.

The denunciation shall only have effect in regard to the notifying Power, and one year after the notification has reached the Netherland Government.

Article 9

A register kept by the Netherland Ministry for Foreign Affairs shall give the date of the deposit of ratifications made in virtue of Article 5, paragraphs 3 and 4, as well as the date on which the notifications of adhesion (Article 6, paragraph 2), or of denunciation (Article 8, paragraph 1) were received.

Each contracting Power is entitled to have access to this register and to be supplied with duly certified extracts.

In faith whereof the plenipotentiaries have appended their signatures to the present Convention.

Done at The Hague, the 18th October, 1907, in a single copy, which shall remain deposited in the archives of the Netherland Government, and duly certified copies of which shall be sent, through the diplomatic channel, to the Powers which have been invited to the Second Peace Conference.

Annex to the Convention
Regulations Respecting the Laws and Customs of War on Land

SECTION I — ON BELLIGERENTS

CHAPTER I — *The Qualifications of Belligerents*

Article 1

The laws, rights, and duties of war apply not only to armies, but also to militia and volunteer corps fulfilling the following conditions:

1. To be commanded by a person responsible for his subordinates;
2. To have a fixed distinctive emblem recognizable at a distance;
3. To carry arms openly; and
4. To conduct their operations in accordance with the laws and customs of war.

In countries where militia or volunteer corps constitute the army, or form part of it, they are included under the denomination 'army'.

Article 2

The inhabitants of a territory which has not been occupied,[1] who, on the approach of the enemy, spontaneously take up arms to resist the invading troops without having had time to organize themselves in accordance with Article 1, shall be regarded as belligerents if they carry arms openly and if they respect the laws and customs of war.

Article 3

The armed forces of the belligerent parties may consist of combatants and non-combatants. In the case of capture by the enemy, both have a right to be treated as prisoners of war.

CHAPTER II — *Prisoners of War*

Article 4

Prisoners of war are in the power of the hostile Government, but not of the individuals or corps who capture them.

They must be humanely treated.

All their personal belongings, except arms, horses, and military papers, remain their property.

---

[1] In the authentic French text: 'La population d'un territoire non occupé . . .' The official UK translation renders these words, more faithfully than the US translation used here, as 'inhabitants of a territory not under occupation . . .'

Article 5

Prisoners of war may be interned in a town, fortress, camp, or other place, and bound not to go beyond certain fixed limits; but they can not be confined except as an indispensable measure of safety and only while the circumstances which necessitate the measure continue to exist.

Article 6

The State may utilize the labor of prisoners of war according to their rank and aptitude, officers excepted. The tasks shall not be excessive and shall have no connection with the operations of the war.

Prisoners may be authorized to work for the public service, for private persons, or on their own account.

Work done for the State is paid for at the rates in force for work of a similar kind done by soldiers of the national army, or, if there are none in force, at a rate according to the work executed.

When the work is for other branches of the public service or for private persons the conditions are settled in agreement with the military authorities.

The wages of the prisoners shall go towards improving their position, and the balance shall be paid them on their release, after deducting the cost of their maintenance.

Article 7

The Government into whose hands prisoners of war have fallen is charged with their maintenance.

In the absence of a special agreement between the belligerents, prisoners of war shall be treated as regards board, lodging, and clothing on the same footing as the troops of the Government who captured them.

Article 8

Prisoners of war shall be subject to the laws, regulations, and orders in force in the army of the State in whose power they are. Any act of insubordination justifies the adoption towards them of such measures of severity as may be considered necessary.

Escaped prisoners who are retaken before being able to rejoin their own army or before leaving the territory occupied by the army which captured them are liable to disciplinary punishment.

Prisoners who, after succeeding in escaping, are again taken prisoners, are not liable to any punishment on account of the previous flight.

Article 9

Every prisoner of war is bound to give, if he is questioned on the subject, his true name and rank, and if he infringes this rule, he is liable to have the advantages given to prisoners of his class curtailed.

Article 10

Prisoners of war may be set at liberty on parole if the laws of their country allow, and, in such cases, they are bound, on their personal honor, scrupulously to fulfil, both towards their own Government and the Government by whom they were made prisoners, the engagements they have contracted.

In such cases their own Government is bound neither to require of nor accept from them any service incompatible with the parole given.

Article 11

A prisoner of war can not be compelled to accept his liberty on parole; similarly the hostile Government is not obliged to accede to the request of the prisoner to be set at liberty on parole.

Article 12

Prisoners of war liberated on parole and recaptured bearing arms against the Government to whom they had pledged their honor, or against the allies of that Government, forfeit their right to be treated as prisoners of war, and can be brought before the courts.

Article 13

Individuals who follow an army without directly belonging to it, such as newspaper correspondents and reporters, sutlers and contractors, who fall into the enemy's hands and whom the latter thinks expedient to detain, are entitled to be treated as prisoners of war, provided they are in possession of a certificate from the military authorities of the army which they were accompanying.

Article 14

An inquiry office for prisoners of war is instituted on the commencement of hostilities in each of the belligerent States, and, when necessary, in neutral countries which have received belligerents in their territory. It is the function of this office to reply to all inquiries about the prisoners. It receives from the various services concerned full information respecting internments and transfers, releases on parole, exchanges, escapes, admissions into hospital, deaths, as well as other information necessary to enable it to make out and keep up to date an individual return for each prisoner of war. The office must state in this return the regimental number, name and surname, age, place of origin, rank, unit, wounds, date and place of capture, internment, wounding, and death, as well as any observations of a special character. The individual return shall be sent to the Government of the other belligerent after the conclusion of peace.

It is likewise the function of the inquiry office to receive and collect all objects of personal use, valuables, letters, etc., found on the field of battle or left by prisoners who have been released on parole, or exchanged, or who have escaped, or died in hospitals or ambulances, and to forward them to those concerned.

Article 15

Relief societies for prisoners of war, which are properly constituted in accordance with the laws of their country and with the object of serving as the channel for charitable effort shall receive from the belligerents, for themselves and their duly accredited agents every facility for the efficient performance of their humane task within the bounds imposed by military necessities and administrative regulations. Agents of these societies may be admitted to the places of internment for the purpose of distributing relief, as also to the halting places of repatriated prisoners, if furnished with a personal permit by the military authorities, and on giving an undertaking in writing to comply with all measures of order and police which the latter may issue.

Article 16

Inquiry offices enjoy the privilege of free postage. Letters, money orders, and valuables, as well as parcels by post, intended for prisoners of war, or dispatched by them, shall be exempt from all postal duties in the countries of origin and destination, as well as in the countries they pass through.

Presents and relief in kind for prisoners of war shall be admitted free of all import or other duties, as well as of payments for carriage by the State railways.

Article 17

Officers taken prisoners shall receive the same rate of pay as officers of corresponding rank in the country where they are detained, the amount to be ultimately refunded by their own Government.

Article 18

Prisoners of war shall enjoy complete liberty in the exercise of their religion, including attendance at the services of whatever church they may belong to, on the sole condition that they comply with the measures of order and police issued by the military authorities.

Article 19

The wills of prisoners of war are received or drawn up in the same way as for soldiers of the national army.

The same rules shall be observed regarding death certificates as well as for the burial of prisoners of war, due regard being paid to their grade and rank.

Article 20

After the conclusion of peace, the repatriation of prisoners of war shall be carried out as quickly as possible.

CHAPTER III — *The Sick and Wounded*

Article 21

The obligations of belligerents with regard to the sick and wounded are governed by the Geneva Convention.[2]

SECTION II — HOSTILITIES

CHAPTER I — *Means of Injuring the Enemy,
Sieges, and Bombardments*

Article 22

The right of belligerents to adopt means of injuring the enemy is not unlimited.

Article 23

In addition to the prohibitions provided by special Conventions, it is especially forbidden —

(*a*) To employ poison or poisoned weapons;

(*b*) To kill or wound treacherously individuals belonging to the hostile nation or army;

(*c*) To kill or wound an enemy who, having laid down his arms, or having no longer means of defence, has surrendered at discretion;

(*d*) To declare that no quarter will be given;

(*e*) To employ arms, projectiles, or material calculated to cause unnecessary suffering;

(*f*) To make improper use of a flag of truce, of the national flag or of the military insignia and uniform of the enemy, as well as the distinctive badges of the Geneva Convention;

---

[2] This was a reference to the 1906 Geneva Convention for the Amelioration of the Condition of the Wounded and Sick in Armies in the Field, which replaced the 1864 Geneva Convention as between states parties to both agreements.

(*g*) To destroy or seize the enemy's property, unless such destruction or seizure be imperatively demanded by the necessities of war;

(*h*) To declare abolished, suspended, or inadmissible in a court of law the rights and actions of the nationals of the hostile party.

A belligerent is likewise forbidden to compel the nationals of the hostile party to take part in the operations of war directed against their own country, even if they were in the belligerent's service before the commencement of the war.

Article 24
Ruses of war and the employment of measures necessary for obtaining information about the enemy and the country are considered permissible.

Article 25
The attack or bombardment, by whatever means, of towns, villages, dwellings, or buildings which are undefended is prohibited.

Article 26
The officer in command of an attacking force must, before commencing a bombardment, except in cases of assault, do all in his power to warn the authorities.

Article 27
In sieges and bombardments all necessary steps must be taken to spare, as far as possible, building dedicated to religion, art, science, or charitable purposes, historic monuments, hospitals, and places where the sick and wounded are collected, provided they are not being used at the time for military purposes.

It is the duty of the besieged to indicate the presence of such buildings or places by distinctive and visible signs, which shall be notified to the enemy beforehand.

Article 28
The pillage of a town or place, even when taken by assault, is prohibited.

CHAPTER II — *Spies*

Article 29
A person can only be considered a spy when, acting clandestinely or on false pretences, he obtains or endeavors to obtain information in the zone of operations of a belligerent, with the intention of communicating it to the hostile party.

Thus, soldiers not wearing a disguise who have penetrated into the zone of operations of the hostile army, for the purpose of obtaining information, are not considered spies. Similarly, the following are not considered spies: Soldiers and civilians, carrying out their mission openly, intrusted with the delivery of despatches intended either for their own army or for the enemy's army. To this class belong likewise persons sent in balloons for the purpose of carrying despatches and, generally, of maintaining communications between the different parts of an army or a territory.

Article 30

A spy taken in the acts shall not be punished without previous trial.

Article 31

A spy who, after rejoining the army to which he belongs, is subsequently captured by the enemy, is treated as a prisoner of war, and incurs no responsibility for his previous acts of espionage.

CHAPTER III — *Flags of Truce*

Article 32

A person is regarded as a parlementaire who has been authorized by one of the belligerents to enter into communication with the other, and who advances bearing a white flag. He has a right to inviolability, as well as the trumpeter, bugler or drummer, the flag-bearer and interpreter who may accompany him.

Article 33

The commander to whom a parlementaire is sent is not in all cases obliged to receive him.

He may take all the necessary steps to prevent the parlementaire taking advantage of his mission to obtain information.

In case of abuse, he has the right to detain the parlementaire temporarily.

Article 34

The parlementaire loses his rights of inviolability if it is proved in a clear and incontestable manner that he has taken advantage of his privileged position to provoke or commit an act of treason.

CHAPTER IV — *Capitulations*

Article 35

Capitulations agreed upon between the contracting Parties must take into account the rules of military honor.

Once settled, they must be scrupulously observed by both parties.

CHAPTER V — *Armistices*

Article 36

An armistice suspends military operations by mutual agreement between the belligerent parties. If its duration is not defined, the belligerent parties may resume operations at any time, provided always that the enemy is warned within the time agreed upon, in accordance with the terms of the armistice.

Article 37

An armistice may be general or local. The first suspends the military operations of the belligerent States everywhere; the second only between certain fractions of the belligerent armies and within a fixed radius.

Article 38

An armistice must be notified officially and in good time to the competent authorities and to the troops. Hostilities are suspended immediately after the notification, or on the date fixed.

Article 39

It rests with the contracting Parties to settle, in the terms of the armistice, what communications may be held in the theatre of war with the inhabitants and between the inhabitants of one belligerent State and those of the other.

Article 40

Any serious violation of the armistice by one of the parties gives the other party the right of denouncing it, and even, in cases of urgency, of recommencing hostilities immediately.

Article 41

A violation of the terms of the armistice by private persons acting on their own initiative only entitles the injured party to demand the punishment of the offenders or, if necessary, compensation for the losses sustained.

SECTION III — MILITARY AUTHORITY OVER THE TERRITORY OF THE HOSTILE STATE

Article 42

Territory is considered occupied when it is actually placed under the authority of the hostile army.

The occupation extends only to the territory where such authority has been established and can be exercised.

Article 43

The authority of the legitimate power having in fact passed into the hands of the occupant, the latter shall take all the measures in his power to restore, and ensure, as far as possible, public order and safety,[3] while respecting, unless absolutely prevented, the laws in force in the country.

Article 44

A belligerent is forbidden to force the inhabitants of territory occupied by it to furnish information about the army of the other belligerent, or about its means of defense.

Article 45

It is forbidden to compel the inhabitants of occupied territory to swear allegiance to the hostile Power.

Article 46

Family honor and rights, the lives of persons, and private property, as well as religious convictions and practice, must be respected.

Private property can not be confiscated.

Article 47

Pillage is formally forbidden.

Article 48

If, in the territory occupied, the occupant collects the taxes, dues, and tolls imposed for the benefit of the State, he shall do so, as far as is possible, in accordance with the rules of assessment and incidence in force, and shall in consequence be bound to defray the expenses of the administration of the occupied territory to the same extent as the legitimate Government was so bound.

Article 49

If, in addition to the taxes mentioned in the above article, the occupant levies other money contributions in the occupied territory, this shall only be for the needs of the army or of the administration of the territory in question.

Article 50

No general penalty, pecuniary or otherwise, shall be inflicted upon the population on account of the acts of individuals for which they can not be regarded as jointly and severally responsible.

Article 51

No contribution shall be collected except under a written order, and on the responsibility of a commander-in-chief.

The collection of the said contribution shall only be effected as far as possible in accordance with the rules of assessment and incidence of the taxes in force.

For every contribution a receipt shall be given to the contributors.

[3] In the authentic French text: 'l'ordre et la vie publics'.

Article 52

Requisitions in kind and services shall not be demanded from municipalities or inhabitants except for the needs of the army of occupation. They shall be in proportion to the resources of the country, and of such a nature as not to involve the inhabitants in the obligation of taking part in military operations against their own country.

Such requisitions and services shall only be demanded on the authority of the commander in the locality occupied.

Contributions in kind shall as far as possible be paid for in cash; if not, a receipt shall be given and the payment of the amount due shall be made as soon as possible.

Article 53

An army of occupation can only take possession of cash, funds, and realizable securities which are strictly the property of the State, depots of arms, means of transport, stores and supplies, and, generally, all movable property belonging to the State which may be used for military operations.

All appliances, whether on land, at sea, or in the air, adapted for the transmission of news, or for the transport of persons or things, exclusive of cases governed by naval law, depots of arms, and, generally, all kinds of munitions of war, may be seized, even if they belong to private individuals, but must be restored and compensation fixed when peace is made.

Article 54

Submarine cables connecting an occupied territory with a neutral territory shall not be seized or destroyed except in the case of absolute necessity. They must likewise be restored and compensation fixed when peace is made.

Article 55

The occupying State shall be regarded only as administrator and usufructuary of public buildings, real estate, forests, and agricultural estates belonging to the hostile State, and situated in the occupied country. It must safeguard the capital of these properties, and administer them in accordance with the rules of usufruct.

Article 56

The property of municipalities, that of institutions dedicated to religion, charity and education, the arts and sciences, even when State property, shall be treated as private property.

All seizure of, destruction or wilful damage done to institutions of this character, historic monuments, works of art and science, is forbidden, and should be made the subject of legal proceedings.

CONCLUDING NOTES

Signatures, Ratifications, Accessions, and Successions[4]

State (* denotes Reservation: see below)	Date of Signature		Date of Ratification (r), Accession (a), or Succession (s)		
Argentina	18 October	1907	—		
*Austria-Hungary	18 October	1907	27 November	1909	r
Belgium	18 October	1907	8 August	1910	r
Bolivia	18 October	1907	27 November	1909	r
Brazil	18 October	1907	5 January	1914	r
Bulgaria	18 October	1907	—		
Byelorussian SSR[5]			4 June	1962	s
Chile	18 October	1907	—		
China			10 May	1917	a
Colombia	18 October	1907	—		
Cuba	18 October	1907	22 February	1912	r
Denmark	18 October	1907	27 November	1909	r
Dominican Republic	18 October	1907	16 May	1958	r
Ecuador	18 October	1907	—		
El Salvador	18 October	1907	27 November	1909	r
Ethiopia			5 August	1935	a
Fiji[5]			2 April	1973	s
Finland[6]			30 December	1918	a
France	18 October	1907	7 October	1910	r
*Germany	18 October	1907	27 November	1909	r
German Democratic Republic[5]			9 February	1959	s
Great Britain	18 October	1907	27 November	1909	r
Greece	18 October	1907	—		
Guatemala	18 October	1907	15 March	1911	r
Haiti	18 October	1907	2 February	1910	r
Italy	18 October	1907	—		
*Japan	18 October	1907	13 December	1911	r
Liberia			4 February	1914	a

[4] Information supplied in communications from the Netherlands Ministry of Foreign Affairs between December 1979 and April 1981. For a list, supplied by the same source, of eighteen states bound by the very similar terms of 1899 Hague Convention II, see the prefatory note above, p. 44.

[5] By letters dated 1 April 1980 and 16 March 1981 the Netherlands Ministry of Foreign Affairs confirmed that these cases constituted successions. *Re* USSR and Byelorussia, see above, p. 41, n. 3.

[6] By letter dated 12 May 1980 the Netherlands Ministry of Foreign Affairs stated (*a*) Finland's accession on 30 December 1918 to this and other 1907 Hague Conventions and to the 1907 Hague Declaration was initially regarded as provisional, pending the final resolution of Finland's international status; (*b*) after consultation with the other contracting powers, the Depositary stated on 9 June 1922 that Finland's accession should be regarded as final and complete; and (*c*) the Conventions and the Declaration entered into force for Finland on 9 June 1922.

State (*denotes Reservation: see below)	Date of Signature		Date of Ratification (r), Accession (a), or Succession (s)		
Luxembourg	18 October	1907	5 September	1912	r
Mexico	18 October	1907	27 November	1909	r
*Montenegro	18 October	1907	—		
Netherlands	18 October	1907	27 November	1909	r
Nicaragua			16 December	1909	a
Norway	18 October	1907	19 September	1910	r
Panama	18 October	1907	11 September	1911	r
Paraguay	18 October	1907	—		
Persia	18 October	1907	—		
Peru	18 October	1907	—		
Poland			9 May	1925	a
Portugal	18 October	1907	13 April	1911	r
Romania	18 October	1907	1 March	1912	r
*Russia	18 October	1907	27 November	1909	r
Serbia	18 October	1907	—		
Siam	18 October	1907	12 March	1910	r
South Africa[5]			10 March	1978	s
Sweden	18 October	1907	27 November	1909	r
Switzerland	18 October	1907	12 May	1910	r
*Turkey	18 October	1907	—		
Uruguay	18 October	1907	—		
USA	18 October	1907	27 November	1909	r
USSR[5]			7 March	1955	s
Venezuela	18 October	1907	—		

Total Number of Parties Listed: 37

Note on Entry into Force for States Parties

In accordance with Article 7, the Convention entered into force on 26 January 1910 for the states which had ratified it sixty days earlier, on 27 November 1909. For each of the other ratifying states, and for each of the acceding states (apart from Finland), the Convention formally entered into force sixty days after the date indicated in the right-hand column above.

Denunciations

None

Reservations

Austria-Hungary, Germany, Japan, Montenegro, and *Russia* all, at signature, made reservation of Article 44 of the annexed Regulations. At ratification, all of them (with the exception of Montenegro, which did not ratify) maintained their reservations.

Turkey, at signature, made reservation of Article 3 of the Convention. It did not ratify the Convention.

6. 1907 Hague Convention V Respecting the Rights and Duties of Neutral Powers and Persons in Case of War on Land

PREFATORY NOTE

The term 'neutrality' in the laws of war refers to the legal position of states which do not actively participate in a given armed conflict: it may thus describe the position of a large number of states during a large number of conflicts. It should be distinguished from other uses of the term, for example to describe the permanent status of a state neutralized by special treaty. In this latter case, particular duties arise in peace as well as in war, and in war the state may have a treaty obligation to remain neutral.

The concept of neutrality in war emerged with the early development of international maritime law. The rapid growth and increasing importance of international trade in the eighteenth and nineteenth centuries, which led maritime states to seek a means of resisting belligerent interference with neutral trade, became the foundation for the contemporary development of neutrality. By the end of the nineteenth century the legal status of neutrality on land and sea was widely accepted, but there were divergent views about specific neutral rights and duties.

Neutral rights and duties in land warfare had been the subject of several articles in 1899 Hague Convention II on land warfare, but were then much more extensively enumerated in 1907 Hague Convention V. At the time of its adoption, 1907 Hague Convention V was regarded as being largely declaratory of customary international law. To the extent that the Convention may be considered customary international law, it would be binding on all states and its 'general participation clause' (Article 20) would cease to be relevant. In hostilities since 1907, including both world wars, the Convention was frequently referred to by both neutrals and belligerents.

However, many developments since the conclusion of the Convention have raised questions about the traditional concept of neutrality and the customary law relating to it. Only a few such developments can be mentioned here. The Convention puts much emphasis on the idea of impartiality towards all belligerents. But when the 1919 Covenant of the League of Nations and the 1928 Kellogg–Briand Pact placed certain restrictions on the right to resort to force, this inevitably raised questions as to the legitimacy of impartiality in the face of an unlawful resort to force. During the Second World War, certain neutral states, without going so far as to actually join in the hostilities, took non-violent discriminatory measures against states regarded as unlawfully resorting to force. This departure from parts of the traditional law of neutrality has at times been called 'qualified neutrality', and some contend that a new legal category of 'non-belligerency' began to emerge, releasing neutral states from certain traditional neutral duties but still requiring avoidance of active participation in hostilities. However, others suggest that the concept of non-belligerency, while describing the actual behaviour of some states, runs counter to the traditional requirement of impartiality and at present does not possess full standing in international law. In this view, the traditional notion of impartiality remains an important characteristic of neutrality in the true sense of the term.

The adoption of the United Nations Charter in 1945 increased the controversy over the status of the traditional concept of neutrality. Some suggest that the customary law of neutrality is incompatible with the international legal regime established by the UN Charter. This contention rests on the combined effect of Article 2(5) which requires UN members to give the UN every assistance in any action it takes, Article 25 which requires UN members to accept and comply with the decisions of the Security Council, and the articles in Chapter VII. The preferable view is to regard the traditional concept of neutrality as having been modified, but not totally superseded, by the UN Charter. As far as UN member states are concerned, they would be free to be neutral if, in a given armed conflict, the UN (for whatever reason) does not act under Chapter VII of the Charter. Such an outcome is particularly likely in the many cases in which the Security Council is unable (for example, through use of the veto) to reach agreement. As for the position of non-members, Article 2(6) provides that the UN shall ensure that non-members act in accordance with the principles set forth in Article 2. However, if the term 'ensure' is interpreted as meaning 'influence' rather than 'coerce', then non-members may remain neutral even if the UN acts. In all such situations, the law relating to neutrality is applicable.

The continuing validity of the concept of neutrality is indicated by the many references to neutral states, neutral territory, etc., which are to be found in international agreements concluded since the establishment of the United Nations: for example, the four 1949 Geneva Conventions refer to neutral powers, countries, and territory; and 1977 Geneva Protocol I refers to 'neutral and other States not Parties to the conflict'.

Date of signature:	18 October 1907
Entry into force:	26 January 1910
Depositary:	Netherlands
Authentic lanuage:	French
Text reprinted from:	J. B. Scott (ed.), *The Hague Conventions and Declarations of 1899 and 1907*, Oxford University Press, New York, 3rd edn., 1918, pp. 133–40. (English translation by US Department of State, with minor corrections by J. B. Scott.)
Also published in:	3 *Martens NRG, 3ème sér.* (1862–1910) 504–32 (Fr. Ger.);
	100 *BFSP* (1906–1907) 359–64 (Fr.);
	2 *AJIL* (1908) Supplement 117–27 (Eng. Fr.);
	205 *CTS* (1907) 299–304 (Fr.)

Convention (V) Respecting the Rights and Duties of Neutral Powers and Persons in Case of War on Land

His Majesty the German Emperor, King of Prussia; [etc.] :

With a view to laying down more clearly the rights and duties of neutral Powers in case of war on land and regulating the position of the belligerents who have taken refuge in neutral territory;

Being likewise desirous of defining the meaning of the term 'neutral', pending the possibility of settling, in its entirety, the position of neutral individuals in their relations with the belligerents;

Have resolved to conclude a Convention to this effect, and have, in consequence, appointed the following as their plenipotentiaries:

[Here follow the names of the plenipotentiaries.]

Who, after having deposited their full powers, found in good and due form, have agreed upon the following provisions:

CHAPTER I — *The Rights and Duties of Neutral Powers*

Article 1

The territory of neutral Powers is inviolable.

Article 2

Belligerents are forbidden to move troops or convoys of either munitions of war or supplies across the territory of a neutral Power.

Article 3

Belligerents are likewise forbidden to —

(*a*) Erect on the territory of a neutral Power a wireless telegraphy station or other apparatus for the purpose of communicating with belligerent forces on land or sea;

(*b*) Use of any installation of this kind established by them before the war on the territory of a neutral Power for purely military purposes, and which has not been opened for the service of public messages.

Article 4

Corps of combatants can not be formed nor recruiting agencies opened on territory of a neutral Power to assist the belligerents.

Article 5

A neutral Power must not allow any of the acts referred to in Articles 2 to 4 to occur on its territory.

It is not called upon to punish acts in violation of its neutrality unless the said acts have been committed on its own territory.

Article 6

The responsibility of a neutral Power is not engaged by the fact of persons crossing the frontier separately to offer their services to one of the belligerents.

Article 7

A neutral Power is not called upon to prevent the export or transport, on behalf of one or other of the belligerents, of arms, munitions of war, or, in general, of anything which can be of use to an army or a fleet.

Article 8

A neutral Power is not called upon to forbid or restrict the use on behalf of the belligerents of telegraph or telephone cables or of wireless telegraphy apparatus belonging to it or to companies or private individuals.

Article 9

Every measure of restriction or prohibition taken by a neutral Power in regard to the matters referred to in Articles 7 and 8 must be impartially applied by it to both belligerents.

A neutral Power must see to the same obligation being observed by companies or private individuals owning telegraph or telephone cables or wireless telegraphy apparatus.

Article 10

The fact of a neutral Power resisting, even by force, attempts to violate its neutrality can not be regarded as a hostile act.

CHAPTER II — *Belligerents Interned and Wounded*
Tended in Neutral Territory

Article 11

A neutral Power which receives on its territory troops belonging to the belligerent armies shall intern them, as far as possible, at a distance from the theatre of war.

It may keep them in camps and even confine them in fortresses or in places set apart for this purpose.

It shall decide whether officers can be left at liberty on giving their parole not to leave the neutral territory without permission.

Article 12

In the absence of a special convention to the contrary, the neutral Power shall supply the interned with the food, clothing, and relief required by humanity.

At the conclusion of peace the expenses caused by the internment shall be made good.

Article 13

A neutral Power which receives escaped prisoners of war shall leave them at liberty. If it allows them to remain in its territory it may assign them a place of residence.

The same rule applies to prisoners of war brought by troops taking refuge in the territory of a neutral Power.

Article 14

A neutral Power may authorize the passage over its territory of the sick and wounded belonging to the belligerent armies, on condition that the trains bringing them shall carry neither personnel nor war material. In such a case, the neutral Power is bound to take whatever measures of safety and control are necessary for the purpose.

The sick or wounded brought under these conditions into neutral territory by one of the belligerents, and belonging to the hostile party, must be guarded by the neutral Power so as to ensure their not taking part again in the military operations. The same duty shall devolve on the neutral State with regard to wounded or sick of the other army who may be committed to its care.

Article 15

The Geneva Convention applies to sick and wounded interned in neutral territory.

CHAPTER III — *Neutral Persons*

Article 16

The nationals of a State which is not taking part in the war are considered as neutrals.

Article 17

A neutral can not avail himself of his neutrality —

(*a*) If he commits hostile acts against a belligerent;

(*b*) If he commits acts in favor of a belligerent, particularly if he voluntarily enlists in the ranks of the armed force of one of the parties.

In such a case, the neutral shall not be more severely treated by the belligerent as against whom he has abandoned his neutrality than a national of the other belligerent State could be for the same act.

Article 18

The following acts shall not be considered as committed in favor of one belligerent in the sense of Article 17, letter (*b*):

(*a*) Supplies furnished or loans made to one of the belligerents, provided that the person who furnishes the supplies or who makes the loans lives neither in the territory of the other party nor in the territory occupied by him, and that the supplies do not come from these territories;

(*b*) Services rendered in matters of police or civil administration.

CHAPTER IV — *Railway Material*

Article 19

Railway material coming from the territory of neutral Powers, whether it be the property of the said Powers or of companies or private persons, and recognizable as such, shall not be requisitioned or utilized by a belligerent except where and to the extent that it is absolutely necessary. It shall be sent back as soon as possible to the country of origin.

A neutral Power may likewise, in case of necessity, retain and utilize to an equal extent material coming from the territory of the belligerent Power.

Compensation shall be paid by one party or the other in proportion to the material used, and to the period of usage.

CHAPTER V — *Final Provisions*

Article 20

The provisions of the present Convention do not apply except between contracting Powers, and then only if all the belligerents are parties to the Convention.

Article 21

The present Convention shall be ratified as soon as possible.

The ratifications shall be deposited at The Hague.

The first deposit of ratifications shall be recorded in a procès-verbal signed by the representatives of the Powers which take part therein and by the Netherland Minister for Foreign Affairs.

The subsequent deposits of ratifications shall be made by means of a written notification, addressed to the Netherland Government and accompanied by the instrument of ratification.

A duly certified copy of the procès-verbal relative to the first deposit of ratifications, of the notifications mentioned in the preceding paragraph, and of the instruments of ratification shall be immediately sent by the Netherland Government, through the diplomatic channel, to the Powers invited to the Second Peace

Conference as well as to the other Powers which have adhered to the Convention. In the cases contemplated in the preceding paragraph, the said Government shall at the same time inform them of the date on which it received the notification.

Article 22

Non-signatory Powers may adhere to the present Convention.

The Power which desires to adhere notifies its intention in writing to the Netherland Government, forwarding to it the act of adhesion, which shall be deposited in the archives of the said Government.

This Government shall immediately forward to all the other Powers a duly certified copy of the notification as well as of the act of adhesion, mentioning the date on which it received the notification.

Article 23

The present Convention shall come into force, in the case of the Powers which were a party to the first deposit of ratifications, sixty days after the date of the procès-verbal of this deposit, and, in the case of the Powers which ratify subsequently or which adhere, sixty days after the notification of their ratification or of their adhesion has been received by the Netherland Government.

Article 24

In the event of one of the contracting Powers wishing to denounce the present Convention, the denunciation shall be notified in writing to the Netherland Government, which shall immediately communicate a duly certified copy of the notification to all the other Powers, informing them at the same time of the date on which it was received.

The denunciation shall only have effect in regard to the notifying Power, and one year after the notification has reached the Netherland Government.

Article 25

A register kept by the Netherland Ministry of Foreign Affairs shall give the date of the deposit of ratifications made in virtue of Article 21, paragraphs 3 and 4, as well as the date on which the notifications of adhesion (Article 22, paragraph 2) or of denunciation (Article 24, paragraph 1) have been received.

Each contracting Power is entitled to have access to this register and to be supplied with duly certified extracts from it.

In faith whereof the plenipotentiaries have appended their signatures to the present Convention.

Done at The Hague, the 18th October, 1907, in a single copy, which shall remain deposited in the archives of the Netherland Government, and duly certified copies of which shall be sent, through the diplomatic channel, to the Powers which have been invited to the Second Peace Conference.

CONCLUDING NOTES

Signatures, Ratifications, Accessions, and Successions[1]

State (* denotes Reservation: see below)	Date of Signature		Date of Ratification (*r*), Accession (*a*), or Succession (*s*)		
*Argentina	18 October	1907	—		
Austria-Hungary	18 October	1907	27 November	1909	*r*
Belgium	18 October	1907	8 August	1910	*r*
Bolivia	18 October	1907	27 November	1909	*r*
Brazil	18 October	1907	5 January	1914	*r*
Bulgaria	18 October	1907	—		
Byelorussian SSR[2]			4 June	1962	*s*
Chile	18 October	1907	—		
China			15 January	1910	*a*
Colombia	18 October	1907	—		
Cuba	18 October	1907	22 February	1912	*r*
Denmark	18 October	1907	27 November	1909	*r*
Dominican Republic	18 October	1907			
Ecuador	18 October	1907	—		
El Salvador	18 October	1907	27 November	1909	*r*
Ethiopia			5 August	1935	*a*
Finland[3]			30 December	1918	*a*
France	18 October	1907	7 October	1910	*r*
Germany	18 October	1907	27 November	1909	*r*
German Democratic Republic[2]			9 February	1959	*s*
*Great Britain	18 October	1907	—		
Greece	18 October	1907	—		
Guatemala	18 October	1907	15 March	1911	*r*
Haiti	18 October	1907	2 February	1910	*r*
Italy	18 October	1907	—		
Japan	18 October	1907	13 December	1911	*r*
Liberia			4 February	1914	*a*

[1] Information supplied in communications from the Netherlands Ministry of Foreign Affairs between December 1979 and April 1981.

[2] By letters dated 1 April 1980 and 16 March 1981 the Netherlands Ministry of Foreign Affairs confirmed that these cases constituted successions. *Re* USSR and Byelorussia, see above, p. 41, n. 3.

[3] The Depositary states that Finland's accession became effective on 9 June 1922. See above, p. 58, n. 6.

State (* denotes Reservation: see below)	Date of Signature		Date of Ratification (r), Accession (a), or Succession (s)		
Luxembourg	18 October	1907	5 September	1912	r
Mexico	18 October	1907	27 November	1909	r
Montenegro	18 October	1907	—		
Netherlands	18 October	1907	27 November	1909	r
Nicaragua			16 December	1909	a
Norway	18 October	1907	19 September	1910	r
Panama	18 October	1907	11 September	1911	r
Paraguay	18 October	1907	—		
Persia	18 October	1907	—		
Peru	18 October	1907	—		
Poland			9 May	1925	a
Portugal	18 October	1907	13 April	1911	r
Romania	18 October	1907	1 March	1912	r
Russia	18 October	1907	27 November	1909	r
Serbia	18 October	1907	—		
Siam	18 October	1907	12 March	1910	r
Spain	18 October	1907	18 March	1913	r
Sweden	18 October	1907	27 November	1909	r
Switzerland	18 October	1907	12 May	1910	r
Turkey	18 October	1907	—		
Uruguay	18 October	1907	—		
USA	18 October	1907	27 November	1909	r
USSR[2]			7 March	1955	s
Venezuela	18 October	1907	—		

Total Number of Parties Listed: 34

Note on Entry into Force for States Parties

In accordance with Article 23, the Convention entered into force on 26 January 1910 for the states which had ratified it sixty days earlier, on 27 November 1909. For each of the other ratifying states, and for each of the acceding states (apart from Finland), the Convention formally entered into force sixty days after the date indicated in the right-hand column above.

Denunciations

None

Reservations

Argentina, at signature, made reservation of Article 19. It did not ratify the Convention.

Great Britain, at signature, made reservation of Articles 16, 17, and 18. It did not ratify the Convention.

7. 1907 Hague Convention VI Relating to the Status of Enemy Merchant Ships at the Outbreak of Hostilities

PREFATORY NOTE

International law once recognized that, during peacetime, states could perform an act of reprisal (technically called 'embargo') whereby an injured state could prevent the ships of a state committing an unlawful act from leaving its ports in order to compel the offending state to make reparations for the act committed. When war seemed imminent, the opposing states could impose such an embargo on enemy merchant ships in port to facilitate capture and confiscation of such ships once war had broken out. However, the use of such reprisals during peacetime would now run up against the UN Charter's requirement to settle disputes by peaceful means and its prohibition of the threat or use of force.

International law recognized that, at the outbreak of war, enemy merchant ships in port were subject to embargo for the purpose of their capture and confiscation, and that such ships at sea were subject to capture and confiscation, even if the ship's officers were ignorant of the outbreak of war. Beginning with the outbreak of the Crimean War in 1854, some states followed the practice of imposing no embargo on belligerent merchant ships in enemy ports at the outbreak of war, allowing such ships a reasonable period of grace to depart before becoming liable to capture and confiscation. Some states also followed the practice of granting immunity from seizure to belligerent merchant ships which had left their last port of departure before the outbreak of war, and whose officers were unaware of the existence of a state of war. Despite these occasional usages, state practice was not uniform.

1907 Hague Convention VI, adopted at the Second Hague Peace Conference, was the first codification of binding rules on the status of enemy merchant ships at the outbreak of hostilities.

Many states failed to ratify the Convention. It contains a 'general participation clause' (Article 6) which affects its technical application in hostilities where not all belligerents are parties to the Convention. During the First World War, observance of the Convention was far from uniform. Great Britain regarded reciprocity and a high degree of uniformity of practice as essential, and therefore denounced the Convention in 1925. France followed suit in 1939. At the outbreak of the Second World War, Great Britain and France did not grant a period of grace to enemy merchant ships in port, and enemy merchant ships (in port or on the high seas) were liable to seizure and confiscation. Other states adopted the same practice. In view of this state practice, it is unlikely that the favourable treatment of belligerent merchant ships in enemy ports at the outbreak of hostilities can be regarded as part of customary international law.

The declining relevance of the Convention may be attributed to two principal factors. First, the Convention does not apply to merchant ships capable of conversion into warships, and therefore the practice of constructing merchant ships which by their design can be quickly converted into warships has reduced the Convention's application accordingly. Second, the military importance of merchant ships which are not converted into warships (to accompany and service warships or to perform other war-related functions) has reduced the likelihood that such ships would not be seized and confiscated by belligerents at the outbreak of hostilities.

Date of signature:	18 October 1907
Entry into force:	26 January 1910
Depositary:	Netherlands
Authentic language:	French
Text reprinted from:	J. B. Scott (ed.), *The Hague Conventions and Declarations of 1899 and 1907*, Oxford University Press, New York, 3rd edn., 1918, pp. 141–5. (English translation by US Department of State, with minor corrections by J. B. Scott.)
Also published in:	3 *Martens NRG, 3ème sér.* (1862–1910) 533–56 (Fr. Ger.);
	100 *BFSP* (1906–1907) 365–77 (Fr.);
	UKTS 10 (1910), Cd. 5031 (Eng. Fr.);
	CXII *UKPP* (1910) 101 (Eng. Fr.);
	2 *AJIL* (1908) Supplement 127–33 (Eng. Fr.);
	205 *CTS* (1907) 305–18 (Fr.)

Convention (VI) Relating to the Status of Enemy Merchant Ships at the Outbreak of Hostilities

His Majesty the German Emperor, King of Prussia; [etc.] :

Anxious to ensure the security of international commerce against the surprises of war, and wishing, in accordance with modern practice, to protect as far as possible operations undertaken in good faith and in process of being carried out before the outbreak of hostilities, have resolved to conclude a Convention to this effect, and have appointed the following persons as their plenipotentiaries:

[Here follow the names of plenipotentiaries.]

Who, after having deposited their full powers, found in good and due form, have agreed upon the following provisions:

Article 1

When a merchant ship belonging to one of the belligerent Powers is at the commencement of hostilities in an enemy port, it is desirable that it should be allowed to depart freely, either immediately, or after a reasonable number of days of grace, and to proceed, after being furnished with a pass, direct to its port of destination or any other port indicated.

The same rule should apply in the case of a ship which has left its last port of departure before the commencement of the war and entered a port belonging to the enemy while still ignorant that hostilities had broken out.

Article 2

A merchant ship unable, owing to circumstances of *force majeure*, to leave the enemy port within the period contemplated in the above article, or which was not allowed to leave, can not be confiscated.

The belligerent may only detain it, without payment of compensation, but subject to the obligation of restoring it after the war, or requisition it on payment of compensation.

Article 3

Enemy merchant ships which left their last port of departure before the commencement of the war, and are encountered on the high seas while still ignorant of the outbreak of hostilities can not be confiscated. They are only liable to detention on the understanding that they shall be restored after the war without compensation, or to be requisitioned, or even destroyed, on payment of compensation, but in such cases provision must be made for the safety of the persons on board as well as the security of the ship's papers.

After touching at a port in their own country or at a neutral port, these ships are subject to the laws and customs of maritime war.

Article 4

Enemy cargo on board the vessels referred to in Articles 1 and 2 is likewise liable to be detained and restored after the termination of the war without payment of compensation, or to be requisitioned on payment of compensation, with or without the ship.

The same rule applies in the case of cargo on board the vessels referred to in Article 3.

Article 5

The present Convention does not affect merchant ships whose build shows that they are intended for conversion into war-ships.

Article 6

The provisions of the present Convention do not apply except between contracting Powers, and then only if all the belligerents are parties to the Convention.

Article 7

The present Convention shall be ratified as soon as possible.

The ratifications shall be deposited at The Hague.

The first deposit of ratifications shall be recorded in a procès-verbal signed by the representatives of the Powers which take part therein and by the Netherland Minister for Foreign Affairs.

The subsequent deposits of ratifications shall be made by means of a written notification addressed to the Netherland Government and accompanied by the instrument of ratification.

A duly certified copy of the procès-verbal relative to the first deposit of ratifications, of the notifications mentioned in the preceding paragraph, as well as of the instruments of ratification, shall be at once sent by the Netherland Government, through the diplomatic channel, to the Powers invited to the Second Peace Conference, as well as to the other Powers which have adhered to the Convention. In the cases contemplated in the preceding paragraph, the said Government shall at the same time inform them of the date on which it received the notification.

Article 8

Non-signatory Powers may adhere to the present Convention.

The Power which desires to adhere notifies in writing its intention to the Netherland Government, forwarding to it the act of adhesion, which shall be deposited in the archives of the said Government.

The said Government shall at once transmit to all the other Powers a duly certified copy of the notification as well as of the act of adhesion, stating the date on which it received the notification.

Article 9

The present Convention shall come into force, in the case of the Powers which were a party to the first deposit of ratifications, sixty days after the date of the procès-verbal of that deposit, and, in the case of the Powers which ratify subsequently or which adhere, sixty days after the notification of their ratification or of their adhesion has been received by the Netherland Government.

Article 10

In the event of one of the contracting Powers wishing to denounce the present Convention, the denunciation shall be notified in writing to the Netherland Government, which shall at once communicate a certified copy of the notification to all the other Powers, informing them of the date on which it was received.

The denunciation shall only have effect in regard to the notifying

Power, and one year after the notification has reached the Netherland Government.

Article 11

A register kept by the Ministry of Foreign Affairs shall give the date of the deposit of ratifications made in virtue of Article 7, paragraphs 3 and 4, as well as the date on which the notifications of adhesion (Article 8, paragraph 2) or of denunciation (Article 10, paragraph 1) have been received.

Each contracting Power is entitled to have access to this register and to be supplied with certified extracts from it.

In faith whereof the plenipotentiaries have appended to the present Convention their signatures.

Done at The Hague, the 18th October, 1907, in a single copy, which shall remain deposited in the archives of the Netherland Government, and duly certified copies of which shall be sent through the diplomatic channel, to the Powers which have been invited to the Second Peace Conference.

CONCLUDING NOTES

Signatures, Ratifications, Accessions, and Successions[1]

State (*denotes Reservation: see below)	Date of Signature		Date of Ratification (r), Accession (a), or Succession (s)		
Argentina	18 October	1907	—		
Austria-Hungary	18 October	1907	27 November	1909	r
Belgium	18 October	1907	8 August	1910	r
Bolivia	18 October	1907	—		
Brazil	18 October	1907	5 January	1914	r
Bulgaria	18 October	1907	—		
Byelorussian SSR[2]			4 June	1962	s
Chile	18 October	1907	—		
China			10 May	1917	a
Colombia	18 October	1907	—		
Cuba	18 October	1907	22 February	1912	r
Denmark	18 October	1907	27 November	1909	r
Dominican Republic	18 October	1907	—		
Ecuador	18 October	1907	—		
El Salvador	18 October	1907	27 November	1909	r
Ethiopia			5 August	1935	a

[1] Information supplied in communications from the Netherlands Ministry of Foreign Affairs between December 1979 and April 1981.

[2] By letters dated 1 April 1980 and 16 March 1981 the Netherlands Ministry of Foreign Affairs confirmed that these cases constituted successions. *Re* USSR and Byelorussia, see above, p. 41, n. 3.

State (* denotes Reservation: see below)	Date of Signature		Date of Ratification (r), Accession (a), or Succession (s)		
Finland[3]			30 December	1918	a
France[4]	18 October	1907	7 October	1910	r
*Germany	18 October	1907	27 November	1909	r
German Democratic Republic[2]			9 February	1959	s
Great Britain[4]	18 October	1907	27 November	1909	r
Greece	18 October	1907	—		
Guatemala	18 October	1907	15 March	1911	r
Haiti	18 October	1907	2 February	1910	r
Italy	18 October	1907	—		
Japan	18 October	1907	13 December	1911	r
Liberia			4 February	1914	a
Luxembourg	18 October	1907	5 September	1912	r
Mexico	18 October	1907	27 November	1909	r
Montenegro	18 October	1907	—		
Netherlands	18 October	1907	27 November	1909	r
Nicaragua			16 December	1909	a
Norway	18 October	1907	19 September	1910	r
Panama	18 October	1907	11 September	1911	r
Paraguay	18 October	1907	—		
Persia	18 October	1907	—		
Peru	18 October	1907	—		
Poland			31 May	1935	a
Portugal	18 October	1907	13 April	1911	r
Romania	18 October	1907	1 March	1912	r
*Russia	18 October	1907	27 November	1909	r
Serbia	18 October	1907	—		
Siam	18 October	1907	12 March	1910	r
Spain	18 October	1907	18 March	1913	r
Sweden	18 October	1907	27 November	1909	r
Switzerland	18 October	1907	12 May	1910	r
Turkey	18 October	1907	—		
Uruguay	18 October	1907	—		
USSR[2]			7 March	1955	s
Venezuela	18 October	1907	—		

Total Number of Parties Listed: 33

Note on Entry into Force for States Parties

In accordance with Article 9, the Convention entered into force on 26 January 1910 for the states which had ratified it sixty days earlier, on 27 November

---

[3] The Depositary states that Finland's accession became effective on 9 June 1922. See above, p. 58, n. 6.

[4] France and Great Britain denounced the Convention: see below.

1909. For each of the other ratifying states, and for each of the acceding states (apart from Finland), the Convention formally entered into force sixty days after the date indicated in the right-hand column above.

Denunciations

Great Britain denounced the Convention on 14 November 1925.
France denounced it on 13 July 1939.
    In accordance with Article 10, these denunciations became effective one year after each of the dates indicated here.

Reservations

Germany and *Russia*, at signature, made reservation of Article 3, and of Article 4, paragraph 2. At ratification, they maintained their reservations.[5]

---

[5] The German and Russian delegations considered that these provisions established an inequality between states in imposing financial burdens on those powers which, lacking naval stations in different parts of the world, were not in a position to take vessels which they had seized into a port, but found themselves compelled to destroy them. J. B. Scott (ed.), *The Hague Conventions and Declarations of 1899 and 1907*, p. 145, n. 2.

8. 1907 Hague Convention VII Relating to the Conversion of Merchant Ships into Warships

PREFATORY NOTE

There has traditionally been a clear distinction between the treatment, in time of war, of enemy warships and enemy merchant ships. Warships could be attacked and destroyed, or captured with title to the ship immediately passing to the capturing state. Merchant ships, on the other hand, were generally immune from attack and destruction, and although they could be captured, title to a ship could only pass after adjudication in the prize courts of the capturing state. However, if a merchant vessel refused to stop, actively resisted search and seizure, directly assisted its own state's warships or attacked enemy warships, any immunity from attack and destruction was forfeited.

The question of whether merchant ships could legitimately be converted into warships arose in 1870 at the outbreak of the Franco-Prussian War. At that time, the North German Confederation possessed relatively few warships and the King of Prussia (as President of the Confederation) formulated a plan to convert merchant ships into warships. France considered the proposed plan a violation of the prohibition of privateering contained in the 1856 Declaration of Paris, and requested Great Britain to intervene. Great Britain declared that the plan was not synonymous with a revival of privateering and therefore refused to object. Nevertheless, the Prussian plan was never put into effect. However, on subsequent occasions other states adopted the practice of securing merchant ships for conversion into warships at the outbreak of a war.

During the Russo-Japanese War of 1904–5, the conversion at sea of certain Russian merchant ships into warships, enabling them to capture neutral ships, led to a consideration of the matter at the Second Hague Peace Conference of 1907. The result was Hague Convention VII, which attempted to set forth a regime under which merchant ships could be converted so as to legitimately acquire the status of warships. The Convention contains a 'general participation clause' (Article 7) which affects its technical application in hostilities where not all belligerents are parties to the Convention.

The regime established by the Convention is regarded as unsatisfactory because it did not resolve the issues of whether conversion may be performed on the high seas and whether a converted merchant ship may convert back to a merchant ship before the termination of the war.

During the First and Second World Wars, belligerents employed the practice of converting merchant ships into warships, but controversy remained over the place of conversion, the legitimacy of re-conversion, and the status of merchant ships which have not been openly converted. Moreover, the actions of belligerents during both wars challenged the traditional immunity of merchant ships from attack and destruction. To the extent that the non-combatant status of merchant ships is undermined, the practical relevance of a distinction between combatant and non-combatant ships is obviously reduced.

Date of signature: 18 October 1907
Entry into force: 26 January 1910
Depositary: Netherlands
Authentic language: French
Text reprinted from: J. B. Scott (ed.), *The Hague Conventions and Declarations of 1899 and 1907*, Oxford University Press, New York, 3rd edn., 1918, pp. 146–50. (English translation by US Department of State, with minor corrections by J. B. Scott.)
Also published in: 3 *Martens NRG*, 3*ème sér.* (1862–1910) 557–79 (Fr. Ger.);
                          100 *BFSP* (1906–1907) 377–89 (Fr.);
                          UKTS 11 (1910), Cd. 5115 (Eng. Fr.);
                          CXII *UKPP* (1910) 125 (Eng. Fr.);
                          2 *AJIL* (1908) Supplement 133–8 (Eng. Fr.);
                          205 *CTS* (1907) 319–31 (Fr.)

Convention (VII) Relating to the Conversion of Merchant Ships into War-ships

His Majesty the German Emperor, King of Prussia; [etc.] :

Whereas it is desirable, in view of the incorporation in time of war of merchant ships in the fighting fleet, to define the conditions subject to which this operation may be effected;

Whereas, however, the contracting Powers have been unable to come to an agreement on the question whether the conversion of a merchant ship into a war-ship may take place upon the high seas, it is understood that the question of the place where such conversion is effected remains outside the scope of this agreement and is in no way affected by the following rules;

Being desirous of concluding a Convention to this effect, have appointed the following as their plenipotentiaries:

[Here follow the names of plenipotentiaries.]

Who, after having deposited their full powers, found in good and due form, have agreed upon the following provisions:

Article 1

A merchant ship converted into a war-ship can not have the rights and duties accruing to such vessels unless it is placed under the direct authority, immediate control, and responsibility of the Power whose flag it flies.

Article 2

Merchant ships converted into war-ships must bear the external marks which distinguish the war-ships of their nationality.

Article 3

The commander must be in the service of the State and duly commissioned by the competent authorities. His name must figure on the list of the officers of the fighting fleet.

Article 4

The crew must be subject to military discipline.

Article 5

Every merchant ship converted into a war-ship must observe in its operations the laws and customs of war.

Article 6

A belligerent who converts a merchant ship into a war-ship must, as soon as possible, announce such conversion in the list of war-ships.

Article 7

The provisions of the present Convention do not apply except between contracting Powers, and then only if all the belligerents are parties to the Convention.

Article 8

The present Convention shall be ratified as soon as possible.

The ratifications shall be deposited at The Hague.

The first deposit of ratifications shall be recorded in a procès-verbal signed by the representatives of the Powers who take part therein and by the Netherland Minister for Foreign Affairs.

The subsequent deposits of ratifications shall be made by means of a written notification, addressed to the Netherland Government and accompanied by the instrument of ratification.

A duly certified copy of the procès-verbal relative to the first deposit of ratifications, of the notifications mentioned in the preceding paragraph, as well as of the instruments of ratification, shall be at once sent by the Netherland Government, through the diplomatic channel, to the Powers invited to the Second Peace Conference, as well as to the other Powers which have adhered to the Convention. In the cases contemplated in the preceding paragraph the said Government shall at the same time inform them of the date on which it received the notification.

Article 9

Non-signatory Powers may adhere to the present Convention.

The Power which desires to ahdere notifies its intention in writing to the Netherland Government, forwarding to it the act of adhesion, which shall be deposited in the archives of the said Government.

That Government shall at once transmit to all the other Powers a duly certified copy of the notification as well as of the act of adhesion, stating the date on which it received the notification.

Article 10

The present Convention shall come into force, in the case of the Powers which were a party to the first deposit of ratifications, sixty days after the date of the procès-verbal of this deposit, and, in the case of the Powers which ratify subsequently or which adhere, sixty days after the notification of their ratification or of their adhesion has been received by the Netherland Government.

Article 11

In the event of one of the contracting Powers wishing to denounce the present Convention, the denunciation shall be notified in writing to the Netherland Government, which shall at once communicate a duly certified copy of the notification to all the other Powers, informing them of the date on which it was received.

The denunciation shall only have effect in regard to the notifying Power, and one year after the notification has reached the Netherland Government.

Article 12

A register kept by the Netherland Ministry for Foreign Affairs shall give the date of the deposit of ratifications made in virtue of Article 8, paragraphs 3 and 4, as well as the date on which the notifications of adhesion (Article 9, paragraph 2) or of denunciation (Article 11, paragraph 1) have been received.

Each contracting Power is entitled to have access to this register and to be supplied with duly certified extracts from it.

In faith whereof the plenipotentiaries have appended their signatures to the present Convention.

Done at The Hague, the 18th October, 1907, in a single copy, which shall remain deposited in the archives of the Netherland Government, and duly certified copies of which shall be sent, through the diplomatic channel, to the Powers which have been invited to the Second Peace Conference.

CONCLUDING NOTES

Signatures, Ratifications, Accessions and Successions [1]

State (* denotes Reservation: see below)	Date of Signature		Date of Ratification (r), Accession (a), or Succession (s)		
Argentina	18 October	1907	—		
Austria-Hungary	18 October	1907	27 November	1909	r
Belgium	18 October	1907	8 August	1910	r
Bolivia	18 October	1907	—		
Brazil	18 October	1907	5 January	1914	r
Bulgaria	18 October	1907	—		
Byelorussian SSR[2]			4 June	1962	s
Chile	18 October	1907	—		
China			10 May	1917	a
Colombia	18 October	1907	—		
Cuba	18 October	1907	—		
Denmark	18 October	1907	27 November	1909	r
Ecuador	18 October	1907	—		
El Salvador	18 October	1907	27 November	1909	r
Ethiopia			5 August	1935	a
Fiji[2]			2 April	1973	s
Finland[3]			30 December	1918	a
France	18 October	1907	7 October	1910	r
Germany	18 October	1907	27 November	1909	r
German Democratic Republic[2]			9 February	1959	s
Great Britain	18 October	1907	27 November	1909	r
Greece	18 October	1907	—		
Guatemala	18 October	1907	15 March	1911	r
Haiti	18 October	1907	2 February	1910	r
Italy	18 October	1907	—		
Japan	18 October	1907	13 December	1911	r
Liberia			4 February	1914	a
Luxembourg	18 October	1907	5 September	1912	r
Mexico	18 October	1907	27 November	1909	r
Montenegro	18 October	1907	—		
Netherlands	18 October	1907	27 November	1909	r
Nicaragua			16 December	1909	a
Norway	18 October	1907	19 September	1910	r
Panama	18 October	1907	11 September	1911	r

[1] Information supplied in communications from the Netherlands Ministry of Foreign Affairs between December 1979 and April 1981.

[2] By letters dated 1 April 1980 and 16 March 1981 the Netherlands Ministry of Foreign Affairs confirmed that these cases constituted successions. *Re* USSR and Byelorussia, see above, p. 41, n. 3.

[3] The Depositary states that Finland's accession became effective on 9 June 1922. See above, p. 58, n. 6.

State (* denotes Reservation: see below)	Date of Signature		Date of Ratification (*r*), Accession (*a*), or Succession (*s*)		
Paraguay	18 October	1907	—		
Persia	18 October	1907	—		
Peru	18 October	1907	—		
Poland			31 May	1935	*a*
Portugal	18 October	1907	13 April	1911	*r*
Romania	18 October	1907	1 March	1912	*r*
Russia	18 October	1907	27 November	1909	*r*
Serbia	18 October	1907	—		
Siam	18 October	1907	12 March	1910	*r*
South Africa[2]			10 March	1978	*s*
Spain	18 October	1907	18 March	1913	*r*
Sweden	18 October	1907	27 November	1909	*r*
Switzerland	18 October	1907	12 May	1910	*r*
*Turkey	18 October	1907	—		
USSR[2]			7 March	1955	*s*
Venezuela	18 October	1907	—		

Total Number of Parties Listed: 34

Note on Entry into Force for States Parties

In accordance with Article 10, the Convention entered into force on 26 January 1910 for the states which had ratified it sixty days earlier, on 27 November 1909. For each of the other ratifying states, and for each of the acceding states (apart from Finland), the Convention formally entered into force sixty days after the date indicated in the right-hand column above.

Denunciations

None

Reservation[4]

Turkey, at signature, referred in its reservation to its declaration at the Conference on 9 October 1907: 'The Imperial Ottoman Government does not engage to recognize as vessels of war, ships which, being in its waters or on the high seas under a merchant flag, are converted on the opening of hostilities.' It did not ratify the Convention.

[4] English version from J. B. Scott (ed.), *The Hague Conventions and Declarations of 1899 and 1907*, p. 150.

9. 1907 Hague Convention VIII
Relative to the Laying of
Automatic Submarine Contact Mines

PREFATORY NOTE

The employment of mines in naval warfare dates from at least the siege of Antwerp in 1584-5, but they were not used widely before the nineteenth century. During the Russo-Japanese War of 1904-5, mines which exploded through contact were laid near Port Arthur and resulted in extensive damage to neutral shipping, even after the war. These indiscriminate effects demonstrated the need for regulation of this kind of mine warfare.

At the Second Hague Peace Conference of 1907, the question of regulating the use of mines was raised with the hope of providing security for neutral shipping. Germany and other states objected to the British proposal that unanchored automatic contact mines should simply be prohibited. Objection was also raised to the British proposal that the use of mines for establishing or maintaining a commercial blockade should be prohibited. The compromise which was reached was embodied in Hague Convention VIII. The Convention contains a 'general participation clause' (Article 7) which affects its technical application in hostilities where not all belligerents are parties to the Convention.

The regime thus established has come to be regarded as unsatisfactory. Although substantial limitations are imposed upon the use of automatic contact mines, the Convention (particularly through Articles 2 and 3) leaves a large measure of discretion to belligerents. Some have suggested that the effect has been to proscribe only minelaying of an openly indiscriminate nature. In this light, it should be noted that Great Britain signed and ratified the Convention subject to the reservation that the failure of the Convention to prohibit a particular act cannot be regarded as preventing Great Britain from contesting the legitimacy of any such act. Other states also entered reservations.

During the First and Second World Wars, there were numerous violations of the provisions of the Convention, which led belligerents to take certain actions, many of them justified as reprisals (such as the establishment of war zones and permanent minefields and the use of the so-called long-distance blockade). Moreover, the Second World War saw the introduction of newer types of mines (acoustic and magnetic) which did not require impact with the hull of a ship to explode.

Some suggest that the development of new types of mines not specifically addressed by the Convention weakens its relevance. Even if the Convention's principles could be applied by analogy to new types of mines, the practice of states in the two World Wars raises questions as to the extent to which the Convention remains relevant as an instrument of control in naval warfare. Moreover, some suggest that the Convention has actually provided belligerents with arguments which would otherwise have no justification.

Even if the value of the Convention is diminished, the more general principles of the laws of war relating to interference with neutral shipping remain as applicable to the use of mines as to other means of naval warfare.

With respect to the use of mines in land warfare, see Protocol I to the 1981 UN Weapons Convention.

Date of signature:	18 October 1907
Entry into force:	26 January 1910
Depositary:	Netherlands
Authentic language:	French
Text reprinted from:	J. B. Scott (ed.), *The Hague Conventions and Declarations of 1899 and 1907*, Oxford University Press, New York, 3rd edn., 1918, pp. 151-6. (English translation by US Department of State, with minor corrections by J. B. Scott.)
Also published in:	3 *Martens NRG, 3ème sér.* (1862–1910) 580–603 (Fr. Ger.);
	100 *BFSP* (1906–1907) 389–401 (Fr.);
	UKTS 12 (1910), Cd. 5116 (Eng. Fr.);
	CXII *UKPP* (1910) 149 (Eng. Fr.);
	2 *AJIL* (1908) Supplement 138–45 (Eng. Fr.);
	205 *CTS* (1907) 331–44 (Fr.)

Convention (VIII)
Relative to the Laying of
Automatic Submarine Contact Mines

His Majesty the German Emperor, King of Prussia; [etc.]:

Inspired by the principle of the freedom of sea routes, the common highway of all nations;

Seeing that, although the existing position of affairs makes it impossible to forbid the employment of automatic submarine contact mines, it is nevertheless desirable to restrict and regulate their employment in order to mitigate the severity of war and to ensure, as far as possible, to peaceful navigation the security to which it is entitled, despite the existence of war;

Until such time as it is found possible to formulate rules on the subject which shall ensure to the interests involved all the guarantees desirable;

Have resolved to conclude a Convention for this purpose, and have appointed the following as their plenipotentiaries:

[Here follow the names of plenipotentiaries.]

Who, after having deposited their full powers, found in good and due form, have agreed upon the following provisions:

Article 1

It is forbidden —

1. To lay unanchored automatic contact mines, except when they are so constructed as to become harmless one hour at most after the person who laid them ceases to control them;

2. To lay anchored automatic contact mines which do not become harmless as soon as they have broken loose from their moorings;

3. To use torpedoes which do not become harmless when they have missed their mark.

Article 2

It is forbidden to lay automatic contact mines off the coast and ports of the enemy, with the sole object of intercepting commercial shipping.

Article 3

When anchored automatic contact mines are employed, every possible precaution must be taken for the security of peaceful shipping.

The belligerents undertake to do their utmost to render these mines harmless within a limited time, and, should they cease to be under surveillance, to notify the danger zones as soon as military exigencies permit, by a notice addressed to ship owners, which must also be communicated to the Governments through the diplomatic channel.

Article 4

Neutral Powers which lay automatic contact mines off their coasts must observe the same rules and take the same precautions as are imposed on belligerents.

The neutral Power must inform ship owners, by a notice issued in advance, where automatic contact mines have been laid. This notice must be communicated at once to the Governments through the diplomatic channel.

Article 5

At the close of the war, the contracting Powers undertake to do their utmost to remove the mines which they have laid, each Power removing its own mines.

As regards anchored automatic contact mines laid by one of the belligerents off the coast of the other, their position must be notified to the other party by the Power which laid them, and each Power must proceed with the least possible delay to remove the mines in its own waters.

Article 6

The contracting Powers which do not at present own perfected mines of the pattern contemplated in the present Convention, and which, consequently, could not at present carry out the rules laid down in Articles 1 and 3, undertake to convert the *matériel* of their mines as soon as possible, so as to bring it into conformity with the foregoing requirements.

Article 7

The provisions of the present Convention do not apply except between contracting Powers, and then only if all the belligerents are parties to the Convention.

Article 8

The present Convention shall be ratified as soon as possible.

The ratifications shall be deposited at The Hague.

The first deposit of ratifications shall be recorded in a procès-verbal signed by the representatives of the Powers which take part therein and by the Netherland Minister for Foreign Affairs.

The subsequent deposits of ratifications shall be made by means of a written notification addressed to the Netherland Government and accompanied by the instrument of ratification.

A duly certified copy of the procès-verbal relative to the first deposit of ratifications, of the notifications mentioned in the preceding paragraph, as well as of the instruments of ratification, shall be at once sent, by the Netherland Government, through the diplomatic channel, to the Powers invited to the Second Peace Conference, as well as to the other Powers which have adhered to the Convention. In the cases contemplated in the preceding paragraph, the said Government shall inform them at the same time of the date on which it has received the notification.

Article 9

Non-signatory Powers may adhere to the present Convention.

The Power which desires to adhere notifies in writing its intention to the Netherland Government, transmitting to it the act of adhesion, which shall be deposited in the archives of the said Government.

This Government shall at once transmit to all the other Powers a duly certified copy of the notification as well as of the act of adhesion, stating the date on which it received the notification.

Article 10

The present Convention shall come into force, in the case of the Powers which were a party to the first deposit of ratifications, sixty days after the date of the procès-verbal of this deposit, and, in the case of the Powers which ratify subsequently or adhere, sixty days after the notification of their ratification or of their adhesion has been received by the Netherland Government.

Article 11

The present Convention shall remain in force for seven years, dating from the sixtieth day after the date of the first deposit of ratifications.

Unless denounced, it shall continue in force after the expiration of this period.

The denunciation shall be notified in writing to the Netherland Government, which shall at once communicate a duly certified copy of the notification to all the Powers, informing them of the date on which it was received.

The denunciation shall only have effect in regard to the notifying Power, and six months after the notification has reached the Netherland Government.

Article 12

The contracting Powers undertake to reopen the question of the employment of automatic contact mines six months before the expriation of the period contemplated in the first paragraph of the preceding article, in the event of the question not having been already reopened and settled by the Third Peace Conference.

If the contracting Powers conclude a fresh Convention relative to the employment of mines, the present Convention shall cease to be applicable from the moment it comes into force.

Article 13

A register kept by the Netherland Ministry for Foreign Affairs shall give the date of the deposit of ratifications made in virtue of Article 8, paragraphs 3 and 4, as well as the date on which the notifications of adhesion (Article 9, paragraph 2) or of denunciation (Article 11, paragraph 3) have been received.

Each contracting Power is entitled to have access to this register and to be supplied with duly certified extracts from it.

In faith whereof the plenipotentiaries have appended their signatures to the present Convention.

Done at The Hague, the 18th October, 1907, in a single copy, which shall remain deposited in the archives of the Netherland Government, and duly certified copies of which shall be sent, through the diplomatic channel, to the Powers which have been invited to the Second Peace Conference.

CONCLUDING NOTES

Signatures, Ratifications, Accessions, and Successions[1]

State (*denotes Reservation etc.: see below)	Date of Signature		Date of Ratification (*r*), Accession (*a*), or Succession (*s*)		
Argentina	18 October	1907	—		
Austria-Hungary	18 October	1907	27 November	1909	*r*
Belgium	18 October	1907	8 August	1910	*r*
Bolivia	18 October	1907	—		
Brazil	18 October	1907	5 January	1914	*r*
Bulgaria	18 October	1907	—		
Chile	18 October	1907	—		
China			10 May	1917	*a*
Colombia	18 October	1907	—		
Cuba	18 October	1907	—		
Denmark	18 October	1907	27 November	1909	*r*
*Dominican Republic	18 October	1907	—		
Ecuador	18 October	1907	—		
El Salvador	18 October	1907	27 November	1909	*r*
Ethiopia			5 August	1935	*a*
Fiji[2]			2 April	1973	*s*
Finland[3]			30 December	1918	*a*
*France	18 October	1907	7 October	1910	*r*
*Germany	18 October	1907	27 November	1909	*r*
*Great Britain	18 October	1907	27 November	1909	*r*
Greece	18 October	1907	—		
Guatemala	18 October	1907	15 March	1911	*r*
Haiti	18 October	1907	2 February	1910	*r*
Italy	18 October	1907	—		
Japan	18 October	1907	13 December	1911	*r*
Liberia			4 February	1914	*a*
Luxembourg	18 October	1907	5 September	1912	*r*
Mexico	18 October	1907	27 November	1909	*r*
Netherlands	18 October	1907	27 November	1909	*r*
Nicaragua			16 December	1909	*a*
Norway	18 October	1907	19 September	1910	*r*
Panama	18 October	1907	11 September	1911	*r*
Paraguay	18 October	1907	—		
Persia	18 October	1907	—		
Peru	18 October	1907	—		

[1] Information supplied in communications from the Netherlands Ministry of Foreign Affairs between December 1979 and April 1981.

[2] By letter dated 1 April 1980 the Netherlands Ministry of Foreign Affairs confirmed that these cases constituted successions.

[3] The Depositary states that Finland's accession became effective on 9 June 1922. See above, p. 58, n. 6.

State (* denotes Reservation etc.: see below)	Date of Signature		Date of Ratification (*r*), Accession (*a*), or Succession (*s*)		
Romania	18 October	1907	1 March	1912	*r*
Serbia	18 October	1907	—		
*Siam	18 October	1907	12 March	1910	*r*
South Africa²			10 March	1978	*s*
Switzerland	18 October	1907	12 May	1910	*r*
*Turkey	18 October	1907	—		
Uruguay	18 October	1907	—		
USA	18 October	1907	27 November	1909	*r*
Venezuela	18 October	1907	—		

Total Number of Parties Listed: 27

Note on Entry into Force for States Parties

In accordance with Article 10, the Convention entered into force on 26 January 1910 for the states which had ratified it sixty days earlier, on 27 November 1909. For each of the other ratifying states, and for each of the acceding states (apart from Finland), the Convention formally entered into force sixty days after the date indicated in the right-hand column above.

Denunciations

None

Reservations etc.[4]

All the following reservations were made at signature; and all were maintained at ratification, except in the two cases, which are noted, where states making reservations did not ratify.

Dominican Republic made reservation of Article 1, paragraph 1. It did not ratify the Convention.

France and *Germany* made reservation of Article 2.

Great Britain: '. . . the mere fact that this Convention does not prohibit a particular act or proceeding must not be held to debar His Britannic Majesty's Government from contesting its legitimacy.'

Siam made reservation of Article 1, paragraph 1.

Turkey referred in its reservation to its declarations at the Conference on 9 October 1907: 'The Imperial Ottoman delegation can not at the present time undertake any engagement whatever for perfected systems which are not yet universally known . . . Given the exceptional situation created by treaties in force of the straits of the Dardanelles and the Bosphorus, straits which are an integral part of the territory, the Imperial Government could not in any way subscribe to any undertaking tending to limit the means

---

[4] This list, based on information supplied by the Netherlands Ministry of Foreign Affairs, contains English versions from J. B. Scott (ed.), *The Hague Conventions and Declarations of 1899 and 1907*, p. 156.

of defence that it may deem necessary to employ for these straits in case of war or with the aim of causing its neutrality to be respected . . . The Imperial Ottoman delegation can not at the present time take part in any engagement as regards the conversion mentioned in Article 6.' Turkey did not ratify the Convention.

10. 1907 Hague Convention IX Concerning Bombardment by Naval Forces in Time of War

PREFATORY NOTE

In land warfare, the customary principle regarding bombardment (later codified in Article 25 of the Regulations annexed to both 1899 Hague Convention II and 1907 Hague Convention IV) prohibited the bombardment by land forces of undefended targets. The principle was based on the notion that an undefended target was open to immediate entry and occupation, and bombardment would only cause unnecessary destruction.

In naval warfare, it was recognized that enemy coastal targets which were defended could be bombarded by naval forces, whether such forces were acting in cooperation with a besieging army or independently. However, the question as to whether or not undefended coastal targets could be bombarded by naval forces remained controversial. Unlike in land warfare, the entry and occupation of undefended coastal targets by naval forces was relatively rare: however, the objective of eliminating an enemy's military resources remained.

At the meeting of the Institute of International Law held in Cambridge in 1895, a committee was appointed to examine the question of naval bombardment, and its report led the Institute in 1896 to adopt a body of rules which declared that the law of bombardment should be the same in both land and naval warfare. These rules were placed before states for their consideration, but were not accepted.

States failed to reach agreement on the subject at the First Hague Peace Conference of 1899, and deferred the matter to a later conference. At the Second Hague Peace Conference of 1907, the agreement reached on a regime to govern naval bombardment was embodied in Hague Convention IX. The Convention prohibits naval bombardment of undefended ports, towns, villages, dwellings or buildings, but (in implicit recognition of the different character of naval warfare) excludes from the prohibition coastal targets which represent a military objective or whose local authorities refuse to comply with legitimate requisitions for supplies necessary for the immediate use of the naval force. The Convention contains a 'general participation clause' (Article 8) which affects its technical application in hostilities where not all belligerents are parties to the Convention.

Hague Convention IX was first applied during the Turco-Italian War of 1911–12. During the First World War, the bombardment of English coastal towns by German naval forces was not in accordance with principles embodied in the Convention because the bombardment affected the civilian population and had no strictly military purpose. During the Second World War, the indiscriminate nature of some naval bombardments conducted by belligerents did not conform to the principles embodied in the Convention.

In the application of the Convention, the importance of determining whether or not a target represents a military objective is clear. It has been suggested that, in view of subsequent developments, the list of military targets provided in the Convention may no longer be regarded as exhaustive. In this view, certain other targets (for example, communications systems) which belligerents have come to regard as capable of use for military purposes may also be subject to bombardment by naval forces.

Date of signature:	18 October 1907
Entry into force:	26 January 1910
Depositary:	Netherlands
Authentic language:	French
Text reprinted from:	J. B. Scott (ed.), *The Hague Conventions and Declarations of 1899 and 1907*, Oxford University Press, New York, 3rd edn., 1918, pp. 157-62. (English translation by US Department of State, with minor corrections by J. B. Scott.)
Also published in:	3 *Martens NRG, 3ème sér.* (1862-1910) 604-29 (Fr. Ger.);
	100 *BFSP* (1906-1907) 401-15 (Fr.);
	UKTS 13 (1910), Cd. 5117 (Eng. Fr.);
	CXII *UKPP* (1910) 173 (Eng. Fr.);
	2 *AJIL* (1908) Supplement 146-53 (Eng. Fr.);
	205 *CTS* (1907) 345-59 (Fr.)

Convention (IX) Concerning Bombardment by Naval Forces in Time of War

His Majesty the German Emperor, King of Prussia; [etc.]:

Animated by the desire to realize the wish expressed by the First Peace Conference respecting the bombardment by naval forces of undefended ports, towns, and villages;

Whereas it is expedient that bombardments by naval forces should be subject to rules of general application which would safeguard the rights of the inhabitants and assure the preservation of the more important buildings, by applying as far as possible to this operation of war the principles of the Regulation of 1899 respecting the laws and customs of land war;

Actuated, accordingly, by the desire to serve the interests of humanity and to diminish the severity and disasters of war;

Have resolved to conclude a Convention to this effect, and have, for this purpose, appointed the following as their plenipotentiaries:

[Here follow the names of the plenipotentiaries.]

Who, after depositing their full powers, found in good and due form, have agreed upon the following provisions:

CHAPTER I — *The Bombardment of Undefended Ports,
Towns, Villages, Dwellings, or Buildings*

Article 1
The bombardment by naval forces of undefended ports, towns, villages, dwellings, or buildings is forbidden.
A place cannot be bombarded solely because automatic submarine contact mines are anchored off the harbor.

Article 2
Military works, military or naval establishments, depots of arms or war *matériel*, workshops or plant which could be utilized for the needs of the hostile fleet or army, and the ships of war in the harbor, are not, however, included in this prohibition. The commander of a naval force may destroy them with artillery, after a summons followed by a reasonable time of waiting, if all other means are impossible, and when the local authorities have not themselves destroyed them within the time fixed.
He incurs no responsibility for any unavoidable damage which may be caused by a bombardment under such circumstances.
If for military reasons immediate action is necessary, and no delay can be allowed the enemy, it is understood that the prohibition to bombard the undefended town holds good, as in the case given in paragraph 1, and that the commander shall take all due measures in order that the town may suffer as little harm as possible.

Article 3
After due notice has been given, the bombardment of undefended ports, towns, villages, dwellings, or buildings may be commenced, if the local authorities, after a formal summons has been made to them, decline to comply with requisitions for provisions or supplies necessary for the immediate use of the naval force before the place in question.
These requisitions shall be in proportion to the resources of the place. They shall only be demanded in the name of the commander of the said naval force, and they shall, as far as possible, be paid for in cash; if not, they shall be evidenced by receipts.

Article 4
Undefended ports, towns, villages, dwellings, or buildings may not be bombarded on account of failure to pay money contributions.

CHAPTER II — *General Provisions*

Article 5

In bombardments by naval forces all the necessary measures must be taken by the commander to spare as far as possible sacred edifices, buildings used for artistic, scientific, or charitable purposes, historic monuments, hospitals, and places where the sick or wounded are collected, on the understanding that they are not used at the same time for military purposes.

It is the duty of the inhabitants to indicate such monuments, edifices, or places by visible signs, which shall consist of large, stiff rectangular panels divided diagonally into two colored triangular portions, the upper portion black, the lower portion white.

Article 6

If the military situation permits, the commander of the attacking naval force, before commencing the bombardment, must do his utmost to warn the authorities.

Article 7

A town or place, even when taken by storm, may not be pillaged.

CHAPTER III — *Final Provisions*

Article 8

The provisions of the present Convention do not apply except between contracting Powers, and then only if all the belligerents are parties to the Convention.

Article 9

The present Convention shall be ratified as soon as possible.

The ratifications shall be deposited at The Hague.

The first deposit of ratifications shall be recorded in a procès-verbal signed by the representatives of the Powers which take part therein and by the Netherland Minister of Foreign Affairs.

The subsequent deposits of ratifications shall be made by means of a written notification addressed to the Netherland Government and accompanied by the instrument of ratification.

A duly certified copy of the procès-verbal relative to the first deposit of ratifications, of the notifications mentioned in the preceding paragraph, as well as of the instruments of ratification, shall be at once sent by the Netherland Government, through the diplomatic channel, to the Powers invited to the Second Peace Conference, as well as to the other Powers which have adhered to the Convention.

In the cases contemplated in the preceding paragraph, the said Government shall inform them at the same time of the date on which it received the notification.

Article 10

Non-signatory Powers may adhere to the present Convention.

The Power which desires to adhere shall notify its intention to the Netherland Government, forwarding to it the act of adhesion, which shall be deposited in the archives of the said Government.

This Government shall immediately forward to all the other Powers a duly certified copy of the notification, as well as of the act of adhesion, mentioning the date on which it received the notification.

Article 11

The present Convention shall come into force, in the case of the Powers which were a party to the first deposit of ratifications, sixty days after the date of the procès-verbal of that deposit, and, in the case of the Powers which ratify subsequently or which adhere, sixty days after the notification of their ratification or of their adhesion has been received by the Netherland Government.

Article 12

In the event of one of the contracting Powers wishing to denounce the present Convention, the denunciation shall be notified in writing to the Netherland Government, which shall at once communicate a duly certified copy of the notification to all the other Powers informing them of the date on which it was received.

The denunciation shall only have effect in regard to the notifying Power, and one year after the notification has reached the Netherland Government.

Article 13

A register kept by the Netherland Minister for Foreign Affairs shall give the date of the deposit of ratifications made in virtue of Article 9, paragraphs 3 and 4, as well as the date on which the notifications of adhesion (Article 10, paragraph 2) or of denunciation (Article 12, paragraph 1) have been received.

Each contracting Power is entitled to have access to this register and to be supplied with duly certified extracts from it.

In faith whereof the plenipotentiaries have appended their signatures to the present Convention.

Done at The Hague, the 18th October, 1907, in a single copy, which shall remain deposited in the archives of the Netherland Government, and duly certified copies of which shall be sent, through the diplomatic channel, to the Powers which have been invited to the Second Peace Conference.

CONCLUDING NOTES

Signatures, Ratifications, Accessions, and Successions[1]

State (* denotes Reservation: see below)	Date of Signature		Date of Ratification (r), Accession (a), or Succession (s)		
Argentina	18 October	1907	—		
Austria-Hungary	18 October	1907	27 November	1909	r
Belgium	18 October	1907	8 August	1910	r
Bolivia	18 October	1907	27 November	1909	r
Brazil	18 October	1907	5 January	1914	r
Bulgaria	18 October	1907	—		
Byelorussian SSR[2]			4 June	1962	s
*Chile	18 October	1907			
China			15 January	1910	a
Colombia	18 October	1907	—		
Cuba	18 October	1907	22 February	1912	r
Denmark	18 October	1907	27 November	1909	r
Dominican Republic	18 October	1907			
Ecuador	18 October	1907	—		
El Salvador	18 October	1907	27 November	1909	r
Ethiopia			5 August	1935	a
Fiji[2]			2 April	1973	s
Finland[3]			30 December	1918	a
*France	18 October	1907	7 October	1910	r
*Germany	18 October	1907	27 November	1909	r
German Democratic Republic[2]			9 February	1959	s
*Great Britain	18 October	1907	27 November	1909	r
Greece	18 October	1907	—		
Guatemala	18 October	1907	15 March	1911	r
Haiti	18 October	1907	2 February	1910	r
Italy	18 October	1907	—		
*Japan	18 October	1907	13 December	1911	r
Liberia			4 February	1914	a
Luxembourg	18 October	1907	5 September	1912	r
Mexico	18 October	1907	27 November	1909	r

[1] Information supplied in communications from the Netherlands Ministry of Foreign Affairs between December 1979 and April 1981.

[2] By letters dated 1 April 1980 and 16 March 1981 the Netherlands Ministry of Foreign Affairs confirmed that these cases constituted successions. *Re* USSR and Byelorussia, see above, p. 41, n. 3.

[3] The Depositary states that Finland's accession became effective on 9 June 1922. See above, p. 58, n. 6.

State (* denotes Reservation: see below)	Date of Signature		Date of Ratification (*r*), Accession (*a*), or Succession (*s*)		
Montenegro	18 October	1907	—		
Netherlands	18 October	1907	27 November	1909	*r*
Nicaragua			16 December	1909	*a*
Norway	18 October	1907	19 September	1910	*r*
Panama	18 October	1907	11 September	1911	*r*
Paraguay	18 October	1907	—		
Persia	18 October	1907	—		
Peru	18 October	1907	—		
Poland			31 May	1935	*a*
Portugal	18 October	1907	13 April	1911	*r*
Romania	18 October	1907	1 March	1912	*r*
Russia	18 October	1907	27 November	1909	*r*
Serbia	18 October	1907	—		
Siam	18 October	1907	12 March	1910	*r*
South Africa[2]			10 March	1978	*s*
Spain			24 February	1913	*a*
Sweden	18 October	1907	27 November	1909	*r*
Switzerland	18 October	1907	12 May	1910	*r*
Turkey	18 October	1907	—		
Uruguay	18 October	1907	—		
USA	18 October	1907	27 November	1909	*r*
USSR[2]			7 March	1955	*s*
Venezuela	18 October	1907	—		

Total Number of Parties Listed: 37

Note on Entry into Force for States Parties

In accordance with Article 11, the Convention entered into force on 26 January 1910 for the states which had ratified it sixty days earlier, on 27 November 1909. For each of the other ratifying states, and for each of the acceding states (apart from Finland), the Convention formally entered into force sixty days after the date indicated in the right-hand column above.

Denunciations

None

Reservations

Chile, at signature, made reservation of Article 3. It did not ratify the Convention.

France, Germany, Great Britain, and Japan all, at signature, made reservation of Article 1, paragraph 2. At ratification, all of them maintained their reservations.

11. 1907 Hague Convention XI Relative to Certain Restrictions with Regard to the Exercise of the Right of Capture in Naval War

PREFATORY NOTE

This Convention deals with three aspects of capture in naval war: postal correspondence; the exemption from capture of certain vessels; and the treatment of crews of enemy merchant ships. The Convention contains a 'general participation clause' which affects its technical application in hostilities where not all belligerents are parties. To the extent that aspects of the Convention may be considered customary international law, those aspects would be applicable to all states and the Convention's 'general participation clause' (Article 9) would cease to be relevant.

Postal Correspondence

During the nineteenth century there was no general rule granting postal correspondence immunity from seizure. Any immunities resulted from bilateral treaties and were thereby restricted in application.

At the Second Hague Peace Conference of 1907, the status of postal correspondence in time of war was examined and made subject to regulation. Hague Convention XI provides for the immunity from capture of the postal correspondence (as distinct from parcel post) of neutrals or belligerents which may be found aboard a neutral or enemy ship on the high seas, providing that the mail is not on its way to or from a blockaded port. If the ship is detained, such postal correspondence must be forwarded with the least possible delay.

Although the articles in the Convention relating to postal correspondence are still technically binding, the practice of belligerents during the two world wars has reduced the significance of these provisions. In many cases, enemy merchant vessels were sunk without warning rather than seized, and as a result any correspondence they were carrying was destroyed. In other cases, the use of the mails to forward propaganda, war-related information, and contraband led to postal correspondence being subject to seizure, examination, and either censorship or confiscation. If states regard such practices as compatible with the Convention then the notion of 'inviolability', which is stressed in Articles 1 and 2, has clearly been qualified.

Exemption from capture of certain vessels

The capture of enemy vessels has traditionally been one of the most important means of conducting naval warfare. Customary international law recognized the right of capture, but imposed important restrictions: for example, an enemy warship or merchant ship within neutral jurisdiction was not liable to capture. There were also immunities of a more general nature, such as the exemption of certain types of vessel from capture. Small coastal fishing or trading boats as well as ships engaged in scientific discovery and research were regarded as immune from capture so long as they did not engage in hostilities.

The customary immunity of hospital ships from capture was codified in 1899 Hague Convention III, 1907 Hague Convention X, and then in 1949 Geneva Convention II, which is the currently applicable agreement. The provisions on hospital ships of the 1949 Convention have been extended in Section II of 1977 Geneva Protocol I. (Note also that hospital ships are exempted from certain payments by the 1904 Hague Convention for the Exemption of Hospital Ships, in Time of War, from the Payment of All Dues and Taxes Imposed for the Benefit of the State, which is still in force.)

Hague Convention XI provides for the immunity of small coastal fishing or trading boats, and vessels on a scientific, religious or philanthropic mission, so long as the vessel pursues its normal functions, does not engage in hostilities, and does not serve the commercial interests of the enemy.

In many instances during both world wars, the customary immunity of small coastal fishing and trading boats was not observed in practice. In some cases, action taken against coastal vessels was attributable to the belligerent use of coastal vessels for intelligence purposes: by failing to restrict activity to innocent employment, such vessels thereby forfeited their immunity. The exemption from capture of religious, scientific and philanthropic vessels was interpreted very restrictively by belligerents, and any immunity of particular humanitarian vessels came to rely upon the express agreement of belligerents.

Crews of captured enemy merchant ships

During the nineteenth century, customary international law recognized that the captured officers and crews of enemy merchant ships could be made prisoners of war. Hague Convention XI contains provisions restricting this earlier customary practice by defining circumstances in which the captain and/or officers and/or crew cannot be made prisoners of war. During both world wars, the practice of interning officers and crews with enemy nationality, which frequently resulted in their being made prisoners of war, has diminished the significance of the Convention in that respect. However, in general belligerents have refrained from detaining officers and crews with neutral nationality so long as they have not participated in hostilities against the captor.

Date of signature:	18 October 1907
Entry into force:	26 January 1910
Depositary:	Netherlands
Authentic language:	French
Text reprinted from:	J. B. Scott (ed.), *The Hague Conventions and Declarations of 1899 and 1907*, Oxford University Press, New York, 3rd edn., 1918, pp. 182-7. (English translation by US Department of State, with minor corrections by J. B. Scott.)
Also published in:	3 *Martens NRG, 3ème sér.* (1862-1910) 663-87 (Fr. Ger.);
	100 *BFSP* (1906-1907) 422-34 (Fr.);
	UKTS 14 (1910), Cd. 5118 (Eng. Fr.);
	CXII *UKPP* (1910) 199 (Eng. Fr.);
	2 *AJIL* (1908) Supplement 167-74 (Eng. Fr.);
	205 *CTS* (1907) 367-80 (Fr.)

Convention (XI) Relative to Certain Restrictions with Regard to the Exercise of the Right of Capture in Naval War

His Majesty the German Emperor, King of Prussia: [etc.] :

Recognizing the necessity of more effectively ensuring than hitherto the equitable application of law to the international relations of maritime Powers in time of war;

Considering that, for this purpose, it is expedient, in giving up or, if necessary, in harmonizing for the common interest certain conflicting practices of long standing, to commence codifying in regulations of general application the guarantees due to peaceful commerce and legitimate business, as well as the conduct of hostilities by sea; that it is expedient to lay down in written mutual engagements the principles which have hitherto remained in the uncertain domain of controversy or have been left to the discretion of Governments;

That, from henceforth, a certain number of rules may be made, without affecting the common law now in force with regard to the matters which that law has left unsettled;

Have appointed the following as their plenipotentiaries:

[Here follow the names of plenipotentiaries.]

Who, after having deposited their full powers, found in good and due form, have agreed upon the following provisions:

CHAPTER I — *Postal Correspondence*

Article 1

The postal correspondence of neutrals or belligerents, whatever its official or private character may be, found on the high seas on board a neutral or enemy ship, is inviolable. If the ship is detained, the correspondence is forwarded by the captor with the least possible delay.

The provisions of the preceding paragraph do not apply, in case of violation of blockade, to correspondence destined for or proceeding from a blockaded port.

Article 2

The inviolability of postal correspondence does not exempt a neutral mail ship from the laws and customs of maritime war as to neutral merchant ships in general. The ship, however, may not be searched except when absolutely necessary, and then only with as much consideration and expedition as possible.

CHAPTER II — *The Exemption from Capture of Certain Vessels*

Article 3

Vessels used exclusively for fishing along the coast or small boats employed in local trade are exempt from capture, as well as their appliances, rigging, tackle, and cargo.

They cease to be exempt as soon as they take any part whatever in hostilities.

The contracting Powers agree not to take advantage of the harmless character of the said vessels in order to use them for military purposes while preserving their peaceful appearance.

Article 4

Vessels charged with religious, scientific, or philanthropic missions are likewise exempt from capture.

CHAPTER III — *Regulations Regarding the Crews of Enemy Merchant Ships Captured by a Belligerent*

Article 5

When an enemy merchant ship is captured by a belligerent, such of its crew as are nationals of a neutral State are not made prisoners of war.

The same rule applies in the case of the captain and officers likewise nationals of a neutral State, if they promise formally in writing not to serve on an enemy ship while the war lasts.

Article 6

The captain, officers, and members of the crew, when nationals of the enemy State, are not made prisoners of war, on condition that they make a formal promise in writing, not to undertake, while hostilities last, any service connected with the operations of the war.

Article 7

The names of the persons retaining their liberty under the conditions laid down in Article 5, paragraph 2, and in Article 6, are notified by the belligerent captor to the other belligerent. The latter is forbidden knowingly to employ the said persons.

Article 8

The provisions of the three preceding articles do not apply to ships taking part in the hostilities.

CHAPTER IV — *Final Provisions*

Article 9

The provisions of the present Convention do not apply except between contracting Powers, and then only if all the belligerents are parties to the Convention.

Article 10

The present Convention shall be ratified as soon as possible.

The ratifications shall be deposited at The Hague.

The first deposit of ratifications shall be recorded in a procès-verbal signed by the representatives of the Powers taking part therein and by the Netherland Minister for Foreign Affairs.

Subsequent deposits of ratifications shall be made by means of a written notification, addressed to the Netherland Government and accompanied by the instrument of ratification.

A duly certified copy of the procès-verbal relative to the first deposit of ratifications, of the notifications mentioned in the preceding paragraph, as well as of the instruments of ratification, shall be at once sent by the Netherland Government, through the diplomatic channel, to the Powers invited to the Second Peace Conference, as well as to the other Powers which have adhered to the Convention. In the cases contemplated in the preceding paragraph, the said Government shall inform them at the same time of the date on which it received the notification.

Article 11

Non-signatory Powers may adhere to the present Convention.

The Power which desires to adhere notifies its intention in writing to the Netherland Government, forwarding to it the act of adhesion, which shall be deposited in the archives of the said Government.

This Government shall at once transmit to all the other Powers a duly certified copy of the notification as well as of the act of adhesion, mentioning the date on which it received the notification.

Article 12

The present Convention shall come into force in the case of the Powers which were a party to the first deposit of ratifications, sixty days after the procès-verbal of that deposit, and, in the case of the Powers which ratify subsequently or which adhere, sixty days after the notification of their ratification has been received by the Netherland Government.

Article 13

In the event of one of the contracting Powers wishing to denounce the present Convention, the denunciation shall be notified in writing to the Netherland Government, which shall at once communicate a duly certified copy of the notification to all the other Powers informing them of the date on which it was received.

The denunciation shall only have effect in regard to the notifying Power, and one year after the notification has reached the Netherland Government.

Article 14

A register kept by the Netherland Ministry for Foreign Affairs shall give the date of the deposit of ratifications made in virtue of Article 10, paragraphs 3 and 4, as well as the date on which the notifications of adhesion (Article 11, paragraph 2) or of denunciation (Article 13, paragraph 1) have been received.

Each contracting Power is entitled to have access to this register and to be supplied with duly certified extracts from it.

In faith whereof the plenipotentiaries have appended their signatures to the present Convention.

Done at The Hague, the 18th October, 1907, in a single copy, which shall remain deposited in the archives of the Netherland Government, and duly certified copies of which shall be sent, through the diplomatic channel, to the Powers invited to the Second Peace Conference.

CONCLUDING NOTES

Signatures, Ratifications, Accessions, and Successions[1]

State	Date of Signature		Date of Ratification (*r*), Accession (*a*), or Succession (*s*)		
Argentina	18 October	1907	—		
Austria-Hungary	18 October	1907	27 November	1909	*r*
Belgium	18 October	1907	8 August	1910	*r*
Bolivia	18 October	1907	—		
Brazil	18 October	1907	5 January	1914	*r*
Bulgaria	18 October	1907	—		
Chile	18 October	1907	—		
China			10 May	1917	*a*
Colombia	18 October	1907	—		
Cuba	18 October	1907	—		

[1] Information supplied in communications from the Netherlands Ministry of Foreign Affairs between December 1979 and April 1981.

State	Date of Signature		Date of Ratification (*r*), Accession (*a*), or Succession (*s*)		
Denmark	18 October	1907	27 November	1909	*r*
Dominican Republic	18 October	1907	—		
Ecuador	18 October	1907	—		
El Salvador	18 October	1907	27 November	1909	*r*
Ethiopia			5 August	1935	*a*
Fiji[2]			2 April	1973	*s*
Finland[3]			30 December	1918	*a*
France	18 October	1907	7 October	1910	*r*
Germany	18 October	1907	27 November	1909	*r*
Great Britain	18 October	1907	27 November	1909	*r*
Greece	18 October	1907	—		
Guatemala	18 October	1907	15 March	1911	*r*
Haiti	18 October	1907	2 February	1910	*r*
Italy	18 October	1907	—		
Japan	18 October	1907	13 December	1911	*r*
Liberia			4 February	1914	*a*
Luxembourg	18 October	1907	5 September	1912	*r*
Mexico	18 October	1907	27 November	1909	*r*
Netherlands	18 October	1907	27 November	1909	*r*
Nicaragua			16 December	1909	*a*
Norway	18 October	1907	19 September	1910	*r*
Panama	18 October	1907	11 September	1911	*r*
Paraguay	18 October	1907	—		
Persia	18 October	1907	—		
Peru	18 October	1907	—		
Poland			31 May	1935	*a*
Portugal	18 October	1907	13 April	1911	*r*
Romania	18 October	1907	1 March	1912	*r*
Serbia	18 October	1907	—		
Siam	18 October	1907	12 March	1910	*r*
South Africa[2]			10 March	1978	*s*
Spain	18 October	1907	18 March	1913	*r*
Sweden	18 October	1907	27 November	1909	*r*
Switzerland	18 October	1907	12 May	1910	*r*
Turkey	18 October	1907	—		
Uruguay	18 October	1907	—		
USA	18 October	1907	27 November	1909	*r*
Venezuela	18 October	1907	—		

Total Number of Parties Listed: 31

[2] By letter dated 1 April 1980 the Netherlands Ministry of Foreign Affairs confirmed that these cases constituted successions.

[3] The Depositary states that Finland's accession became effective on 9 June 1922. See above, p. 58, n. 6.

Note on Entry into Force for States Parties

In accordance with Article 12, the Convention entered into force on 26 January 1910 for the states which had ratified it sixty days earlier, on 27 November 1909. For each of the other ratifying states, and for each of the acceding states (apart from Finland), the Convention formally entered into force sixty days after the date indicated in the right-hand column above.

Denunciations

None

Reservations

None

12. 1907 Hague Convention XIII Concerning the Rights and Duties of Neutral Powers in Naval War

PREFATORY NOTE

The general remarks on neutrality in the prefatory note to 1907 Hague Convention V on neutrality in land war are also germane to this Convention. Like 1907 Hague Convention V, this Convention was regarded at the time of its adoption as being largely declaratory of customary international law; and to the extent that this Convention may be considered customary international law, it would be binding on all states and its 'general participation clause' (Article 28) would cease to be relevant.

This Convention *inter alia* prohibits hostile acts by belligerents in neutral ports and waters, and in turn requires a neutral state to use the means at its disposal to prevent such acts.

However, in practice belligerents have occasionally departed from certain provisions of the Convention. For example, there have been several instances in which a belligerent has acted within neutral waters, claiming that this was done because the neutral state was unable or unwilling to assert its neutral rights as against the other belligerent. In addition, different interpretations regarding other neutral rights and duties have led to varying state practice. Despite these problems, however, the Convention has been widely referred to by both neutrals and belligerents in twentieth-century conflicts, including both world wars.

Certain other international agreements have a bearing on neutrality in naval war, including: 1856 Paris Declaration on maritime law, 1907 Hague Convention VII on the conversion of merchant ships, 1907 Hague Convention VIII on automatic submarine mines, 1907 Hague Convention XI on the right of capture, the unratified 1907 Hague Convention XII on an International Prize Court, the unratified 1909 Declaration of London on the laws of naval war, and 1949 Geneva Convention II on wounded, sick, and shipwrecked.

Date of signature:	18 October 1907
Entry into force:	26 January 1910
Depositary:	Netherlands
Authentic language:	French
Text reprinted from:	J. B. Scott (ed.), *The Hague Conventions and Declarations of 1899 and 1907*, Oxford University Press, New York, 3rd edn., 1918, pp. 209–19. (English translation by US Department of State, with minor corrections by J. B. Scott.)
Also published in:	3 *Martens NRG, 3ème sér.* (1862–1910) 713–44 (Fr. Ger.);

100 *BFSP* (1906–1907) 448–54 (Fr.);
2 *AJIL* (1908) Supplement 202–16 (Eng. Fr.);
205 *CTS* (1907) 395–402 (Fr.)

Convention (XIII) Concerning the Rights and Duties of Neutral Powers in Naval War

His Majesty the German Emperor, King of Prussia; [etc.]:

With a view to harmonizing the divergent views which, in the event of naval war, are still held on the relations between neutral Powers and belligerent Powers, and to anticipating the difficulties to which such divergence of views might give rise;

Seeing that, even if it is not possible at present to concert measures applicable to all circumstances which may in practice occur, it is nevertheless undeniably advantageous to frame, as far as possible, rules of general application to meet the case where war has unfortunately broken out;

Seeing that, in cases not covered by the present Convention, it is expedient to take into consideration the general principles of the law of nations;

Seeing that it is desirable that the Powers should issue detailed enactments to regulate the results of the attitude of neutrality when adopted by them;

Seeing that it is, for neutral Powers, an admitted duty to apply these rules impartially to the several belligerents;

Seeing that, in this category of ideas, these rules should not, in principle, be altered, in the course of the war, by a neutral Power, except in a case where experience has shown the necessity for such change for the protection of the rights of that Power;

Have agreed to observe the following common rules, which can not however modify provisions laid down in existing general treaties, and have appointed as their plenipotentiaries, namely:

[Here follow the names of plenipotentiaries.]

Who, after having deposited their full powers, found in good and due form, have agreed upon the following provisions:

Article 1

Belligerents are bound to respect the sovereign rights of neutral Powers and to abstain, in neutral territory or neutral waters, from any act which would, if knowingly permitted by any Power, constitute a violation of neutrality.

Article 2

Any act of hostility, including capture and the exercise of the right of search, committed by belligerent war-ships in the territorial waters of a neutral Power, constitutes a violation of neutrality and is strictly forbidden.

Article 3

When a ship has been captured in the territorial waters of a neutral Power, this Power must employ, if the prize is still within its jurisdiction, the means at its disposal to release the prize with its officers and crew, and to intern the prize crew.

If the prize is not in the jurisdiction of the neutral Power, the captor Government, on the demand of that Power, must liberate the prize with its officers and crew.

Article 4

A prize court can not be set up by a belligerent on neutral territory or on a vessel in neutral waters.

Article 5

Belligerents are forbidden to use neutral ports and waters as a base of naval operations against their adversaries, and in particular to erect wireless telegraphy stations or any apparatus for the purpose of communicating with the belligerent forces on land or sea.

Article 6

The supply, in any manner, directly or indirectly, by a neutral Power to a belligerent Power, of war-ships, ammunition, or war material of any kind whatever, is forbidden.

Article 7

A neutral Power is not bound to prevent the export or transit, for the use of either belligerent, of arms, ammunition, or, in general, of anything which could be of use to an army or fleet.

Article 8

A neutral Government is bound to employ the means at its disposal to prevent the fitting out or arming of any vessel within its jurisdiction which it has reason to believe is intended to cruise, or engage in hostile operations, against a Power with which that Government is at peace. It is also bound to display the same vigilance to prevent the departure from its jurisdiction of any vessel intended to cruise, or engage in hostile operations, which had been adapted entirely or partly within the said jurisdiction for use in war.

Article 9

A neutral Power must apply impartially to the two belligerents the conditions, restrictions, or prohibitions made by it in regard to the admission into its ports, roadsteads, or territorial waters, of belligerent war-ships or of their prizes.

Nevertheless, a neutral Power may forbid a belligerent vessel which has failed to conform to the orders and regulations made by it, or which has violated neutrality, to enter its ports or roadsteads.

Article 10

The neutrality of a Power is not affected by the mere passage through its territorial waters of war-ships or prizes belonging to belligerents.

Article 11

A neutral Power may allow belligerent war-ships to employ its licensed pilots.

Article 12

In the absence of special provisions to the contrary in the legislation of a neutral Power, belligerent war-ships are not permitted to remain in the ports, roadsteads, or territorial waters of the said Power for more than twenty-four hours, except in the cases covered by the present Convention.

Article 13

If a Power which has been informed of the outbreak of hostilities learns that a belligerent war-ship is in one of its ports or roadsteads, or in its territorial waters, it must notify the said ship to depart within twenty-four hours or within the time prescribed by local regulations.

Article 14

A belligerent war-ship may not prolong its stay in a neutral port beyond the permissible time except on account of damage or stress of weather. It must depart as soon as the cause of the delay is at an end.

The regulations as to the question of the length of time which these vessels may remain in neutral ports, roadsteads, or waters, do not apply to war-ships devoted exclusively to religious, scientific, or philanthropic purposes.

Article 15

In the absence of special provisions to the contrary in the legislation of a neutral Power, the maximum number of war-ships belonging to a belligerent which may be in one of the ports or roadsteads of that Power simultaneously shall be three.

Article 16

When war-ships belonging to both belligerents are present simultaneously in a neutral port or roadstead, a period of not less than twenty-four hours must elapse between the departure of the ship belonging to one belligerent and the departure of the ship belonging to the other.

The order of departure is determined by the order of arrival, unless the ship which arrived first is so circumstanced that an extension of its stay is permissible.

A belligerent war-ship may not leave a neutral port or roadstead until twenty-four hours after the departure of a merchant ship flying the flag of its adversary.

Article 17

In neutral ports and roadsteads belligerent war-ships may only carry out such repairs as are absolutely necessary to render them seaworthy, and may not add in any manner whatsoever to their fighting force. The local authorities of the neutral Power shall decide what repairs are necessary, and these must be carried out with the least possible delay.

Article 18

Belligerent war-ships may not make use of neutral ports, roadsteads, or territorial waters for replenishing or increasing their supplies of war material or their armament, or for completing their crews.

Article 19

Belligerent war-ships may only revictual in neutral ports or roadsteads to bring up their supplies to the peace standard.

Similarly these vessels may only ship sufficient fuel to enable them to reach the nearest port in their own country. They may, on the other hand, fill up their bunkers built to carry fuel, when in neutral countries which have adopted this method of determining the amount of fuel to be supplied.

If, in accordance with the law of the neutral Power, the ships are not supplied with coal within twenty-four hours of their arrival, the permissible duration of their stay is extended by twenty-four hours.

Article 20

Belligerent war-ships which have shipped fuel in a port belonging to a neutral Power may not within the succeeding three months replenish their supply in a port of the same Power.

Article 21

A prize may only be brought into a neutral port on account of unseaworthiness, stress of weather, or want of fuel or provisions.

It must leave as soon as the circumstances which justified its entry are at an end. If it does not, the neutral Power must order it to leave at once; should it fail to obey, the neutral Power must employ the means at its disposal to release it with its officers and crew and to intern the prize crew.

Article 22

A neutral Power must, similarly, release a prize brought into one of its ports under circumstances other than those referred to in Article 21.

Article 23

A neutral Power may allow prizes to enter its ports and road-steads, whether under convoy or not, when they are brought there to be sequestrated pending the decision of a Prize Court. It may have the prize taken to another of its ports.

If the prize is convoyed by a war-ship, the prize crew may go on board the convoying ship.

If the prize is not under convoy, the prize crew are left at liberty.

Article 24

If, notwithstanding the notification of the neutral Power, a belligerent ship of war does not leave a port where it is not entitled to remain, the neutral Power is entitled to take such measures as it considers necessary to render the ship incapable of taking the sea during the war, and the commanding officer of the ship must facilitate the execution of such measures.

When a belligerent ship is detained by a neutral Power, the officers and crew are likewise detained.

The officers and crew thus detained may be left in the ship or kept either on another vessel or on land, and may be subjected to the measures of restriction which it may appear necessary to impose upon them. A sufficient number of men for looking after the vessel must, however, be always left on board.

The officers may be left at liberty on giving their word not to quit the neutral territory without permission.

Article 25

A neutral Power is bound to exercise such surveillance as the means at its disposal allow to prevent any violation of the provisions of the above articles occurring in its ports or roadsteads or in its waters.

Article 26

The exercise by a neutral Power of the rights laid down in the present Convention can under no circumstances be considered as an unfriendly act by one or other belligerent who has accepted the articles relating thereto.

Article 27

The contracting Powers shall communicate to each other in due course all laws, proclamations, and other enactments regulating in their respective countries the status of belligerent war-ships in their ports and waters, by means of a communication addressed to the Government of the Netherlands, and forwarded immediately by that Government to the other contracting Powers.

Article 28

The provisions of the present Convention do not apply except between contracting Powers, and then only if all the belligerents are parties to the Convention.

Article 29

The present Convention shall be ratified as soon as possible.

The ratifications shall be deposited at The Hague.

The first deposit of ratifications shall be recorded in a procès-verbal signed by the representatives of the Powers which take part therein and by the Netherland Minister for Foreign Affairs.

The subsequent deposits of ratifications shall be made by means of a written notification addressed to the Netherland Government and accompanied by the instrument of ratification.

A duly certified copy of the procès-verbal relative to the first deposit of ratifications, of the ratifications mentioned in the preceding paragraph, as well as of the instruments of ratification, shall be at once sent by the Netherland Government, through the diplomatic channel, to the Powers invited to the Second Peace Conference, as well as to the other Powers which have adhered to the Convention. In the cases contemplated in the preceding paragraph, the said Government shall inform them at the same time of the date on which it received the notification.

Article 30

Non-signatory Powers may adhere to the present Convention.

The Power which desires to adhere notifies in writing its intention to the Netherland Government, forwarding to it the act of adhesion, which shall be deposited in the archives of the said Government.

That Government shall at once transmit to all the other Powers a duly certified copy of the notification as well as of the act of adhesion, mentioning the date on which it received the notification.

Article 31

The present Convention shall come into force in the case of the Powers which were a party to the first deposit of the ratifications, sixty days after the date of the procès-verbal of that deposit, and, in the case of the Powers who ratify subsequently or who adhere, sixty days after the notification of their ratification or of their decision has been received by the Netherland Government.

Article 32

In the event of one of the contracting Powers wishing to denounce the Present Convention, the denunciation shall be notified in writing to the Netherland Government, who shall at once communicate a duly certified copy of the notification to all the other Powers, informing them of the date on which it was received.

The denunciation shall only have effect in regard to the notifying Power, and one year after the notification has been made to the Netherland Government.

Article 33

A register kept by the Netherland Ministry for Foreign Affairs shall give the date of the deposit of ratifications made by Article 29, paragraphs 3 and 4, as well as the date on which the notifications of adhesion (Article 30, paragraph 2) or of denunciation (Article 32, paragraph 1) have been received.

Each contracting Power is entitled to have access to this register and to be supplied with duly certified extracts.

In faith whereof the plenipotentiaries have appended their signatures to the present Convention.

Done at The Hague, the 18th October, 1907, in a single copy, which shall remain deposited in the archives of the Netherland Government, and duly certified copies of which shall be sent, through the diplomatic channel, to the Powers which have been invited to the Second Peace Conference.

CONCLUDING NOTES

Signatures, Ratifications, Accessions, and Successions[1]

State (* denotes Reservation: see below)	Date of Signature		Date of Ratification (*r*), Accession (*a*), or Succession (*s*)		
Argentina	18 October	1907	—		
Austria-Hungary	18 October	1907	27 November	1909	*r*
Belgium	18 October	1907	8 August	1910	*r*
Bolivia	18 October	1907	—		
Brazil	18 October	1907	5 January	1914	*r*
Bulgaria	18 October	1907	—		
Byelorussian SSR[2]			4 June	1962	*s*
Chile	18 October	1907	—		
*China			15 January	1910	*a*
Colombia	18 October	1907	—		
Denmark	18 October	1907	27 November	1909	*r*
*Dominican Republic	18 October	1907	—		
Ecuador	18 October	1907	—		
El Salvador	18 October	1907	27 November	1909	*r*
Ethiopia			5 August	1935	*a*
Finland[3]			30 December	1918	*a*
France	18 October	1907	7 October	1910	*r*
*Germany	18 October	1907	27 November	1909	*r*
German Democratic Republic[2]			9 February	1959	*s*
*Great Britain	18 October	1907	—		
Greece	18 October	1907	—		
Guatemala	18 October	1907	15 March	1911	*r*
Haiti	18 October	1907	2 February	1910	*r*
Italy	18 October	1907	—		
*Japan	18 October	1907	13 December	1911	*r*
Liberia			4 February	1914	*a*
Luxembourg	18 October	1907	5 September	1912	*r*
Mexico	18 October	1907	27 November	1909	*r*
Montenegro	18 October	1907	—		
Netherlands	18 October	1907	27 November	1909	*r*
Nicaragua			16 December	1909	*a*
Norway	18 October	1907	19 September	1910	*r*
Panama	18 October	1907	11 September	1911	*r*

[1] Information supplied in communications from the Netherlands Ministry of Foreign Affairs between December 1979 and April 1981.

[2] By letters dated 1 April 1980 and 16 March 1981 the Netherlands Ministry of Foreign Affairs confirmed that these cases constituted successions. *Re* USSR and Byelorussia, see above, p. 41, n. 3.

[3] The Depositary states that Finland's accession became effective on 9 June 1922. See above, p. 58, n. 6.

State (* denotes Reservation: see below)	Date of Signature		Date of Ratification (r), Accession (a), or Succession (s)		
Paraguay	18 October	1907	—		
*Persia	18 October	1907	—		
Peru	18 October	1907	—		
Portugal	18 October	1907	13 April	1911	r
Romania	18 October	1907	1 March	1912	r
Russia	18 October	1907	27 November	1909	r
Serbia	18 October	1907	—		
*Siam	18 October	1907	12 March	1910	r
Sweden	18 October	1907	27 November	1909	r
Switzerland	18 October	1907	12 May	1910	r
*Turkey	18 October	1907	—.		
Uruguay	18 Ocotber	1907			
*USA			3 December	1909	a
USSR[2]			7 March	1955	s
Venezuela	18 October	1907	—		

Total Number of Parties Listed: 30

Note on Entry into Force for States Parties

In accordance with Article 31, the Convention entered into force on 26 January 1910 for the states which had ratified it sixty days earlier, on 27 November 1909. For each of the other ratifying states, and for each of the acceding states (apart from Finland), the Convention formally entered into force sixty days after the date indicated in the right-hand column above.

Denunciations

None

Reservations[4]

China, at accession, made reservation of Article 14, paragraph 2; Article 19, paragraph 3; and Article 27.

Dominican Republic, at signature, made reservation of Article 12. It did not ratify the Convention.

Germany, at signature, made reservation of Articles 11, 12, 13, and 20. At ratification, it maintained its reservation.

Great Britain, at signature, made reservation of Articles 19 and 23. It did not ratify the Convention.

Japan, at signature, made reservation of Articles 19 and 23. At ratification, it maintained its reservation.

Persia, at signature, made reservation of Articles 12, 19, and 21. It did not ratify the Convention.

---

[4] This list, based on information supplied by the Netherlands Ministry of Foreign Affairs, contains English versions from J. B. Scott (ed.), *The Hague Conventions and Declarations of 1899 and 1907*, pp. 218–19.

Siam, at signature, made reservation of Articles 12, 19, and 23. At ratification, it maintained its reservation.

Turkey, at signature, referred in its reservation to its declaration at the Conference on 9 October 1907 concerning Article 10: 'The Ottoman delegation declares that the straits of the Dardanelles and the Bosphorus can not in any case be referred to by Article 10. The Imperial Government could undertake no engagement whatever tending to limit its undoubted rights over these straits.' It did not ratify the Convention.

USA, at accession: 'That the United States adheres to the said Convention, subject to the reservation and exclusion of its Article 23 and with the understanding that the last clause of Article 3 thereof implies the duty of a neutral power to make the demand therein mentioned for the return of a ship captured within the neutral jurisdiction and no longer within that jurisdiction.'

13. 1923 Hague Rules of Aerial Warfare

PREFATORY NOTE

The 1923 Hague Draft Rules were never adopted in legally binding form, but at the time of their conclusion they were regarded as an authoritative attempt to clarify and formulate rules of air warfare, and largely corresponded to customary rules and general principles underlying the laws of war on land and at sea.

Apart from siege warfare, bombing from the air is probably the form of warfare which most directly affects non-combatants. Yet (except for the 1907 Hague Declaration on balloons, which is of limited value) there is in fact no single international agreement in force which exclusively addresses either air warfare in general or bombing in particular. However, many binding international agreements, adopted both before and since the 1923 Hague Draft Rules, have a considerable bearing on the subject.

The first codifications of rules of air warfare were the 1899 and 1907 Hague Declarations relating to balloons. 1899 Hague Declaration 1, prohibiting the launching of projectiles and explosives from balloons and other methods of a similar nature, entered into force in 1900 but, in accordance with its terms, expired after five years. It was replaced by the similar 1907 Hague Declaration (XIV) prohibiting the discharge of projectiles and explosives from balloons, which entered into force in 1909 and is still technically binding. However, the 1907 Declaration is of relatively minor contemporary significance. First, many important states (including France, Germany, Italy, Japan and Russia) never signed or acceded to it; and in 1942 one of the two great powers bound under it, the USA, announced that it would not observe its terms. (Like 1899 Hague Declaration 1, the 1907 Hague Declaration on balloons contains a 'general participation clause' which affects its technical application in hostilities where not all belligerents are parties.) Second, state practice has further reduced the significance of the 1907 Declaration: during the 1911–12 Turco-Italian War, Italy employed balloons to spot and bomb enemy troops; during the First World War dirigibles and aircraft were employed; and during the Second World War aircraft were used on an unprecedented scale, and in 1944–5 Japan sent some balloons carrying small bombs over the USA. Third, although the Declaration does contain a reference to 'other new methods of a similar nature', which can be interpreted as including aircraft, its particular reference to balloons is now more or less obsolete.

In addition to the 1899 and 1907 Hague Declarations on balloons, the Regulations annexed to both 1899 Hague Convention II and 1907 Hague Convention IV make brief reference to air warfare. In Articles 29 and 53 the reference is explicit, and in Articles 25, 26, and 27 it is implied.

The subject of air warfare was further considered at the meeting of the Institute of International Law held in Madrid in 1911. The Institute recommended that air warfare must not pose a greater danger to the civilian population than land or sea warfare, but this was not acted upon by states.

The experience of the First World War demonstrated the need for air warfare to be regulated by a comprehensive code, but the heightened awareness of the military potential of aircraft was a serious obstacle to reaching agreement. Article 38 of the 1919 Paris Aerial Navigation Convention left all parties with complete freedom of action in time of war, and the 1921–2 Washington Conference on the Limitation of Armament failed to produce an agreement on air warfare. States represented at the Washington Conference did agree to appoint a Commission of Jurists (composed of representatives of the USA, Great Britain, France, Italy, Japan, and the Netherlands, and under the chairmanship of John Bassett Moore of the USA) to study the subject and to report its conclusions to each of the governments represented in its membership.

The Commission met in The Hague, and in February 1923 adopted a General Report on the Revision of the Rules of Warfare, Part II of which was the Rules of Aerial Warfare. (Part I was the Rules for the Control of Radio in Time of War.) The USA proposed that the draft rules be incorporated into a treaty for general acceptance, but these rules were never adopted in legally binding form.

The most important provisions may be those relating to bombing, particularly the principle that aerial bombardment to terrorize the civilian population or destroy and damage private property is prohibited. In the period following the Commission's Report, several states announced that they would comply with the regime.

Shortly after the formulation of the Hague Draft Rules, an important agreement having a bearing on air warfare was concluded: the 1925 Geneva Protocol on gas and bacteriological warfare. At the 1932–4 Geneva Disarmament Conference the issue of air warfare was discussed; although the General Commission of the Conference adopted a resolution on air bombardment, no binding agreement was reached. The 1936 London Procès-Verbal on submarine warfare against merchant ships was regarded by various states as also being applicable to military aircraft in operations against merchant shipping.

Before the Second World War, the actions of the Italian air force during the invasion of Ethiopia, the German air force during the Spanish civil war, and the Japanese air force during the invasion of China, demonstrated the need for binding rules on air bombardment. On 21 June 1938 the British Prime Minister, Neville Chamberlain, enunciated in the House of Commons three fundamental principles of international law applicable to warfare from the air: (1) direct attack against the civilian population is unlawful; (2) targets for air bombardment must be legitimate, identifiable military objectives; and (3) reasonable care must be taken in attacking military objectives to avoid bombardment of a civilian population in the neighbourhood. These principles were embodied in a resolution which the League of Nations Assembly unanimously adopted on 30 September 1938.

During the Second World War, the practice of indiscriminate bombardment seriously challenged the application of the most fundamental principles developed in respect of air warfare. To the extent that such practices continue, the significance of certain principles embodied in the 1923 Hague Draft Rules will be called into greater question.

In the period since the Second World War, certain provisions of other international agreements (for example, the four 1949 Geneva Conventions, the 1954 Hague Cultural Property Convention, 1977 Geneva Protocol I, and the 1981 UN Weapons Convention) have expressly or impliedly addressed particular aspects of air warfare.

The fact remains that, unlike either land or sea warfare, there is no formally binding agreement which exclusively addresses air warfare. However, in addition to the various treaty articles which do relate to air warfare, certain general principles underlying the laws of war are considered to be applicable in air warfare, even if in practice their application is not free from difficulty.

The text reproduced here consists of the draft articles only, without the commentary which accompanied them. Complete versions of the commentary are to be found in the sources listed under 'Also published in' below.

Text reprinted from: 17 *AJIL* (1923) Supplement 245–60
Also published in: UK *Misc.* 14 (1924), Cmd. 2201 (Eng.);
                          XXVII *UKPP* (1924) 1017 (Eng.);
                          32 *AJIL* (1938) Supplement 12–56 (Eng.)

Rules of Aerial Warfare

CHAPTER I — *Applicability: Classification and Marks*

Article 1

The rules of aerial warfare apply to all aircraft, whether lighter or heavier than air, irrespective of whether they are, or are not, capable of floating on the water.

Article 2

The following shall be deemed to be public aircraft:
(a) military aircraft;
(b) non-military aircraft exclusively employed in the public service.
All other aircraft shall be deemed to be private aircraft.

Article 3

A military aircraft shall bear an external mark indicating its nationality and military character.

Article 4

A public non-military aircraft employed for customs or police purposes shall carry papers evidencing the fact that it is exclusively employed in the public service. Such an aircraft shall bear an external mark indicating its nationality and its public non-military character.

Article 5

Public non-military aircraft other than those employed for customs or police purposes shall in time of war bear the same external marks, and for the purposes of these rules shall be treated on the same footing, as private aircraft.

Article 6

Aircraft not comprised in Articles 3 and 4 and deemed to be private aircraft shall carry such papers and bear such external marks as are required by the rules in force in their own country. These marks must indicate their nationality and character.

Article 7

The external marks required by the above articles shall be so affixed that they cannot be altered in flight. They shall be as large as is practicable and shall be visible from above, from below and from each side.

Article 8

The external marks, prescribed by the rules in force in each state, shall be notified promptly to all other Powers.

Modifications adopted in time of peace of the rules prescribing external marks shall be notified to all other Powers before they are brought into force.

Modifications of such rules adopted at the outbreak of war or during hostilities shall be notified by each Power as soon as possible to all other Powers and at latest when they are communicated to its own fighting forces.

Article 9

A belligerent non-military aircraft, whether public or private, may be converted into a military aircraft, provided that the conversion is effected within the jurisdiction of the belligerent state to which the aircraft belongs and not on the high seas.

Article 10

No aircraft may possess more than one nationality.

CHAPTER II — *General Principles*

Article 11

Outside the jurisdiction of any state, belligerent or neutral, all aircraft shall have full freedom of passage through the air and of alighting.

Article 12

In time of war any state, whether belligerent or neutral, may forbid or regulate the entrance, movement or sojourn of aircraft within its jurisdiction.

CHAPTER III — *Belligerents*

Article 13
Military aircraft are alone entitled to exercise belligerent rights.

Article 14
A military aircraft shall be under the command of a person duly commissioned or enlisted in the military service of the state; the crew must be exclusively military.

Article 15
Members of the crew of a military aircraft shall wear a fixed distinctive emblem of such character as to be recognizable at a distance in case they become separated from their aircraft.

Article 16
No aircraft other than a belligerent military aircraft shall engage in hostilities in any form.

The term 'hostilities' includes the transmission during flight of military intelligence for the immediate use of a belligerent.

No private aircraft, when outside the jurisdiction of its own country, shall be armed in time of war.

Article 17
The principles laid down in the Geneva Convention, 1906, and the convention for the Adaptation of the said Convention to Maritime War (No. X of 1907) shall apply to aerial warfare and to flying ambulances, as well as to the control over flying ambulances exercised by a belligerent commanding officer.

In order to enjoy the protection and privileges allowed to mobile medical units by the Geneva Convention, 1906, flying ambulances must bear the distinctive emblem of the Red Cross in addition to the usual distinguishing marks.

CHAPTER IV — *Hostilities*

Articles 18
The use of tracer, incendiary or explosive projectiles by or against aircraft is not prohibited.

This provision applies equally to states which are parties to the Declaration of St'Petersburg, 1868, and to those which are not.

Article 19
The use of false external marks is forbidden.

Article 20

When an aircraft has been disabled, the occupants when endeavoring to escape by means of a parachute must not be attacked in the course of their descent.

Article 21

The use of aircraft for the purpose of disseminating propaganda shall not be treated as an illegitimate means of warfare.

Members of the crews of such aircraft must not be deprived of their rights as prisoners of war on the charge that they have committed such an act.

Bombardment

Article 22

Aerial bombardment for the purpose of terrorizing the civilian population, of destroying or damaging private property not of military character, or of injuring non-combatants is prohibited.

Article 23

Aerial bombardment for the purpose of enforcing compliance with requisitions in kind or payment of contributions in money is prohibited.

Article 24

(1) Aerial bombardment is legitimate only when directed at a military objective, that is to say, an object of which the destruction or injury would constitute a distinct military advantage to the belligerent.

(2) Such bombardment is legitimate only when directed exclusively at the following objectives: military forces; military works; military establishments or depots; factories constituting important and well-known centres engaged in the manufacture of arms, ammunition or distinctively military supplies; lines of communication or transportation used for military purposes.

(3) The bombardment of cities, towns, villages, dwellings or buildings not in the immediate neighborhood of the operations of land forces is prohibited. In cases where the objectives specified in paragraph 2 are so situated, that they cannot be bombarded without the indiscriminate bombardment of the civilian population, the aircraft must abstain from bombardment.

(4) In the immediate neighborhood of the operations of land forces, the bombardment of cities, towns, villages, dwellings or buildings is legitimate provided that there exists a reasonable presumption that the military concentration is sufficiently important

to justify such bombardment, having regard to the danger thus caused to the civilian population.

(5) A belligerent state is liable to pay compensation for injuries to person or to property caused by the violation by any of its officers or forces of the provisions of this article.

Article 25

In bombardment by aircraft, all necessary steps must be taken by the commander to spare as far as possible buildings dedicated to public worship, art, science, or charitable purposes, historic monuments, hospital ships, hospitals and other places where the sick and wounded are collected, provided such buildings, objects or places are not at the time used for military purposes. Such buildings, objects and places must by day be indicated by marks visible to aircraft. The use of marks to indicate other buildings, objects, or places than those specified above is to be deemed an act of perfidy. The marks used as aforesaid shall be in the case of buildings protected under the Geneva Convention the red cross on a white ground, and in the case of other protected buildings a large rectangular panel divided diagonally into two pointed triangular portions, one black and the other white.

A belligerent who desires to secure by night the protection for the hospitals and other privileged buildings above mentioned must take the necessary measures to render the special signs referred to sufficiently visible.

Article 26

The following special rules are adopted for the purpose of enabling states to obtain more efficient protection for important historic monuments situated within their territory, provided that they are willing to refrain from the use of such monuments and a surrounding zone for military purposes, and to accept a special régime for their inspection.

(1) A state shall be entitled, if it sees fit, to establish a zone of protection round such monuments situated in its territory. Such zones shall in time of war enjoy immunity from bombardment.

(2) The monuments round which a zone is to be established shall be notified to other Powers in peace time through the diplomatic channel; the notification shall also indicate the limits of the zones. The notification may not be withdrawn in time of war.

(3) The zone of protection may include, in addition to the area actually occupied by the monument or group of monuments, an outer zone, not exceeding 500 metres in width, measured from the circumference of the said area.

(4) Marks clearly visible from aircraft either by day or by night

will be employed for the purpose of ensuring the identification by belligerent airmen of the limits of the zones.

(5) The marks on the monuments themselves will be those defined in Article 25. The marks employed for indicating the surrounding zones will be fixed by each state adopting the provisions of this article, and will be notified to other Powers at the same time as the monuments and zones are notified.

(6) Any abusive use of the marks indicating the zones referred to in paragraph 5 will be regarded as an act of perfidy.

(7) A state adopting the provisions of this article must abstain from using the monument and the surrounding zone for military purposes, or for the benefit in any way whatever of its military organization, or from committing within such monument or zone any act with a military purpose in view.

(8) An inspection committee consisting of three neutral representatives accredited to the state adopting the provisions of this article, or their delegates, shall be appointed for the purpose of ensuring that no violation is committed of the provisions of paragraph 7. One of the members of the committee of inspection shall be the representative (or his delegate) of the state to which has been entrusted the interests of the opposing belligerent.

Espionage

Article 27

Any person on board a belligerent or neutral aircraft is to be deemed a spy only if acting clandestinely or on false pretences he obtains or seeks to obtain, while in the air, information within belligerent jurisdiction or in the zone of operations of a belligerent with the intention of communicating it to the hostile party.

Article 28

Acts of espionage committed after leaving the aircraft by members of the crew of an aircraft or by passengers transported by it are subject to the provisions of the Land Warfare Regulations.

Article 29

Punishment of the acts of espionage referred to in Articles 27 and 28 is subject to Articles 30 and 31 of the Land Warfare Regulations.

CHAPTER V — *Military Authority over Enemy and Neutral Aircraft and Persons on Board*

Article 30

In case a belligerent commanding officer considers that the presence of aircraft is likely to prejudice the success of the operations in which he is engaged at the moment, he may prohibit the passing of neutral aircraft in the immediate vicinity of his forces or may oblige them to follow a particular route. A neutral aircraft which does not conform to such directions, of which it has had notice issued by the belligerent commanding officer, may be fired upon.

Article 31

In accordance with the principles of Article 53 of the Land Warfare Regulations, neutral private aircraft found upon entry in the enemy's jurisdiction by a belligerent occupying force may be requisitioned, subject to the payment of full compensation.

Article 32

Enemy public aircraft, other than those treated on the same footing as private aircraft, shall be subject to confiscation without prize proceedings.

Article 33

Belligerent non-military aircraft, whether public or private, flying within the jurisdiction of their own state, are liable to be fired upon unless they make the nearest available landing on the approach of enemy military aircraft.

Article 34

Belligerent non-military aircraft, whether public or private, are liable to be fired upon, if they fly (1) within the jurisdiction of the enemy, or (2) in the immediate vicinity thereof and outside the jurisdiction of their own state or (3) in the immediate vicinity of the military operations of the enemy by land or sea.

Article 35

Neutral aircraft flying within the jurisdiction of a belligerent, and warned of the approach of military aircraft of the opposing belligerent, must make the nearest available landing. Failure to do so exposes them to the risk of being fired upon.

Article 36

When an enemy military aircraft falls into the hands of a belligerent, the members of the crew and the passengers, if any, may be made prisoners of war.

The same rule applies to the members of the crew and the passengers, if any, of an enemy public non-military aircraft, except that in the case of public non-military aircraft devoted exclusively to the transport of passengers, the passengers will be entitled to be released unless they are in the service of the enemy, or are enemy nationals fit for military service.

If an enemy private aircraft falls into the hands of a belligerent, members of the crew who are enemy nationals or who are neutral nationals in the service of the enemy, may be made prisoners of war. Neutral members of the crew, who are not in the service of the enemy, are entitled to be released if they sign a written undertaking not to serve in any enemy aircraft while hostilities last. Passengers are entitled to be released unless they are in the service of the enemy or are enemy nationals fit for military service, in which cases they may be made prisoners of war.

Release may in any case be delayed if the military interests of the belligerent so require.

The belligerent may hold as prisoners of war any member of the crew or any passenger whose service in a flight at the close of which he has been captured has been of special and active assistance to the enemy.

The names of individuals released after giving a written undertaking in accordance with the third paragraph of this article will be notified to the opposing belligerent, who must not knowingly employ them in violation of their undertaking.

Article 37

Members of the crew of a neutral aircraft which has been detained by a belligerent shall be released unconditionally, if they are neutral nationals and not in the service of the enemy. If they are enemy nationals or in the service of the enemy, they may be made prisoners of war.

Passengers are entitled to be released unless they are in the service of the enemy or are enemy nationals fit for military service, in which cases they may be made prisoners of war.

Release may in any case be delayed if the military interests of the belligerent so require.

The belligerent may hold as prisoners of war any member of the crew or any passenger whose service in a flight at the close of which he has been captured has been of special and active assistance to the enemy.

Article 38

Where under the provisions of Articles 36 and 37 it is provided that members of the crew or passengers may be made prisoners of war, it is to be understood that, if they are not members of the armed forces, they shall be entitled to treatment not less favourable than that accorded to prisoners of war.

CHAPTER VI — *Belligerent Duties towards Neutral States and Neutral Duties towards Belligerent States*

Article 39

Belligerent aircraft are bound to respect the rights of neutral Powers and to abstain within the jurisdiction of a neutral state from the commission of any act which it is the duty of that state to prevent.

Article 40

Belligerent military aircraft are forbidden to enter the jurisdiction of a neutral state.

Article 41

Aircraft on board vessels of war, including aircraft-carriers, shall be regarded as part of such vessel.

Article 42

A neutral government must use the means at its disposal to prevent the entry within its jurisdiction of belligerent military aircraft and to compel them to alight if they have entered such jurisdiction.

A neutral government shall use the means at its disposal to intern any belligerent military aircraft which is within its jurisdiction after having alighted for any reason whatsoever, together with its crew and the passengers, if any.

Article 43

The personnel of a disabled belligerent military aircraft rescued outside neutral waters and brought into the jurisdiction of a neutral state by a neutral military aircraft and there landed shall be interned.

Article 44

The supply in any manner, directly or indirectly, by a neutral government to a belligerent Power of aircraft, parts of aircraft, or material, supplies or munitions required for aircraft is forbidden.

Article 45

Subject to the provisions of Article 46, a neutral Power is not bound to prevent the export or transit on behalf of a belligerent of aircraft, parts of aircraft, or material, supplies or munitions for aircraft.

Article 46

A neutral government is bound to use the means at its disposal:

(1) To prevent the departure from its jurisdiction of an aircraft in a condition to make a hostile attack against a belligerent Power, or carrying or accompanied by appliances or materials the mounting

or utilization of which would enable it to make a hostile attack, if there is reason to believe that such aircraft is destined for use against a belligerent Power;

(2) To prevent the departure of an aircraft the crew of which includes any member of the combatant forces of a belligerent Power;

(3) To prevent work upon an aircraft designed to prepare it to depart in contravention of the purposes of this article.

On the departure by air of any aircraft despatched by persons or companies in neutral jurisdiction to the order of a belligerent Power, the neutral government must prescribe for such aircraft a route avoiding the neighborhood of the military operations of the opposing belligerent, and must exact whatever guarantees may be required to ensure that the aircraft follows the route prescribed.

Article 47

A neutral state is bound to take such steps as the means at its disposal permit to prevent within its jurisdiction aerial observation of the movements, operations or defenses of one belligerent, with the intention of informing the other belligerent.

This provision applies equally to a belligerent military aircraft on board a vessel of war.

Article 48

The action of a neutral Power in using force or other means at its disposal in the exercise of its rights or duties under these rules cannot be regarded as a hostile act.

CHAPTER VII — *Visit and Search, Capture and Condemnation*

Article 49

Private aircraft are liable to visit and search and to capture by belligerent military aircraft.

Article 50

Belligerent military aircraft have the right to order public non-military and private aircraft to alight in or proceed for visit and search to a suitable locality reasonably accessible.

Refusal, after warning, to obey such orders to alight or to proceed to such a locality for examination exposes an aircraft to the risk of being fired upon.

Article 51

Neutral public non-military aircraft, other than those which are to be treated as private aircraft, are subject only to visit for the purpose of the verification of their papers.

Article 52
Enemy private aircraft are liable to capture in all circumstances.

Article 53
A neutral private aircraft is liable to capture if it:
(a) resists the legitimate exercise of belligerent rights;
(b) violates a prohibition of which it has had notice issued by a belligerent commanding officer under Article 30;
(c) is engaged in unneutral service;
(d) is armed in time of war when outside the jurisdiction of its own country;
(e) has no external marks or uses false marks;
(f) has no papers or insufficient or irregular papers;
(g) is manifestly out of the line between the point of departure and the point of destination indicated in its papers and after such enquiries as the belligerent may deem necessary, no good cause is shown for the deviation. The aircraft, together with its crew and passengers, if any, may be detained by the belligerent, pending such enquiries.
(h) carries, or itself constitutes, contraband of war;
(i) is engaged in breach of a blockade duly established and effectively maintained;
(k) has been transferred from belligerent to neutral nationality at a date and in circumstances indicating an intention of evading the consequences to which an enemy aircraft, as such, is exposed.
Provided that in each case, (except k), the ground for capture shall be an act carried out in the flight in which the neutral aircraft came into belligerent hands, i.e. since it left its point of departure and before it reached its point of destination.

Article 54
The papers of a private aircraft will be regarded as insufficient or irregular if they do not establish the nationality of the aircraft and indicate the names and nationalities of the crew and passengers, the points of departure and destination of the flight, together with particulars of the cargo and the conditions under which it is transported. The logs must also be included.

Article 55
Capture of an aircraft or of goods on board an aircraft shall be made the subject of prize proceedings, in order that any neutral claim may be duly heard and determined.

Article 56
A private aircraft captured upon the ground that it has no external

marks or is using false marks, or that it is armed in time of war outside the jurisdiction of its own country, is liable to condemnation.

A neutral private aircraft captured upon the ground that it has disregarded the direction of a belligerent commanding officer under Article 30 is liable to condemnation, unless it can justify its presence within the prohibited zone.

In all other cases, the prize court in adjudicating upon any case of capture of an aircraft or its cargo, or of postal correspondence on board an aircraft, shall apply the same rules as would be applied to a merchant vessel or its cargo or to postal correspondence on board a merchant vessel.

Article 57

Private aircraft which are found upon visit and search to be enemy aircraft may be destroyed if the belligerent commanding officer finds it necessary to do so, provided that all persons on board have first been placed in safety and all the papers of the aircraft have been preserved.

Article 58

Private aircraft which are found upon visit and search to be neutral aircraft liable to condemnation upon the ground of unneutral service, or upon the ground that they have no external marks or are bearing false marks, may be destroyed, if sending them in for adjudication would be impossible or would imperil the safety of the belligerent aircraft or the success of the operations in which it is engaged. Apart from the cases mentioned above, a neutral private aircraft must not be destroyed except in the gravest military emergency, which would not justify the officer in command in releasing it or sending it in for adjudication.

Article 59

Before a neutral private aircraft is destroyed, all persons on board must be placed in safety, and all the papers of the aircraft must be preserved.

A captor who had destroyed a neutral private aircraft must bring the capture before the prize court, and must first establish that he was justified in destroying it under Article 58. If he fails to do this, parties interested in the aircraft or its cargo are entitled to compensation. If the capture is held to be invalid, though the act of destruction is held to have been justifiable, compensation must be paid to the parties interested in place of the restitution to which they would have been entitled.

Article 60

Where a neutral private aircraft is captured on the ground that it is carrying contraband, the captor may demand the surrender of any absolute contraband on board, or may proceed to the destruction of such absolute contraband, if sending in the aircraft for adjudication is impossible or would imperil the safety of the belligerent aircraft or the success of the operations in which it is engaged. After entering in the log book of the aircraft the delivery or destruction of the goods, and securing, in original or copy, the relevant papers of the aircraft, the captor must allow the neutral aircraft to continue its flight.

The provisions of the second paragraph of Article 59 will apply where absolute contraband on board a neutral private aircraft is handed over or destroyed.

CHAPTER VIII — *Definitions*

Article 61

The term 'military' throughout these rules is to be read as referring to all branches of the forces, i.e. the land forces, the naval forces and the air forces.

Article 62

Except so far as special rules are here laid down and except also so far as the provisions of Chapter VII of these rules or international conventions indicate that maritime law and procedure are applicable, aircraft personnel engaged in hostilities come under the laws of war and neutrality applicable to land troops in virtue of the custom and practice of international law and of the various declarations and conventions to which the states concerned are parties.

14. 1925 Geneva Protocol for the Prohibition of the Use in War of Asphyxiating, Poisonous or Other Gases, and of Bacteriological Methods of Warfare

PREFATORY NOTE

At the First Hague Peace Conference of 1899, Hague Declaration 2 prohibited the use of projectiles the sole object of which is the diffusion of asphyxiating or deleterious gases. As mentioned in the prefatory note to that document, 1899 Hague Declaration 2 was derived from the customary rules prohibiting the use of poison and materials causing unnecessary suffering.

At the conclusion of the First World War, articles in various peace treaties reiterated and in some respects enlarged the prohibition embodied in the 1899 Declaration. For example, Article 171 of the 1919 Treaty of Versailles stated: 'The use of asphyxiating, poisonous or other gases and all analogous liquids, materials or devices being prohibited, their manufacture and importation are strictly forbidden in Germany.' (This was a ban on possession as well as use.) The 1922 Treaty of Washington on the Use of Submarines and Noxious Gases in Warfare prohibited the use of 'asphyxiating, poisonous or other gases, and all analogous liquids, materials or devices' but did not enter into force.

The 1925 Geneva Protocol was adopted by the International Conference on the Control of the International Trade in Arms, Munitions, and Implements of War, which had been convened by the Council of the League of Nations and met in Geneva in May and June 1925. Under the Protocol, so far as the states parties were not already parties to treaties prohibiting the use in war of asphyxiating, poisonous, or other gases, and of all analogous liquids, materials, and devices, the states accepted this prohibition; and they also extended it to the use of bacteriological methods of warfare. Like earlier agreements referred to above, the 1925 Geneva Protocol was derived from the general principles of customary international law prohibiting the use of poison and materials causing unnecessary suffering.

The Protocol is regarded as having two main flaws. First, its terms leave considerable room for divergent interpretations of the prohibitions embodied therein. States have taken different positions on whether or not tear-gas and other normally non-lethal gases, or herbicides and similar agents, fall within the Protocol's prohibitions. As regards tear-gas, an early attempt at clarification was made in 1930. On 2 December 1930, in the Preparatory Commission for the Disarmament Conference, the British Government submitted a memorandum drawing attention to 'a serious ambiguity' in the wording of the Protocol, namely that where the English text referred to 'asphyxiating, poisonous or other gases', the equally authentic French text had 'similaires' rather than 'other'. The memorandum said that the British Government took the view that under the Protocol the use of 'other' gases, including lachrymatory (i.e. tear) gases, was prohibited. In reply, the French delegate stated unequivocally: 'The

French Government . . . considers that the use of lachrymatory gases is covered by the prohibition arising out of the Geneva Protocol of 1925.' Eleven other members of the Commission expressed their governments' endorsement of this Anglo-French interpretation. Only the USA (not at that time a party to the Protocol) dissented. It did so partly on the grounds that it would be inconsistent to prohibit the use in warfare of gases which could still continue to be used within states in peacetime for police purposes. On 22 January 1975, in connection with the US ratification of the Protocol, the President made a statement affirming the US understanding of the scope of the Protocol as not extending to control agents and chemical herbicides, but announced that as a matter of policy the use of such substances would be restricted. On 2 February 1970 the British Foreign Secretary announced a significant and controversial change of the UK position when he said in a written answer in the House of Commons: '. . . we regard CS and other such gases . . . as being outside the scope of the Geneva Protocol.' This unilateral reinterpretation of the Protocol relied on a claimed distinction between CS smoke and older forms of tear-gas as they had existed in 1930.

Since 1966, the UN General Assembly has adopted several resolutions calling for strict observance of the principles of the 1925 Geneva Protocol: GA Resolution 2603A (XXIV) of 16 December 1969 interprets the Protocol, declaring that it prohibits the use in international armed conflicts of: '(a) Any chemical agents of warfare — chemical substances, whether gaseous liquid or solid — which might be employed because of their direct toxic effects on man, animals or plants; (b) Any biological agents of warfare — living organisms, whatever their nature, or infective material derived from them — which are intended to cause disease or death in man, animals or plants, and which depend for their effects on their ability to multiply in the person, animal or plant attacked.'

The second main flaw in the Protocol is that a number of states have become parties to it subject to the reservation that the Protocol is binding only in relation to other states bound by it and shall cease to be binding if the enemy or its allies fail to respect the prohibitions embodied therein. In other words, the Protocol is regarded by such states as containing not an absolute prohibition of the use of such weapons, but only an agreement not to use such weapons first.

The observance of the Protocol has been uneven. Italy used gas in 1935–6 during its invasion of Ethiopia. At the outbreak of the Second World War, several states, including Germany, declared that they would observe the prohibitions of the Protocol subject to reciprocity. In military operations during the Second World War, gas and bacteriological weapons were not used to any great extent. The most important exception was the Japanese use of gas in China between 1937 and 1945. In so far as the belligerents refrained from using such weapons (of which they had stocks) in warfare, this was due to a variety of factors which included fear of retaliation in kind. In conflicts since the Second World War, the use of toxic gases has often been alleged; and also, occasionally, the use of bacteriological weapons. In most such cases at least one party to the conflict was not a party to the Protocol.

The majority view is that, given the large number of states presently bound by the 1925 Geneva Protocol, the prohibitions embodied in the Protocol should be viewed as having become a part of customary international law. As customary international law, the Protocol would be applicable to all states and not merely those which have formally ratified or adhered to the instrument. However, some suggest that the controversy over the Protocol's interpretation, as well as the character of reservations, have reduced the Protocol's usefulness as a guide to customary international law in this area. The weight of opinion appears to recognize that at least the first use of lethal chemical and biological weapons is prohibited by customary international law. Less consensus exists on the status under customary international law of non-lethal chemical and biological weapons. However, the distinction between lethal and non-lethal agents is very difficult to draw.

Biological weapons are now also the subject of the 1972 Convention on the Prohibition of the Development, Production and Stockpiling of Bacteriological (Biological) and Toxin Weapons and on their Destruction, which entered into force in 1975.

The 1925 Geneva Protocol has been cited as the basis for establishing the illegality of certain contemporary weapons whose use in hostilities is not explicitly regulated by written agreement. In particular, it has been suggested that the effects of nuclear weapons imply, by analogy, that their use is prohibited by the 1925 Geneva Protocol as well as by the customary principles prohibiting the use of poison and materials causing unnecessary suffering. Others suggest that such an analogy only indicates that the use of nuclear weapons is prohibited if directed against non-military objectives, or against military targets which cannot be destroyed without serious loss of life or injury to health. Still others find difficulty in prohibiting nuclear weapons by such an analogy and consider that, in the absence of any express prohibition, the use of such weapons may in some circumstances be permitted.

Date of signature:	17 June 1925
Entry into force:	8 February 1928 (But see note on pp. 143–4 below.)
Depositary:	France
Authentic languages:	French and English
Text reprinted from:	XCIV *LNTS* (1929) 65–74
Also published in:	26 *Martens NRG, 3ème sér.* (1932–1933) 643–50 (Eng. Fr.);
	126 *BFSP* (1927) 324–5 (Eng.);
	UKTS 24 (1930), Cmd. 3604 (Eng. Fr.);
	XXXII *UKPP* (1929–1930) 293 (Eng. Fr.);
	25 *AJIL* (1931) Supplement 94–6 (Eng.)

Protocol for the Prohibition of the Use in War of Asphyxiating, Poisonous or Other Gases, and of Bacteriological Methods of Warfare

THE UNDERSIGNED PLENIPOTENTIARIES, in the name of their respective Governments:

Whereas the use in war of asphyxiating, poisonous or other gases, and of all analogous liquids materials or devices, has been justly condemned by the general opinion of the civilised world; and

Whereas the prohibition of such use has been declared in Treaties to which the majority of Powers of the world are Parties; and

To the end that this prohibition shall be universally accepted as a part of International Law, binding alike the conscience and the practice of nations;

DECLARE:

That the High Contracting Parties, so far as they are not already Parties to Treaties prohibiting such use, accept this prohibition, agree to extend this prohibition to the use of bacteriological methods of warfare and agree to be bound as between themselves according to the terms of this declaration.

The High Contracting Parties will exert every effort to induce other States to accede to the present Protocol. Such accession will be notified to the Government of the French Republic, and by the latter to all signatory and acceding Powers, and will take effect on the date of the notification by the Government of the French Republic.

The present Protocol, of which the French and English texts are both authentic, shall be ratified as soon as possible. It shall bear to-day's date.

The ratifications of the present Protocol shall be addressed to the Government of the French Republic, which will at once notify the deposit of such ratification to each of the signatory and acceding Powers.

The instruments of ratification of and accession to the present Protocol will remain deposited in the archives of the Government of the French Republic.

The present Protocol will come into force for each signatory Power as from the date of deposit of its ratification, and, from that moment, each Power will be bound as regards other Powers which have already deposited their ratifications.

In witness whereof the Plenipotentiaries have signed the present Protocol.

Done at Geneva in a single copy, the seventeenth day of June, One Thousand Nine Hundred and Twenty-Five.

CONCLUDING NOTES

Signatures, Ratifications, Accessions, and Successions[1]			
State (* denotes Reservation etc.: see below)	Date of Signature		Date of Ratification (r), Accession (a), or Succession (s)[2]
Argentina			12 May 1969 *a*
*Australia			24 May 1930 *a*
Austria	17 June	1925	9 May 1928 *r*
Barbados[3]			16 July 1976 *s*
*Belgium	17 June	1925	4 December 1928 *r*
Bhutan			19 February 1979 *a*
Brazil	17 June	1925	28 August 1970 *r*
*Bulgaria	17 June	1925	7 March 1934 *r*
*Canada	17 June	1925	6 May 1930 *r*
Central African Republic			31 July 1970 *a*
Ceylon			20 January 1954 *a*
*Chile	17 June	1925	2 July 1935 *r*
China			24 August 1929 *a*
*China, People's Republic of			16 July 1952 *s*
Cuba			24 June 1966 *a*
Cyprus			29 November 1966 *s*
*Czechoslovakia	17 June	1925	16 August 1938 *r*
Denmark	17 June	1925	5 May 1930 *r*
Dominican Republic			8 December 1970 *a*
Ecuador			16 September 1970 *a*
Egypt	17 June	1925	6 December 1928 *r*
El Salvador	17 June	1925	—
*Estonia	17 June	1925	28 August 1931 *r*
Ethiopia	17 June	1925	7 October 1935 *r*
*Fiji			21 March 1973 *s*
Finland	17 June	1925	26 June 1929 *r*
*France	17 June	1925	10 May 1926 *r*
Gambia			5 November 1966 *s*
Germany	17 June	1925	25 April 1929 *r*
German Democratic Republic[4]			2 March 1959 *s*
Ghana			3 May 1967 *a*

[1] Information supplied in communications from the French Ministry of Foreign Affairs between April 1980 and April 1981, supplemented by various volumes of *LNTS*.

[2] The dates for accessions given below are the dates on which such accessions become effective. In most cases, instruments of accession were deposited on an earlier date. See below, 'Note on Entry into Force for States Parties'.

[3] In notifying succession, Barbados withdrew from the reservation made by Great Britain.

[4] On 2 March 1959 the German Democratic Republic, through the Czechoslovak Embassy in Paris, communicated a declaration confirming the application of the Protocol; and it confirmed this on 21 October 1974.

State (* denotes Reservation etc.: see below)	Date of Signature		Date of Ratification (r), Accession (a), or Succession (s)		
*Great Britain and Empire[5]	17 June	1925	9 April	1930	r
Greece	17 June	1925	30 May	1931	r
Holy See			18 October	1966	a
Hungary			11 October	1952	a
Iceland			2 November	1967	a
*India	17 June	1925	9 April	1930	r
Indonesia			21 January	1971	s
*Iraq			8 September	1931	a
*Ireland			29 August	1930	a
*Israel			20 February	1969	a
Italy	17 June	1925	3 April	1928	r
Ivory Coast			27 July	1970	a
Jamaica			28 July	1970	s
Japan	17 June	1925	21 May	1970	r
*Jordan			20 January	1977	a
Kenya			6 July	1970	a
*Kuwait			15 December	1971	a
Latvia	17 June	1925	3 June	1931	r
Lebanon			17 April	1969	a
Lesotho			10 March	1972	s
Liberia			17 June	1927	a
*Libya			29 December	1971	a
Lithuania	17 June	1925	15 June	1933	r
Luxembourg	17 June	1925	1 September	1936	r
Madagascar			2 August	1967	a
Malawi			14 September	1970	a
Malaysia			10 December	1970	a
Maldives			27 December	1966	s
Malta			9 October	1970	s
Mauritius			23 December	1970	s
Mexico			28 May	1932	a
Monaco			6 January	1967	a
*Mongolia			6 December	1968	a
Morocco			13 October	1970	a
Nepal			9 May	1969	a
*Netherlands[6]	17 June	1925	31 October	1930	r
*New Zealand			24 May	1930	a
Nicaragua	17 June	1925	—		
Niger			5 April	1967	s
*Nigeria			15 October	1968	a
Norway	17 June	1925	27 July	1932	r
*Pakistan			15 April	1960	s

[5] On signing, the British declared that their signature 'does not bind India or any British Dominion which is a separate Member of the League of Nations and does not separately sign or adhere to the Protocol.'

[6] Including the Netherlands Indies, Surinam and Curacao.

State (* denotes Reservation etc.: see below)	Date of Signature		Date of Ratification (r), Accession (a), or Succession (s)		
Panama			4 December	1970	a
Papua New Guinea			2 December	1980	s
Paraguay[7]			22 October	1933	a
Persia			5 November	1929	a
Philippines			8 June	1973	a
Poland	17 June	1925	4 February	1929	r
*Portugal	17 June	1925	1 July	1930	r
Qatar			18 October	1976	a
*Romania	17 June	1925	23 August	1929	r
Rwanda			11 May	1964	s
Saudi Arabia			27 January	1971	a
Senegal			20 July	1977	a
*Serbs, Croats and Slovenes, Kingdom of[8]	17 June	1925	12 April	1929	r
Siam	17 June	1925	6 June	1931	r
Sierra Leone			20 March	1967	a
*South Africa			24 May	1930	a
*Spain	17 June	1925	22 August	1929	r
Sudan			17 December	1980	a
Sweden	17 June	1925	25 April	1930	r
Switzerland	17 June	1925	12 July	1932	r
*Syria			17 December	1968	a
Tanganyika			22 April	1963	u
Togo			5 April	1971	a
Tonga			19 July	1971	s
Trinidad and Tobago			24 November	1970	s
Tunisia			12 July	1967	a
Turkey	17 June	1925	5 October	1929	r
Uganda			24 May	1965	a
Upper Volta			3 March	1971	a
Uruguay	17 June	1925	12 April	1977	r
*USA	17 June	1925	10 April	1975	r
*USSR			5 April	1928	a
Venezuela	17 June	1925	8 February	1928	r
*Vietnam			11 December	1980	a
Yemen Arab Republic (North)			17 March	1971	a

Total Number of Parties Listed: 106

Note on Entry into Force for States Parties

According to the Depositary, the Protocol entered into force on 8 February 1928. That was the date of the second ratification, by Venezuela. (However, it could be argued that the Protocol had already been in force as between

---

[7] Notification regularized on 13 January 1969.   [8] Since 1930, Yugoslavia.

France and Liberia, the latter having acceded on 17 June 1927.) For each of the other ratifying states, the Protocol entered into force on the date (given in the right-hand column above) of deposit of the instrument of ratification. For each of the acceding states it entered into force on the date (given in the right-hand column above) when the French government gave notification of the accession concerned to the other signatory and acceding powers: this date is often several days, or even several months, later than the date of deposit of the instrument of accession by the acceding state with the French government.

Denunciations

None

Reservations etc.[9]

All the following reservations were made at ratification, accession or succession.

Australia, Belgium, Bulgaria, Canada, Chile, Czechoslovakia, Estonia, Fiji, Great Britain and Empire, India, Iraq, Netherlands, New Zealand, Nigeria, Pakistan, Portugal, Romania, South Africa, USSR and *Vietnam* all made reservations similar to those of France.

China, People's Republic of, stated that it would implement the provisions the provisions of the Protocol 'provided that all the other contracting and acceding powers observe them reciprocally'.

France: '(1) The said Protocol is only binding on the Government of the French Republic as regards States which have signed or ratified it or which may accede to it. (2) The said Protocol shall *ipso facto* cease to be binding on the Government of the French Republic in regard to any enemy State whose armed forces or whose Allies fail to respect the prohibitions laid down in the Protocol.'

Ireland made reservations similar to those of France; but it withdrew these reservations with effect from 10 February 1972.

Israel: 'The Protocol is binding on the State of Israel only in respect of those States which have signed and ratified it or have acceded thereto. The Protocol shall *ipso facto* cease to be binding on the State of Israel in respect of any enemy State whose armed forces or those of its allies, or regular or irregular forces, or groups or individuals operating from its territory do not comply with the prohibitions which are the subject of this Protocol.'

Jordan stated that its accession 'shall not in any way imply recognition of Israel' and 'shall not entail for it the obligation to conclude with Israel any of the arrangements indicated in the Protocol'. Jordan 'undertakes to observe the obligations contained in the Protocol in relation to those States which have entered into similar undertakings'. The undertakings entered into by Jordan 'shall not apply in relation to those States whose armed forces, regular or otherwise, do not observe the provisions' of the Protocol.

Kuwait: 'The accession of the State of Kuwait to this Protocol does not in any way imply recognition of Israel nor the establishment with Israel of relations governed by this Protocol. In the case of a breach of the prohibition referred

---

[9] This list is based on the sources referred to in footnote 1 above, and also (for the period since 1945) on various volumes of *UKTS* and *AJIL*.

to in this Protocol by any of the parties to it, the State of Kuwait will not be bound to apply the provisions of the Protocol to such party.'

Libya: Accession 'does not imply recognition of nor the establishment of relations of any kind with Israel'. Libya is only bound 'in regard to those States which are bound by the Protocol and . . . will cease to be bound by the Protocol in respect of those States whose forces or whose allies' armed forces do not respect the prohibition which is the object of the Protocol'.

Mongolia: 'In the case of violation of this prohibition by any State in respect of the People's Republic of Mongolia or their allies, the government of the People's Republic of Mongolia will not consider itself bound by the obligations of the Protocol as regards that State.'

Serbs, Croats and Slovenes, Kingdom of: The Protocol shall cease to be binding 'in regard to any enemy State whose armed forces or whose Allies fail to respect the prohibitions laid down in the Protocol'.

Spain declares the Protocol 'as compulsory *ipso facto* and without special agreement in relation to any other Member [of the League of Nations] or State accepting and executing the same obligation, that is to say, on condition of reciprocity'.

Syria: Accession 'shall under no circumstances signify recognition of Israel and cannot lead to entry into dealings with the latter on the subject of the provisions laid down by this Protocol'.

USA: 'The said Protocol shall cease to be binding on the Government of the United States with respect to the use in war of asphyxiating, poisonous or other gases, and of all analogous liquids, materials or devices, in regard to an enemy state if such state or any of its allies fails to respect the prohibition laid down in the Protocol.'

15. 1936 London Procès-Verbal Relating to the Rules of Submarine Warfare Set Forth in Part IV of the Treaty of London of 22 April 1930

PREFATORY NOTE

This agreement (also known as the 1936 London Protocol) is one of several which relate to the long-standing and difficult question of action by belligerents in relation to merchant ships.

At the outbreak of the First World War, the traditional rules of naval warfare were given general recognition by belligerents, but the practice of belligerents soon called the traditional régime into question. In particular, Germany began to use submarines against merchant ships, and this practice (justified by Germany primarily as reprisals) has been regarded as seriously violating the principle distinguishing combatants from non-combatants in naval warfare; however, that principle was difficult to apply due to the arming of British merchant ships. Other belligerents followed these practices, and the conduct of naval warfare significantly weakened the traditional immunity of merchant ships from attack.

After the First World War, it was hoped that the authority of the traditional rules of naval warfare could be restored. At the conclusion of the 1921–2 Washington Conference on the Limitation of Armament, the United States, Great Britain, France, Italy, Japan, and certain other states signed (in addition to a treaty limiting naval armaments) the 1922 Washington Treaty Relating to the Use of Submarines and Noxious Gases in Warfare. The treaty required the ratification of all signatories in order to enter into force; France did not ratify, and hence the treaty did not become formally binding.

On 22 April 1930 the International Treaty for the Limitation and Reduction of Naval Armament was signed in London by eleven states. Nine of them ratified the Treaty in 1930, and two in 1936. Although primarily an agreement on arms limitation, one part of the Treaty related to the laws of war: Part IV, which consisted of one article, Article 22. This set forth rules regarding the use of submarines in warfare, and explicitly stated that they 'are accepted as established rules of international law'. According to Article 23, Part IV was to remain in force without limit of time. Consequently, when the remainder of the 1930 London Naval Treaty expired on 31 December 1936, Part IV (i.e. Article 22) remained in force.

With a view to enlarging the number of states expressly accepting the provisions embodied in Article 22 of the 1930 London Naval Treaty, representatives of the eleven states which had signed the 1930 Treaty, meeting in London, signed a Procès-Verbal on 6 November 1936 which incorporated verbatim the provisions of Article 22 of the 1930 London Naval Treaty, and also provided for the accession of other states without limit of time. Many states, including in 1936 both Germany and the Soviet Union, acceded to the Procès-Verbal.

By the outbreak of the Second World War, forty-eight states (including almost all of the belligerents involved in the war) had become parties to the Procès-Verbal.

The provisions of the 1936 London Procès-Verbal were included in the naval regulations issued by many states to their naval forces. They were also referred to in the preamble to the 1937 Nyon Agreement (concluded by eight states) as being declaratory of international law. In addition, these provisions were regarded by various states as also being applicable to military aircraft in operations against enemy merchant shipping.

After the outbreak of the Second World War, unrestricted submarine and air warfare by Germany against merchant ships was regarded as violating both the Procès-Verbal and the customary principles embodied therein. Germany recognized the obligations of the Procès-Verbal, but contended that its actions were justified as measures of reprisal, and that the British integration of merchant shipping into its military effort prevented German compliance with the Procès-Verbal. Soon thereafter, Great Britain and France adopted retaliatory measures and stated that one of the reasons for this was Germany's violation of the Procès-Verbal. In the Pacific both of the major naval belligerents adopted a policy of unrestricted submarine and air warfare against merchant ships.

A particular difficulty in the implementation of the Procès-Verbal relates to the danger to which a submarine is exposed if it surfaces which it has to do to fulfil the obligations incumbent on surface ships.

In the trials of Admirals Doenitz and Raeder at Nuremberg in 1945–6, the International Military Tribunal found the accused had violated the Procès-Verbal, but because it recognized that the United States and Great Britain had also carried on unrestricted submarine warfare, it was neither prepared to hold them guilty, nor to assess their sentences, on the basis of such violations.

Although the Procès-Verbal was not very effective in regulating belligerent conduct during the war, the International Military Tribunal at Nuremberg did not imply that this agreement no longer possessed the status of law. Indeed, despite the great practical difficulty of distinguishing combatants from non-combatants, the Nuremberg Judgment can be interpreted as assuming the continuing validity of the Procès-Verbal. None the less, the practice of belligerents during the two world wars and the changing nature of naval warfare continue to raise questions as to the extent to which the principles embodied in the Procès-Verbal may remain applicable.

Date of signature: 6 November 1936
Entry into force: 6 November 1936
Depositary: United Kingdom
Authentic languages: English and French
Text reprinted from: CLXXIII *LNTS* (1936–1937) 353–7
Also published in: 33 *Martens NRG, 3ème sér.* (1937) 3–5 (Eng. Fr.);
                  140 *BFSP* (1936) 300–2 (Eng.);
                  UKTS 29 (1936), Cmd. 5302 (Eng. Fr.);
                  XXVIII *UKPP* (1936–1937) 693 (Eng. Fr.);
                  31 *AJIL* (1937) Supplement 137–9 (Eng.)

Procès-Verbal Relating to the Rules of Submarine Warfare Set Forth in Part IV of the Treaty of London of April 22 1930

Whereas the Treaty for the Limitation and Reduction of Naval Armaments signed in London on the 22nd April, 1930, has not been ratified by all the signatories;

And whereas the said Treaty will cease to be in force after the 31st December, 1936, with the exception of Part IV thereof, which sets forth rules as to the action of submarines with regard to merchant ships as being established rules of international law, and remains in force without limit of time;

And whereas the last paragraph of Article 22 in the said Part IV states that the High Contracting Parties invite all other Powers to express their assent to the said rules;

And whereas the Governments of the French Republic and the Kingdom of Italy have confirmed their acceptance of the said rules resulting from the signature of the said Treaty;

And whereas all the signatories of the said Treaty desire that as great a number of Powers as possible should accept the rules contained in the said Part IV as established rules of international law;

The undersigned, representatives of their respective Governments, bearing in mind the said Article 22 of the Treaty, hereby request the Government of the United Kingdom of Great Britain and Northern Ireland forthwith to communicate the said rules, as annexed hereto, to the Governments of all Powers which are not signatories of the said Treaty, with an invitation to accede thereto definitely and without limit of time.

RULES

'(1) In their action with regard to merchant ships, submarines must conform to the rules of International Law to which surface vessels are subject.

'(2) In particular, except in the case of persistent refusal to stop on being duly summoned, or of active resistance to visit or search, a warship, whether surface vessel or submarine, may not sink or render incapable of navigation a merchant vessel without having first placed passengers, crew and ship's papers in a place of safety. For this purpose the ship's boats are not regarded as a place of safety unless the safety of the passengers and crew is assured, in the existing sea and weather conditions, by the proximity of land, or the presence of another vessel which is in a position to take them on board.'

Signed in London, the 6th day of November, nineteen hundred and thirty-six.

CONCLUDING NOTES

Signatures, Accessions, and Successions[1]

State	Date of Signature[2]	Date of Accession (*a*), or Succession (*s*)	
Afghanistan		25 May	1937 *a*
Albania		3 March	1937 *a*
Australia	6 November 1936		
Austria		1 April	1937 *a*
Belgium		23 December	1936 *a*
Brazil		31 December	1937 *a*
Bulgaria		1 March	1937 *a*
Canada	6 November 1936		
Costa Rica		7 July	1937 *a*
Czechoslovakia		14 September	1937 *a*
Denmark		21 April	1937 *a*
Egypt		23 June	1937 *a*
El Salvador		24 November	1937 *a*
Estonia		26 June	1937 *a*
Fiji		6 March	1973 *s*
Finland		18 February	1937 *a*
France	6 November 1936		
Germany		23 November	1936 *a*
Greece		11 January	1937 *a*
Guatemala		8 September	1938 *a*
Haiti		23 January	1937 *a*
Holy See		16 March	1937 *a*
Hungary		8 December	1937 *a*
India	6 November 1936		
Iran		21 January	1939 *a*
Iraq		27 December	1937 *a*
Ireland	6 November 1936		
Italy	6 November 1936		
Japan	6 November 1936		
Latvia		7 March	1938 *a*

[1] Information supplied in communications from the UK Foreign and Commonwealth Office between December 1979 and January 1981.

[2] Like the 1856 Paris Declaration and the 1868 St. Petersburg Declaration, the 1936 London Procès-Verbal became binding on the signatory states without need of ratification.

State	Date of Signature	Date of Accession (*a*), or Succession (*s*)		
Lithuania		27 January	1938	*a*
Mexico		3 January	1938	*a*
Nepal		27 January	1937	*a*
Netherlands		30 September	1937	*a*
New Zealand	6 November 1936			
Norway		21 May	1937	*a*
Panama		26 February	1937	*a*
Peru		3 June	1937	*a*
Poland		21 July	1937	*a*
Saudi Arabia		11 June	1937	*a*
Siam		12 January	1938	*a*
South Africa	6 November 1936			
Sweden		15 February	1937	*a*
Switzerland		22 May	1937	*a*
Tonga		7 July	1971	*s*
Turkey		7 July	1937	*a*
United Kingdom	6 November 1936			
USA	6 November 1936			
USSR		27 December	1936	*a*
Yugoslavia		19 April	1937	*a*

Total Number of Parties Listed: 50

Note on Entry into Force for States Parties

The Procès-Verbal entered into force for each state on the date of its respective signature or accession.

Denunciations

None

Reservations

None

16. 1946 Judgment of the International Military Tribunal at Nuremberg: Extracts on Crimes Against International Law

PREFATORY NOTE

The principal international agreements on the laws of war concluded before 1945 contain inadequate references to the punishment of violations. For example, Article 3 of 1907 Hague Convention IV only recognizes in rather general terms a state's responsibility for acts committed by its armed forces, and provides for the payment of compensation for violations of the Regulations annexed to the Convention; and there are also some rather vague references to compensation and to proceedings in Articles 53 and 56 of the Regulations.

Despite this relative dearth of formal provisions, there have been many civil and criminal cases involving the laws of war. Some cases concerned the question of the punishment of violations by enemy individuals. For example, at the end of the First World War, Articles 227 to 230 of the Treaty of Versailles required Germany to surrender for trial members of its armed forces charged with violations of the laws of war. By subsequent arrangement with Allied governments, Germany itself tried German offenders on charges formulated by the Allies, but very few were convicted.

The overwhelming majority of those accused of committing crimes against international law in the Second World War were tried (whether during or after the war) by national courts, or by military courts established by occupying states. In addition, some members of armed forces were tried by their own national military courts.

However, the best known Second World War trials were those held by the International Military Tribunals at Nuremberg and Tokyo. During the course of the war, the Allied governments had resolved in both unilateral and joint statements to ensure an effective post-war punishment of enemy individuals violating the laws of war. On 8 August 1945 the USA, Britain, France, and the USSR concluded in London an Agreement for the Prosecution and Punishment of the Major War Criminals of the European Axis; and nineteen other states adhered to this Agreement, seventeen of them before the trial began. The Agreement provided for the establishment of an International Military Tribunal for the trial of war criminals whose offences had no particular geographical location. Annexed to the Agreement was the Charter of the Tribunal which established the jurisdiction of the Tribunal and set forth principles to be applied by it. The trial began in Nuremberg on 20 November 1945. There were twenty-two defendants, of whom all but three were found guilty in the Judgment, which was rendered on 30 September and 1 October 1946.

The trial of Japanese major war criminals by the International Military Tribunal for the Far East was based on the same principles as the Nuremberg trial: it was convened in Tokyo on 3 May 1946 and judgment was rendered on 4–12 November 1948.

In reaching its verdict, the Nuremberg Tribunal focused attention on many issues of central importance to the application of the laws of war, including the responsibility of individuals to observe international law, the question of obedience to superior orders, the concepts of 'war crimes' and 'crimes against humanity', and questions relating to jurisdiction and fair trial. On many of these matters, the doctrines recognized at Nuremberg have come to be known as the 'Nuremberg principles'.

The United Nations has on a number of occasions concerned itself with the Nuremberg principles. On 11 December 1946 the UN General Assembly unanimously adopted Resolution 95(I) which affirmed 'the principles of international law recognized by the Charter of the Nuremberg Tribunal and the judgment of the Tribunal'. In 1950 the International Law Commission of the UN adopted a statement formulating those principles.

The sheer length of the Nuremberg Judgment (it runs to over 170 printed pages), and the range of issues and evidence it covers, make any choice of extracts difficult. The two extracts reprinted below have been selected because of their general relevance to war crimes and to the application of the law.

The first extract is taken from the beginning of the Judgment, and simply sets forth Article 6 of the Tribunal's Charter, with its definitions of 'crimes against peace' (relating to *jus ad bellum*), and of 'war crimes' and 'crimes against humanity' (comprehending *jus in bello*). It is acts falling under the latter headings which are of particular interest so far as the law governing the actual conduct of armed hostilities is concerned. Note that, as defined by the Charter, 'crimes against humanity' may include acts committed against fellow-citizens, and even certain acts committed before the war.

The second extract, taken from a later part of the Judgment, elaborates on what Article 6 of the Charter states concerning war crimes. Four points may be noted. First, the Judgment (here as elsewhere) refers much more to war crimes in the strict sense, as defined by Article 6(b), than to crimes against humanity. Second, the Charter's definition of war crimes was recognized by the Tribunal as being in accord with existing international law. Third, to determine the applicability of a particular international agreement on the laws of war, reference must be made to its specific terms (such as the 'general participation clause' found in early conventions) which may affect its formal application. Fourth, if any international agreement can be regarded as embodying customary international law, its provisions are fully binding on all states, whatever the particular terms of the agreement.

Text reprinted from: *Trial of the Major War Criminals before the International Military Tribunal, Nuremberg*, vol. XXII, IMT Secretariat, Nuremberg, 1948, pp. 413–14 and 497.

Also published in: *The Trial of German Major War Criminals: Proceedings of the International Military Tribunal Sitting at Nuremberg Germany*, Part 22, HMSO, London, 1950, pp. 412–13 and 467;

Annual Digest and Reports of Public International Law Cases 1946, Butterworth, London, 1951, pp. 204 and 212

Judgment (Extracts)

The Charter Provisions

The individual defendants are indicted under Article 6 of the Charter, which is as follows:

'Article 6. The Tribunal established by the Agreement referred to in Article 1 hereof for the trial and punishment of the major war criminals of the European Axis countries shall have the power to try and punish persons who, acting in the interests of the European Axis countries, whether as individuals or as members of organizations, committed any of the following crimes:

'The following acts, or any of them, are crimes coming within the jurisdiction of the Tribunal for which there shall be individual responsibility:

'(a) Crimes against Peace: namely, planning, preparation, initiation, or waging of a war of aggression, or a war in violation of international treaties, agreements, or assurances, or participation in a common plan or conspiracy for the accomplishment of any of the foregoing:

'(b) War Crimes: namely, violations of the laws or customs of war. Such violations shall include, but not be limited to, murder, ill-treatment, or deportation to slave labor or for any other purpose of civilian population of or in occupied territory, murder or ill-treatment of prisoners of war or persons on the seas, killing of hostages, plunder of public or private property, wanton destruction of cities, towns, or villages, or devastation not justified by military necessity:

'(c) Crimes against Humanity: namely, murder, extermination, enslavement, deportation, and other inhumane acts committed against any civilian population, before or during the war, or persecutions on political, racial or religious grounds in execution of or in connection with any crime within the jurisdiction of the Tribunal, whether or not in violation of the domestic law of the country where perpetrated.

'Leaders, organizers, instigators, and accomplices participating in the formulation or execution of a common plan or conspiracy to commit any of the foregoing crimes are responsible for all acts performed by any persons in execution of such plan.'

*   *   *

The Law Relating to War Crimes and Crimes Against Humanity

The Tribunal is of course bound by the Charter, in the definition which it gives both of War Crimes and Crimes against Humanity. With respect to War Crimes, however, as has already been pointed out, the crimes defined by Article 6, section (b) of the Charter were already recognized as War Crimes under international law. They were covered by Articles 46, 50, 52, and 56 of the Hague Convention of 1907, and Articles 2, 3, 4, 46, and 51 of the Geneva Convention of 1929. That violations of these provisions constituted crimes for which the guilty individuals were punishable is too well settled to admit of argument.

But it is argued that the Hague Convention does not apply in this case, because of the 'general participation' clause in Article 2 of the Hague Convention of 1907. That clause provided:

'The provisions contained in the regulations (Rules of Land Warfare) referred to in Article I, as well as in the present convention, do not apply except between contracting powers, and then only if all the belligerents are parties to the convention.'

Several of the belligerents in the recent war were not parties to this convention.

In the opinion of the Tribunal it is not necessary to decide this question. The rules of land warfare expressed in the convention undoubtedly represented an advance over existing international law at the time of their adoption. But the convention expressly stated that it was an attempt 'to revise the general laws and customs of war,' which it thus recognized to be then existing, but by 1939 these rules laid down in the convention were recognized by all civilized nations, and were regarded as being declaratory of the laws and customs of war which are referred to in Article 6(b) of the Charter.

17. 1948 United Nations Convention on the Prevention and Punishment of the Crime of Genocide

PREFATORY NOTE

The practices of the German government before and during the Second World War, and particularly the mass murder of millions of people during the war, led after the war to a formal consideration of the question of genocide. The term 'genocide' was first used by the Polish scholar Raphael Lemkin in his book *Axis Rule in Occupied Europe*, published in the USA in 1944, in which he defined it as 'the destruction of a nation or of an ethnic group'.

The Convention was the result of extensive negotiations at the United Nations. On 2 November 1946 the delegations of Cuba, India, and Panama requested the UN Secretary-General to include in the agenda of the General Assembly the question of the prevention and punishment of genocide. On 11 December 1946 the General Assembly unanimously adopted Resolution 96 (I), which affirmed that genocide is a crime under international law and requested that the Economic and Social Council undertake studies which would lead to the drafting of a convention on genocide. On 28 March 1947 the ECOSOC called upon the UN Secretary-General to draft such a convention. The resulting text was considered by various bodies of the UN. On 3 March 1948 the ECOSOC established the UN *Ad Hoc* Committee on Genocide, and instructed it to prepare a draft convention on genocide (taking into consideration the draft convention prepared by the Secretariat). The *Ad Hoc* Committee's draft was considered by certain UN bodies, and on 26 August 1948 the ECOSOC transmitted the draft convention to the General Assembly.

After further revision, the General Assembly adopted Resolution 260 (III) on 9 December 1948. Part A of the Resolution approved the text of the Convention, annexed thereto, and proposed that it be submitted to states for their signature and ratification, or accession; Part B invited the International Law Commission to study the possibility of establishing an international judicial organ, possibly in the form of a criminal chamber of the International Court of Justice, for the trial of persons charged with genocide; and Part C referred to extending the application of the Convention to administered territories.

Several points should be mentioned. First, the prohibition of genocide can be regarded as a principle of customary international law. Second, the Convention confirms that genocide, whether committed in time of war or peace, is a crime under international law. Third, while the term 'homicide' relates to the destruction of individual human beings, the term 'genocide' relates exclusively to the destruction of human groups. Fourth, the Convention's definition of genocide includes acts other than killing. Fifth, the Convention defines punishable acts as including not only the crime of genocide itself, but also conspiracy, incitement, attempts, and complicity in relation to the crime. Sixth, to constitute genocide, prohibited acts must be accompanied by the intent to partially or completely destroy a particular group. Seventh, the practical value of the Convention's provisions relating to punishment, and particularly the emphasis on trial by a tribunal in the state in which the act was committed (Article VI), has been questioned.

Date of signature:	Signed on 11 December 1948, and open for signature (see Article XI) until 31 December 1949.
Entry into force:	12 January 1951
Depositary:	United Nations
Authentic languages:	Chinese, English, French, Russian, and Spanish
Text reprinted from:	78 *UNTS* (1951) 277–323
Also published in:	151 *BFSP* (1948) 682–7 (Eng.);
	UKTS 58 (1970), Cmnd. 4421 (Ch. Eng. Fr. Rus. Sp.);
	XXIII *UKPP* (1970–1971) 675 (Ch. Eng. Fr. Rus. Sp.);
	45 *AJIL* (1951) Supplement 7–13 (Eng.)

Convention on the Prevention and Punishment of the Crime of Genocide

THE CONTRACTING PARTIES,

HAVING CONSIDERED the declaration made by the General Assembly of the United Nations in its resolution 96 (I) dated 11 December 1946 that genocide is a crime under international law, contrary to the spirit and aims of the United Nations and condemned by the civilized world;

RECOGNIZING that at all periods of history genocide has inflicted great losses on humanity; and

BEING CONVINCED that, in order to liberate mankind from such an odious scourge, international co-operation is required,

HEREBY AGREE AS HEREINAFTER PROVIDED:

Article I

The Contracting Parties confirm that genocide, whether committed in time of peace or in time of war, is a crime under international law which they undertake to prevent and to punish.

Article II

In the present Convention, genocide means any of the following acts committed with intent to destroy, in whole or in part, a national, ethnical, racial or religious group, as such:

    (*a*) Killing members of the group;

    (*b*) Causing serious bodily or mental harm to members of the group;

    (*c*) Deliberately inflicting on the group conditions of life calculated to bring about its physical destruction in whole or in part;

    (*d*) Imposing measures intended to prevent births within the group;

(*e*) Forcibly transferring children of the group to another group.

Article III

The following acts shall be punishable:
(*a*) Genocide;
(*b*) Conspiracy to commit genocide;
(*c*) Direct and public incitement to commit genocide;
(*d*) Attempt to commit genocide;
(*e*) Complicity in genocide.

Article IV

Persons commiting genocide or any of the other acts enumerated in article III shall be punished, whether they are constitutionally responsible rulers, public officials or private individuals.

Article V

The Contracting Parties undertake to enact, in accordance with their respective Constitutions, the necessary legislation to give effect to the provisions of the present Convention and, in particular, to provide effective penalties for persons guilty of genocide or of any of the other acts enumerated in article III.

Article VI

Persons charged with genocide or any of the other acts enumerated in article III shall be tried by a competent tribunal of the State in the territory of which the act was committed, or by such international penal tribunal as may have jurisdiction with respect to those Contracting Parties which shall have accepted its jurisdiction.

Article VII

Genocide and the other acts enumerated in article III shall not be considered as political crimes for the purpose of extradition.

The Contracting Parties pledge themselves in such cases to grant extradition in accordance with their laws and treaties in force.

Article VIII

Any Contracting Party may call upon the competent organs of the United Nations to take such action under the Charter of the United Nations as they consider appropriate for the prevention and suppression of acts of genocide or any of the other acts enumerated in article III.

Article IX

Disputes between the Contracting Parties relating to the interpretation, application or fulfilment of the present Convention, including those relating to the responsibility of a State for genocide or for any of the other acts enumerated in article III, shall be submitted to the International Court of Justice at the request of any of the parties to the dispute.

Article X

The present Convention, of which the Chinese, English, French, Russian and Spanish texts are equally authentic, shall bear the date of 9 December 1948.

Article XI

The present Convention shall be open until 31 December 1949 for signature on behalf of any Member of the United Nations and of any non-member State to which an invitation to sign has been addressed by the General Assembly.

The present Convention shall be ratified, and the instruments of ratification shall be deposited with the Secretary-General of the United Nations.

After 1 January 1950 the present Convention may be acceded to on behalf of any Member of the United Nations and of any non-member State which has received an invitation as aforesaid.

Instruments of accession shall be deposited with the Secretary-General of the United Nations.

Article XII

Any Contracting Party may at any time, by notification addressed to the Secretary-General of the United Nations, extend the application of the present Convention to all or any of the territories for the conduct of whose foreign relations that Contracting Party is responsible.

Article XIII

On the day when the first twenty instruments of ratification or accession have been deposited, the Secretary-General shall draw up a *procès-verbal* and transmit a copy thereof to each Member of the United Nations and to each of the non-member States contemplated in article XI.

The present Convention shall come into force on the ninetieth day following the date of deposit of the twentieth instrument of ratification or accession.

Any ratification or accession effected subsequent to the latter date shall become effective on the ninetieth day following the deposit of the instrument of ratification or accession.

Article XIV

The present Convention shall remain in effect for a period of ten years as from the date of its coming into force.

It shall thereafter remain in force for successive periods of five years for such Contracting Parties as have not denounced it at least six months before the expiration of the current period.

Denunciation shall be effected by a written notification addressed to the Secretary-General of the United Nations.

Article XV

If, as a result of denunciations, the number of Parties to the present Convention should become less than sixteen, the Convention shall cease to be in force as from the date on which the last of these denunciations shall become effective.

Article XVI

A request for the revision of the present Convention may be made at any time by any Contracting Party by means of a notification in writing addressed to the Secretary-General.

The General Assembly shall decide upon the steps, if any, to be taken in respect of such request.

Article XVII

The Secretary-General of the United Nations shall notify all Members of the United Nations and the non-member States contemplated in article XI of the following:

(*a*) Signatures, ratifications and accessions received in accordance with article XI;

(*b*) Notifications received in accordance with article XII;

(*c*) The date upon which the present Convention comes into force in accordance with article XIII;

(*d*) Denunciations received in accordance with article XIV;

(*e*) The abrogation of the Convention in accordance with article XV;

(*f*) Notifications received in accordance with article XVI.

Article XVIII

The original of the present Convention shall be deposited in the archives of the United Nations.

A certified copy of the Convention shall be transmitted to each Member of the United Nations and to each of the non-member States contemplated in article XI.

Article XIX

The present Convention shall be registered by the Secretary-General of the United Nations on the date of its coming into force.

CONCLUDING NOTES

Signatures, Ratifications, Accessions, and Successions[1]

State (* denotes Reservation etc.: see below)	Date of Signature		Date of Ratification (r), Accession (a), or Succession (s)		
Afghanistan			22 March	1956	a
*Albania			12 May	1955	a
*Algeria			31 October	1963	a
*Argentina			5 June	1956	a
*Australia[2]	11 December	1948	8 July	1949	r
Austria			19 March	1958	a
Bahamas			5 August	1975	s
Barbados			14 January	1980	a
*Belgium[3]	12 December	1949	5 September	1951	r
Bolivia	11 December	1948	—		
*Brazil	11 December	1948	15 April	1952	r
*Bulgaria			21 July	1950	a
*Burma	30 December	1949	14 March	1956	r
*Byelorussian SSR	16 December	1949	11 August	1954	r
Cambodia			14 October	1950	a
Canada	28 November	1949	3 September	1952	r
*Ceylon			12 October	1950	a
Chile	11 December	1948	3 June	1953	r
*China, Republic of[4]	20 July	1949	19 July	1951	r
Colombia	12 August	1949	27 October	1959	r
Congo, Democratic Republic of (now Zaire)			31 May	1962	s
Costa Rica			14 October	1950	a

[1] Information supplied in communications from the Treaty Section of the United Nations between January 1980 and February 1981, supplemented by various volumes of *UNTS* and of the annual UN publication entitled *Multilateral Treaties in Respect of Which the Secretary-General Performs Depositary Functions: List of Signatures, Ratifications, Accessions, etc.*

[2] At ratification, Australia extended the application of the Convention to all territories for the conduct of whose foreign relations Australia is responsible.

[3] By note received on 13 March 1952, Belgium extended the application of the Convention to Belgian Congo and Ruanda-Urundi.

[4] On 29 September 1972 the Depositary received a communication from the Foreign Minister of the People's Republic of China stating: '1. With regard to the multilateral treaties signed, ratified or acceded to by the defunct Chinese government before the establishment of the Government of the People's Republic of China, my Government will examine their contents before making a decision in the light of the circumstances as to whether or not they should be recognized. 2. As from October 1, 1949, the day of the founding of the People's Republic of China, the Chiang Kai-shek clique has no right at all to represent China. Its signature and ratification of, or accession to, any multilateral treaties by usurping the name of "China" are all illegal and null and void . . .'

State (* denotes Reservation etc.: see below)	Date of Signature		Date of Ratification (r), Accession (a), or Succession (s)		
*Cuba	28 December	1949	4 March	1953	r
*Czechoslovakia	28 December	1949	21 December	1950	r
Denmark	28 September	1949	15 June	1951	r
Dominican Republic	11 December	1948	—		
*Ecuador	11 December	1948	21 December	1949	r
Egypt	12 December	1948	8 February	1952	r
El Salvador	27 April	1949	28 September	1950	r
Ethiopia	11 December	1948	1 July	1949	r
Fiji			11 January	1973	s
*Finland			18 December	1959	a
France	11 December	1948	14 October	1950	r
Gambia			29 December	1978	a
*German Democratic Republic			27 March	1973	a
Germany, Federal Republic of[5]			24 November	1954	a
Ghana			24 December	1958	a
*Greece	29 December	1949	8 December	1954	r
Guatemala	22 June	1949	13 January	1950	r
Haiti	11 December	1948	14 October	1950	r
Honduras	22 April	1949	5 March	1952	r
*Hungary			7 January	1952	a
Iceland	14 May	1949	29 August	1949	r
*India	29 November	1949	27 August	1959	r
Iran	8 December	1949	14 August	1956	r
Iraq			20 January	1959	a
Ireland			22 June	1976	a
Israel	17 August	1949	9 March	1950	r
Italy			4 June	1952	a
Jamaica			23 September	1968	a
Jordan			3 April	1950	a
Korea, Republic of (South)			14 October	1950	a
Laos			8 December	1950	a
Lebanon	30 December	1949	17 December	1953	r
Lesotho			29 November	1974	a
Liberia	11 December	1948	9 June	1950	r
Mali			16 July	1974	a
Mexico	14 December	1948	22 July	1952	r
Monaco			30 March	1950	a

[5] At accession, the Federal Republic of Germany stated that the Convention would also apply to *Land Berlin*. In a note received by the Depositary on 27 December 1973 the German Democratic Republic objected to this. Subsequent communications were received from these states and also from others: France, UK, USA, USSR, and Ukrainian SSR.

State (* denotes Reservation etc.: see below)	Date of Signature		Date of Ratification (r), Accession (a), or Succession (s)		
*Mongolia			5 January	1967	a
*Morocco			24 January	1958	a
Nepal			17 January	1969	a
*Netherlands			20 June	1966	a
New Zealand	25 November	1949	28 December	1978	r
Nicaragua			29 January	1952	a
*Norway	11 December	1948	22 July	1949	r
Pakistan	11 December	1948	12 October	1957	r
Panama	11 December	1948	11 January	1950	r
Paraguay	11 December	1948	—		
Peru	11 December	1948	24 February	1960	r
*Philippines	11 December	1948	7 July	1950	r
*Poland			14 November	1950	a
*Romania			2 November	1950	a
*Rwanda			16 April	1975	a
Saudi Arabia			13 July	1950	a
*Spain			13 September	1968	a
Sweden	30 December	1949	27 May	1952	r
Syria			25 June	1955	a
Tonga			16 February	1972	a
Tunisia			29 November	1956	a
Turkey			31 July	1950	a
*Ukrainian SSR	16 December	1949	15 November	1954	r
*United Kingdom[6]			30 January	1970	a
Upper Volta			14 September	1965	a
Uruguay	11 December	1948	11 July	1967	r
USA	11 December	1948	—		
*USSR	16 December	1949	3 May	1954	r
*Venezuela			12 July	1960	a
*Vietnam, Republic of (South)			11 August	1950	a
Yugoslavia	11 December	1948	29 August	1950	r

Total Number of Parties Listed: 86

Note on Entry into Force for States Parties

In accordance with Article XIII, the Convention entered into force on 12 January 1951 for the states which had ratified it ninety or more days earlier. For each of the other ratifying states, and for each of the acceding states, the Convention formally entered into force ninety days after the date indicated in the right-hand column above.

Denunciations

None

[6] At accession, and also in a subsequent notification received on 2 June 1970, the UK extended the application of the Convention to certain territories for whose conduct of international relations the UK is responsible.

Reservations etc.[7]

Except where otherwise stated, all of the following were (in the case of signatory states) made at signature and maintained at ratification; or (in the case of acceding states) made at accession. All were the subject of specific or general objections: the objections are listed separately in the following section.[8]

Albania, Bulgaria, Byelorussian SSR, Czechoslovakia, Romania, and *Ukrainian SSR* all made reservations identical to that of USSR.

Algeria 'does not consider itself bound by Article IX of the Convention, which confers on the International Court of Justice jurisdiction in all disputes relating to the said Convention . . . No provision of Article VI . . . shall be interpreted as depriving its tribunals of jurisdiction in cases of genocide or other acts enumerated in Article III which have been committed on its territory or as conferring such jurisdiction on foreign tribunals. International tribunals may, as an exceptional measure, be recognized as having jurisdiction, in cases in which the Algerian Government has given its express approval.' Algeria 'does not accept the terms of Article XII . . . and considers that all of the provisions of the said Convention should apply to Non-Self-Governing Territories, including Trust Territories.'

Argentina reserved the right not to submit to the procedure laid down in Article IX 'any dispute relating directly or indirectly to the territories referred to in its reservation to Article XII.' On Article XII: 'If any other Contracting Party extends the application of the Convention to territories under the sovereignty of the Argentine Republic, this extension shall in no way affect the rights and duties of the Republic.'

Burma, at ratification only, stated that nothing in Article VI 'shall be construed as depriving the courts and tribunals of the Union of jurisdiction or as giving foreign courts and tribunals jurisdiction over any cases of genocide or any of the other acts enumerated in Article III committed within the Union territory.' Article VIII 'shall not apply to the Union.'

Finland: '. . . Subject to the provisions of Article 47, paragraph 2, of the Constitution Act, 1919, concerning the impeachment of the President of the Republic of Finland.'

German Democratic Republic made a reservation identical to that of USSR, but stating, additionally, that Article XI 'deprives a number of States of the opportunity to become Parties to the Convention. As the Convention regulates matters affecting the interests of all States, it should be open to participation by all States whose policies are guided by the purposes and principles of the Charter of the United Nations.'

Hungary 'reserves its rights with regard to the provisions of Article IX . . . which grant wide jurisdiction to the International Court at The Hague, and with

---

[7] This list is based on the sources referred to in footnote 1 above. The objections, listed in the following section, are from the same sources.

[8] Controversy over the effect to be given to reservations to the Convention led the UN General Assembly, on 16 November 1950, to request an Advisory Opinion of the International Court of Justice. On 28 May 1951 the ICJ gave an Advisory Opinion. The significance of the issue goes beyond the Genocide Convention to the law of treaties in general. See 'Reservations to the Convention on the Prevention and Punishment of the Crime of Genocide: Advisory Opinion of May 28th, 1951', *ICJ Reports*, 1951, pp. 15–55.

regard to the provisions of Article XII which do not define the obligations of countries having colonies with regard to questions of colonial exploitation and to acts which might be described as genocide.'

India, at ratification only, declared that, for the submission of any dispute in terms of Article IX to the jurisdiction of the ICJ, the consent of all the parties to the dispute is required in each case.

Mongolia made a reservation identical to that of USSR, but drawing attention, additionally, 'to the discriminatory character of Article XI . . . under the terms of which a number of States are precluded from acceding to the Convention and declares that the Convention deals with matters which affect the interests of all States and it should, therefore, be open for accession by all States.'

Morocco, with reference to Article VI, 'considers that Moroccan courts and tribunals alone have jurisdiction with respect to acts of genocide committed within the territory of the Kingdom of Morocco. The competence of international courts may be admitted exceptionally in cases with respect to which the Moroccan Government has given its specific agreement. With reference to Article IX . . . no dispute relating to the interpretation, application or fulfilment of the present Convention can be brought before the International Court of Justice, without the prior agreement of the parties to the dispute.'

Philippines, at ratification only, with reference to Article IV, stated *inter alia* that this does not override 'the existing immunities from judicial processes guaranteed certain public officials by the Constitution of the Philippines.' With reference to Article VII, the Government does not undertake to give effect to this 'until the Congress of the Philippines has enacted the necessary legislation defining and punishing the crime of genocide . . .' With reference to Articles VI and IX, 'nothing contained in said articles shall be construed as depriving Philippine courts of jurisdiction over all cases of genocide committed within Philippine territory save only in those cases where the Philippine Government consents to have the decision of the Philippine courts reviewed by either of the international tribunals referred to in said articles.' With further reference to Article IX, the Philippines 'does not consider the said article to extend the concept of State responsibility beyond that recognized by the generally accepted principles of international law.'

Poland 'does not regard itself as bound' by Article IX, 'since the agreement of all the parties to a dispute is a necessary condition in each specific case for submission to the International Court of Justice.' Poland 'does not accept the provisions' of Article XII, 'considering that the Convention should apply to Non-Self-Governing Territories, including Trust Territories.'

Rwanda and *Spain* made reservation of Article IX.

USSR: 'The Soviet Union does not consider as binding upon itself the provisions of Article IX which provides that disputes between the Contracting Parties with regard to the interpretation, application and implementation of the present Convention shall be referred for examination to the International Court at the request of any party to the dispute, and declares that, as regards the International Court's jurisdiction in respect of disputes concerning the interpretation, application and implementation of the Convention, the Soviet Union will, as hitherto, maintain the position that in each particular case the agreement of all parties to the dispute is essential for the submission of any particular dispute to the International Court for decision . . .

The USSR declares that it is not in agreement with Article XII of the Convention and considers that all the provisions of the Convention should extend to Non-Self-Governing Territories, including Trust Territories.'

Venezuela: 'With reference to Article VI, notice is given that any proceedings to which Venezuela may be a party before an international penal tribunal would be invalid without Venezuela's prior express acceptance of the jurisdiction of such international tribunal. With reference to Article VII, notice is given that the laws in force in Venezuela do not permit the extradition of Venezuelan nationals. With reference to Article IX, the reservation is made that the submission of a dispute to the International Court of Justice shall be regarded as valid only when it takes place with Venezuela's approval, signified by the express conclusion of a prior agreement in each case.'

Objections

Except where otherwise indicated, the objections were made at ratification or accession by the objecting state.

Australia, in communications of 15 November 1950 and 19 January 1951, stated that it does not accept the reservations made by Bulgaria, Byelorussian SSR, Czechoslovakia, Philippines, Poland, Romania, Ukrainian SSR, and USSR.

Belgium 'does not accept the reservations made by Bulgaria, Byelorussian SSR, Czechoslovakia, Poland, Romania, Ukrainian SSR and USSR.'

Brazil stated that it objects to the reservations made by eight states (identical list to Australia's, see above), adding that these reservations are 'compatible with the object and purpose of the Convention. The position taken by the Government of Brazil is founded on the Advisory Opinion of the International Court of Justice of 28 May 1951 and on the resolution adopted by the sixth session of the General Assembly on 12 January 1952, on reservations to multilateral conventions. The Brazilian Government reserves the right to draw any such legal consequences as it may deem fit from its formal objection to the above-mentioned reservations.'

Ceylon, in a communication received on 6 February 1951, stated that it does not accept the reservations made by Romania.

China, Republic of, in communications received on 15 November 1954, 13 September 1955, and 25 July 1956, stated that it objects to the reservations made by Albania, Bulgaria, Burma, Byelorussian SSR, Czechoslovakia, Hungary, Poland, Romania, Ukrainian SSR, and USSR. It 'considers the above-mentioned reservations as incompatible with the object and purpose of the Convention and, therefore, by virtue of the Advisory Opinion of the International Court of Justice of 28 May 1951, would not regard the above-mentioned States as being Parties to the Convention.'

Cuba made an identical objection to that of Belgium.

Ecuador, in communications received on 31 March and 21 August 1950, and 9 January 1951, objected to the reservations made by seven states (identical list to Belgium's, see above), adding that 'they do not apply to Ecuador.'

Greece: 'We have not accepted and do not accept any reservation which has already been made or which may hereafter be made by the countries signatory to this instrument or by countries which have acceded or may hereafter accede thereto.'

Netherlands 'considers the reservations made by Albania, Algeria, Bulgaria, Byelorussian SSR, Czechoslovakia, Hungary, India, Morocco, Poland, Romania, Ukrainian SSR and USSR in respect of Article IX . . . to be incompatible with the object and purpose of the Convention. The Government of the Kingdom of the Netherlands therefore does not deem any State which has made or which will make such reservation a party to the Convention.'

Norway, in a communication received on 10 April 1952, stated that it does not accept the reservations made by the Philippines.

United Kingdom, at accession and in a further communication of 21 November 1975, stated that it does not accept the reservations to Articles IV, VII, VIII, IX, or XII made by twenty states (that is, every state which made reservations except Finland).

Vietnam, Republic of (South), in a communication received on 3 November 1950, stated that it could not accept the reservations submitted by Bulgaria, Byelorussian SSR, Czechoslovakia, Philippines, Ukrainian SSR, and USSR, or by any other state.

18. 1949 Geneva Convention I for the Amelioration of the Condition of the Wounded and Sick in Armed Forces in the Field

PREFATORY NOTE

The four 1949 Geneva Conventions: General

On 12 August 1949 a diplomatic conference in Geneva approved the text of four conventions which have come to be adhered to by more states than any other agreements on the laws of war. They deal respectively with (I) wounded and sick in armed forces in the field; (II) wounded, sick and shipwrecked in armed forces at sea; (III) prisoners of war; and (IV) civilians.

The central concern of all four 1949 Geneva Conventions is thus the protection of victims of war. Since 1864, when a Geneva Convention on wounded was adopted, several binding international agreements have been concluded which address various aspects of this question. The 1949 Conventions were the outgrowth of efforts undertaken before the Second World War to draft new conventions; and they were also the product of the experience of the war itself.

During the Second World War, existing conventions relating to the protection of war victims had benefited significant numbers, but events had also confirmed the need to revise and extend the laws of war. First, in many areas the law was insufficiently clear and precise. Second, even in areas of relative clarity and precision, violations of the law highlighted the need for more specific provisions about monitoring the observance of the law and punishing violations.

After the Second World War the International Committee of the Red Cross formulated proposals to adapt and develop international humanitarian law applicable in armed conflicts. Between 1945 and 1948 a series of consultations, in which experts from various states participated, resulted in the preparation of draft conventions. At the 17th International Conference of the Red Cross, held in Stockholm in 1948, these were amended and approved for submission to a diplomatic conference.

The Diplomatic Conference for the Establishment of International Conventions for the Protection of Victims of War, held in Geneva from 21 April to 12 August 1949, was attended by the representatives of sixty-four states. Convened by the Swiss government (as Depositary of the Geneva Conventions), the Conference had as its stated purpose the revision of (1) the 1929 Geneva Convention for the Relief of Wounded and Sick in Armies in the Field; (2) 1907 Hague Convention X for the Adaptation to Maritime Warfare of the Principles of the 1906 Geneva Convention; and (3) the 1929 Geneva Convention Relative to the Treatment of Prisoners of War. In addition, the Conference was to establish (4) a Convention for the Protection of Civilian Persons in Time of War. The four ICRC draft conventions were taken as the sole negotiating texts, and the outcome was the four 1949 Geneva Conventions.

The four Conventions are linked not only by certain general principles, but more specifically by certain common articles. Such common articles are found among the general provisions at the beginning of each Convention, among the provisions relating to execution of each Convention, and in the concluding procedural provisions. Full expositions of all the provisions of the Conventions are to be found in the four volumes entitled *The Geneva Conventions of 12 August 1949: Commentary*, prepared under the general editorship of Jean S. Pictet and published by the ICRC between 1952 and 1960.

In view of the large number of states parties to the 1949 Geneva Conventions and the status which the Conventions have acquired in the international community, it is reasonable to assume that the Conventions are (at least in large part) declaratory of customary international law. This is particularly the case in respect of the general principles contained therein.

1977 Geneva Protocol I specifically states that it supplements the four 1949 Geneva Conventions; and 1977 Geneva Protocol II specifically states that it develops and supplements Article 3 common to the four 1949 Geneva Conventions.

1949 Geneva Convention I

This Convention, relating to wounded and sick on land, was preceded by several other international agreements on this subject: those of 1864, 1906, and 1929. In 1864 the Swiss government convened a conference in Geneva to consider a draft convention which had been prepared by the Geneva Committee (which later became the ICRC). This led to the adoption of the 1864 Geneva Convention for the Amelioration of the Condition of the Wounded in Armies in the Field.

In 1868 a diplomatic conference was convened by the Swiss government in Geneva to clarify certain provisions of the 1864 Geneva Convention and, in particular, to extend the Convention's principles to naval warfare. Although the 1868 Additional Articles Relating to the Condition of the Wounded in War were not ratified and did not enter into force, during the 1870-1 Franco-Prussian War and the 1898 Spanish-American War the belligerents agreed to observe their provisions.

The Final Act of the First Hague Peace Conference of 1899 recommended that a conference be convened for the revision of the 1864 Geneva Convention. Such a conference was convened by the Swiss government in Geneva in 1906. On the basis of proposals submitted to it by the ICRC, the conference adopted the 1906 Geneva Convention for the Amelioration of the Condition of the Wounded and Sick in Armies in the Field, which considerably developed the earlier Convention. As between parties to both agreements, the 1906 Geneva Convention replaced the 1864 Geneva Convention. Article 21 of the Regulations annexed to both 1899 Hague Convention II and 1907 Hague Convention IV specifically referred to the obligations of belligerents regarding the sick and wounded as being governed by the applicable Geneva Convention.

The experience of the First World War indicated the need to adapt the 1906 Geneva Convention to modern warfare. In 1929 the Swiss government convened a diplomatic conference in Geneva partly for the purpose of revising the 1906 Geneva Convention (and partly for the purpose of adopting a convention on prisoners of war). The conference adopted the 1929 Geneva Convention for the Amelioration of the Condition of the Wounded and Sick in Armies in the Field. As between parties, the 1929 Geneva Convention replaced the earlier conventions. It contained fewer revisions than had the 1906 Convention.

In 1937, after consultation with various experts, a further draft convention was formulated by the ICRC and was submitted to the 16th International Conference of the Red Cross held in London in 1938. In January 1939 the Swiss government transmitted the ICRC draft to states as a basis for a diplomatic conference which the Swiss government planned to convene in Geneva in early 1940. However, the outbreak of the Second World War intervened. As noted above, the process of drafting a new agreement only resumed after the war.

1949 Geneva Convention I represents a revised and enlarged version of the 1929 Geneva Convention on wounded and sick, and replaces the earlier conventions as between parties. The 1949 Convention follows the traditional lines and the fundamental principles governing earlier versions of the Convention, but the conditions of modern warfare necessitated the restriction of the privileges of medical personnel and equipment in enemy hands. Virtually all provisions have been given greater precision.

Date of signature:	Signed on 12 August 1949, and open for signature (see Article 56) until 12 February 1950.
Entry into force:	21 October 1950
Depositary:	Switzerland
Authentic languages:	English and French
Text reprinted from:	*Final Record of the Diplomatic Conference of Geneva of 1949*, Federal Political Department, Berne, n.d., vol. 1, pp. 205-18.
Also published in:	75 *UNTS* (1950) 31-83 (Eng. Fr.);
	157 *BFSP* (1950) 234-61 (Eng.);
	UKTS 39 (1958), Cmnd. 550 (Eng. Fr.);
	XXXII *UKPP* (1958-1959) 11 (Eng. Fr.)

Geneva Convention for the Amelioration of the Condition of the Wounded and Sick in Armed Forces in the Field of August 12, 1949

The undersigned Plenipotentiaries of the Governments represented at the Diplomatic Conference held at Geneva from April 21 to August 12, 1949, for the purpose of revising the Geneva Convention for the Relief of the Wounded and Sick in Armies in the Field of July 27, 1929, have agreed as follows:

CHAPTER I — *General Provisions*

Article 1

The High Contracting Parties undertake to respect and to ensure respect for the present Convention in all circumstances.

Article 2

In addition to the provisions which shall be implemented in peacetime, the present Convention shall apply to all cases of declared war or of any other armed conflict which may arise between two or more of the High Contracting Parties, even if the state of war is not recognized by one of them.

The Convention shall also apply to all cases of partial or total occupation of the territory of a High Contracting Party, even if the said occupation meets with no armed resistance.

Although one of the Powers in conflict may not be a party to the present Convention, the Powers who are parties thereto shall remain bound by it in their mutual relations. They shall furthermore be bound by the Convention in relation to the said Power, if the latter accepts and applies the provisions thereof.

Article 3

In the case of armed conflict not of an international character occurring in the territory of one of the High Contracting Parties, each Party to the conflict shall be bound to apply, as a minimum, the following provisions:

(1) Persons taking no active part in the hostilities, including members of armed forces who have laid down their arms and those placed *hors de combat* by sickness, wounds, detention, or any other cause, shall in all circumstances be treated humanely, without any adverse distinction founded on race, colour, religion or faith, sex, birth or wealth, or any other similar criteria.

To this end, the following acts are and shall remain prohibited at any time and in any place whatsoever with respect to the above-mentioned persons:

(a) violence to life and person, in particular murder of all kinds, mutilation, cruel treatment and torture;

(b) taking of hostages;

(c) outrages upon personal dignity, in particular humiliating and degrading treatment;

(d) the passing of sentences and the carrying out of executions without previous judgment pronounced by a regularly constituted court, affording all the judicial guarantees which are recognized as indispensable by civilized peoples.

(2) The wounded and sick shall be collected and cared for.

An impartial humanitarian body, such as the International Committee of the Red Cross, may offer its services to the Parties to the conflict.

The Parties to the conflict should further endeavour to bring into force, by means of special agreements, all or part of the other provisions of the present Convention.

The application of the preceding provisions shall not affect the legal status of the Parties to the conflict.

Article 4

Neutral Powers shall apply by analogy the provisions of the

present Convention to the wounded and sick, and to members of the medical personnel and to chaplains of the armed forces of the Parties to the conflict, received or interned in their territory, as well as to dead persons found.

Article 5

For the protected persons who have fallen into the hands of the enemy, the present Convention shall apply until their final repatriation.

Article 6

In addition to the agreements expressly provided for in Articles 10, 15, 23, 28, 31, 36, 37 and 52, the High Contracting Parties may conclude other special agreements for all matters concerning which they may deem it suitable to make separate provision. No special agreement shall adversely affect the situation of the wounded and sick, of members of the medical personnel or of chaplains, as defined by the present Convention, nor restrict the rights which it confers upon them.

Wounded and sick, as well as medical personnel and chaplains, shall continue to have the benefit of such agreements as long as the Convention is applicable to them, except where express provisions to the contrary are contained in the aforesaid or in subsequent agreements, or where more favourable measures have been taken with regard to them by one or other of the Parties to the conflict.

Article 7

Wounded and sick, as well as members of the medical personnel and chaplains, may in no circumstances renounce in part or in entirety the rights secured to them by the present Convention, and by the special agreements referred to in the foregoing Article, if such there be.

Article 8

The present Convention shall be applied with the cooperation and under the scrutiny of the Protecting Powers whose duty it is to safeguard the interests of the Parties to the conflict. For this purpose, the Protecting Powers may appoint, apart from their diplomatic or consular staff, delegates from amongst their own nationals or the nationals of other neutral Powers. The said delegates shall be subject to the approval of the Power with which they are to carry out their duties.

The Parties to the conflict shall facilitate to the greatest extent possible, the task of the representatives or delegates of the Protecting Powers.

The representatives or delegates of the Protecting Powers shall not in any case exceed their mission under the present Convention. They shall, in particular, take account of the imperative necessities of security of the State wherein they carry out their duties. Their activities shall only be restricted as an exceptional and temporary measure when this is rendered necessary by imperative military necessities.

Article 9

The provisions of the present Convention constitute no obstacle to the humanitarian activities which the International Committee of the Red Cross or any other impartial humanitarian organization may, subject to the consent of the Parties to the conflict concerned, undertake for the protection of wounded and sick, medical personnel and chaplains, and for their relief.

Article 10

The High Contracting Parties may at any time agree to entrust to an organization which offers all guarantees of impartiality and efficacy the duties incumbent on the Protecting Powers by virtue of the present Convention.

When wounded and sick, or medical personnel and chaplains do not benefit or cease to benefit, no matter for what reason, by the activities of a Protecting Power or of an organization provided for in the first paragraph above, the Detaining Power shall request a neutral State, or such an organization, to undertake the functions performed under the present Convention by a Protecting Power designated by the Parties to a conflict.

If protection cannot be arranged accordingly, the Detaining Power shall request or shall accept, subject to the provisions of this Article, the offer of the services of a humanitarian organization, such as the International Committee of the Red Cross, to assume the humanitarian functions performed by Protecting Powers under the present Convention.

Any neutral Power or any organization invited by the Power concerned or offering itself for these purposes, shall be required to act with a sense of responsibility towards the Party to the conflict on which persons protected by the present Convention depend, and shall be required to furnish sufficient assurances that it is in a position to undertake the appropriate functions and to discharge them impartially.

No derogation from the preceding provisions shall be made by special agreements between Powers one of which is restricted, even temporarily, in its freedom to negotiate with the other Power or its allies by reason of military events, more particularly where the whole, or a substantial part, of the territory of the said Power is occupied.

Whenever, in the present Convention, mention is made of a Protecting Power, such mention also applies to substitute organizations in the sense of the present Article.

Article 11

In cases where they deem it advisable in the interest of protected persons, particularly in cases of disagreement between the Parties to the conflict as to the application or interpretation of the provisions of the present Convention, the Protecting Powers shall lend their good offices with a view to settling the disagreement.

For this purpose, each of the Protecting Powers may, either at the invitation of one Party or on its own initiative, propose to the Parties to the conflict a meeting of their representatives, in particular of the authorities responsible for the wounded and sick, members of medical personnel and chaplains, possibly on neutral territory suitably chosen. The Parties to the conflict shall be bound to give effect to the proposals made to them for this purpose. The Protecting Powers may, if necessary, propose for approval by the Parties to the conflict, a person belonging to a neutral Power or delegated by the International Committee of the Red Cross, who shall be invited to take part in such a meeting.

CHAPTER II — *Wounded and Sick*

Article 12

Members of the armed forces and other persons mentioned in the following Article, who are wounded or sick, shall be respected and protected in all circumstances.

They shall be treated humanely and cared for by the Party to the conflict in whose power they may be, without any adverse distinction founded on sex, race, nationality, religion, political opinions, or any other similar criteria. Any attempts upon their lives, or violence to their persons, shall be strictly prohibited; in particular, they shall not be murdered or exterminated, subjected to torture or to biological experiments; they shall not wilfully be left without medical assistance and care, nor shall conditions exposing them to contagion or infection be created.

Only urgent medical reasons will authorize priority in the order of treatment to be administered.

Women shall be treated with all consideration due to their sex.

The Party to the conflict which is compelled to abandon wounded or sick to the enemy shall, as far as military considerations permit, leave with them a part of its medical personnel and material to assist in their care.

Article 13

The present Convention shall apply to the wounded and sick belonging to the following categories:

(1) Members of the armed forces of a Party to the conflict, as well as members of militias or volunteer corps forming part of such armed forces.

(2) Members of other militias and members of other volunteer corps, including those of organized resistance movements, belonging to a Party to the conflict and operating in or outside their own territory, even if this territory is occupied, provided that such militias or volunteer corps, including such organized resistance movements, fulfil the following conditions:

   (a) that of being commanded by a person responsible for his subordinates;

   (b) that of having a fixed distinctive sign recognizable at a distance;

   (c) that of carrying arms openly;

   (d) that of conducting their operations in accordance with the laws and customs of war.

(3) Members of regular armed forces who profess allegiance to a Government or an authority not recognized by the Detaining Power.

(4) Persons who accompany the armed forces without actually being members thereof, such as civil members of military aircraft crews, war correspondents, supply contractors, members of labour units or of services responsible for the welfare of the armed forces, provided that they have received authorization from the armed forces which they accompany.

(5) Members of crews, including masters, pilots and apprentices of the merchant marine and the crews of civil aircraft of the Parties to the conflict, who do not benefit by more favourable treatment under any other provisions in international law.

(6) Inhabitants of a non-occupied territory who, on the approach of the enemy, spontaneously take up arms to resist the invading forces, without having had time to form themselves into regular armed units, provided they carry arms openly and respect the laws and customs of war.

Article 14

Subject to the provisions of Article 12, the wounded and sick of a belligerent who fall into enemy hands shall be prisoners of war, and the provisions of international law concerning prisoners of war shall apply to them.

Article 15

At all times, and particularly after an engagement, Parties to the conflict shall, without delay, take all possible measures to search for and collect the wounded and sick, to protect them against pillage and ill-treatment, to ensure their adequate care, and to search for the dead and prevent their being despoiled.

Whenever circumstances permit, an armistice or a suspension of fire shall be arranged, or local arrangements made, to permit the removal, exchange and transport of the wounded left on the battlefield.

Likewise, local arrangements may be concluded between Parties to the conflict for the removal or exchange of wounded and sick from a besieged or encircled area, and for the passage of medical and religious personnel and equipment on their way to that area.

Article 16

Parties to the conflict shall record as soon as possible, in respect of each wounded, sick or dead person of the adverse Party falling into their hands, any particulars which may assist in his identification.

These records should if possible include:

(*a*) designation of the Power on which he depends;
(*b*) army, regimental, personal or serial number;
(*c*) surname;
(*d*) first name or names;
(*e*) date of birth;
(*f*) any other particulars shown on his identity card or disc;
(*g*) date and place of capture or death;
(*h*) particulars concerning wounds or illness, or cause of death.

As soon as possible the above mentioned information shall be forwarded to the Information Bureau described in Article 122 of the Geneva Convention relative to the Treatment of Prisoners of War of August 12, 1949, which shall transmit this information to the Power on which these persons depend through the intermediary of the Protecting Power and of the Central Prisoners of War Agency.

Parties to the conflict shall prepare and forward to each other through the same bureau, certificates of death or duly authenticated lists of the dead. They shall likewise collect and forward through the same bureau one half of a double identity disc, last wills or other documents of importance to the next of kin, money and in general all articles of an intrinsic or sentimental value, which are found on the dead. These articles, together with unidentified articles, shall be sent in sealed packets, accompanied by statements giving all particulars necessary for the identification of the deceased owners, as well as by a complete list of the contents of the parcel.

Article 17

Parties to the conflict shall ensure that burial or cremation of the dead, carried out individually as far as circumstances permit, is preceded by a careful examination, if possible by a medical examination, of the bodies, with a view to confirming death, establishing identity and enabling a report to be made. One half of the double identity disc, or the identity disc itself if it is a single disc, should remain on the body.

Bodies shall not be cremated except for imperative reasons of hygiene or for motives based on the religion of the deceased. In case of cremation, the circumstances and reasons for cremation shall be stated in detail in the death certificate or on the authenticated list of the dead.

They shall further ensure that the dead are honourably interred, if possible according to the rites of the religion to which they belonged, that their graves are respected, grouped if possible according to the nationality of the deceased, properly maintained and marked so that they may always be found. For this purpose, they shall organize at the commencement of hostilities an Official Graves Registration Service, to allow subsequent exhumations and to ensure the identification of bodies, whatever the site of the graves, and the possible transportation to the home country. These provisions shall likewise apply to the ashes, which shall be kept by the Graves Registration Service until proper disposal thereof in accordance with the wishes of the home country.

As soon as circumstances permit, and at latest at the end of hostilities, these Services shall exchange, through the Information Bureau mentioned in the second paragraph of Article 16, lists showing the exact location and markings of the graves, together with particulars of the dead interred therein.

Article 18

The military authorities may appeal to the charity of the inhabitants voluntarily to collect and care for, under their direction, the wounded and sick, granting persons who have responded to this appeal the necessary protection and facilities. Should the adverse Party take or retake control of the area, he shall likewise grant these persons the same protection and the same facilities.

The military authorities shall permit the inhabitants and relief societies, even in invaded or occupied areas, spontaneously to collect and care for wounded or sick of whatever nationality. The civilian population shall respect these wounded and sick, and in particular abstain from offering them violence.

No one may ever be molested or convicted for having nursed the wounded or sick.

The provisions of the present Article do not relieve the occupying Power of its obligation to give both physical and moral care to the wounded and sick.

CHAPTER III — *Medical Units and Establishments*

Article 19

Fixed establishments and mobile medical units of the Medical Service may in no circumstances be attacked, but shall at all times be respected and protected by the Parties to the conflict. Should they fall into the hands of the adverse Party, their personnel shall be free to pursue their duties, as long as the capturing Power has not itself ensured the necessary care of the wounded and sick found in such establishments and units.

The responsible authorities shall ensure that the said medical establishments and units are, as far as possible, situated in such a manner that attacks against military objectives cannot imperil their safety.

Article 20

Hospital ships entitled to the protection of the Geneva Convention for the Amelioration of the Condition of Wounded, Sick and Shipwrecked Members of Armed Forces at Sea of August 12, 1949, shall not be attacked from the land.

Article 21

The protection to which fixed establishments and mobile medical units of the Medical Service are entitled shall not cease unless they are used to commit, outside their humanitarian duties, acts harmful to the enemy. Protection may, however, cease only after a due warning has been given, naming, in all appropriate cases, a reasonable time limit, and after such warning has remained unheeded.

Article 22

The following conditions shall not be considered as depriving a medical unit or establishment of the protection guaranteed by Article 19:

(1) That the personnel of the unit or establishment are armed, and that they use the arms in their own defence, or in that of the wounded and sick in their charge.
(2) That in the absence of armed orderlies, the unit or establishment is protected by a picket or by sentries or by an escort.
(3) That small arms and ammunition taken from the wounded and sick and not yet handed to the proper service, are found in the unit or establishment.
(4) That personnel and material of the veterinary service are found in the unit or establishment, without forming an integral part thereof.
(5) That the humanitarian activities of medical units and establishments or of their personnel extend to the care of civilian wounded or sick.

Article 23

In time of peace, the High Contracting Parties and, after the outbreak of hostilities, the Parties thereto, may establish in their own territory and, if the need arises, in occupied areas, hospital zones and localities so organized as to protect the wounded and sick from the effects of war, as well as the personnel entrusted with the organization and administration of these zones and localities and with the care of the persons therein assembled.

Upon the outbreak and during the course of hostilities, the Parties concerned may conclude agreements on mutual recognition of the hospital zones and localities they have created. They may for this purpose implement the provisions of the Draft Agreeement annexed to the present Convention, with such amendments as they may consider necessary.

The Protecting Powers and the International Committee of the Red Cross are invited to lend their good offices in order to facilitate the institution and recognition of these hospital zones and localities.

CHAPTER IV — *Personnel*

Article 24

Medical personnel exclusively engaged in the search for, or the collection, transport or treatment of the wounded or sick, or in the prevention of disease, staff exclusively engaged in the administration of medical units and establishments, as well as chaplains attached to the armed forces, shall be respected and protected in all circumstances.

Article 25

Members of the armed forces specially trained for employment, should the need arise, as hospital orderlies, nurses or auxiliary stretcher-bearers, in the search for or the collection, transport or treatment of the wounded and sick shall likewise be respected and protected if they are carrying out these duties at the time when they come into contact with the enemy or fall into his hands.

Article 26

The staff of National Red Cross Societies and that of other Voluntary Aid Societies, duly recognized and authorized by their Governments, who may be employed on the same duties as the personnel named in Article 24, are placed on the same footing as the personnel named in the said Article, provided that the staff of such societies are subject to military laws and regulations.

Each High Contracting Party shall notify to the other, either in time of peace, or at the commencement of or during hostilities, but in any case before actually employing them, the names of the societies which it has authorized, under its responsibility, to render assistance to the regular medical service of its armed forces.

Article 27

A recognized Society of a neutral country can only lend the assistance of its medical personnel and units to a Party to the conflict with the previous consent of its own Government and the authorization of the Party to the conflict concerned. That personnel and those units shall be placed under the control of that Party to the conflict.

The neutral Government shall notify this consent to the adversary of the State which accepts such assistance. The Party to the conflict who accepts such assistance is bound to notify the adverse Party thereof before making any use of it.

In no circumstances shall this assistance be considered as interference in the conflict.

The members of the personnel named in the first paragraph shall be duly furnished with the identity cards provided for in Article 40 before leaving the neutral country to which they belong.

Article 28

Personnel designated in Articles 24 and 26 who fall into the hands of the adverse Party, shall be retained only in so far as the state of health, the spiritual needs and the number of prisoners of war require.

Personnel thus retained shall not be deemed prisoners of war. Nevertheless they shall at least benefit by all the provisions of the

Geneva Convention relative to the Treatment of Prisoners of War of August 12, 1949. Within the framework of the military laws and regulations of the Detaining Power, and under the authority of its competent service, they shall continue to carry out, in accordance with their professional ethics, their medical and spiritual duties on behalf of prisoners of war, preferably those of the armed forces to which they themselves belong. They shall further enjoy the following facilities for carrying out their medical or spiritual duties:

(a) They shall be authorized to visit periodically the prisoners of war in labour units or hospitals outside the camp. The Detaining Power shall put at their disposal the means of transport required.

(b) In each camp the senior medical officer of the highest rank shall be responsible to the military authorities of the camp for the professional activity of the retained medical personnel. For this purpose, from the outbreak of hostilities, the Parties to the conflict shall agree regarding the corresponding seniority of the ranks of their medical personnel, including those of the societies designated in Article 26. In all questions arising out of their duties, this medical officer, and the chaplains, shall have direct access to the military and medical authorities of the camp who shall grant them the facilities they may require for correspondence relating to these questions.

(c) Although retained personnel in a camp shall be subject to its internal discipline, they shall not, however, be required to perform any work outside their medical or religious duties.

During hostilities the Parties to the conflict shall make arrangements for relieving where possible retained personnel, and shall settle the procedure of such relief.

None of the preceding provisions shall relieve the Detaining Power of the obligations imposed upon it with regard to the medical and spiritual welfare of the prisoners of war.

Article 29

Members of the personnel designated in Article 25 who have fallen into the hands of the enemy, shall be prisoners of war, but shall be employed on their medical duties in so far as the need arises.

Article 30

Personnel whose retention is not indispensable by virtue of the provisions of Article 28 shall be returned to the Party to the conflict to whom they belong, as soon as a road is open for their return and military requirements permit.

Pending their return, they shall not be deemed prisoners of war.

Nevertheless they shall at least benefit by all the provisions of the Geneva Convention relative to the Treatment of Prisoners of War of August 12, 1949. They shall continue to fulfil their duties under the orders of the adverse Party and shall preferably be engaged in the care of the wounded and sick of the Party to the conflict to which they themselves belong.

On their departure, they shall take with them the effects, personal belongings, valuables and instruments belonging to them.

Article 31

The selection of personnel for return under Article 30 shall be made irrespective of any consideration of race, religion or political opinion, but preferably according to the chronological order of their capture and their state of health.

As from the outbreak of hostilities, Parties to the conflict may determine by special agreement the percentage of personnel to be retained, in proportion to the number of prisoners and the distribution of the said personnel in the camps.

Article 32

Persons designated in Article 27 who have fallen into the hands of the adverse Party may not be detained.

Unless otherwise agreed, they shall have permission to return to their country, or if this is not possible, to the territory of the Party to the conflict in whose service they were, as soon as a route for their return is open and military considerations permit.

Pending their release, they shall continue their work under the direction of the adverse Party; they shall preferably be engaged in the care of the wounded and sick of the Party to the conflict in whose service they were.

On their departure, they shall take with them their effects, personal articles and valuables and the instruments, arms and if possible the means of transport belonging to them.

The Parties to the conflict shall secure to this personnel, while in their power, the same food, lodging, allowances and pay as are granted to the corresponding personnel of their armed forces. The food shall in any case be sufficient as regards quantity, quality and variety to keep the said personnel in a normal state of health.

CHAPTER V — *Buildings and Material*

Article 33

The material of mobile medical units of the armed forces which fall into the hands of the enemy, shall be reserved for the care of wounded and sick.

The buildings, material and stores of fixed medical establishments of the armed forces shall remain subject to the laws of war, but may not be diverted from their purpose as long as they are required for the care of wounded and sick. Nevertheless, the commanders of forces in the field may make use of them, in case of urgent military necessity, provided that they make previous arrangements for the welfare of the wounded and sick who are nursed in them.

The material and stores defined in the present Article shall not be intentionally destroyed.

Article 34

The real and personal property of aid societies which are admitted to the privileges of the Convention shall be regarded as private property.

The right of requisition recognized for belligerents by the laws and customs of war shall not be exercised except in case of urgent necessity, and only after the welfare of the wounded and sick has been ensured.

CHAPTER VI — *Medical Transports*

Article 35

Transports of wounded and sick or of medical equipment shall be respected and protected in the same way as mobile medical units.

Should such transports or vehicles fall into the hands of the adverse Party, they shall be subject to the laws of war, on condition that the Party to the conflict who captures them shall in all cases ensure the care of the wounded and sick they contain.

The civilian personnel and all means of transport obtained by requisition shall be subject to the general rules of international law.

Article 36

Medical aircraft, that is to say, aircraft exclusively employed for the removal of wounded and sick and for the transport of medical personnel and equipment, shall not be attacked, but shall be respected by the belligerents, while flying at heights, times and on routes specifically agreed upon between the belligerents concerned.

They shall bear, clearly marked, the distinctive emblem prescribed in Article 38, together with their national colours, on their lower, upper and lateral surfaces. They shall be provided with any other markings or means of identification that may be agreed upon between the belligerents upon the outbreak or during the course of hostilities.

Unless agreed otherwise, flights over enemy or enemy-occupied territory are prohibited.

Medical aircraft shall obey every summons to land. In the event of a landing thus imposed, the aircraft with its occupants may continue its flight after examination, if any.

In the event of an involuntary landing in enemy or enemy-occupied territory, the wounded and sick, as well as the crew of the aircraft shall be prisoners of war. The medical personnel shall be treated according to Article 24 and the Articles following.

Article 37

Subject to the provisions of the second paragraph, medical aircraft of Parties to the conflict may fly over the territory of neutral Powers, land on it in case of necessity, or use it as a port of call. They shall give the neutral Powers previous notice of their passage over the said territory and obey all summons to alight, on land or water. They will be immune from attack only when flying on routes, at heights and at times specifically agreed upon between the Parties to the conflict and the neutral Power concerned.

The neutral Powers may, however, place conditions or restrictions on the passage or landing of medical aircraft on their territory. Such possible conditions or restrictions shall be applied equally to all Parties to the conflict.

Unless agreed otherwise between the neutral Power and the Parties to the conflict, the wounded and sick who are disembarked, with the consent of the local authorities, on neutral territory by medical aircraft, shall be detained by the neutral Power, where so required by international law, in such a manner that they cannot again take part in operations of war. The cost of their accommodation and internment shall be borne by the Power on which they depend.

CHAPTER VII — *The Distinctive Emblem*

Article 38

As a compliment to Switzerland, the heraldic emblem of the red cross on a white ground, formed by reversing the Federal colours, is retained as the emblem and distinctive sign of the Medical Service of armed forces.

Nevertheless, in the case of countries which already use as emblem, in place of the red cross, the red crescent or the red lion and sun on a white ground, those emblems are also recognized by the terms of the present Convention.

Article 39

Under the direction of the competent military authority, the emblem shall be displayed on the flags, armlets and on all equipment employed in the Medical Service.

Article 40

The personnel designated in Article 24 and in Articles 26 and 27 shall wear, affixed to the left arm, a water-resistant armlet bearing the distinctive emblem, issued and stamped by the military authority.

Such personnel, in addition to wearing the identity disc mentioned in Article 16, shall also carry a special identity card bearing the distinctive emblem. This card shall be water-resistant and of such size that it can be carried in the pocket. It shall be worded in the national language, shall mention at least the surname and first names, the date of birth, the rank and the service number of the bearer, and shall state in what capacity he is entitled to the protection of the present Convention. The card shall bear the photograph of the owner and also either his signature or his finger-prints or both. It shall be embossed with the stamp of the military authority.

The identity card shall be uniform throughout the same armed forces and, as far as possible, of a similar type in the armed forces of the High Contracting Parties. The Parties to the conflict may be guided by the model which is annexed, by way of example, to the present Convention. They shall inform each other, at the outbreak of hostilities, of the model they are using. Identity cards should be made out, if possible, at least in duplicate, one copy being kept by the home country.

In no circumstances may the said personnel be deprived of their insignia or identity cards nor of the right to wear the armlet. In case of loss, they shall be entitled to receive duplicates of the cards and to have the insignia replaced.

Article 41

The personnel designated in Article 25 shall wear, but only while carrying out medical duties, a white armlet bearing in its centre the distinctive sign in miniature; the armlet shall be issued and stamped by the military authority.

Military identity documents to be carried by this type of personnel shall specify what special training they have received, the temporary character of the duties they are engaged upon, and their authority for wearing the armlet.

Article 42

The distinctive flag of the Convention shall be hoisted only over such medical units and establishments as are entitled to be respected under the Convention, and only with the consent of the military authorities.

In mobile units, as in fixed establishments, it may be accompanied by the national flag of the Party to the conflict to which the unit or establishment belongs.

Nevertheless, medical units which have fallen into the hands of the enemy shall not fly any flag other than that of the Convention.

Parties to the conflict shall take the necessary steps, in so far as military considerations permit, to make the distinctive emblems indicating medical units and establishments clearly visible to the enemy land, air or naval forces, in order to obviate the possibility of any hostile action.

Article 43

The medical units belonging to neutral countries, which may have been authorized to lend their services to a belligerent under the conditions laid down in Article 27, shall fly, along with the flag of the Convention, the national flag of that belligerent, wherever the latter makes use of the faculty conferred on him by Article 42.

Subject to orders to the contrary by the responsible military authorities, they may, on all occasions, fly their national flag, even if they fall into the hands of the adverse Party.

Article 44

With the exception of the cases mentioned in the following paragraphs of the present Article, the emblem of the Red Cross on a white ground and the words 'Red Cross', or 'Geneva Cross' may not be employed, either in time of peace or in time of war, except to indicate or to protect the medical units and establishments, the personnel and material protected by the present Convention and other Conventions dealing with similar matters. The same shall apply to the emblems mentioned in Article 38, second paragraph, in respect of the countries which use them. The National Red Cross Societies and other Societies designated in Article 26 shall have the right to use the distinctive emblem conferring the protection of the Convention only within the framework of the present paragraph.

Furthermore, National Red Cross (Red Crescent, Red Lion and Sun) Societies may, in time of peace, in accordance with their national legislation, make use of the name and emblem of the Red Cross for their other activities which are in conformity with the principles laid down by the International Red Cross Conferences. When those activities are carried out in time of war, the conditions for the use of the emblem shall be such that it cannot be considered as conferring the protection of the Convention; the emblem shall be comparatively small in size and may not be placed on armlets or on the roofs of buildings.

The international Red Cross organizations and their duly authorized personnel shall be permitted to make use, at all times, of the emblem of the Red Cross on a white ground.

As an exceptional measure, in conformity with national legislation and with the express permission of one of the National Red Cross (Red Crescent, Red Lion and Sun) Societies, the emblem of the Convention may be employed in time of peace to identify vehicles used as ambulances and to mark the position of aid stations exclusively assigned to the purpose of giving free treatment to the wounded or sick.

CHAPTER VIII — *Execution of the Convention*

Article 45

Each Party to the conflict, acting through its Commanders-in-Chief, shall ensure the detailed execution of the preceding Articles, and provide for unforeseen cases, in conformity with the general principles of the present Convention.

Article 46

Reprisals against the wounded, sick, personnel, buildings or equipment protected by the Convention are prohibited.

Article 47

The High Contracting Parties undertake, in time of peace as in time of war, to disseminate the text of the present Convention as widely as possible in their respective countries, and, in particular, to include the study thereof in their programmes of military and, if possible, civil instruction, so that the principles thereof may become known to the entire population, in particular to the armed fighting forces, the medical personnel and the chaplains.

Article 48

The High Contracting Parties shall communicate to one another through the Swiss Federal Council and, during hostilities, through the Protecting Powers, the official translations of the present Convention, as well as the laws and regulations which they may adopt to ensure the application thereof.

CHAPTER IX — *Repression of Abuses and Infractions*

Article 49

The High Contracting Parties undertake to enact any legislation necessary to provide effective penal sanctions for persons committing, or ordering to be committed, any of the grave breaches of the present Convention defined in the following Article.

Each High Contracting Party shall be under the obligation to search for persons alleged to have committed, or to have ordered to be committed, such grave breaches, and shall bring such persons, regardless of their nationality, before its own courts. It may also, if it prefers, and in accordance with the provisions of its own legislation, hand such persons over for trial to another High Contracting Party concerned, provided such High Contracting Party has made out a *prima facie* case.

Each High Contracting Party shall take measures necessary for the suppression of all acts contrary to the provisions of the present Convention other than the grave breaches defined in the following Article.

In all circumstances, the accused persons shall benefit by safeguards of proper trial and defence, which shall not be less favourable than those provided by Article 105 and those following of the Geneva Convention relative to the Treatment of Prisoners of War of August 12, 1949.

Article 50

Grave breaches to which the preceding Article relates shall be those involving any of the following acts, if committed against persons or property protected by the Convention: wilful killing, torture or inhuman treatment, including biological experiments, wilfully causing great suffering or serious injury to body or health, and extensive destruction and appropriation of property, not justified by military necessity and carried out unlawfully and wantonly.

Article 51

No High Contracting Party shall be allowed to absolve itself or any other High Contracting Party of any liability incurred by itself or by another High Contracting Party in respect of breaches referred to in the preceding Article.

Article 52

At the request of a Party to the conflict, an enquiry shall be instituted, in a manner to be decided between the interested Parties, concerning any alleged violation of the Convention.

If agreement has not been reached concerning the procedure for the enquiry, the Parties should agree on the choice of an umpire who will decide upon the procedure to be followed.

Once the violation has been established, the Parties to the conflict shall put an end to it and shall repress it with the least possible delay.

Article 53

The use by individuals, societies, firms or companies either public or private, other than those entitled thereto under the present Convention, of the emblem or the designation 'Red Cross' or 'Geneva Cross', or any sign or designation constituting an imitation thereof, whatever the object of such use, and irrespective of the date of its adoption, shall be prohibited at all times.

By reason of the tribute paid to Switzerland by the adoption of the reversed Federal colours, and of the confusion which may arise between the arms of Switzerland and the distinctive emblem of the Convention, the use by private individuals, societies or firms, of the arms of the Swiss Confederation, or of marks constituting an imitation thereof, whether as trade-marks or commerical marks, or as parts of such marks, or for a purpose contrary to commerical honesty, or in circumstances capable of wounding Swiss national sentiment, shall be prohibited at all times.

Nevertheless, such High Contracting Parties as were not party to the Geneva Convention of July 27, 1929, may grant to prior users of the emblems, designations, signs or marks designated in the first paragraph, a time limit not to exceed three years from the coming into force of the present Convention to discontinue such use, provided that the said use shall not be such as would appear, in time of war, to confer the protection of the Convention.

The prohibition laid down in the first paragraph of the present Article shall also apply, without effect on any rights acquired through prior use, to the emblems and marks mentioned in the second paragraph of Article 38.

Article 54

The High Contracting Parties shall, if their legislation is not already adequate, take measures necessary for the prevention and repression, at all times, of the abuses referred to under Article 53.

FINAL PROVISIONS

Article 55

The present Convention is established in English and in French. Both texts are equally authentic.

The Swiss Federal Council shall arrange for official translations of the Convention to be made in the Russian and Spanish languages.

Article 56

The present Convention, which bears the date of this day, is open to signature until February 12, 1950, in the name of the Powers represented at the Conference which opened at Geneva on April 21, 1949; furthermore, by Powers not represented at that Conference, but which are parties to the Geneva Conventions of 1864, 1906 or 1929 for the Relief of the Wounded and Sick in Armies in the Field.

Article 57

The present Convention shall be ratified as soon as possible and the ratifications shall be deposited at Berne.

A record shall be drawn up of the deposit of each instrument of ratification and certified copies of this record shall be transmitted by the Swiss Federal Council to all the Powers in whose name the Convention has been signed, or whose accession has been notified.

Article 58

The present Convention shall come into force six months after not less than two instruments of ratification have been deposited.

Thereafter, it shall come into force for each High Contracting Party six months after the deposit of the instrument of ratification.

Article 59

The present Convention replaces the Conventions of August 22, 1864, July 6, 1906, and July 27, 1929, in relations between the High Contracting Parties.

Article 60

From the date of its coming into force, it shall be open to any Power in whose name the present Convention has not been signed, to accede to this Convention.

Article 61

Accessions shall be notified in writing to the Swiss Federal Council, and shall take effect six months after the date on which they are received.

The Swiss Federal Council shall communicate the accessions to all the Powers in whose name the Convention has been signed, or whose accession has been notified.

Article 62

The situations provided for in Articles 2 and 3 shall give immediate effect to ratifications deposited and accessions notified by the Parties to the conflict before or after the beginning of hostilities or occupation. The Swiss Federal Council shall communicate by the quickest method any ratifications or accessions received from Parties to the conflict.

Article 63

Each of the High Contracting Parties shall be at liberty to denounce the present Convention.

The denunciation shall be notified in writing to the Swiss Federal Council, which shall transmit it to the Governments of all the High Contracting Parties.

The denunciation shall take effect one year after the notification thereof has been made to the Swiss Federal Council. However, a denunciation of which notification has been made at a time when the denouncing Power is involved in a conflict shall not take effect until peace has been concluded, and until after operations connected with the release and repatriation of the persons protected by the present Convention have been terminated.

The denunciation shall have effect only in respect of the denouncing Power. It shall in no way impair the obligations which the Parties to the conflict shall remain bound to fulfil by virtue of the principles of the law of nations, as they result from the usages established among civilized peoples, from the laws of humanity and the dictates of the public conscience.

Article 64

The Swiss Federal Council shall register the present Convention with the Secretariat of the United Nations. The Swiss Federal Council shall also inform the Secretariat of the United Nations of all ratifications, accessions and denunciations received by it with respect to the present Convention.

IN WITNESS WHEREOF the undersigned, having deposited their respective full powers, have signed the present Convention.

DONE at Geneva this twelfth day of August 1949, in the English and French languages. The original shall be deposited in the archives of the Swiss Confederation. The Swiss Federal Council shall transmit certified copies thereof to each of the signatory and acceding States.

[Annexes omitted]

CONCLUDING NOTES

The concluding notes for 1949 Geneva Convention I are combined with those for the other three 1949 Geneva Conventions and are to be found after the end of 1949 Geneva Convention IV, below, p. 326.

19. 1949 Geneva Convention II for the Amelioration of the Condition of Wounded, Sick and Shipwrecked Members of Armed Forces at Sea

PREFATORY NOTE

The protection of wounded, sick and shipwrecked armed forces at sea was formally considered at the 1868 Geneva Conference which adopted the 1868 Additional Articles Relating to the Condition of Wounded in War. These Articles extended to naval forces the protections of the 1864 Geneva Convention. Although the 1868 Additional Articles were not ratified and did not enter into force, during the 1870–1 Franco-Prussian War and the 1898 Spanish-American War the belligerents agreed to observe their provisions.

At the request of the Swiss government, the ICRC prepared a new draft, but before a diplomatic conference could be convened in Geneva, Tsar Nicholas II took the initiative to convene the First Hague Peace Conference in 1899 and proposed that the Conference, among other things, consider the adaptation to naval warfare of the 1864 Geneva Convention. The Conference adopted 1899 Hague Convention III for the Adaptation to Maritime Warfare of the Principles of the Geneva Convention of 22 August 1864.

At the Second Hague Peace Conference of 1907, the provisions of 1899 Hague Convention III were revised and greatly enlarged, and then embodied in 1907 Hague Convention X for the Adaptation to Maritime Warfare of the Principles of the Geneva Convention. 1907 Hague Convention X replaced 1899 Hague Convention III as between parties to both agreements. Where 1899 Hague Convention III had been based on the adaptation of the principles of the 1864 Geneva Convention, 1907 Hague Convention X was based on the 1906 Geneva Convention. The revision of the 1906 Geneva Convention at the 1929 Geneva diplomatic conference, together with developments in the methods of warfare, demonstrated the need to revise 1907 Hague Convention X.

In 1937, after consultation with various experts, the ICRC formulated a draft convention which revised 1907 Hague Convention X. In January 1939, the Swiss government transmitted the ICRC draft convention to states as a basis for a diplomatic conference which the Swiss government planned to convene in Geneva in early 1940. However, the outbreak of the Second World War intervened. As indicated in the general prefatory note to the four 1949 Geneva Conventions, the process of drafting a new agreement only resumed after the war.

1949 Geneva Convention II represents a greatly enlarged version of 1907 Hague Convention X and replaces the earlier convention as between parties. Both 1899 Hague Convention III and 1907 Hague Convention X are now no longer in force. As an extension of the protection given to wounded and sick armed forces in land warfare, 1949 Geneva Convention II embodies the same basic principles as those set forth in 1949 Geneva Convention I. Compared with the 1868 Additional Articles and 1907 Hague Convention X, 1949 Geneva Convention II is considerably enlarged. It closely adapts the detailed provisions of 1949 Geneva Convention I and establishes other provisions which are obviously applicable only to naval warfare.

Date of signature: Signed on 12 August 1949, and open for signature (see Article 55) until 12 February 1950.
Entry into force: 21 October 1950
Depositary: Switzerland
Authentic languages: English and French
Text reprinted from: *Final Record of the Diplomatic Conference of Geneva of 1949*, Federal Political Department, Berne, n.d., vol. 1, pp. 225–36.
Also published in: 75 *UNTS* (1950) 85–133 (Eng. Fr.);
                          157 *BFSP* (1950) 262–83 (Eng.);
                          UKTS 39 (1958), Cmnd. 550 (Eng. Fr.);
                          XXXII *UKPP* (1958–1959) 11 (Eng. Fr.)

Geneva Convention for the Amelioration of the Condition of Wounded, Sick and Shipwrecked Members of Armed Forces at Sea of August 12, 1949

The undersigned Plenipotentiaries of the Governments represented at the Diplomatic Conference held at Geneva from April 21 to August 12, 1949, for the purpose of revising the Xth Hague Convention of October 18, 1907, for the Adaptation to Maritime Warfare of the Principles of the Geneva Convention of 1906, have agreed as follows:

CHAPTER I — *General Provisions*

Article 1

The High Contracting Parties undertake to respect and to ensure respect for the present Convention in all circumstances.

Article 2

In addition to the provisions which shall be implemented in peacetime, the present Convention shall apply to all cases of declared war or of any other armed conflict which may arise between two or more of the High Contracting Parties, even if the state of war is not recognized by one of them.

The Convention shall also apply to all cases of partial or total occupation of the territory of a High Contracting Party, even if the said occupation meets with no armed resistance.

Although one of the Powers in conflict may not be a party to the present Convention, the Powers who are parties thereto shall remain bound by it in their mutual relations. They shall furthermore be bound by the Convention in relation to the said Power, if the latter accepts and applies the provisions thereof.

Article 3

In the case of armed conflict not of an international character occurring in the territory of one of the High Contracting Parties, each Party to the conflict shall be bound to apply, as a minimum, the following provisions:

(1) Persons taking no active part in the hostilities, including members of armed forces who have laid down their arms and those placed *hors de combat* by sickness, wounds, detention, or any other cause, shall in all circumstances be treated humanely, without any adverse distinction founded on race, colour, religion or faith, sex, birth or wealth, or any other similar criteria.

To this end, the following acts are and shall remain prohibited at any time and in any place whatsoever with respect to the above-mentioned persons:

(a) violence to life and person, in particular murder of all kinds, mutilation, cruel treatment and torture;

(b) taking of hostages;

(c) outrages upon personal dignity, in particular, humiliating and degrading treatment;

(d) the passing of sentences and the carrying out of executions without previous judgment pronounced by a regularly constituted court, affording all the judicial guarantees which are recognized as indispensable by civilized peoples.

(2) The wounded, sick and shipwrecked shall be collected and cared for.

An impartial humanitarian body, such as the International Committee of the Red Cross, may offer its services to the Parties to the conflict.

The Parties to the conflict should further endeavour to bring into force, by means of special agreements, all or part of the other provisions of the present Convention.

The application of the preceding provisions shall not affect the legal status of the Parties to the conflict.

Article 4

In case of hostilities between land and naval forces of Parties to the conflict, the provisions of the present Convention shall apply only to forces on board ship.

Forces put ashore shall immediately become subject to the provisions of the Geneva Convention for the Amelioration of the Condition of the Wounded and Sick in Armed Forces in the Field of August 12, 1949.

Article 5

Neutral Powers shall apply by analogy the provisions of the present Convention to the wounded, sick and shipwrecked, and to members of the medical personnel and to chaplains of the armed forces of the Parties to the conflict received or interned in their territory, as well as to dead persons found.

Article 6

In addition to the agreements expressly provided for in Articles 10, 18, 31, 38, 39, 40, 43 and 53, the High Contracting Parties may conclude other special agreements for all matters concerning which they may deem it suitable to make separate provision. No special agreement shall adversely affect the situation of wounded, sick and shipwrecked persons, of members of the medical personnel or of chaplains, as defined by the present Convention, nor restrict the rights which it confers upon them.

Wounded, sick, and shipwrecked persons, as well as medical personnel and chaplains, shall continue to have the benefit of such agreements as long as the Convention is applicable to them, except where express provisions to the contrary are contained in the aforesaid or in subsequent agreements, or where more favourable measures have been taken with regard to them by one or other of the Parties to the conflict.

Article 7

Wounded, sick and shipwrecked persons, as well as members of the medical personnel and chaplains, may in no circumstances renounce in part or in entirety the rights secured to them by the present Convention, and by the special agreements referred to in the foregoing Article, if such there be.

Article 8

The present Convention shall be applied with the cooperation and under the scrutiny of the Protecting Powers whose duty it is to safeguard the interests of the Parties to the conflict. For this purpose, the Protecting Powers may appoint, apart from their diplomatic or consular staff, delegates from amongst their own nationals or the nationals of other neutral Powers. The said delegates shall be subject to the approval of the Power with which they are to carry out their duties.

The Parties to the conflict shall facilitate to the greatest extent possible the task of the representatives or delegates of the Protecting Powers.

The representatives or delegates of the Protecting Powers shall not in any case exceed their mission under the present Convention. They shall, in particular, take account of the imperative necessities of security of the State wherein they carry out their duties. Their activities shall only be restricted as an exceptional and temporary measure when this is rendered necessary by imperative military necessities.

Article 9

The provisions of the present Convention constitute no obstacle to the humanitarian activities which the International Committee of the Red Cross or any other impartial humanitarian organization may, subject to the consent of the Parties to the conflict concerned, undertake for the protection of wounded, sick and shipwrecked persons, medical personnel and chaplains, and for their relief.

Article 10

The High Contracting Parties may at any time agree to entrust to an organization which offers all guarantees of impartiality and efficacy the duties incumbent on the Protecting Powers by virtue of the present Convention.

When wounded, sick and shipwrecked, or medical personnel and chaplains do not benefit or cease to benefit, no matter for what reason, by the activities of a Protecting Power or of an organization provided for in the first paragraph above, the Detaining Power shall request a neutral State, or such an organization, to undertake the functions performed under the present Convention by a Protecting Power designated by the Parties to a conflict.

If protection cannot be arranged accordingly, the Detaining Power shall request or shall accept, subject to the provisions of this Article, the offer of the services of a humanitarian organization, such as the International Committee of the Red Cross, to assume the humanitarian functions performed by Protecting Powers under the present Convention.

Any neutral Power, or any organization invited by the Power concerned or offering itself for these purposes, shall be required to act with a sense of responsibility towards the Party to the conflict on which persons protected by the present Convention depend, and shall be required to furnish sufficient assurances that it is in a position to undertake the appropriate functions and to discharge them impartially.

No derogation from the preceding provisions shall be made by special agreements between Powers one of which is restricted, even temporarily, in its freedom to negotiate with the other Power or its allies by reason of military events, more particularly where the whole, or a substantial part, of the territory of the said Power is occupied.

Whenever, in the present Convention, mention is made of a Protecting Power, such mention also applies to substitute organizations in the sense of the present Article.

Article 11

In cases where they deem it advisable in the interest of protected persons, particularly in cases of disagreement between the Parties to the conflict as to the application or interpretation of the provisions of the present Convention, the Protecting Powers shall lend their good offices with a view to settling the disagreement.

For this purpose, each of the Protecting Powers may, either at the invitation of one Party or on its own initiative, propose to the Parties to the conflict a meeting of their representatives, in particular of the authorities responsible for the wounded, sick and shipwrecked, medical personnel and chaplains, possibly on neutral territory suitably chosen. The Parties to the conflict shall be bound to give effect to the proposals made to them for this purpose. The Protecting Powers may, if necessary, propose for approval by the Parties to the conflict, a person belonging to a neutral Power or delegated by the International Committee of the Red Cross, who shall be invited to take part in such a meeting.

CHAPTER II — *Wounded, Sick and Shipwrecked*

Article 12

Members of the armed forces and other persons mentioned in the following Article, who are at sea and who are wounded, sick or shipwrecked, shall be respected and protected in all circumstances, it being understood that the term 'shipwreck' means shipwreck from any cause and includes forced landings at sea by or from aircraft.

Such persons shall be treated humanely and cared for by the Parties to the conflict in whose power they may be, without any adverse distinction founded on sex, race, nationality, religion, political opinions, or any other similar criteria. Any attempts upon their lives, or violence to their persons, shall be strictly prohibited; in particular, they shall not be murdered or exterminated, subjected to torture or to biological experiments; they shall not wilfully be left without medical assistance and care, nor shall conditions exposing them to contagion or infection be created.

Only urgent medical reasons will authorize priority in the order of treatment to be administered.

Women shall be treated with all consideration due to their sex.

Article 13

The present Convention shall apply to the wounded, sick and shipwrecked at sea belonging to the following categories:

(1) Members of the armed forces of a Party to the conflict, as well as members of militias or volunteer corps forming part of such armed forces.

(2) Members of other militias and members of other volunteer corps, including those of organized resistance movements, belonging to a Party to the conflict and operating in or outside their own territory, even if this territory is occupied, provided that such militias or volunteer corps, including such organized resistance movements, fulfil the following conditions:

(a) that of being commanded by a person responsible for his subordinates;

(b) that of having a fixed distinctive sign recognizable at a distance;

(c) that of carrying arms openly;

(d) that of conducting their operations in accordance with the laws and customs of war.

(3) Members of regular armed forces who profess allegiance to a a Government or an authority not recognized by the Detaining Power.

(4) Persons who accompany the armed forces without actually being members thereof, such as civilian members of military aircraft crews, war correspondents, supply contractors, members of labour units or of services responsible for the welfare of the armed forces, provided that they have received authorization from the armed forces which they accompany.

(5) Members of crews, including masters, pilots and apprentices of the merchant marine and the crews of civil aircraft of the Parties to the conflict, who do not benefit by more favourable treatment under any other provisions of international law.

(6) Inhabitants of a non-occupied territory who, on the approach of the enemy, spontaneously take up arms to resist the invading forces, without having had time to form themselves into regular armed units, provided they carry arms openly and respect the laws and customs of war.

Article 14

All warships of a belligerent Party shall have the right to demand that the wounded, sick or shipwrecked on board military hospital ships, and hospital ships belonging to relief societies or to private individuals, as well as merchant vessels, yachts and other craft shall be surrendered, whatever their nationality, provided that the wounded and sick are in a fit state to be moved and that the warship can provide adequate facilities for necessary medical treatment.

Article 15

If wounded, sick or shipwrecked persons are taken on board a neutral warship or a neutral military aircraft, it shall be ensured, where so required by international law, that they can take no further part in operations of war.

Article 16

Subject to the provisions of Article 12, the wounded, sick and shipwrecked of a belligerent who fall into enemy hands shall be prisoners of war, and the provisions of international law concerning prisoners of war shall apply to them. The captor may decide, according to circumstances, whether it is expedient to hold them, or to convey them to a port in the captor's own country, to a neutral port or even to a port in enemy territory. In the last case, prisoners of war thus returned to their home country may not serve for the duration of the war.

Article 17

Wounded, sick or shipwrecked persons who are landed in neutral ports with the consent of the local authorities, shall, failing arrangements to the contrary between the neutral and the belligerent Powers, be so guarded by the neutral Power, where so required by international law, that the said persons cannot again take part in operations of war.

The costs of hospital accommodation and internment shall be borne by the Power on whom the wounded, sick or shipwrecked persons depend.

Article 18

After each engagement, Parties to the conflict shall, without delay, take all possible measures to search for and collect the shipwrecked, wounded and sick, to protect them against pillage and ill-treatment, to ensure their adequate care, and to search for the dead and prevent their being despoiled.

Whenever circumstances permit, the Parties to the conflict shall conclude local arrangements for the removal of the wounded and sick by sea from a besieged or encircled area and for the passage of medical and religious personnel and equipment on their way to that area.

Article 19

The Parties to the conflict shall record as soon as possible, in respect of each shipwrecked, wounded, sick or dead person of the adverse Party falling into their hands, any particulars which may assist in his identification. These records should if possible include:

(*a*) designation of the Power on which he depends;
(*b*) army, regimental, personal or serial number;
(*c*) surname;
(*d*) first name or names;
(*e*) date of birth;
(*f*) any other particulars shown on his identity card or disc;
(*g*) date and place of capture or death;
(*h*) particulars concerning wounds or illness, or cause of death.

As soon as possible the above-mentioned information shall be forwarded to the information bureau described in Article 122 of the Geneva Convention relative to the Treatment of Prisoners of War of August 12, 1949, which shall transmit this information to the Power on which these persons depend through the intermediary of the Protecting Power and of the Central Prisoners of War Agency.

Parties to the conflict shall prepare and forward to each other through the same bureau, certificates of death or duly authenticated lists of the dead. They shall likewise collect and forward through the same bureau one half of the double identity disc, or the identity disc itself if it is a single disc, last wills or other documents of importance to the next of kin, money and in general all articles of an intrinsic or sentimental value, which are found on the dead. These articles, together with unidentified articles, shall be sent in sealed packets, accompanied by statements giving all particulars necessary for the identification of the deceased owners, as well as by a complete list of the contents of the parcel.

Article 20

Parties to the conflict shall ensure that burial at sea of the dead, carried out individually as far as circumstances permit, is preceded by a careful examination, if possible by a medical examination, of the bodies, with a view to confirming death, establishing identity and enabling a report to be made. Where a double identity disc is used, one half of the disc should remain on the body.

If dead persons are landed, the provisions of the Geneva Convention for the Amelioration of the Condition of the Wounded and Sick in Armed Forces in the Field of August 12, 1949, shall be applicable.

Article 21

The Parties to the conflict may appeal to the charity of commanders of neutral merchant vessels, yachts or other craft, to take on board and care for wounded, sick or shipwrecked persons, and to collect the dead.

Vessels of any kind responding to this appeal, and those having of their own accord collected wounded, sick or shipwrecked persons, shall enjoy special protection and facilities to carry out such assistance.

They may, in no case, be captured on account of any such transport; but, in the absence of any promise to the contrary, they shall remain liable to capture for any violations of neutrality they may have committed.

CHAPTER III -- *Hospital Ships*

Article 22

Military hospital ships, that is to say, ships built or equipped by the Powers specially and solely with a view to assisting the wounded, sick and shipwrecked, to treating them and to transporting them, may in no circumstances be attacked or captured, but shall at all times be respected and protected, on condition that their names and descriptions have been notified to the Parties to the conflict ten days before those ships are employed.

The characteristics which must appear in the notification shall include registered gross tonnage, the length from stem to stern and the number of masts and funnels.

Article 23

Establishments ashore entitled to the protection of the Geneva Convention for the Amelioration of the Condition of the Wounded and Sick in Armed Forces in the Field of August 12, 1949, shall be protected from bombardment or attack from the sea.

Article 24

Hospital ships utilized by National Red Cross Societies, by officially recognized relief societies or by private persons shall have the same protection as military hospital ships and shall be exempt from capture, if the Party to the conflict on which they depend has given them an official commission and in so far as the provisions of Article 22 concerning notification have been complied with.

These ships must be provided with certificates from the responsible authorities, stating that the vessels have been under their control while fitting out and on departure.

Article 25

Hospital ships utilized by National Red Cross Societies, officially recognized relief societies, or private persons of neutral countries shall have the same protection as military hospital ships and shall be exempt from capture, on condition that they have placed themselves under the control of one of the Parties to the conflict, with the previous consent of their own governments and with the authorization of the Party to the conflict concerned, in so far as the provisions of Article 22 concerning notification have been complied with.

Article 26

The protection mentioned in Articles 22, 24 and 25 shall apply to hospital ships of any tonnage and to their lifeboats, wherever they are operating. Nevertheless, to ensure the maximum comfort and security, the Parties to the conflict shall endeavour to utilize, for the transport of wounded, sick and shipwrecked over long distances and on the high seas, only hospital ships of over 2,000 tons gross.

Article 27

Under the same conditions as those provided for in Articles 22 and 24, small craft employed by the State or by the officially recognized lifeboat institutions for coastal rescue operations, shall also be respected and protected, so far as operational requirements permit.

The same shall apply so far as possible to fixed coastal installations used exclusively by these craft for their humanitarian missions.

Article 28

Should fighting occur on board a warship, the sick-bays shall be respected and spared as far as possible. Sick-bays and their equipment shall remain subject to the laws of warfare, but may not be diverted from their purpose so long as they are required for the wounded and sick. Nevertheless, the commander into whose power they have fallen may, after ensuring the proper care of the wounded and sick who are accommodated therein, apply them to other purposes in case of urgent military necessity.

Article 29

Any hospital ship in a port which falls into the hands of the enemy shall be authorized to leave the said port.

Article 30

The vessels described in Articles 22, 24, 25 and 27 shall afford relief and assistance to the wounded, sick and shipwrecked without distinction of nationality.

The High Contracting Parties undertake not to use these vessels for any military purpose.

Such vessels shall in no wise hamper the movements of the combatants.

During and after an engagement, they will act at their own risk.

Article 31

The Parties to the conflict shall have the right to control and search the vessels mentioned in Articles 22, 24, 25 and 27. They can refuse assistance from these vessels, order them off, make them take a certain course, control the use of their wireless and other means of communication, and even detain them for a period not exceeding seven days from the time of interception, if the gravity of the circumstances so requires.

They may put a commissioner temporarily on board whose sole task shall be to see that orders given in virtue of the provisions of the preceding paragraph are carried out.

As far as possible, the Parties to the conflict shall enter in the log of the hospital ship, in a language he can understand, the orders they have given the captain of the vessel.

Parties to the conflict may, either unilaterally or by particular agreements, put on board their ships neutral observers who shall verify the strict observation of the provisions contained in the present Convention.

Article 32

Vessels described in Articles 22, 24, 25 and 27 are not classed as warships as regards their stay in a neutral port.

Article 33

Merchant vessels which have been transformed into hospital ships cannot be put to any other use throughout the duration of hostilities.

Article 34

The protection to which hospital ships and sick-bays are entitled shall not cease unless they are used to commit, outside their humanitarian duties, acts harmful to the enemy. Protection may, however, cease only after due warning has been given, naming in all appropriate cases a reasonable time limit, and after such warning has remained unheeded.

In particular, hospital ships may not possess or use a secret code for their wireless or other means of communication.

Article 35

The following conditions shall not be considered as depriving hospital ships or sick-bays of vessels of the protection due to them:

(1) The fact that the crews of ships or sick-bays are armed for the maintenance of order, for their own defence or that of the sick and wounded.

(2) The presence on board of apparatus exclusively intended to facilitate navigation or communication.

(3) The discovery on board hospital ships or in sick-bays of portable arms and ammunition taken from the wounded, sick and shipwrecked and not yet handed to the proper service.

(4) The fact that the humanitarian activities of hospital ships and sick-bays of vessels or of the crews extend to the care of wounded, sick or shipwrecked civilians.

(5) The transport of equipment and of personnel intended exclusively for medical duties, over and above the normal requirements.

CHAPTER IV — *Personnel*

Article 36

The religious, medical and hospital personnel of hospital ships and their crews shall be respected and protected; they may not be captured during the time they are in the service of the hospital ship, whether or not there are wounded and sick on board.

Article 37

The religious, medical and hospital personnel assigned to the medical or spiritual care of the persons designated in Articles 12 and 13 shall, if they fall into the hands of the enemy, be respected and protected; they may continue to carry out their duties as long as this is necessary for the care of the wounded and sick. They shall afterwards be sent back as soon as the Commander-in-Chief, under whose authority they are, considers it practicable. They may take with them, on leaving the ship, their personal property.

If, however, it proves necessary to retain some of this personnel owing to the medical or spiritual needs of prisoners of war, everything possible shall be done for their earliest possible landing.

Retained personnel shall be subject, on landing, to the provisions of the Geneva Convention for the Amelioration of the Condition of the Wounded and Sick in Armed Forces in the Field of August 12, 1949.

CHAPTER V — *Medical Transports*

Article 38

Ships chartered for that purpose shall be authorized to transport equipment exclusively intended for the treatment of wounded and sick members of armed forces or for the prevention of disease, provided that the particulars regarding their voyage have been notified to the adverse Power and approved by the latter. The adverse Power shall preserve the right to board the carrier ships, but not to capture them or seize the equipment carried.

By agreement amongst the Parties to the conflict, neutral observers may be placed on board such ships to verify the equipment carried. For this purpose, free access to the equipment shall be given.

Article 39

Medical aircraft, that is to say, aircraft exclusively employed for the removal of the wounded, sick and shipwrecked, and for the transport of medical personnel and equipment, may not be the object of attack, but shall be respected by the Parties to the conflict, while flying at heights, at times and on routes specifically agreed upon between the Parties to the conflict concerned.

They shall be clearly marked with the distinctive emblem prescribed in Article 41, together with their national colours, on their lower, upper and lateral surfaces. They shall be provided with any other markings or means of identification which may be agreed upon between the Parties to the conflict upon the outbreak or during the course of hostilities.

Unless agreed otherwise, flights over enemy or enemy-occupied territory are prohibited.

Medical aircraft shall obey every summons to alight on land or water. In the event of having thus to alight, the aircraft with its occupants may continue its flight after examination, if any.

In the event of alighting involuntarily on land or water in enemy or enemy-occupied territory, the wounded, sick and shipwrecked, as well as the crew of the aircraft shall be prisoners of war. The medical personnel shall be treated according to Articles 36 and 37.

Article 40

Subject to the provisions of the second paragraph, medical aircraft of Parties to the conflict may fly over the territory of neutral Powers, land thereon in case of necessity, or use it as a port of call. They shall give neutral Powers prior notice of their passage over the said territory, and obey every summons to alight, on land or water. They will be immune from attack only when flying on routes, at heights and at times specifically agreed upon between the Parties to the conflict and the neutral Power concerned.

The neutral Powers may, however, place conditions or restrictions on the passage or landing of medical aircraft on their territory. Such possible conditions or restrictions shall be applied equally to all Parties to the conflict.

Unless otherwise agreed between the neutral Powers and the Parties to the conflict, the wounded, sick or shipwrecked who are disembarked with the consent of the local authorities on neutral territory by medical aircraft shall be detained by the neutral Power, where so required by international law, in such a manner that they cannot again take part in operations of war. The cost of their accommodation and internment shall be borne by the Power on which they depend.

CHAPTER VI — *The Distinctive Emblem*

Article 41

Under the direction of the competent military authority, the emblem of the red cross on a white ground shall be displayed on the flags, armlets and on all equipment employed in the Medical Service.

Nevertheless, in the case of countries which already use as emblem, in place of the red cross, the red crescent or the red lion and sun on a white ground, these emblems are also recognized by the terms of the present Convention.

Article 42

The personnel designated in Articles 36 and 37 shall wear, affixed to the left arm, a water-resistant armlet bearing the distinctive emblem, issued and stamped by the military authority.

Such personnel, in addition to wearing the identity disc mentioned in Article 19, shall also carry a special identity card bearing the distinctive emblem. This card shall be water-resistant and of such size that it can be carried in the pocket. It shall be worded in the national language, shall mention at least the surname and first names, the date of birth, the rank and the service number of the bearer, and shall state in what capacity he is entitled to the protection of the present Convention. The card shall bear the photograph of the owner and also either his signature or his finger-prints or both. It shall be embossed with the stamp of the military authority.

The identity card shall be uniform throughout the same armed forces and, as far as possible, of a similar type in the armed forces of the High Contracting Parties. The Parties to the conflict may be guided by the model which is annexed, by way of example, to the present Convention. They shall inform each other, at the outbreak of hostilities, of the model they are using. Identity cards should be made out, if possible, at least in duplicate, one copy being kept by the home country.

In no circumstances may the said personnel be deprived of their insignia or identity cards nor of the right to wear the armlet. In case of loss they shall be entitled to receive duplicates of the cards and to have the insignia replaced.

Article 43

The ships designated in Articles 22, 24, 25 and 27 shall be distinctively marked as follows:

(*a*) All exterior surfaces shall be white.
(*b*) One or more dark red crosses, as large as possible, shall be painted and displayed on each side of the hull and on the horizontal surfaces, so placed as to afford the greatest possible visibility from the sea and from the air.

All hospital ships shall make themselves known by hoisting their national flag and further, if they belong to a neutral state, the flag of the Party to the conflict whose direction they have accepted. A white flag with a red cross shall be flown at the mainmast as high as possible.

Lifeboats of hospital ships, coastal lifeboats and all small craft used by the Medical Service shall be painted white with dark red crosses prominently displayed and shall, in general, comply with the identification system prescribed above for hospital ships.

The above-mentioned ships and craft, which may wish to ensure by night and in times of reduced visibility the protection to which they are entitled, must, subject to the assent of the Party to the conflict under whose power they are, take the necessary measures to render their painting and distinctive emblems sufficiently apparent.

Hospital ships which, in accordance with Article 31, are provisionally detained by the enemy, must haul down the flag of the Party to the conflict in whose service they are or whose direction they have accepted.

Coastal lifeboats, if they continue to operate with the consent of the Occupying Power from a base which is occupied, may be allowed, when away from their base, to continue to fly their own national colours along with a flag carrying a red cross on a white ground, subject to prior notification to all the Parties to the conflict concerned.

All the provisions in this Article relating to the red cross shall apply equally to the other emblems mentioned in Article 41.

Parties to the conflict shall at all times endeavour to conclude mutual agreements, in order to use the most modern methods available to facilitate the identification of hospital ships.

Article 44

The distinguishing signs referred to in Article 43 can only be used, whether in time of peace or war, for indicating or protecting the ships therein mentioned, except as may be provided in any other international Convention or by agreement between all the Parties to the conflict concerned.

Article 45

The High Contracting Parties shall, if their legislation is not already adequate, take the measures necessary for the prevention and repression, at all times, of any abuse of the distinctive signs provided for under Article 43.

CHAPTER VII — *Execution of the Convention*

Article 46

Each Party to the conflict, acting through its Commanders-in-Chief, shall ensure the detailed execution of the preceding Articles and provide for unforeseen cases, in conformity with the general principles of the present Convention.

Article 47

Reprisals against the wounded, sick and shipwrecked persons, the personnel, the vessels or the equipment protected by the Convention are prohibited.

Article 48

The High Contracting Parties undertake, in time of peace as in time of war, to disseminate the text of the present Convention as widely as possible in their respective countries, and, in particular, to include the study thereof in their programmes of military and, if possible, civil instruction, so that the principles thereof may become known to the entire population, in particular to the armed fighting forces, the medical personnel and the chaplains.

Article 49

The High Contracting Parties shall communicate to one another through the Swiss Federal Council and, during hostilities, through the Protecting Powers, the official translations of the present Convention, as well as the laws and regulations which they may adopt to ensure the application thereof.

CHAPTER VIII — *Repression of Abuses and Infractions*

Article 50

The High Contracting Parties undertake to enact any legislation necessary to provide effective penal sanctions for persons committing, or ordering to be committed, any of the grave breaches of the present Convention defined in the following Article.

Each High Contracting Party shall be under the obligation to search for persons alleged to have committed, or to have ordered to be committed, such grave breaches, and shall bring such persons, regardless of their nationality, before its own courts. It may also, if it prefers, and in accordance with the provisions of its own legislation, hand such persons over for trial to another High Contracting Party concerned, provided such High Contracting Party has made out a *prima facie* case.

Each High Contracting Party shall take measures necessary for the suppression of all acts contrary to the provisions of the present Convention other than the grave breaches defined in the following Article.

In all circumstances, the accused persons shall benefit by safeguards of proper trial and defence, which shall not be less favourable than those provided by Article 105 and those following of the Geneva Convention relative to the Treatment of Prisoners of War of August 12, 1949.

Article 51

Grave breaches to which the preceding Article relates shall be those involving any of the following acts, if committed against persons or property protected by the Convention: wilful killing, torture or inhuman treatment, including biological experiments, wilfully causing great suffering or serious injury to body or health, and extensive destruction and appropriation of property, not justified by military necessity and carried out unlawfully and wantonly.

Article 52

No High Contracting Party shall be allowed to absolve itself or any other High Contracting Party of any liability incurred by itself or by another High Contracting Party in respect of breaches referred to in the preceding Article.

Article 53

At the request of a Party to the conflict, an enquiry shall be instituted, in a manner to be decided between the interested Parties, concerning any alleged violation of the Convention.

If agreement has not been reached concerning the procedure for the enquiry, the Parties should agree on the choice of an umpire, who will decide upon the procedure to be followed.

Once the violation has been established, the Parties to the conflict shall put an end to it and shall repress it with the least possible delay.

FINAL PROVISIONS

Article 54

The present Convention is established in English and in French. Both texts are equally authentic.

The Swiss Federal Council shall arrange for official translations of the Convention to be made in the Russian and Spanish languages.

Article 55

The present Convention, which bears the date of this day, is open to signature until February 12, 1950, in the name of the Powers represented at the Conference which opened at Geneva on April 21, 1949; furthermore, by Powers not represented at that Conference, but which are parties to the Xth Hague Convention of October 18, 1907, for the adaptation to Maritime Warfare of the principles of the Geneva Convention of 1906, or to the Geneva Conventions of 1864, 1906 or 1929 for the Relief of the Wounded and Sick in Armies in the Field.

Article 56

The present Convention shall be ratified as soon as possible and the ratifications shall be deposited at Berne.

A record shall be drawn up of the deposit of each instrument of ratification and certified copies of this record shall be transmitted by the Swiss Federal Council to all the Powers in whose name the Convention has been signed, or whose accession has been notified.

Article 57

The present Convention shall come into force six months after not less than two instruments of ratification have been deposited.

Thereafter, it shall come into force for each High Contracting Party six months after the deposit of the instrument of ratification.

Article 58

The present Convention replaces the Xth Hague Convention of October 18, 1907, for the adaptation to Maritime Warfare of the principles of the Geneva Convention of 1906, in relations between the High Contracting Parties.

Article 59

From the date of its coming into force, it shall be open to any Power in whose name the present Convention has not been signed, to accede to this Convention.

Article 60

Accessions shall be notified in writing to the Swiss Federal Council, and shall take effect six months after the date on which they are received.

The Swiss Federal Council shall communicate the accessions to all the Powers in whose name the Convention has been signed, or whose accession has been notified.

Article 61

The situations provided for in Articles 2 and 3 shall give immediate effect to ratifications deposited and accessions notified by the Parties to the conflict before or after the beginning of hostilities or occupation. The Swiss Federal Council shall communicate by the quickest method any ratifications or accessions received from Parties to the conflict.

Article 62

Each of the High Contracting Parties shall be at liberty to denounce the present Convention.

The denunciation shall be notified in writing to the Swiss Federal Council, which shall transmit it to the Governments of all the High Contracting Parties.

The denunciation shall take effect one year after the notification thereof has been made to the Swiss Federal Council. However, a denunciation of which notification has been made at a time when the denouncing Power is involved in a conflict shall not take effect until peace has been concluded, and until after operations connected with the release and repatriation of the persons protected by the present Convention have been terminated.

The denunciation shall have effect only in respect of the denouncing Power. It shall in no way impair the obligations which the Parties to the conflict shall remain bound to fulfil by virtue of the principles of the law of nations, as they result from the usages established among civilized peoples, from the laws of humanity and the dictates of the public conscience.

Article 63

The Swiss Federal Council shall register the present Convention with the Secretariat of the United Nations. The Swiss Federal Council shall also inform the Secretariat of the United Nations of all ratifications, accessions and denunciations received by it with respect to the present Convention.

IN WITNESS WHEREOF the undersigned, having deposited their respective full powers, have signed the present Convention.

DONE at Geneva this twelfth day of August 1949, in the English and French languages. The original shall be deposited in the Archives of the Swiss Confederation. The Swiss Federal Council shall transmit certified copies thereof to each of the signatory and acceding States.

[Annex omitted]

CONCLUDING NOTES

The concluding notes for 1949 Geneva Convention II are combined with those for the other three 1949 Geneva Conventions and are to be found after the end of 1949 Geneva Convention IV, below, p. 326.

20. 1949 Geneva Convention III Relative to the Treatment of Prisoners of War

PREFATORY NOTE

The treatment of prisoners of war is one question with which the laws of war have traditionally been particularly concerned. The issue was formally considered at the Brussels Conference of 1874. Twelve articles in the 1874 Brussels Declaration established a regime governing prisoners of war; and although the Declaration was not ratified and did not enter into force, its provisions found expression in subsequent international agreements.

At the Hague Peace Conferences of 1899 and 1907 further consideration was given to the matter, and seventeen articles relating to prisoners of war were included in the Regulations annexed to both 1899 Hague Convention II and 1907 Hague Convention IV. (There were also some articles relevant to prisoners of war in some of the other 1907 Hague Conventions.)

During the First World War the incompleteness and the lack of precision of the seventeen articles in the Hague Regulations became apparent. These deficiencies were partly overcome by special agreements reached between belligerents in 1917 and 1918. In 1921, the 10th International Conference of the Red Cross held in Geneva (the first such conference held after the First World War) recommended that a convention on the treatment of prisoners of war be adopted.

In 1929 the Swiss government convened a diplomatic conference in Geneva partly for the purpose of adopting a convention on prisoners of war (and partly to revise the 1906 Geneva Convention on wounded and sick). The conference considered a draft convention prepared by the ICRC, and adopted the 1929 Geneva Convention Relative to the Treatment of Prisoners of War. The 1929 Geneva Convention supplemented rather than replaced the provisions on prisoners of war contained in the Hague Regulations of 1899 and 1907.

Before the Second World War there were efforts to improve the protection afforded to prisoners of war under the 1929 Geneva Convention. The events of the Second World War showed that, valuable as the 1929 Convention undoubtedly was for countless prisoners, it nevertheless required revision in many areas. For example, there was a need to broaden the categories of person entitled to prisoner-of-war status. After the war, as indicated in the general prefatory note to the four Geneva Conventions, the process of drafting a new agreement got under way.

1949 Geneva Convention III represents a greatly enlarged version of the 1929 Geneva Convention on prisoners of war, which it replaced as between parties to both agreements. Some provisions are much more explicit and comprehensive than in the earlier convention; other provisions are a logical development of those in the earlier convention; and still other provisions represent entirely new regulations which address previously unregulated problems or which depart from earlier rules which no longer retained their validity. A major controversy relating to the 1949 Convention, arising particularly after the Korean and Vietnam Wars, has been the long-standing question of repatriating prisoners of war against their will at the conclusion of hostilities.

Date of signature: Signed on 12 August 1949, and open for signature (see Article 136) until 12 February 1950.
Entry into force: 21 October 1950
Depositary: Switzerland
Authentic languages: English and French
Text reprinted from: *Final Record of the Diplomatic Conference of Geneva of 1949*, Federal Political Department, Berne, n.d., vol. 1, pp. 243–76
Also published in: 75 *UNTS* (1950) 135–285 (Eng. Fr.);
                            157 *BFSP* (1950) 284–355 (Eng.);
                            UKTS 39 (1958), Cmnd. 550 (Eng. Fr.);
                            XXXII *UKPP* (1958–1959) 11 (Eng. Fr.);
                            47 *AJIL* (1953) Supplement 119–177 (Eng.)

Geneva Convention Relative to the Treatment of Prisoners of War of August 12, 1949

The undersigned Plenipotentiaries of the Governments represented at the Diplomatic Conference held at Geneva from April 21 to August 12, 1949, for the purpose of revising the Convention concluded at Geneva on July 27, 1929, relative to the Treatment of Prisoners of War, have agreed as follows:

PART I – GENERAL PROVISIONS

Article 1

The High Contracting Parties undertake to respect and to ensure respect for the present Convention in all circumstances.

Article 2

In addition to the provisions which shall be implemented in peace time, the present Convention shall apply to all cases of declared war or of any other armed conflict which may arise between two or more of the High Contracting Parties, even if the state of war is not recognized by one of them.

The Convention shall also apply to all cases of partial or total occupation of the territory of a High Contracting Party, even if the said occupation meets with no armed resistance.

Although one of the Powers in conflict may not be a party to the present Convention, the Powers who are parties thereto shall remain bound by it in their mutual relations. They shall futhermore be bound by the Convention in relation to the said Power, if the latter accepts and applies the provisions thereof.

Article 3

In the case of armed conflict not of an international character occurring in the territory of one of the High Contracting Parties, each Party to the conflict shall be bound to apply, as a minimum, the following provisions:

(1) Persons taking no active part in the hostilities, including members of armed forces who have laid down their arms and those placed *hors de combat* by sickness, wounds, detention, or any other cause, shall in all circumstances be treated humanely, without any adverse distinction founded on race, colour, religion or faith, sex, birth or wealth, or any other similar criteria.

   To this end, the following acts are and shall remain prohibited at any time and in any place whatsoever with respect to the above-mentioned persons:

   (a) violence to life and person, in particular murder of all kinds, mutilation, cruel treatment and torture;

   (b) taking of hostages;

   (c) outrages upon personal dignity, in particular, humiliating and degrading treatment;

   (d) the passing of sentences and the carrying out of executions without previous judgment pronounced by a regularly constituted court affording all the judicial guarantees which are recognized as indispensable by civilized peoples.

(2) The wounded and sick shall be collected and cared for.

An impartial humanitarian body, such as the International Committee of the Red Cross, may offer its services to the Parties to the conflict.

The Parties to the conflict should further endeavour to bring into force, by means of special agreements, all or part of the other provisions of the present Convention.

The application of the preceding provisions shall not affect the legal status of the Parties to the conflict.

Article 4

A. Prisoners of war, in the sense of the present Convention, are persons belonging to one of the following categories, who have fallen into the power of the enemy:

(1) Members of the armed forces of a Party to the conflict as well as members of militias or volunteer corps forming part of such armed forces.

(2) Members of other militias and members of other volunteer corps, including those of organized resistance movements, belonging to a Party to the conflict and operating in or outside their own territory, even if this territory is occupied, provided that such militias or volunteer corps, including such organized resistance movements, fulfil the following conditions:

(*a*) that of being commanded by a person responsible for his subordinates;

(*b*) that of having a fixed distinctive sign recognizable at a distance;

(*c*) that of carrying arms openly;

(*d*) that of conducting their operations in accordance with the laws and customs of war.

(3) Members of regular armed forces who profess allegiance to a government or an authority not recognized by the Detaining Power.

(4) Persons who accompany the armed forces without actually being members thereof, such as civilian members of military aircraft crews, war correspondents, supply contractors, members of labour units or of services responsible for the welfare of the armed forces, provided that they have received authorization from the armed forces which they accompany, who shall provide them for that purpose with an identity card similar to the annexed model.

(5) Members of crews, including masters, pilots and apprentices, of the merchant marine and the crews of civil aircraft of the Parties to the conflict, who do not benefit by more favourable treatment under any other provisions of international law.

(6) Inhabitants of a non-occupied territory, who on the approach of the enemy spontaneously take up arms to resist the invading forces, without having had time to form themselves into regular armed units, provided they carry arms openly and respect the laws and customs of war.

B. The following shall likewise be treated as prisoners of war under the present Convention:

(1) Persons belonging, or having belonged, to the armed forces of the occupied country, if the occupying Power considers it necessary by reason of such allegiance to intern them, even though it has originally liberated them while hostilities were going on outside the territory it occupies, in particular where such persons have made an unsuccessful attempt to rejoin the armed forces to which they belong and which

are engaged in combat, or where they fail to comply with a summons made to them with a view to internment.

(2) The persons belonging to one of the categories enumerated in the present Article, who have been received by neutral or non-belligerent Powers on their territory and whom these Powers are required to intern under international law, without prejudice to any more favourable treatment which these Powers may choose to give and with the exception of Articles 8, 10, 15, 30, fifth paragraph, 58–67, 92, 126 and, where diplomatic relations exist between the Parties to the conflict and the neutral or non-belligerent Power concerned, those Articles concerning the Protecting Power. Where such diplomatic relations exist, the Parties to a conflict on whom these persons depend shall be allowed to perform towards them the functions of a Protecting Power as provided in the present Convention, without prejudice to the functions which these Parties normally exercise in conformity with diplomatic and consular usage and treaties.

C. This Article shall in no way affect the status of medical personnel and chaplains as provided for in Article 33 of the present Convention.

Article 5

The present Convention shall apply to the persons referred to in Article 4 from the time they fall into the power of the enemy and until their final release and repatriation.

Should any doubt arise as to whether persons, having committed a belligerent act and having fallen into the hands of the enemy, belong to any of the categories enumerated in Article 4, such persons shall enjoy the protection of the present Convention until such time as their status has been determined by a competent tribunal.

Article 6

In addition to the agreements expressly provided for in Articles 10, 23, 28, 33, 60, 65, 66, 67, 72, 73, 75, 109, 110, 118, 119, 122 and 132, the High Contracting Parties may conclude other special agreements for all matters concerning which they may deem it suitable to make separate provision. No special agreement shall adversely affect the situation of prisoners of war, as defined by the present Convention, nor restrict the rights which it confers upon them.

Prisoners of war shall continue to have the benefit of such agreements as long as the Convention is applicable to them, except where express provisions to the contrary are contained in the aforesaid or in subsequent agreements, or where more favourable measures have been taken with regard to them by one or other of the Parties to the conflict.

Article 7

Prisoners of war may in no circumstances renounce in part or in entirety the rights secured to them by the present Convention, and by the special agreements referred to in the foregoing Article, if such there be.

Article 8

The present Convention shall be applied with the cooperation and under the scrutiny of the Protecting Powers whose duty it is to safeguard the interests of the Parties to the conflict. For this purpose, the Protecting Powers may appoint, apart from their diplomatic or consular staff, delegates from amongst their own nationals or the nationals of other neutral Powers. The said delegates shall be subject to the approval of the Power with which they are to carry out their duties.

The Parties to the conflict shall facilitate to the greatest extent possible the task of the representatives or delegates of the Protecting Powers.

The representatives or delegates of the Protecting Powers shall not in any case exceed their mission under the present Convention. They shall, in particular, take account of the imperative necessities of security of the State wherein they carry out their duties.

Article 9

The provisions of the present Convention constitute no obstacle to the humanitarian activities which the International Committee of the Red Cross or any other impartial humanitarian organization may, subject to the consent of the Parties to the conflict concerned, undertake for the protection of prisoners of war and for their relief.

Article 10

The High Contracting Parties may at any time agree to entrust to an organization which offers all guarantees of impartiality and efficacy the duties incumbent on the Protecting Powers by virtue of the present Convention.

When prisoners of war do not benefit or cease to benefit, no matter for what reason, by the activities of a Protecting Power or of an organization provided for in the first paragraph above, the Detaining Power shall request a neutral State, or such an organization, to undertake the functions performed under the present Convention by a Protecting Power designated by the Parties to a conflict.

If protection cannot be arranged accordingly, the Detaining Power shall request or shall accept, subject to the provisions of this Article, the offer of the services of a humanitarian organization, such as the International Committee of the Red Cross, to assume the humanitarian functions performed by Protecting Powers under the present Convention.

Any neutral Power or any organization invited by the Power concerned or offering itself for these purposes, shall be required to act with a sense of responsibility towards the Party to the conflict on which persons protected by the present Convention depend, and shall be required to furnish sufficient assurances that it is in a position to undertake the appropriate functions and to discharge them impartially.

No derogation from the preceding provisions shall be made by special agreements between Powers one of which is restricted, even temporarily, in its freedom to negotiate with the other Power or its allies by reason of military events, more particularly where the whole, or a substantial part, of the territory of the said Power is occupied.

Whenever in the present Convention mention is made of a Protecting Power, such mention applies to substitute organizations in the sense of the present Article.

Article 11

In cases where they deem it advisable in the interest of protected persons, particularly in cases of disagreement between the Parties to the conflict as to the application or interpretation of the provisions of the present Convention, the Protecting Powers shall lend their good offices with a view to settling the disagreement.

For this purpose, each of the Protecting Powers may, either at the invitation of one Party or on its own initiative, propose to the Parties to the conflict a meeting of their representatives, and in particular of the authorities responsible for prisoners of war, possibly on neutral territory suitably chosen. The Parties to the conflict shall be bound to give effect to the proposals made to them for this purpose. The Protecting Powers may, if necessary, propose for approval by the Parties to the conflict a person belonging to a neutral Power, or delegated by the International Committee of the Red Cross, who shall be invited to take part in such a meeting.

PART II — GENERAL PROTECTION OF PRISONERS OF WAR

Article 12

Prisoners of war are in the hands of the enemy Power, but not of the individuals or military units who have captured them. Irrespective of the individual responsibilities that may exist, the Detaining Power is responsible for the treatment given them.

Prisoners of war may only be transferred by the Detaining Power to a Power which is a party to the Convention and after the Detaining Power has satisfied itself of the willingness and ability of such transferee Power to apply the Convention. When prisoners of war are transferred under such circumstances, responsibility for the application of the Convention rests on the Power accepting them while they are in its custody.

Nevertheless, if that Power fails to carry out the provisions of the Convention in any important respect, the Power by whom the prisoners of war were transferred shall, upon being notified by the Protecting Power, take effective measures to correct the situation or shall request the return of the prisoners of war. Such requests must be complied with.

Article 13

Prisoners of war must at all times be humanely treated. Any unlawful act or omission by the Detaining Power causing death or seriously endangering the health of a prisoner of war in its custody is prohibited, and will be regarded as a serious breach of the present Convention. In particular, no prisoner of war may be subjected to physical mutilation or to medical or scientific experiments of any kind which are not justified by the medical, dental or hospital treatment of the prisoner concerned and carried out in his interest.

Likewise, prisoners of war must at all times be protected, particularly against acts of violence or intimidation and against insults and public curiosity.

Measures of reprisal against prisoners of war are prohibited.

Article 14

Prisoners of war are entitled in all circumstances to respect for their persons and their honour.

Women shall be treated with all the regard due to their sex and shall in all cases benefit by treatment as favourable as that granted to men.

Prisoners of war shall retain the full civil capacity which they enjoyed at the time of their capture. The Detaining Power may not restrict the exercise, either within or without its own territory, of the rights such capacity confers except in so far as the captivity requires.

Article 15

The Power detaining prisoners of war shall be bound to provide free of charge for their maintenance and for the medical attention required by their state of health.

Article 16

Taking into consideration the provisions of the present Convention relating to rank and sex, and subject to any privileged treatment which may be accorded to them by reason of their state of health, age or professional qualifications, all prisoners of war shall be treated alike by the Detaining Power, without any adverse distinction based on race, nationality, religious belief or political opinions, or any other distinction founded on similar criteria.

PART III — CAPTIVITY

Section I — Beginning of Captivity

Article 17

Every prisoner of war, when questioned on the subject, is bound to give only his surname, first names and rank, date of birth, and army, regimental, personal or serial number, or failing this, equivalent information.

If he wilfully infringes this rule, he may render himself liable to a restriction of the privileges accorded to his rank or status.

Each Party to a conflict is required to furnish the persons under its jurisdiction who are liable to become prisoners of war, with an identity card showing the owner's surname, first names, rank, army, regimental, personal or serial number or equivalent information, and date of birth. The identity card may, furthermore, bear the signature or the fingerprints, or both, of the owner, and may bear, as well, any other information the Party to the conflict may wish to add concerning persons belonging to its armed forces. As far as possible the card shall measure 6.5 × 10 cm. and shall be issued in duplicate. The identity card shall be shown by the prisoner of war upon demand, but may in no case be taken away from him.

No physical or mental torture, nor any other form of coercion, may be inflicted on prisoners of war to secure from them information of any kind whatever. Prisoners of war who refuse to answer may not be threatened, insulted, or exposed to unpleasant or disadvantageous treatment of any kind.

Prisoners of war who, owing to their physical or mental condition, are unable to state their identity, shall be handed over to the medical service. The identity of such prisoners shall be established by all possible means, subject to the provisions of the preceding paragraph.

The questioning of prisoners of war shall be carried out in a language which they understand.

Article 18

All effects and articles of personal use, except arms, horses, military equipment and military documents, shall remain in the possession of prisoners of war, likewise their metal helmets and gas masks and like articles issued for personal protection. Effects and articles used for their clothing or feeding shall likewise remain in their possession, even if such effects and articles belong to their regulation military equipment.

At no time should prisoners of war be without identity documents. The Detaining Power shall supply such documents to prisoners of war who possess none.

Badges of rank and nationality, decorations and articles having above all a personal or sentimental value may not be taken from prisoners of war.

Sums of money carried by prisoners of war may not be taken away from them except by order of an officer, and after the amount and particulars of the owner have been recorded in a special register and an itemized receipt has been given, legibly inscribed with the name, rank and unit of the person issuing the said receipt. Sums in the currency of the Detaining Power, or which are changed into such currency at the prisoner's request, shall be placed to the credit of the prisoner's account as provided in Article 64.

The Detaining Power may withdraw articles of value from prisoners of war only for reasons of security; when such articles are withdrawn, the procedure laid down for sums of money impounded shall apply.

Such objects, likewise sums taken away in any currency other than that of the Detaining Power and the conversion of which has not been asked for by the owners, shall be kept in the custody of the Detaining Power and shall be returned in their initial shape to prisoners of war at the end of their captivity.

Article 19

Prisoners of war shall be evacuated, as soon as possible after their capture, to camps situated in an area far enough from the combat zone for them to be out of danger.

Only those prisoners of war who, owing to wounds or sickness, would run greater risks by being evacuated than by remaining where they are, may be temporarily kept back in a danger zone.

Prisoners of war shall not be unnecessarily exposed to danger while awaiting evacuation from a fighting zone.

Article 20

The evacuation of prisoners of war shall always be effected humanely and in conditions similar to those for the forces of the Detaining Power in their changes of station.

The Detaining Power shall supply prisoners of war who are being evacuated with sufficient food and potable water, and with the necessary clothing and medical attention. The Detaining Power shall take all suitable precautions to ensure their safety during evacuation, and shall establish as soon as possible a list of the prisoners of war who are evacuated.

If prisoners of war must, during evacuation, pass through transit camps, their stay in such camps shall be as brief as possible.

SECTION II — INTERNMENT OF PRISONERS OF WAR

CHAPTER I — *General Observations*

Article 21

The Detaining Power may subject prisoners of war to internment. It may impose on them the obligation of not leaving, beyond certain limits, the camp where they are interned, or if the said camp is fenced in, of not going outside its perimeter. Subject to the provisions of the present Convention relative to penal and disciplinary sanctions, prisoners of war may not be held in close confinement except where necessary to safeguard their health and then only during the continuation of the circumstances which make such confinement necessary.

Prisoners of war may be partially or wholly released on parole or promise, in so far as is allowed by the laws of the Power on which they depend. Such measures shall be taken particularly in cases where this may contribute to the improvement of their state of health. No prisoner of war shall be compelled to accept liberty on parole or promise.

Upon the outbreak of hostilities, each Party to the conflict shall notify the adverse Party of the laws and regulations allowing or forbidding its own nationals to accept liberty on parole or promise. Prisoners of war who are paroled or who have given their promise in conformity with the laws and regulations so notified, are bound on their personal honour scrupulously to fulfil, both towards the

Power on which they depend and towards the Power which has captured them, the engagements of their paroles or promises. In such cases, the Power on which they depend is bound neither to require nor to accept from them any service incompatible with the parole or promise given.

Article 22

Prisoners of war may be interned only in premises located on land and affording every guarantee of hygiene and healthfulness. Except in particular cases which are justified by the interest of the prisoners themselves, they shall not be interned in penitentiaries.

Prisoners of war interned in unhealthy areas, or where the climate is injurious for them, shall be removed as soon as possible to a more favourable climate.

The Detaining Power shall assemble prisoners of war in camps or camp compounds according to their nationality, language and customs, provided that such prisoners shall not be separated from prisoners of war belonging to the armed forces with which they were serving at the time of their capture, except with their consent.

Article 23

No prisoner of war may at any time be sent to, or detained in areas where he may be exposed to the fire of the combat zone, nor may his presence be used to render certain points or areas immune from military operations.

Prisoners of war shall have shelters against air bombardment and other hazards of war, to the same extent as the local civilian population. With the exception of those engaged in the protection of their quarters against the aforesaid hazards, they may enter such shelters as soon as possible after the giving of the alarm. Any other protective measure taken in favour of the population shall also apply to them.

Detaining Powers shall give the Powers concerned, through the intermediary of the Protecting Powers, all useful information regarding the geographical location of prisoner of war camps.

Whenever military considerations permit, prisoner of war camps shall be indicated in the day-time by the letters PW or PG, placed so as to be clearly visible from the air. The Powers concerned may, however, agree upon any other system or marking. Only prisoner of war camps shall be marked as such.

Article 24

Transit or screening camps of a permanent kind shall be fitted out under conditions similar to those described in the present Section, and the prisoners therein shall have the same treatment as in other camps.

CHAPTER II — *Quarters, Food and Clothing of Prisoners of War*

Article 25

Prisoners of war shall be quartered under conditions as favourable as those for the forces of the Detaining Power who are billeted in the same area. The said conditions shall make allowance for the habits and customs of the prisoners and shall in no case be prejudicial to their health.

The foregoing provisions shall apply in particular to the dormitories of prisoners of war as regards both total surface and minimum cubic space, and the general installations, bedding and blankets.

The premises provided for the use of prisoners of war individually or collectively, shall be entirely protected from dampness and adequately heated and lighted, in particular between dusk and lights out. All precautions must be taken against the danger of fire.

In any camps in which women prisoners of war, as well as men, are accommodated, separate dormitories shall be provided for them.

Article 26

The basic daily food rations shall be sufficient in quantity, quality and variety to keep prisoners of war in good health and to prevent loss of weight or the development of nutritional deficiencies. Account shall also be taken of the habitual diet of the prisoners.

The Detaining Power shall supply prisoners of war who work with such additional rations as are necessary for the labour on which they are employed.

Sufficient drinking water shall be supplied to prisoners of war. The use of tobacco shall be permitted.

Prisoners of war shall, as far as possible, be associated with the preparation of their meals; they may be employed for that purpose in the kitchens. Furthermore, they shall be given the means of preparing, themselves, the additional food in their possession.

Adequate premises shall be provided for messing.

Collective disciplinary measures affecting food are prohibited.

Article 27

Clothing, underwear and footwear shall be supplied to prisoners of war in sufficient quantities by the Detaining Power, which shall make allowance for the climate of the region where the prisoners are detained. Uniforms of enemy armed forces captured by the Detaining Power should, if suitable for the climate, be made available to clothe prisoners of war.

The regular replacement and repair of the above articles shall be assured by the Detaining Power. In addition, prisoners of war who work shall receive appropriate clothing, wherever the nature of the work demands.

Article 28

Canteens shall be installed in all camps, where prisoners of war may procure foodstuffs, soap and tobacco and ordinary articles in daily use. The tariff shall never be in excess of local market prices.

The profits made by camp canteens shall be used for the benefit of the prisoners; a special fund shall be created for this purpose. The prisoners' representative shall have the right to collaborate in the management of the canteen and of this fund.

When a camp is closed down, the credit balance of the special fund shall be handed to an international welfare organization, to be employed for the benefit of prisoners of war of the same nationality as those who have contributed to the fund. In case of a general repatriation, such profits shall be kept by the Detaining Power, subject to any agreement to the contrary between the Powers concerned.

CHAPTER III — *Hygiene and Medical Attention*

Article 29

The Detaining Power shall be bound to take all sanitary measures necessary to ensure the cleanliness and heathfulness of camps and to prevent epidemics.

Prisoners of war shall have for their use, day and night, conveniences which conform to the rules of hygiene and are maintained in a constant state of cleanliness. In any camps in which women prisoners of war are accommodated, separate conveniences shall be provided for them.

Also, apart from the baths and showers with which the camps shall be furnished, prisoners of war shall be provided with sufficient water and soap for their personal toilet and for washing their personal laundry; the necessary installations, facilities and time shall be granted them for that purpose.

Article 30

Every camp shall have an adequate infirmary where prisoners of war may have the attention they require, as well as appropriate diet. Isolation wards shall, if necessary, be set aside for cases of contagious or mental disease.

Prisoners of war suffering from serious disease, or whose condition necessitates special treatment, a surgical operation or hospital care, must be admitted to any military or civil medical unit where such treatment can be given, even if their repatriation is contemplated in the near future. Special facilities shall be afforded for the care to be given to the disabled, in particular to the blind, and for their rehabilitation, pending repatriation.

Prisoners of war shall have the attention, preferably, of medical personnel of the Power on which they depend and, if possible, of their nationality.

Prisoners of war may not be prevented from presenting themselves to the medical authorities for examination. The detaining authorities shall, upon request, issue to every prisoner who has undergone treatment, an official certificate indicating the nature of his illness or injury, and the duration and kind of treatment received. A duplicate of this certificate shall be forwarded to the Central Prisoners of War Agency.

The costs of treatment, including those of any apparatus necessary for the maintenance of prisoners of war in good health, particularly dentures and other artificial appliances, and spectacles, shall be borne by the Detaining Power.

Article 31

Medical inspections of prisoners of war shall be held at least once a month. They shall include the checking and the recording of the weight of each prisoner of war. Their purpose shall be, in particular, to supervise the general state of health, nutrition and cleanliness of prisoners and to detect contagious diseases, especially tuberculosis, malaria and venereal disease. For this purpose the most efficient methods available shall be employed, e.g. periodic mass miniature radiography for the early detection of tuberculosis.

Article 32

Prisoners of war who, though not attached to the medical service of their armed forces, are physicians, surgeons, dentists, nurses or medical orderlies, may be required by the Detaining Power to exercise their medical functions in the interests of prisoners of war dependent on the same Power. In that case they shall continue to be prisoners of war, but shall receive the same treatment as corresponding medical personnel retained by the Detaining Power. They shall be exempted from any other work under Article 49.

CHAPTER IV — *Medical Personnel and Chaplains Retained
to Assist Prisoners of War*

Article 33

Members of the medical personnel and chaplains while retained
by the Detaining Power with a view to assisting prisoners of war,
shall not be considered as prisoners of war. They shall, however,
receive as a minimum the benefits and protection of the present
Convention, and shall also be granted all facilities necessary to
provide for the medical care of, and religious ministration to
prisoners of war.

They shall continue to exercise their medical and spiritual functions for the benefit of prisoners of war, preferably those belonging
to the armed forces upon which they depend, within the scope
of the military laws and regulations of the Detaining Power and
under the control of its competent services, in accordance with
their professional etiquette. They shall also benefit by the following
facilities in the exercise of their medical or spiritual functions:

(a) They shall be authorized to visit periodically prisoners of
war situated in working detachments or in hospitals outside
the camp. For this purpose, the Detaining Power shall place
at their disposal the necessary means of transport.

(b) The senior medical officer in each camp shall be responsible
to the camp military authorities for everything connected
with the activities of retained medical personnel. For this
purpose, Parties to the conflict shall agree at the outbreak
of hostilities on the subject of the corresponding ranks of the
medical personnel, including that of societies mentioned in
Article 26 of the Geneva Convention for the Amelioration
of the Condition of the Wounded and Sick in Armed Forces
in the Field of August 12, 1949. This senior medical officer,
as well as chaplains, shall have the right to deal with the
competent authorities of the camp on all questions relating
to their duties. Such authorities shall afford them all necessary facilities for correspondence relating to these questions.

(c) Although they shall be subject to the internal discipline of
the camp in which they are retained, such personnel may not
be compelled to carry out any work other than that concerned with their medical or religious duties.

During hostilities, the Parties to the conflict shall agree concerning
the possible relief of retained personnel and shall settle the procedure
to be followed.

None of the preceding provisions shall relieve the Detaining Power of its obligations with regard to prisoners of war from the medical or spiritual point of view.

CHAPTER V — *Religious, Intellectual and Physical Activities*

Article 34

Prisoners of war shall enjoy complete latitude in the exercise of their religious duties, including attendance at the service of their faith, on condition that they comply with the disciplinary routine prescribed by the military authorities.

Adequate premises shall be provided where religious services may be held.

Article 35

Chaplains who fall into the hands of the enemy Power and who remain or are retained with a view to assisting prisoners of war, shall be allowed to minister to them and to exercise freely their ministry amongst prisoners of war of the same religion, in accordance with their religious conscience. They shall be allocated among the various camps and labour detachments containing prisoners of war belonging to the same forces, speaking the same language or practising the same religion. They shall enjoy the necessary facilities, including the means of transport provided for in Article 33, for visiting the prisoners of war outside their camp. They shall be free to correspond, subject to censorship, on matters concerning their religious duties with the ecclesiastical authorities in the country of detention and with international religious organizations. Letters and cards which they may send for this purpose shall be in addition to the quota provided for in Article 71.

Article 36

Prisoners of war who are ministers of religion, without having officiated as chaplains to their own forces, shall be at liberty, whatever their denomination, to minister freely to the members of their community. For this purpose, they shall receive the same treatment as the chaplains retained by the Detaining Power. They shall not be obliged to do any other work.

Article 37

When prisoners of war have not the assistance of a retained chaplain or of a prisoner of war minister of their faith, a minister belonging to the prisoners' or a similar denomination, or in his absence a qualified layman, if such a course is feasible from a confessional point of view, shall be appointed, at the request of the prisoners concerned, to fill this office. This appointment, subject to the approval of the Detaining Power, shall take place with the agreement of the community of prisoners concerned and, wherever necessary, with the approval of the local religious authorities of the same faith. The person thus appointed shall comply with all regulations established by the Detaining Power in the interests of discipline and military security.

Article 38

While respecting the individual preferences of every prisoner, the Detaining Power shall encourage the practice of intellectual, educational, and recreational pursuits, sports and games amongst prisoners, and shall take the measures necessary to ensure the exercise thereof by providing them with adequate premises and necessary equipment.

Prisoners shall have opportunities for taking physical exercise including sports and games and for being out of doors. Sufficient open spaces shall be provided for this purpose in all camps.

CHAPTER VI – *Discipline*

Article 39

Every prisoner of war camp shall be put under the immediate authority of a responsible commissioned officer belonging to the regular armed forces of the Detaining Power. Such officer shall have in his possession a copy of the present Convention; he shall ensure that its provisions are known to the camp staff and the guard and shall be responsible, under the direction of his government, for its application.

Prisoners of war, with the exception of officers, must salute and show to all officers of the Detaining Power the external marks of respect provided for by the regulations applying in their own forces.

Officer prisoners of war are bound to salute only officers of a higher rank of the Detaining Power; they must, however, salute the camp commander regardless of his rank.

Article 40

The wearing of badges of rank and nationality, as well as of decorations, shall be permitted.

Article 41

In every camp the text of the present Convention and its Annexes and the contents of any special agreement provided for in Article 6, shall be posted, in the prisoners' own language, in places where all may read them. Copies shall be supplied, on request, to the prisoners who cannot have access to the copy which has been posted.

Regulations, orders, notices and publications of every kind relating to the conduct of prisoners of war shall be issued to them in a language which they understand. Such regulations, orders and publications shall be posted in the manner described above and copies shall be handed to the prisoners' representative. Every order and command addressed to prisoners of war individually must likewise be given in a language which they understand.

Article 42

The use of weapons against prisoners of war, especially against those who are escaping or attempting to escape, shall constitute an extreme measure, which shall always be preceded by warnings appropriate to the circumstances.

CHAPTER VII — *Rank of Prisoners of War*

Article 43

Upon the outbreak of hostilities, the Parties to the conflict shall communicate to one another the titles and ranks of all the persons mentioned in Article 4 of the present Convention, in order to ensure equality of treatment between prisoners of equivalent rank. Titles and ranks which are subsequently created shall form the subject of similar communications.

The Detaining Power shall recognize promotions in rank which have been accorded to prisoners of war and which have been duly notified by the Power on which these prisoners depend.

Article 44

Officers and prisoners of equivalent status shall be treated with the regard due to their rank and age.

In order to ensure service in officers' camps, other ranks of the same armed forces who, as far as possible, speak the same language, shall be assigned in sufficient numbers, account being taken of the rank of officers and prisoners of equivalent status. Such orderlies shall not be required to perform any other work.

Supervision of the mess by the officers themselves shall be facilitated in every way.

Article 45

Prisoners of war other than officers and prisoners of equivalent status shall be treated with the regard due to their rank and age.

Supervision of the mess by the prisoners themselves shall be facilitated in every way.

CHAPTER VIII — *Transfer of Prisoners of War After Their Arrival in Camp*

Article 46

The Detaining Power, when deciding upon the transfer of prisoners of war, shall take into account the interests of the prisoners themselves, more especially so as not to increase the difficulty of their repatriation.

The transfer of prisoners of war shall always be effected humanely and in conditions not less favourable than those under which the forces of the Detaining Power are transferred. Account shall always be taken of the climatic conditions to which the prisoners of war are accustomed and the conditions of transfer shall in no case be prejudicial to their health.

The Detaining Power shall supply prisoners of war during transfer with sufficient food and drinking water to keep them in good health, likewise with the necessary clothing, shelter and medical attention. The Detaining Power shall take adequate precautions especially in case of transport by sea or by air, to ensure their safety during transfer, and shall draw up a complete list of all transferred prisoners before their departure.

Article 47

Sick or wounded prisoners of war shall not be transferred as long as their recovery may be endangered by the journey, unless their safety imperatively demands it.

If the combat zone draws closer to a camp, the prisoners of war in the said camp shall not be transferred unless their transfer can be carried out in adequate conditions of safety, or unless they are exposed to greater risks by remaining on the spot than by being transferred.

Article 48

In the event of transfer, prisoners of war shall be officially advised of their departure and of their new postal address. Such notifications shall be given in time for them to pack their luggage and inform their next of kin.

They shall be allowed to take with them their personal effects, and the correspondence and parcels which have arrived for them. The weight of such baggage may be limited, if the conditions of transfer so require, to what each prisoner can reasonably carry, which shall in no case be more than twenty-five kilograms per head.

Mail and parcels addressed to their former camp shall be forwarded to them without delay. The camp commander shall take, in agreement with the prisoners' representative, any measures needed to ensure the transport of the prisoners' community property and of the luggage they are unable to take with them in consequence of restrictions imposed by virtue of the second paragraph of this Article.

The costs of transfers shall be borne by the Detaining Power.

SECTION III — LABOUR OF PRISONERS OF WAR

Article 49.

The Detaining Power may utilize the labour of prisoners of war who are physically fit, taking into account their age, sex, rank and physical aptitude, and with a view particularly to maintaining them in a good state of physical and mental health.

Non-commissioned officers who are prisoners of war shall only be required to do supervisory work. Those not so required may ask for other suitable work which shall, so far as possible, be found for them.

If officers or persons of equivalent status ask for suitable work, it shall be found for them, so far as possible, but they may in no circumstances be compelled to work.

Article 50

Besides work connected with camp administration, installation or maintenance, prisoners of war may be compelled to do only such work as is included in the following classes:

(*a*) agriculture;
(*b*) industries connected with the production or the extraction of raw materials, and manufacturing industries, with the exception of metallurgical, machinery and chemical industries; public works and building operations which have no military character or purpose;
(*c*) transport and handling of stores which are not military in character or purpose;
(*d*) commercial business, and arts and crafts;
(*e*) domestic service;
(*f*) public utility services having no military character or purpose.

Should the above provisions be infringed, prisoners of war shall be allowed to exercise their right of complaint, in conformity with Article 78.

Article 51

Prisoners of war must be granted suitable working conditions, especially as regards accommodation, food, clothing and equipment; such conditions shall not be inferior to those enjoyed by nationals of the Detaining Power employed in similar work; account shall also be taken of climatic conditions.

The Detaining Power, in utilizing the labour of prisoners or war, shall ensure that in areas in which such prisoners are employed, the national legislation concerning the protection of labour, and, more particularly, the regulations for the safety of workers, are duly applied.

Prisoners of war shall receive training and be provided with the means of protection suitable to the work they will have to do and similar to those accorded to the nationals of the Detaining Power. Subject to the provisions of Article 52, prisoners may be submitted to the normal risks run by these civilian workers.

Conditions of labour shall in no case be rendered more arduous by disciplinary measures.

Article 52

Unless he be a volunteer, no prisoner of war may be employed on labour which is of an unhealthy or dangerous nature.

No prisoner of war shall be assigned to labour which would be looked upon as humiliating for a member of the Detaining Power's own forces.

The removal of mines or similar devices shall be considered as dangerous labour.

Article 53

The duration of the daily labour of prisoners of war, including the time of the journey to and fro, shall not be excessive, and must in no case exceed that permitted for civilian workers in the district, who are nationals of the Detaining Power and employed on the same work.

Prisoners of war must be allowed, in the middle of the day's work, a rest of not less than one hour. This rest will be the same as that to which workers of the Detaining Power are entitled, if the latter is of longer duration. They shall be allowed in addition a rest of twenty-four consecutive hours every week, preferably on Sunday or the day of rest in their country of origin. Furthermore, every prisoner who has worked for one year shall be granted a rest of eight consecutive days, during which his working pay shall be paid him.

If methods of labour such as piece work are employed, the length of the working period shall not be rendered excessive thereby.

Article 54

The working pay due to prisoners of war shall be fixed in accordance with the provisions of Article 62 of the present Convention.

Prisoners of war who sustain accidents in connection with work, or who contract a disease in the course, or in consequence of their work, shall receive all the care their condition may require. The Detaining Power shall furthermore deliver to such prisoners of war a medical certificate enabling them to submit their claims to the Power on which they depend, and shall send a duplicate to the Central Prisoners of War Agency provided for in Article 123.

Article 55

The fitness of prisoners of war for work shall be periodically verified by medical examinations at least once a month. The examinations shall have particular regard to the nature of the work which prisoners of war are required to do.

If any prisoner of war considers himself incapable of working, he shall be permitted to appear before the medical authorities of his camp. Physicians or surgeons may recommend that the prisoners who are, in their opinion, unfit for work, be exempted therefrom.

Article 56

The organization and administration of labour detachments shall be similar to those of prisoner of war camps.

Every labour detachment shall remain under the control of and administratively part of a prisoner of war camp. The military authorities and the commander of the said camp shall be responsible, under the direction of their government, for the observance of the provisions of the present Convention in labour detachments.

The camp commander shall keep an up-to-date record of the labour detachments dependent on his camp, and shall communicate it to the delegates of the Protecting Power, of the International Committee of the Red Cross, or of other agencies giving relief to prisoners of war, who may visit the camp.

Article 57

The treatment of prisoners of war who work for private persons, even if the latter are responsible for guarding and protecting them, shall not be inferior to that which is provided for by the present Convention. The Detaining Power, the military authorities and the commander of the camp to which such prisoners belong shall be entirely responsible for the maintenance, care, treatment, and payment of the working pay of such prisoners of war.

Such prisoners of war shall have the right to remain in communication with the prisoners' representatives in the camps on which they depend.

SECTION IV — FINANCIAL RESOURCES OF
PRISONERS OF WAR

Article 58

Upon the outbreak of hostilities, and pending an arrangement on this matter with the Protecting Power, the Detaining Power may determine the maximum amount of money in cash or in any similar form, that prisoners may have in their possession. Any amount in excess, which was properly in their possession and which has been taken or withheld from them, shall be placed to their account, together with any monies deposited by them, and shall not be converted into any other currency without their consent.

If prisoners of war are permitted to purchase services or commodities outside the camp against payment in cash, such payments shall be made by the prisoner himself or by the camp administration who will charge them to the accounts of the prisoners concerned. The Detaining Power will establish the necessary rules in this respect.

Article 59

Cash which was taken from prisoners of war, in accordance with Article 18, at the time of their capture, and which is in the currency of the Detaining Power, shall be placed to their separate accounts, in accordance with the provisions of Article 64 of the present Section.

The amounts, in the currency of the Detaining Power, due to the conversion of sums in other currencies that are taken from the prisoners of war at the same time, shall also be credited to their separate accounts.

Article 60

The Detaining Power shall grant all prisoners of war a monthly advance of pay, the amount of which shall be fixed by conversion, into the currency of the said Power, of the following amounts:

Category I: Prisoners ranking below sergeants: eight Swiss francs.

Category II: Sergeants and other non-commissioned officers, or prisoners of equivalent rank: twelve Swiss francs.

Category III: Warrant officers and commissioned officers below the rank of major or prisoners of equivalent rank: fifty Swiss francs.

Category IV: Majors, lieutenant-colonels, colonels or prisoners of equivalent rank: sixty Swiss francs.

Category V: General officers or prisoners of war of equivalent rank: seventy-five Swiss francs.

However, the Parties to the conflict concerned may by special agreement modify the amount of advances of pay due to prisoners of the preceding categories.

Furthermore, if the amounts indicated in the first paragraph above would be unduly high compared with the pay of the Detaining Power's armed forces or would, for any reason, seriously embarrass the Detaining Power, then, pending the conclusion of a special agreement with the Power on which the prisoners depend to vary the amounts indicated above, the Detaining Power:

(*a*) shall continue to credit the accounts of the prisoners with the amounts indicated in the first paragraph above;

(*b*) may temporarily limit the amount made available from these advances of pay to prisoners of war for their own use, to sums which are reasonable, but which, for Category I, shall never be inferior to the amount that the Detaining Power gives to the members of its own armed forces.

The reasons for any limitations will be given without delay to the Protecting Power.

Article 61

The Detaining Power shall accept for distribution as supplementary pay to prisoners of war sums which the Power on which the prisoners depend may forward to them, on condition that the sums to be paid shall be the same for each prisoner of the same category, shall be payable to all prisoners of that category depending on that Power, and shall be placed in their separate accounts, at the earliest opportunity, in accordance with the provisions of Article 64. Such supplementary pay shall not relieve the Detaining Power of any obligation under this Convention.

Article 62

Prisoners of war shall be paid a fair working rate of pay by the detaining authorities direct. The rate shall be fixed by the said authorities, but shall at no time be less than one-fourth of one Swiss franc for a full working day. The Detaining Power shall inform prisoners of war, as well as the Power on which they depend, through the intermediary of the Protecting Power, of the rate of daily working pay that it has fixed.

Working pay shall likewise be paid by the detaining authorities to prisoners of war permanently detailed to duties or to a skilled or semi-skilled occupation in connection with the administration, installation or maintenance of camps, and to the prisoners who are required to carry out spiritual or medical duties on behalf of their comrades.

The working pay of the prisoners' representative, of his advisers, if any, and of his assistants, shall be paid out of the fund maintained by canteen profits. The scale of this working pay shall be fixed by the prisoners' representative and approved by the camp commander. If there is no such fund, the detaining authorities shall pay these prisoners a fair working rate of pay.

Article 63

Prisoners of war shall be permitted to receive remittances of money addressed to them individually or collectively.

Every prisoner of war shall have at his disposal the credit balance of his account as provided for in the following Article, within the limits fixed by the Detaining Power, which shall make such payments as are requested. Subject to financial or monetary restrictions which the Detaining Power regards as essential, prisoners of war may also have payments made abroad. In this case payments addressed by prisoners of war to dependents shall be given priority.

In any event, and subject to the consent of the Power on which they depend, prisoners may have payments made in their own country, as follows: the Detaining Power shall send to the aforesaid Power through the Protecting Power, a notification giving all the necessary particulars concerning the prisoners of war, the beneficiaries of the payments, and the amount of the sums to be paid, expressed in the Detaining Power's currency. The said notification shall be signed by the prisoners and countersigned by the camp commander. The Detaining Power shall debit the prisoners' account by a corresponding amount; the sums thus debited shall be placed by it to the credit of the Power on which the prisoners depend.

To apply the foregoing provisions, the Detaining Power may usefully consult the Model Regulations in Annex V of the present Convention.

Article 64

The Detaining Power shall hold an account for each prisoner of war, showing at least the following:

(1) The amounts due to the prisoner or received by him as advances of pay, as working pay or derived from any other source; the sums in the currency of the Detaining Power which were taken from him; the sums taken from him and converted at his request into the currency of the said Power.

(2) The payments made to the prisoner in cash, or in any other similar form; the payments made on his behalf and at his request; the sums transferred under Article 63, third paragraph.

Article 65

Every item entered in the account of a prisoner of war shall be countersigned or initialled by him, or by the prisoners' representative acting on his behalf.

Prisoners of war shall at all times be afforded reasonable facilities for consulting and obtaining copies of their accounts, which may likewise be inspected by the representatives of the Protecting Powers at the time of visits to the camp.

When prisoners of war are transferred from one camp to another, their personal accounts will follow them. In case of transfer from one Detaining Power to another, the monies which are their property and are not in the currency of the Detaining Power will follow them. They shall be given certificates for any other monies standing to the credit of their accounts.

The Parties to the conflict concerned may agree to notify to each other at specific intervals through the Protecting Power, the amount of the accounts of the prisoners of war.

Article 66

On the termination of captivity, through the release of a prisoner of war or his repatriation, the Detaining Power shall give him a statement, signed by an authorized officer of that Power, showing the credit balance then due to him. The Detaining Power shall also send through the Protecting Power to the government upon which the prisoner of war depends, lists giving all appropriate particulars of all prisoners of war whose captivity has been terminated by repatriation, release, escape, death or any other means, and showing the amount of their credit balances. Such lists shall be certified on each sheet by an authorized representative of the Detaining Power.

Any of the above provisions of this Article may be varied by mutual agreement between any two Parties to the conflict.

The Power on which the prisoner of war depends shall be responsible for settling with him any credit balance due to him from the Detaining Power on the termination of his captivity.

Article 67

Advances of pay, issued to prisoners of war in conformity with Article 60, shall be considered as made on behalf of the Power on which they depend. Such advances of pay, as well as all payments made by the said Power under Article 63, third paragraph, and

Article 68, shall form the subject of arrangements between the Powers concerned, at the close of hostilities.

Article 68

Any claim by a prisoner of war for compensation in respect of any injury or other disability arising out of work shall be referred to the Power on which he depends, through the Protecting Power. In accordance with Article 54, the Detaining Power will, in all cases, provide the prisoner of war concerned with a statement showing the nature of the injury or disability, the circumstances in which it arose and particulars of medical or hospital treatment given for it. This statement will be signed by a responsible officer of the Detaining Power and the medical particulars certified by a medical officer.

Any claim by a prisoner of war for compensation in respect of personal effects, monies or valuables impounded by the Detaining Power under Article 18 and not forthcoming on his repatriation, or in respect of loss alleged to be due to the fault of the Detaining Power or any of its servants, shall likewise be referred to the Power on which he depends. Nevertheless, any such personal effects required for use by the prisoners of war whilst in captivity shall be replaced at the expense of the Detaining Power. The Detaining Power will, in all cases, provide the prisoner of war with a statement, signed by a responsible officer, showing all available information regarding the reasons why such effects, monies or valuables have not been restored to him. A copy of this statement will be forwarded to the Power on which he depends through the Central Prisoners of War Agency provided for in Article 123.

SECTION V — RELATIONS OF PRISONERS OF WAR WITH THE EXTERIOR

Article 69

Immediately upon prisoners of war falling into its power, the Detaining Power shall inform them and the Powers on which they depend, through the Protecting Power, of the measures taken to carry out the provisions of the present Section. They shall likewise inform the parties concerned of any subsequent modifications of such measures.

Article 70

Immediately upon capture, or not more than one week after arrival at a camp, even if it is a transit camp, likewise in case of sickness or transfer to hospital or to another camp, every prisoner of war shall be enabled to write direct to his family, on the one hand, and to the Central Prisoners of War Agency provided for in Article 123, on the other hand, a card similar, if possible, to the model annexed to the present Convention, informing his relatives of his capture, address and state of health. The said cards shall be forwarded as rapidly as possible and may not be delayed in any manner.

Article 71

Prisoners of war shall be allowed to send and receive letters and cards. If the Detaining Power deems it necessary to limit the number of letters and cards sent by each prisoner of war, the said number shall not be less than two letters and four cards monthly, exclusive of the capture cards provided for in Article 70, and conforming as closely as possible to the models annexed to the present Convention. Further limitations may be imposed only if the Protecting Power is satisfied that it would be in the interests of the prisoners of war concerned to do so owing to difficulties of translation caused by the Detaining Power's inability to find sufficient qualified linguists to carry out the necessary censorship. If limitations must be placed on the correspondence addressed to prisoners of war, they may be ordered only by the Power on which the prisoners depend, possibly at the request of the Detaining Power. Such letters and cards must be conveyed by the most rapid method at the disposal of the Detaining Power; they may not be delayed or retained for disciplinary reasons.

Prisoners of war who have been without news for a long period, or who are unable to receive news from their next of kin or to give them news by the ordinary postal route, as well as those who are at a great distance from their homes, shall be permitted to send telegrams, the fees being charged against the prisoners of war's accounts with the Detaining Power or paid in the currency at their disposal. They shall likewise benefit by this measure in cases of urgency.

As a general rule, the correspondence of prisoners of war shall be written in their native language. The Parties to the conflict may allow correspondence in other languages.

Sacks containing prisoner of war mail must be securely sealed and labelled so as clearly to indicate their contents, and must be addressed to offices of destination.

Article 72

Prisoners of war shall be allowed to receive by post or by any other means individual parcels or collective shipments containing, in particular, foodstuffs, clothing, medical supplies and articles of a religious, educational or recreational character which may meet their needs, including books, devotional articles, scientific equipment, examination papers, musical instruments, sports outfits and materials allowing prisoners of war to pursue their studies or their cultural activities.

Such shipments shall in no way free the Detaining Power from the obligations imposed upon it by virtue of the present Convention.

The only limits which may be placed on these shipments shall be those proposed by the Protecting Power in the interest of the prisoners themselves, or by the International Committee of the Red Cross or any other organization giving assistance to the prisoners, in respect of their own shipments only, on account of exceptional strain on transport or communications.

The conditions for the sending of individual parcels and collective relief shall, if necessary, be the subject of special agreements between the Powers concerned, which may in no case delay the receipt by the prisoners of relief supplies. Books may not be included in parcels of clothing and foodstuffs. Medical supplies shall, as a rule, be sent in collective parcels.

Article 73

In the absence of special agreements between the Powers concerned on the conditions for the receipt and distribution of collective relief shipments, the rules and regulations concerning collective shipments, which are annexed to the present Convention, shall be applied.

The special agreements referred to above shall in no case restrict the right of prisoners' representatives to take possession of collective relief shipments intended for prisoners of war, to proceed to their distribution or to dispose of them in the interest of the prisoners.

Nor shall such agreements restrict the right of representatives of the Protecting Power, the International Committee of the Red Cross or any other organization giving assistance to prisoners of war and responsible for the forwarding of collective shipments, to supervise their distribution to the recipients.

Article 74

All relief shipments for prisoners of war shall be exempt from import, customs and other dues.

Correspondence, relief shipments and authorized remittances of money addressed to prisoners of war or despatched by them through the post office, either direct or through the Information Bureaux provided for in Article 122 and the Central Prisoners of War Agency provided for in Article 123, shall be exempt from any postal dues, both in the countries of origin and destination, and in intermediate countries.

If relief shipments intended for prisoners of war cannot be sent through the post office by reason of weight or for any other cause, the cost of transportation shall be borne by the Detaining Power in all the territories under its control. The other Powers party to the Convention shall bear the cost of transport in their respective territories.

In the absence of special agreements between the Parties concerned, the costs connected with transport of such shipments, other than costs covered by the above exemption, shall be charged to the senders.

The High Contracting Parties shall endeavour to reduce, so far as possible, the rates charged for telegrams sent by prisoners of war, or addressed to them.

Article 75

Should military operations prevent the Powers concerned from fulfilling their obligation to assure the transport of the shipments referred to in Articles 70, 71, 72 and 77, the Protecting Powers concerned, the International Committee of the Red Cross or any other organization duly approved by the Parties to the conflict may undertake to ensure the conveyance of such shipments by suitable means (railway wagons, motor vehicles, vessels or aircraft, etc.). For this purpose, the High Contracting Parties shall endeavour to supply them with such transport and to allow its circulation, especially by granting the necessary safe-conducts.

Such transport may also be used to convey:

(*a*) correspondence, lists and reports exchanged between the Central Information Agency referred to in Article 123 and the National Bureaux referred to in Article 122;

(*b*) correspondence and reports relating to prisoners of war which the Protecting Powers, the International Committee of the Red Cross or any other body assisting the prisoners, exchange either with their own delegates or with the Parties to the conflict.

These provisions in no way detract from the right of any Party to the conflict to arrange other means of transport, if it should so prefer, nor preclude the granting of safe-conducts, under mutually agreed conditions, to such means of transport.

In the absence of special agreements, the costs occasioned by the use of such means of transport shall be borne proportionally by the Parties to the conflict whose nationals are benefited thereby.

Article 76

The censoring of correspondence addressed to prisoners of war or despatched by them shall be done as quickly as possible. Mail shall be censored only by the despatching State and the receiving State, and once only by each.

The examination of consignments intended for prisoners of war shall not be carried out under conditions that will expose the goods contained in them to deterioration; except in the case of written or printed matter, it shall be done in the presence of the addressee, or of a fellow-prisoner duly delegated by him. The delivery to prisoners of individual or collective consignments shall not be delayed under the pretext of difficulties of censorship.

Any prohibition of correspondence ordered by Parties to the conflict, either for military or political reasons, shall be only temporary and its duration shall be as short as possible.

Article 77

The Detaining Powers shall provide all facilities for the transmission, through the Protecting Power or the Central Prisoners of War Agency provided for in Article 123, of instruments, papers or documents intended for prisoners of war or despatched by them, especially powers of attorney and wills.

In all cases they shall facilitate the preparation and execution of such documents on behalf of prisoners of war; in particular, they shall allow them to consult a lawyer and shall take what measures are necessary for the authentication of their signatures.

SECTION VI — RELATIONS BETWEEN PRISONERS OF WAR AND THE AUTHORITIES

CHAPTER I — *Complaints of Prisoners of War Respecting the Conditions of Captivity*

Article 78

Prisoners of war shall have the right to make known to the military authorities in whose power they are, their requests regarding the conditions of captivity to which they are subjected.

They shall also have the unrestricted right to apply to the representatives of the Protecting Powers either through their prisoners' representative or, if they consider it necessary, direct, in order to draw their attention to any points on which they may have complaints to make regarding their conditions of captivity.

These requests and complaints shall not be limited nor considered to be a part of the correspondence quota referred to in Article 71. They must be transmitted immediately. Even if they are recognized to be unfounded, they may not give rise to any punishment.

Prisoners' representatives may send periodic reports on the situation in the camps and the needs of the prisoners of war to the representatives of the Protecting Powers.

CHAPTER II — *Prisoner of War Representatives*

Article 79

In all places where there are prisoners of war, except in those where there are officers, the prisoners shall freely elect by secret ballot, every six months, and also in case of vacancies, prisoners' representatives entrusted with representing them before the military authorities, the Protecting Powers, the International Committee of the Red Cross and any other organization which may assist them. These prisoners' representatives shall be eligible for re-election.

In camps for officers and persons of equivalent status or in mixed camps, the senior officer among the prisoners of war shall be recognized as the camp prisoners' representative. In camps for officers, he shall be assisted by one or more advisers chosen by the officers; in mixed camps, his assistants shall be chosen from among the prisoners of war who are not officers and shall be elected by them.

Officer prisoners of war of the same nationality shall be stationed in labour camps for prisoners of war, for the purpose of carrying out the camp administration duties for which the prisoners of war are responsible. These officers may be elected as prisoners' representatives under the first paragraph of this Article. In such a case the assistants to the prisoners' representatives shall be chosen from among those prisoners of war who are not officers.

Every representative elected must be approved by the Detaining Power before he has the right to commence his duties. Where the Detaining Power refuses to approve a prisoner of war elected by his fellow prisoners of war, it must inform the Protecting Power of the reason for such refusal.

In all cases the prisoners' representative must have the same nationality, language and customs as the prisoners of war whom he represents. Thus, prisoners of war distributed in different sections of a camp, according to their nationality, language or customs, shall have for each section their own prisoners' representative, in accordance with the foregoing paragraphs.

Article 80

Prisoners' representatives shall further the physical, spiritual and intellectual well-being of prisoners of war.

In particular, where the prisoners decide to organize amongst themselves a system of mutual assistance, this organization will be within the province of the prisoners' representative, in addition to the special duties entrusted to him by other provisions of the present Convention.

Prisoners' representatives shall not be held responsible, simply by reason of their duties, for any offences committed by prisoners of war.

Article 81

Prisoners' representatives shall not be required to perform any other work, if the accomplishment of their duties is thereby made more difficult.

Prisoners' representatives may appoint from amongst the prisoners such assistants as they may require. All material facilities shall be granted them, particularly a certain freedom of movement necessary for the accomplishment of their duties (inspection of labour detachments, receipt of supplies, etc.).

Prisoners' representatives shall be permitted to visit premises where prisoners of war are detained, and every prisoner of war shall have the right to consult freely his prisoners' representative.

All facilities shall likewise be accorded to the prisoners' representatives for communication by post and telegraph with the detaining authorities, the Protecting Powers, the International Committee of the Red Cross and their delegates, the Mixed Medical Commissions and the bodies which give assistance to prisoners of war. Prisoners' representatives of labour detachments shall enjoy the same facilities for communication with the prisoners' representatives of the principal camp. Such communications shall not be restricted, nor considered as forming a part of the quota mentioned in Article 71.

Prisoners' representatives who are transferred shall be allowed a reasonable time to acquaint their successors with current affairs.

In case of dismissal, the reasons therefor shall be communicated to the Protecting Power.

CHAPTER III — *Penal and Disciplinary Sanctions*

I. *General Provisions*

Article 82

A prisoner of war shall be subject to the laws, regulations and orders in force in the armed forces of the Detaining Power; the Detaining Power shall be justified in taking judicial or disciplinary measures in respect of any offence committed by a prisoner of war against such laws, regulations or orders. However, no proceedings or punishments contrary to the provisions of this Chapter shall be allowed.

If any law, regulation or order of the Detaining Power shall declare acts committed by a prisoner of war to be punishable, whereas the same acts would not be punishable if commited by a member of the forces of the Detaining Power, such acts shall entail disciplinary punishments only.

Article 83

In deciding whether proceedings in respect of an offence alleged to have been committed by a prisoner of war shall be judicial or disciplinary, the Detaining Power shall ensure that the competent authorities exercise the greatest leniency and adopt, wherever possible, disciplinary rather than judicial measures.

Article 84

A prisoner of war shall be tried only by a military court, unless the existing laws of the Detaining Power expressly permit the civil courts to try a member of the armed forces of the Detaining Power in respect of the particular offence alleged to have been committed by the prisoner of war.

In no circumstances whatever shall a prisoner of war be tried by a court of any kind which does not offer the essential guarantees of independence and impartiality as generally recognized, and, in particular, the procedure of which does not afford the accused the rights and means of defence provided for in Article 105.

Article 85

Prisoners of war prosecuted under the laws of the Detaining Power for acts committed prior to capture shall retain, even if convicted, the benefits of the present Convention.

Article 86

No prisoner of war may be punished more than once for the same act, or on the same charge.

Article 87

Prisoners of war may not be sentenced by the military authorities and courts of the Detaining Power to any penalties except those provided for in respect of members of the armed forces of the said Power who have committed the same acts.

When fixing the penalty, the courts or authorities of the Detaining Power shall take into consideration, to the widest extent possible, the fact that the accused, not being a national of the Detaining Power, is not bound to it by any duty of allegiance, and that he is in its power as the result of circumstances independent of his own will. The said courts or authorities shall be at liberty to reduce the penalty provided for the violation of which the prisoner of war is accused, and shall therefore not be bound to apply the minimum penalty prescribed.

Collective punishment for individual acts, corporal punishment, imprisonment in premises without daylight and, in general, any form of torture or cruelty, are forbidden.

No prisoner of war may be deprived of his rank by the Detaining Power, or prevented from wearing his badges.

Article 88

Officers, non-commissioned officers and men who are prisoners of war undergoing a disciplinary or judicial punishment, shall not be subjected to more severe treatment than that applied in respect of the same punishment to members of the armed forces of the Detaining Power of equivalent rank.

A woman prisoner of war shall not be awarded or sentenced to a punishment more severe, or treated whilst undergoing punishment more severely, than a woman member of the armed forces of the Detaining Power dealt with for a similar offence.

In no case may a woman prisoner of war be awarded or sentenced to a punishment more severe, or treated whilst undergoing punishment more severely, than a male member of the armed forces of the Detaining Power dealt with for a similar offence.

Prisoners of war who have served disciplinary or judicial sentences may not be treated differently from other prisoners of war.

II. *Disciplinary Sanctions*

Article 89

The disciplinary punishments applicable to prisoners of war are the following:

(1) A fine which shall not exceed 50 per cent of the advances of pay and working pay which the prisoner of war would

otherwise receive under the provisions of Articles 60 and 62 during a period of not more than thirty days.

(2) Discontinuance of privileges granted over and above the treatment provided for by the present Convention.

(3) Fatigue duties not exceeding two hours daily.

(4) Confinement.

The punishment referred to under (3) shall not be applied to officers.

In no case shall disciplinary punishments be inhuman, brutal or dangerous to the health of prisoners of war.

Article 90

The duration of any single punishment shall in no case exceed thirty days. Any period of confinement awaiting the hearing of a disciplinary offence or the award of disciplinary punishment shall be deducted from an award pronounced against a prisoner of war.

The maximum of thirty days provided above may not be exceeded, even if the prisoner of war is answerable for several acts at the same time when he is awarded punishment, whether such acts are related or not.

The period between the pronouncing of an award of disciplinary punishment and its execution shall not exceed one month.

When a prisoner of war is awarded a further disciplinary punishment, a period of at least three days shall elapse between the execution of any two of the punishments, if the duration of one of these is ten days or more.

Article 91

The escape of a prisoner of war shall be deemed to have succeded when:

(1) he has joined the armed forces of the Power on which he depends, or those of an allied Power;

(2) he has left the territory under the control of the Detaining Power, or of an ally of the said Power;

(3) he has joined a ship flying the flag of the Power on which he depends, or of an allied Power, in the territorial waters of the Detaining Power, the said ship not being under the control of the last named Power.

Prisoners of war who have made good their escape in the sense of this Article and who are recaptured, shall not be liable to any punishment in respect of their previous escape.

Article 92

A prisoner of war who attempts to escape and is recaptured before having made good his escape in the sense of Article 91 shall be liable only to a disciplinary punishment in respect of this act, even if it is a repeated offence.

A prisoner of war who is recaptured shall be handed over without delay to the competent military authority.

Article 88, fourth paragraph, notwithstanding, prisoners of war punished as a result of an unsuccessful escape may be subjected to special surveillance. Such surveillance must not affect the state of their health, must be undergone in a prisoner of war camp, and must not entail the suppression of any of the safeguards granted them by the present Convention.

Article 93

Escape or attempt to escape, even if it is a repeated offence, shall not be deemed an aggravating circumstance if the prisoner of war is subjected to trial by judicial proceedings in respect of an offence committed during his escape or attempt to escape.

In conformity with the principle stated in Article 83, offences committed by prisoners of war with the sole intention of facilitating their escape and which do not entail any violence against life or limb, such as offences against public property, theft without intention of self-enrichment, the drawing up or use of false papers, or the wearing of civilian clothing, shall occasion disciplinary punishment only.

Prisoners of war who aid or abet an escape or an attempt to escape shall be liable on this count to disciplinary punishment only.

Article 94

If an escaped prisoner of war is recaptured, the Power on which he depends shall be notified thereof in the manner defined in Article 122, provided notification of his escape has been made.

Article 95

A prisoner of war accused of an offence against discipline shall not be kept in confinement pending the hearing unless a member of the armed forces of the Detaining Power would be so kept if he were accused of a similar offence, or if it is essential in the interests of camp order and discipline.

Any period spent by a prisoner of war in confinement awaiting the disposal of an offence against discipline shall be reduced to an absolute minimum and shall not exceed fourteen days.

The provisions of Articles 97 and 98 of this Chapter shall apply to prisoners of war who are in confinement awaiting the disposal of offences against discipline.

Article 96

Acts which constitute offences against discipline shall be investigated immediately.

Without prejudice to the competence of courts and superior military authorities, disciplinary punishment may be ordered only by an officer having disciplinary powers in his capacity as camp commander, or by a responsible officer who replaces him or to whom he has delegated his disciplinary powers.

In no case may such powers be delegated to a prisoner of war or be exercised by a prisoner of war.

Before any disciplinary award is pronounced, the accused shall be given precise information regarding the offences of which he is accused, and given an opportunity of explaing his conduct and of defending himself. He shall be permitted, in particular, to call witnesses and to have recourse, if necessary, to the services of a qualified interpreter. The decision shall be announced to the accused prisoner of war and to the prisoners' representative.

A record of disciplinary punishments shall be maintained by the camp commander and shall be open to inspection by representatives of the Protecting Power.

Article 97

Prisoners of war shall not in any case be transferred to penitentiary establishments (prisons, penitentiaries, convict prisons, etc.) to undergo disciplinary punishment therein.

All premises in which disciplinary punishments are undergone shall conform to the sanitary requirements set forth in Article 25. A prisoner of war undergoing punishment shall be enabled to keep himself in a state of cleanliness, in conformity with Article 29.

Officers and persons of equivalent status shall not be lodged in the same quarters as non-commissioned officers or men.

Women prisoners of war undergoing disciplinary punishment shall be confined in separate quarters from male prisoners of war and shall be under the immediate supervision of women.

Article 98

A prisoner of war undergoing confinement as a disciplinary punishment, shall continue to enjoy the benefits of the provisions of this Convention except in so far as these are necessarily rendered inapplicable by the mere fact that he is confined. In no case may he be deprived of the benefits of the provisions of Articles 78 and 126.

A prisoner of war awarded disciplinary punishment may not be deprived of the prerogatives attached to his rank.

Prisoners of war awarded disciplinary punishment shall be allowed to exercise and to stay in the open air at least two hours daily.

They shall be allowed, on their request, to be present at the daily medical inspections. They shall receive the attention which their state of health requires and, if necessary, shall be removed to the camp infirmary or to a hospital.

They shall have permission to read and write, likewise to send and receive letters. Parcels and remittances of money however, may be withheld from them until the completion of the punishment; they shall meanwhile be entrusted to the prisoners' representative, who will hand over to the infirmary the perishable goods contained in such parcels.

III. *Judicial Proceedings*

Article 99

No prisoner of war may be tried or sentenced for an act which is not forbidden by the law of the Detaining Power or by international law, in force at the time the said act was committed.

No moral or physical coercion may be exerted on a prisoner of war in order to induce him to admit himself guilty of the act of which he is accused.

No prisoner of war may be convicted without having had an opportunity to present his defence and the assistance of a qualified advocate or counsel.

Article 100

Prisoners of war and the Protecting Powers shall be informed as soon as possible of the offences which are punishable by the death sentence under the laws of the Detaining Power.

Other offences shall not thereafter be made punishable by the death penalty without the concurrence of the Power on which the prisoners of war depend.

The death sentence cannot be pronounced on a prisoner of war unless the attention of the court has, in accordance with Article 87, second paragraph, been particularly called to the fact that since the accused is not a national of the Detaining Power, he is not bound to it by any duty of allegiance, and that he is in its power as the result of circumstances independent of his own will.

Article 101

If the death penalty is pronounced on a prisoner of war, the sentence shall not be executed before the expiration of a period of at least six months from the date when the Protecting Power receives, at an indicated address, the detailed communication provided for in Article 107.

Article 102

A prisoner of war can be validly sentenced only if the sentence has been pronounced by the same courts according to the same procedure as in the case of members of the armed forces of the Detaining Power, and if, furthermore, the provisions of the present Chapter have been observed.

Article 103

Judicial investigations relating to a prisoner of war shall be conducted as rapidly as circumstances permit and so that his trial shall take place as soon as possible. A prisoner of war shall not be confined while awaiting trial unless a member of the armed forces of the Detaining Power would be so confined if he were accused of a similar offence, or if it is essential to do so in the interests of national security. In no circumstances shall this confinement exceed three months.

Any period spent by a prisoner of war in confinement awaiting trial shall be deducted from any sentence of imprisonment passed upon him and taken into account in fixing any penalty.

The provisions of Articles 97 and 98 of this Chapter shall apply to a prisoner of war whilst in confinement awaiting trial.

Article 104

In any case in which the Detaining Power has decided to institute judicial proceedings against a prisoner of war, it shall notify the Protecting Power as soon as possible and at least three weeks before the opening of the trial. This period of three weeks shall run as from the day on which such notification reaches the Protecting Power at the address previously indicated by the latter to the Detaining Power.

The said notification shall contain the following information:

(1) Surname and first names of the prisoner of war, his rank, his army, regimental, personal or serial number, his date of birth, and his profession or trade, if any;
(2) Place of internment or confinement;
(3) Specification of the charge or charges on which the prisoner of war is to be arraigned, giving the legal provisions applicable;
(4) Designation of the court which will try the case, likewise the date and place fixed for the opening of the trial.

The same communication shall be made by the Detaining Power to the prisoners' representative.

If no evidence is submitted, at the opening of a trial, that the notification referred to above was received by the Protecting Power, by the prisoner of war and by the prisoners' representative concerned, at least three weeks before the opening of the trial, then the latter cannot take place and must be adjourned.

Article 105

The prisoner of war shall be entitled to assistance by one of his prisoner comrades, to defence by a qualified advocate or counsel of his own choice, to the calling of witnesses and, if he deems necessary, to the services of a competent interpreter. He shall be advised of these rights by the Detaining Power in due time before the trial.

Failing a choice by the prisoner of war, the Protecting Power shall find him an advocate or counsel, and shall have at least one week at its disposal for the purpose. The Detaining Power shall deliver to the said Power, on request, a list of persons qualified to present the defence. Failing a choice of an advocate or counsel by the prisoner of war or the Protecting Power, the Detaining Power shall appoint a competent advocate or counsel to conduct the defence.

The advocate or counsel conducting the defence on behalf of the prisoner of war shall have at his disposal a period of two weeks at least before the opening of the trial, as well as the necessary facilities to prepare the defence of the accused. He may, in particular, freely visit the accused and interview him in private. He may also confer with any witnesses for the defence, including prisoners of war. He shall have the benefit of these facilities until the term of appeal or petition has expired.

Particulars of the charge or charges on which the prisoner of war is to be arraigned, as well as the documents which are generally communicated to the accused by virtue of the laws in force in the armed forces of the Detaining Power, shall be communicated to the accused prisoner of war in a language which he understands, and in good time before the opening of the trial. The same communication in the same circumstances shall be made to the advocate or counsel conducting the defence on behalf of the prisoner of war.

The representatives of the Protecting Power shall be entitled to attend the trial of the case, unless, exceptionally, this is held *in camera* in the interest of State security. In such a case the Detaining Power shall advise the Protecting Power accordingly.

Article 106

Every prisoner of war shall have, in the same manner as the members of the armed forces of the Detaining Power, the right of appeal or petition from any sentence pronounced upon him, with a view to the quashing or revising of the sentence or the re-opening of the trial. He shall be fully informed of his right to appeal or petition and of the time limit within which he may do so.

Article 107

Any judgment and sentence pronounced upon a prisoner of war shall be immediately reported to the Protecting Power in the form of a summary communication, which shall also indicate whether he has the right of appeal with a view to the quashing of the sentence or the re-opening of the trial. This communication shall likewise be sent to the prisoners' representative concerned. It shall also be sent to the accused prisoner of war in a language he understands, if the sentence was not pronounced in his presence. The Detaining Power shall also immediately communicate to the Protecting Power the decision of the prisoner of war to use or to waive his right of appeal.

Furthermore, if a prisoner of war is finally convicted or if a sentence pronounced on a prisoner of war in the first instance is a death sentence, the Detaining Power shall as soon as possible address to the Protecting Power a detailed communication containing:

(1) the precise wording of the finding and sentence;
(2) a summarized report of any preliminary investigation and of the trial, emphasizing in particular the elements of the prosecution and the defence;
(3) notification, where applicable, of the establishment where the sentence will be served.

The communications provided for in the foregoing sub-paragraphs shall be sent to the Protecting Power at the address previously made known to the Detaining Power.

Article 108

Sentences pronounced on prisoners of war after a conviction has become duly enforceable, shall be served in the same establishments and under the same conditions as in the case of members of the armed forces of the Detaining Power. These conditions shall in all cases conform to the requirements of health and humanity.

A woman prisoner of war on whom such a sentence has been pronounced shall be confined in separate quarters and shall be under the supervision of women.

In any case, prisoners of war sentenced to a penalty depriving them of their liberty shall retain the benefit of the provisions of Articles 78 and 126 of the present Convention. Furthermore, they shall be entitled to receive and despatch correspondence, to receive at least one relief parcel monthly, to take regular exercise in the open air, to have the medical care required by their state of health, and the spiritual assistance they may desire. Penalties to which they may be subjected shall be in accordance with the provisions of Article 87, third paragraph.

PART IV — TERMINATION OF CAPTIVITY

Section I — Direct Repatriation and Accommodation in Neutral Countries

Article 109

Subject to the provisions of the third paragraph of this Article, Parties to the conflict are bound to send back to their own country, regardless of number or rank, seriously wounded and seriously sick prisoners of war, after having cared for them until they are fit to travel, in accordance with the first paragraph of the following Article.

Throughout the duration of hostilities, Parties to the conflict shall endeavour, with the cooperation of the neutral Powers concerned, to make arrangements for the accommodation in neutral countries of the sick and wounded prisoners of war referred to in the second paragraph of the following Article. They may, in addition, conclude agreements with a view to the direct repatriation or internment in a neutral country of able-bodied prisoners of war who have undergone a long period of captivity.

No sick or injured prisoner of war who is eligible for repatriation under the first paragraph of this Article, may be repatriated against his will during hostilities.

Article 110

The following shall be repatriated direct:
(1) Incurably wounded and sick whose mental or physical fitness seems to have been gravely diminished.
(2) Wounded and sick who, according to medical opinion, are not likely to recover within one year, whose condition requires treatment and whose mental or physical fitness seems to have been gravely diminished.
(3) Wounded and sick who have recovered, but whose mental or physical fitness seems to have been gravely and permanently diminished.

The following may be accommodated in a neutral country:
(1) Wounded and sick whose recovery may be expected within one year of the date of the wound or the beginning of the illness, if treatment in a neutral country might increase the prospects of a more certain and speedy recovery.

(2) Prisoners of war whose mental or physical health, according to medical opinion, is seriously threatened by continued captivity, but whose accommodation in a neutral country might remove such a threat.

The conditions which prisoners of war accommodated in a neutral country must fulfil in order to permit their repatriation shall be fixed, as shall likewise their status, by agreement between the Powers concerned. In general, prisoners of war who have been accommodated in a neutral country, and who belong to the following categories, should be repatriated:

(1) those whose state of health has deteriorated so as to fulfil the conditions laid down for direct repatriation;
(2) those whose mental or physical powers remain, even after treatment, considerably impaired.

If no special agreements are concluded between the Parties to the conflict concerned, to determine the cases of disablement or sickness entailing direct repatriation or accommodation in a neutral country, such cases shall be settled in accordance with the principles laid down in the Model Agreement concerning direct repatriation and accommodation in neutral countries of wounded and sick prisoners of war and in the Regulations concerning Mixed Medical Commissions annexed to the present Convention.

Article 111

The Detaining Power, the Power on which the prisoners of war depend, and a neutral Power agreed upon by these two Powers, shall endeavour to conclude agreements which will enable prisoners of war to be interned in the territory of the said neutral Power until the close of hostilities.

Article 112

Upon the outbreak of hostilities, Mixed Medical Commissions shall be appointed to examine sick and wounded prisoners of war, and to make all appropriate decisions regarding them. The appointment, duties and functioning of these Commissions shall be in conformity with the provisions of the Regulations annexed to the present Convention.

However, prisoners of war who, in the opinion of the medical authorities of the Detaining Power, are manifestly seriously injured or seriously sick, may be repatriated without having to be examined by a Mixed Medical Commission.

Article 113

Besides those who are designated by the medical authorities of the Detaining Power, wounded or sick prisoners of war belonging to the categories listed below shall be entitled to present themselves for examination by the Mixed Medical Commissions provided for in the foregoing Article:

(1) Wounded and sick proposed by a physician or surgeon who is of the same nationality, or a national of a Party to the conflict allied with the Power on which the said prisoners depend, and who exercises his functions in the camp.

(2) Wounded and sick proposed by their prisoners' representative.

(3) Wounded and sick proposed by the Power on which they depend, or by an organization duly recognized by the said Power and giving assistance to the prisoners.

Prisoners of war who do not belong to one of the three foregoing categories may nevertheless present themselves for examination by Mixed Medical Commissions, but shall be examined only after those belonging to the said categories.

The physician or surgeon of the same nationality as the prisoners who present themselves for examination by the Mixed Medical Commission, likewise the prisoners' representative of the said prisoners, shall have permission to be present at the examination.

Article 114

Prisoners of war who meet with accidents shall, unless the injury is self-inflicted, have the benefit of the provisions of this Convention as regards repatriation or accommodation in a neutral country.

Article 115

No prisoner of war on whom a disciplinary punishment has been imposed and who is eligible for repatriation or for accommodation in a neutral country, may be kept back on the plea that he has not undergone his punishment.

Prisoners of war detained in connection with a judicial prosecution or conviction and who are designated for repatriation or accommodation in a neutral country, may benefit by such measures before the end of the proceedings or the completion of the punishment, if the Detaining Power consents.

Parties to the conflict shall communicate to each other the names of those who will be detained until the end of the proceedings or the completion of the punishment.

Article 116

The cost of repatriating prisoners of war or of transporting them to a neutral country shall be borne, from the frontiers of the Detaining Power, by the Power on which said prisoners depend.

Article 117

No repatriated person may be employed on active military service.

SECTION II — RELEASE AND REPATRIATION OF PRISONERS OF WAR AT THE CLOSE OF HOSTILITIES

Article 118

Prisoners of war shall be released and repatriated without delay after the cessation of active hostilities.

In the absence of stipulations to the above effect in any agreement concluded between the Parties to the conflict with a view to the cessation of hostilities, or failing any such agreement, each of the Detaining Powers shall itself establish and execute without delay a plan of repatriation in conformity with the principle laid down in the foregoing paragraph.

In either case, the measures adopted shall be brought to the knowledge of the prisoners of war.

The costs of repatriation of prisoners of war shall in all cases be equitably apportioned between the Detaining Power and the Power on which the prisoners depend. This apportionment shall be carried out on the following basis:

(*a*) If the two Powers are contiguous, the Power on which the prisoners of war depend shall bear the costs of repatriation from the frontiers of the Detaining Power.

(*b*) If the two Powers are not contiguous, the Detaining Power shall bear the costs of transport of prisoners of war over its own territory as far as its frontier or its port of embarkation nearest to the territory of the Power on which the prisoners of war depend. The Parties concerned shall agree between themselves as to the equitable apportionment of the remaining costs of the repatriation. The conclusion of this agreement shall in no circumstances justify any delay in the repatriation of the prisoners of war.

Article 119

Repatriation shall be effected in conditions similar to those laid down in Articles 46 to 48 inclusive of the present Convention for the transfer of prisoners of war, having regard to the provisions of Article 118 and to those of the following paragraphs.

On repatriation, any articles of value impounded from prisoners of war under Article 18, and any foreign currency which has not been converted into the currency of the Detaining Power, shall be restored to them. Articles of value and foreign currency which, for any reason whatever, are not restored to prisoners of war on repatriation, shall be despatched to the Information Bureau set up under Article 122.

Prisoners of war shall be allowed to take with them their personal effects, and any correspondence and parcels which have arrived for them. The weight of such baggage may be limited, if the conditions of repatriation so require, to what each prisoner can reasonably carry. Each prisoner shall in all cases be authorized to carry at least twenty-five kilograms.

The other personal effects of the repatriated prisoner shall be left in the charge of the Detaining Power which shall have them forwarded to him as soon as it has concluded an agreement to this effect, regulating the conditions of transport and the payment of the costs involved, with the Power on which the prisoner depends.

Prisoners of war against whom criminal proceedings for an indictable offence are pending may be detained until the end of such proceedings, and, if necessary, until the completion of the punishment. The same shall apply to prisoners of war already convicted for an indictable offence.

Parties to the conflict shall communicate to each other the names of any prisoners of war who are detained until the end of proceedings or until punishment has been completed.

By agreement between the Parties to the conflict, commissions shall be established for the purpose of searching for dispersed prisoners of war and of assuring their repatriation with the least possible delay.

SECTION III – DEATH OF PRISONERS OF WAR

Article 120

Wills of prisoners of war shall be drawn up so as to satisfy the conditions of validity required by the legislation of their country of origin, which will take steps to inform the Detaining Power of its requirements in this respect. At the request of the prisoner of war and, in all cases, after death, the will shall be transmitted without delay to the Protecting Power; a certified copy shall be sent to the Central Agency.

Death certificates in the form annexed to the present Convention, or lists certified by a responsible officer, of all persons who die as prisoners of war shall be forwarded as rapidly as possible to the Prisoner of War Information Bureau established in accordance with Article 122. The death certificates or certified lists shall show particulars of identity as set out in the third paragraph of Article 17, and also the date and place of death, the cause of death, the date and place of burial and all particulars necessary to identify the graves.

The burial or cremation of a prisoner of war shall be preceded by a medical examination of the body with a view to confirming death and enabling a report to be made and, where necessary, establishing identity.

The detaining authorities shall ensure that prisoners of war who have died in captivity are honourably buried, if possible according to the rites of the religion to which they belonged, and that their graves are respected, suitably maintained and marked so as to be found at any time. Wherever possible, deceased prisoners of war who depended on the same Power shall be interred in the same place.

Deceased prisoners of war shall be buried in individual graves unless unavoidable circumstances require the use of collective graves. Bodies may be cremated only for imperative reasons of hygiene, on account of the religion of the deceased or in accordance with his express wish to this effect. In case of cremation, the fact shall be stated and the reasons given in the death certificate of the deceased.

In order that graves may always be found, all particulars of burials and graves shall be recorded with a Graves Registration Service established by the Detaining Power. Lists of graves and particulars of the prisoners of war interred in cemeteries and elsewhere shall be transmitted to the Power on which such prisoners of war depended. Responsibility for the care of these graves and for records of any subsequent moves of the bodies shall rest on the Power controlling the territory, if a Party to the present Convention. These provisions shall also apply to the ashes which shall be kept by the Graves Registration Service until proper disposal thereof in accordance with the wishes of the home country.

Article 121

Every death or serious injury of a prisoner of war caused or suspected to have been caused by a sentry, another prisoner of war, or any other person, as well as any death the cause of which is unknown, shall be immediately followed by an official enquiry by the Detaining Power.

A communication on this subject shall be sent immediately to the Protecting Power. Statements shall be taken from witnesses, especially from those who are prisoners of war, and a report including such statements shall be forwarded to the Protecting Power.

If the enquiry indicates the guilt of one or more persons, the Detaining Power shall take all measures for the prosecution of the person or persons responsible.

PART V — INFORMATION BUREAUX AND
RELIEF SOCIETIES FOR PRISONERS OF WAR

Article 122

Upon the outbreak of a conflict and in all cases of occupation, each of the Parties to the conflict shall institute an official Information Bureau for prisoners of war who are in its power. Neutral or non-belligerent Powers who may have received within their territory persons belonging to one of the categories referred to in Article 4, shall take the same action with respect to such persons. The Power concerned shall ensure that the Prisoners of War Information Bureau is provided with the necessary accommodation, equipment and staff to ensure its efficient working. It shall be at liberty to employ prisoners of war in such a Bureau under the conditions laid down in the Section of the present Convention dealing with work by prisoners of war.

Within the shortest possible period, each of the Parties to the conflict shall give its Bureau the information referred to in the fourth, fifth and sixth paragraphs of this Article regarding any enemy person belonging to one of the categories referred to in Article 4, who has fallen into its power. Neutral or non-belligerent Powers shall take the same action with regard to persons belonging to such categories whom they have received within their territory.

The Bureau shall immediately forward such information by the most rapid means to the Powers concerned, through the intermediary of the Protecting Powers and likewise of the Central Agency provided for in Article 123.

This information shall make it possible quickly to advise the next of kin concerned. Subject to the provisions of Article 17, the information shall include, in so far as available to the Information Bureau, in respect of each prisoner of war, his surname, first names, rank, army, regimental, personal or serial number, place and full date of birth, indication of the Power on which he depends, first name of the father and maiden name of the mother, name and address of the person to be informed and the address to which correspondence for the prisoner may be sent.

The Information Bureau shall receive from the various departments concerned information regarding transfers, releases, repatriations, escapes, admissions to hospital, and deaths, and shall transmit such information in the manner described in the third paragraph above.

Likewise, information regarding the state of health of prisoners of war who are seriously ill or seriously wounded shall be supplied regularly, every week if possible.

The Information Bureau shall also be responsible for replying to all enquiries sent to it concerning prisoners of war, including those who have died in captivity; it will make any enquiries necessary to obtain the information which is asked for if this is not in its possession.

All written communications made by the Bureau shall be authenticated by a signature or a seal.

The Information Bureau shall furthermore be charged with collecting all personal valuables, including sums in currencies other than that of the Detaining Power and documents of importance to the next of kin, left by prisoners of war who have been repatriated or released, or who have escaped or died, and shall forward the said valuables to the Powers concerned. Such articles shall be sent by the Bureau in sealed packets which shall be accompanied by statements giving clear and full particulars of the identity of the person to whom the articles belonged, and by a complete list of the contents of the parcel. Other personal effects of such prisoners of war shall be transmitted under arrangements agreed upon between the Parties to the conflict concerned.

Article 123

A Central Prisoners of War Information Agency shall be created in a neutral country. The International Committee of the Red Cross shall, if it deems necessary, propose to the Powers concerned the organization of such an Agency.

The function of the Agency shall be to collect all the information it may obtain through official or private channels respecting prisoners of war, and to transmit it as rapidly as possible to the country of origin of the prisoners of war or to the Power on which they depend. It shall receive from the Parties to the conflict all facilities for effecting such transmissions.

The High Contracting Parties, and in particular those whose nationals benefit by the services of the Central Agency, are requested to give the said Agency the financial aid it may require.

The foregoing provisions shall in no way be interpreted as restricting the humanitarian activities of the International Committee of the Red Cross, or of the relief societies provided for in Article 125.

Article 124

The national Information Bureaux and the Central Information Agency shall enjoy free postage for mail, likewise all the exemptions provided for in Article 74, and further, so far as possible, exemption from telegraphic charges or, at least, greatly reduced rates.

Article 125

Subject to the measures which the Detaining Powers may consider essential to ensure their security or to meet any other reasonable need, the representatives of religious organizations, relief societies, or any other organization assisting prisoners of war, shall receive from the said Powers, for themselves and their duly accredited agents, all necessary facilities for visiting the prisoners, for distributing relief supplies and material, from any source, intended for religious, educational or recreative purposes, and for assisting them in organizing their leisure time within the camps. Such societies or organizations may be constituted in the territory of the Detaining Power or in any other country, or they may have an international character.

The Detaining Power may limit the number of societies and organizations whose delegates are allowed to carry out their activities in its territory and under its supervision, on condition, however, that such limitation shall not hinder the effective operation of adequate relief to all prisoners of war.

The special position of the International Committee of the Red Cross in this field shall be recognized and respected at all times.

As soon as relief supplies or material intended for the above-mentioned purposes are handed over to prisoners of war, or very shortly afterwards, receipts for each consignment, signed by the prisoners' representative, shall be forwarded to the relief society or organization making the shipment. At the same time, receipts for these consignments shall be supplied by the administrative authorities responsible for guarding the prisoners.

PART VI – EXECUTION OF THE CONVENTION

SECTION I – GENERAL PROVISIONS

Article 126

Representatives or delegates of the Protecting Powers shall have permission to go to all places where prisoners of war may be, particularly to places of internment, imprisonment and labour, and shall have access to all premises occupied by prisoners of war; they shall also be allowed to go to the places of departure, passage and arrival of prisoners who are being transferred. They shall be able to interview the prisoners, and in particular the prisoners' representatives, without witnesses, either personally or through an interpreter.

Representatives and delegates of the Protecting Powers shall have full liberty to select the places they wish to visit. The duration and frequency of these visits shall not be restricted. Visits may not be prohibited except for reasons of imperative military necessity, and then only as an exceptional and temporary measure.

The Detaining Power and the Power on which the said prisoners of war depend may agree, if necessary, that compatriots of these prisoners of war be permitted to participate in the visits.

The delegates of the International Committee of the Red Cross shall enjoy the same prerogatives. The appointment of such delegates shall be submitted to the approval of the Power detaining the prisoners of war to be visited.

Article 127

The High Contracting Parties undertake, in time of peace as in time of war, to disseminate the text of the present Convention as widely as possible in their respective countries, and, in particular, to include the study thereof in their programmes of military and, if possible, civil instruction, so that the principles thereof may become known to all their armed forces and to the entire population.

Any military or other authorities, who in time of war assume responsibilities in respect of prisoners of war, must possess the text of the Convention and be specially instructed as to its provisions.

Article 128

The High Contracting Parties shall communicate to one another through the Swiss Federal Council and, during hostilities, through the Protecting Powers, the official translations of the present Convention, as well as the laws and regulations which they may adopt to ensure the application thereof.

Article 129

The High Contracting Parties undertake to enact any legislation necessary to provide effective penal sanctions for persons committing, or ordering to be committed, any of the grave breaches of the present Convention defined in the following Article.

Each High Contracting Party shall be under the obligation to search for persons alleged to have committed, or to have ordered to be committed, such grave breaches, and shall bring such persons, regardless of their nationality, before its own courts. It may also, if it prefers, and in accordance with the provisions of its own legislation, hand such persons over for trial to another High Contracting Party concerned, provided such High Contracting Party has made out a *prima facie* case.

Each High Contracting Party shall take measures necessary for the suppression of all acts contrary to the provisions of the present Convention other than the grave breaches defined in the following Article.

In all circumstances, the accused persons shall benefit by safeguards of proper trial and defence, which shall not be less favourable than those provided by Article 105 and those following of the present Convention.

Article 130

Grave breaches to which the preceding Article relates shall be those involving any of the following acts, if committed against persons or property protected by the Convention: wilful killing, torture or inhuman treatment, including biological experiments, wilfully causing great suffering or serious injury to body or health, compelling a prisoner of war to serve in the forces of the hostile Power, or wilfully depriving a prisoner of war of the rights of fair and regular trial prescribed in this Convention.

Article 131

No High Contracting Party shall be allowed to absolve itself or any other High Contracting Party of any liability incurred by itself or by another High Contracting Party in respect of breaches referred to in the preceding Article.

Article 132

At the request of a Party to the conflict, an enquiry shall be instituted, in a manner to be decided between the interested Parties, concerning any alleged violation of the Convention.

If agreement has not been reached concerning the procedure for the enquiry, the Parties should agree on the choice of an umpire who will decide upon the procedure to be followed.

Once the violation has been established, the Parties to the conflict shall put an end to it and shall repress it with the least possible delay.

SECTION II – FINAL PROVISIONS

Article 133

The present Convention is established in English and in French. Both texts are equally authentic.

The Swiss Federal Council shall arrange for official translations of the Convention to be made in the Russian and Spanish languages.

Article 134

The present Convention replaces the Convention of July 27, 1929, in relations between the High Contracting Parties.

Article 135

In the relations between the Powers which are bound by the Hague Convention respecting the Laws and Customs of War on Land, whether that of July 29, 1899, or that of October 18, 1907, and which are parties to the present Convention, this last Convention shall be complementary to Chapter II of the Regulations annexed to the above-mentioned Conventions of the Hague.

Article 136

The present Convention, which bears the date of this day, is open to signature until February 12, 1950, in the name of the Powers represented at the Conference which opened at Geneva on April 21, 1949; furthermore, by Powers not represented at that Conference, but which are parties to the Convention of July 27, 1929.

Article 137

The present Convention shall be ratified as soon as possible and the ratifications shall be deposited at Berne.

A record shall be drawn up of the deposit of each instrument of ratification and certified copies of this record shall be transmitted by the Swiss Federal Council to all the Powers in whose name the Convention has been signed, or whose accession has been notified.

Article 138

The present Convention shall come into force six months after not less than two instruments of ratification have been deposited.

Thereafter, it shall come into force for each High Contracting Party six months after the deposit of the instrument of ratification.

Article 139

From the date of its coming into force, it shall be open to any Power in whose name the present Convention has not been signed, to accede to this Convention.

Article 140

Accessions shall be notified in writing to the Swiss Federal Council, and shall take effect six months after the date on which they are received.

The Swiss Federal Council shall communicate the accessions to all the Powers in whose name the Convention has been signed, or whose accession has been notified.

Article 141

The situations provided for in Articles 2 and 3 shall give immediate effect to ratifications deposited and accessions notified by the Parties to the conflict before or after the beginning of hostilities or occupation. The Swiss Federal Council shall communicate by the quickest method any ratifications or accessions received from Parties to the conflict.

Article 142

Each of the High Contracting Parties shall be at liberty to denounce the present Convention.

The denunication shall be notified in writing to the Swiss Federal Council, which shall transmit it to the Governments of all the High Contracting Parties.

The denunciation shall take effect one year after the notification thereof has been made to the Swiss Federal Council. However, a denunciation of which notification has been made at a time when the denouncing Power is involved in a conflict shall not take effect until peace has been concluded, and until after operations connected with the release and repatriation of the persons protected by the present Convention have been terminated.

The denunciation shall have effect only in respect of the denouncing Power. It shall in no way impair the obligations which the Parties to the conflict shall remain bound to fulfil by virtue of the principles of the law of nations, as they result from the usages established among civilized peoples, from the laws of humanity and the dictates of the public conscience.

Article 143

The Swiss Federal Council shall register the present Convention with the Secretariat of the United Nations. The Swiss Federal Council shall also inform the Secretariat of the United Nations of all ratifications, accessions and denunciations received by it with respect to the present Convention.

IN WITNESS WHEREOF the undersigned, having deposited their respective full powers, have signed the present Convention.

DONE at Geneva this twelfth day of August 1949, in the English and French languages. The original shall be deposited in the Archives of the Swiss Confederation. The Swiss Federal Council shall transmit certified copies thereof to each of the signatory and acceding States.

[Annexes omitted]

CONCLUDING NOTES

The concluding notes for 1949 Geneva Convention III are combined with those for the other three 1949 Geneva Conventions and are to be found after the end of 1949 Geneva Convention IV, below, p. 326.

21. 1949 Geneva Convention IV
Relative to the Protection of
Civilian Persons in Time of War

PREFATORY NOTE

In the early codification of the laws of war, international agreements were primarily concerned with the treatment of combatants rather than civilians. The 1864 Geneva Convention on wounded made very little reference to civilians. The Regulations annexed to 1899 Hague Convention II and 1907 Hague Convention IV make express reference to civilians primarily in respect of the occupation of territory by enemy armed forces, and even these relatively few provisions are fairly basic in character.

The experience of the First World War showed the inadequacy of these provisions: the technological development of weapons, and the enlarged field of military action introduced thereby, demonstrated that civilians could no longer be regarded as being outside hostilities, and indeed, were exposed to the same (or worse) dangers as combatants.

After the First World War, various International Conferences of the Red Cross considered the protection of civilians in war. In the course of such consideration, the International Committee of the Red Cross prepared a preliminary draft convention on the protection of civilians. However, the general optimism of states regarding the question of war made them reluctant to conclude regulations governing the status of civilians in war. The 1929 Geneva diplomatic conference, which revised the 1906 Geneva Convention on wounded and sick armed forces in land warfare and also adopted the convention on prisoners of war, merely recommended that a study be made with a view to the conclusion of a convention on the protection of civilians.

The ICRC prepared a new and more complete draft convention, which was approved at the 15th International Conference of the Red Cross, held in Tokyo in 1934. In January 1939 the Swiss government transmitted the ICRC draft convention to states as a basis for a diplomatic conference which the Swiss government planned to convene in Geneva in early 1940. However, the outbreak of the Second World War intervened.

For civilian populations, the Second World War had exceptionally damaging effects, including very high casualty rates. The principles embodied in the Hague Regulations were clearly insufficient, and the need to adopt an international agreement for the protection of civilians in time of war became apparent. As indicated in the general prefatory note to the four 1949 Geneva Conventions, the process of drafting such an agreement resumed after the war.

1949 Geneva Convention IV is the first international agreement in the laws of war to exclusively address the treatment of civilians. As such, the Convention is a singular contribution to the law. None the less, the Convention is not regarded as introducing specifically new ideas to international law on the subject. It builds on the small number of pre-existing codified provisions, and it expressly states that it supplements rather than replaces the relevant articles in the Hague Regulations. However, the extent to which the regime protecting civilians has been supplemented by the Convention is substantial: of the four 1949 Geneva Conventions, it is the longest.

Date of signature:	Signed on 12 August 1949, and open for signature (see Article 151) until 12 February 1950.
Entry into force:	21 October 1950
Depositary:	Switzerland
Authentic languages:	English and French
Text reprinted from:	*Final Record of the Diplomatic Conference of Geneva of 1949*, Federal Political Department, Berne, n.d., vol. 1, pp. 297–330
Also published in:	75 *UNTS* (1950) 287–417 (Eng. Fr.);
	157 *BFSP* (1950) 355–423 (Eng.);
	UKTS 39 (1958), Cmnd. 550 (Eng. Fr.);
	XXXII *UKPP* (1958–1959) 11 (Eng. Fr.);
	50 *AJIL* (1956) 724–83 (Eng.)

Geneva Convention Relative to the Protection of Civilian Persons in Time of War of August 12, 1949

The undersigned Plenipotentiaries of the Governments represented at the Diplomatic Conference held at Geneva from April 21 to August 12, 1949, for the purpose of establishing a Convention for the Protection of Civilian Persons in Time of War, have agreed as follows:

PART I – GENERAL PROVISIONS

Article 1

The High Contracting Parties undertake to respect and to ensure respect for the present Convention in all circumstances.

Article 2

In addition to the provisions which shall be implemented in peacetime, the present Convention shall apply to all cases of declared war or of any other armed conflict which may arise between two or more of the High Contracting Parties, even if the state of war is not recognized by one of them.

The Convention shall also apply to all cases of partial or total occupation of the territory of a High Contracting Party, even if the said occupation meets with no armed resistance.

Although one of the Powers in conflict may not be a party to the present Convention, the Powers who are parties thereto shall remain bound by it in their mutual relations. They shall futhermore be bound by the Convention in relation to the said Power, if the latter accepts and applies the provisions thereof.

Article 3

In the case of armed conflict not of an international character occurring in the territory of one of the High Contracting Parties, each Party to the conflict shall be bound to apply, as a minimum, the following provisions:

(1) Persons taking no active part in the hostilities, including members of armed forces who have laid down their arms and those placed *hors de combat* by sickness, wounds, detention, or any other cause, shall in all circumstances be treated humanely, without any adverse distinction founded on race, colour, religion or faith, sex, birth or wealth, or any other similar criteria.

To this end, the following acts are and shall remain prohibited at any time and in any place whatsoever with respect to the above-mentioned persons:

(a) violence to life and person, in particular murder of all kinds, mutilation, cruel treatment and torture;

(b) taking of hostages;

(c) outrages upon personal dignity, in particular humiliating and degrading treatment;

(d) the passing of sentences and the carrying out of executions without previous judgment pronounced by a regularly constituted court, affording all the judicial guarantees which are recognized as indispensable by civilized peoples.

(2) The wounded and sick shall be collected and cared for.

An impartial humanitarian body, such as the International Committee of the Red Cross, may offer its services to the Parties to the conflict.

The Parties to the conflict should further endeavour to bring into force, by means of special agreements, all or part of the other provisions of the present Convention.

The application of the preceding provisions shall not affect the legal status of the Parties to the conflict.

Article 4

Persons protected by the Convention are those who, at a given moment and in any manner whatsoever, find themselves, in case of a conflict or occupation, in the hands of a Party to the conflict or Occupying Power of which they are not nationals.

Nationals of a State which is not bound by the Convention are not protected by it. Nationals of a neutral State who find themselves in the territory of a belligerent State, and nationals of a co-belligerent State, shall not be regarded as protected persons while the State of which they are nationals has normal diplomatic representation in the State in whose hands they are.

The provisions of Part II are, however, wider in application, as defined in Article 13.

Persons protected by the Geneva Convention for the Amelioration of the Condition of the Wounded and Sick in Armed Forces in the Field of August 12, 1949, or by the Geneva Convention for the Amelioration of the Condition of Wounded, Sick and Shipwrecked Members of Armed Forces at Sea of August 12, 1949, or by the Geneva Convention relative to the Treatment of Prisoners of War of August 12, 1949, shall not be considered as protected persons within the meaning of the present Convention.

Article 5

Where, in the territory of a Party to the conflict, the latter is satisfied that an individual protected person is definitely suspected of or engaged in activities hostile to the security of the State, such individual person shall not be entitled to claim such rights and privileges under the present Convention as would, if exercised in the favour of such individual person, be prejudicial to the security of such State.

Where in occupied territory an individual protected person is detained as a spy or saboteur, or as a person under definite suspicion of activity hostile to the security of the Occupying Power, such person shall, in those cases where absolute military security so requires, be regarded as having forfeited rights of communication under the present Convention.

In each case, such persons shall nevertheless be treated with humanity, and in case of trial, shall not be deprived of the rights of fair and regular trial prescribed by the present Convention. They shall also be granted the full rights and privileges of a protected person under the present Convention at the earliest date consistent with the security of the State or Occupying Power, as the case may be.

Article 6

The present Convention shall apply from the outset of any conflict or occupation mentioned in Article 2.

In the territory of Parties to the conflict, the application of the present Convention shall cease on the general close of military operations.

In the case of occupied territory, the application of the present Convention shall cease one year after the general close of military operations; however, the Occupying Power shall be bound, for the duration of the occupation, to the extent that such Power exercises the functions of government in such territory, by the provisions of the following Articles of the present Convention: 1 to 12, 27, 29 to 34, 47, 49, 51, 52, 53, 59, 61 to 77, 143.

Protected persons whose release, repatriation or re-establishment may take place after such dates shall meanwhile continue to benefit by the present Convention.

Article 7

In addition to the agreements expressly provided for in Articles 11, 14, 15, 17, 36, 108, 109, 132, 133 and 149, the High Contracting Parties may conclude other special agreements for all matters concerning which they may deem it suitable to make separate provision. No special agreement shall adversely affect the situation of protected persons, as defined by the present Convention, nor restrict the rights which it confers upon them.

Protected persons shall continue to have the benefit of such agreements as long as the Convention is applicable to them, except where express provisions to the contrary are contained in the aforesaid or in subsequent agreements, or where more favourable measures have been taken with regard to them by one or other of the Parties to the conflict.

Article 8

Protected persons may in no circumstances renounce in part or in entirety the rights secured to them by the present Convention, and by the special agreements referred to in the foregoing Article, if such there be.

Article 9

The present Convention shall be applied with the cooperation and under the scrutiny of the Protecting Powers whose duty it is to safeguard the interests of the Parties to the conflict. For this purpose, the Protecting Powers may appoint, apart from their diplomatic or consular staff, delegates from amongst their own nationals or the nationals of other neutral Powers. The said delegates shall be subject to the approval of the Power with which they are to carry out their duties.

The Parties to the conflict shall facilitate to the greatest extent possible the task of the representatives or delegates of the Protecting Powers.

The representatives or delegates of the Protecting Powers shall not in any case exceed their mission under the present Convention. They shall, in particular, take account of the imperative necessities of security of the State wherein they carry out their duties.

Article 10

The provisions of the present Convention constitute no obstacle to the humanitarian activities which the International Committee of the Red Cross or any other impartial humanitarian organization may, subject to the consent of the Parties to the conflict concerned, undertake for the protection of civilian persons and for their relief.

Article 11

The High Contracting Parties may at any time agree to entrust to an organization which offers all guarantees of impartiality and efficacy the duties incumbent on the Protecting Powers by virtue of the present Convention.

When persons protected by the present Convention do not benefit or cease to benefit, no matter for what reason, by the activities of a Protecting Power or of an organization provided for in the first paragraph above, the Detaining Power shall request a neutral State, or such an organization, to undertake the functions performed under the present Convention by a Protecting Power designated by the Parties to a conflict.

If protection cannot be arranged accordingly, the Detaining Power shall request or shall accept, subject to the provisions of this Article, the offer of the services of a humanitarian organization, such as the International Committee of the Red Cross, to assume the humanitarian functions performed by Protecting Powers under the present Convention.

Any neutral Power or any organization invited by the Power concerned or offering itself for these purposes, shall be required to act with a sense of responsibility towards the Party to the conflict on which persons protected by the present Convention depend, and shall be required to furnish sufficient assurances that it is in a position to undertake the appropriate functions and to discharge them impartially.

No derogation from the preceding provisions shall be made by special agreements between Powers one of which is restricted, even temporarily, in its freedom to negotiate with the other Power or its allies by reason of military events, more particularly where the whole, or a substantial part, of the territory of the said Power is occupied.

Whenever in the present Convention mention is made of a Protecting Power, such mention applies to substitute organizations in the sense of the present Article.

The provisions of this Article shall extend and be adapted to cases of nationals of a neutral State who are in occupied territory or who find themselves in the territory of a belligerent State in which the State of which they are nationals has not normal diplomatic representation.

Article 12

In cases where they deem it advisable in the interest of protected persons, particularly in cases of disagreement between the Parties to the conflict as to the application or interpretation of the provisions of the present Convention, the Protecting Powers shall lend their good offices with a view to settling the disagreement.

For this purpose, each of the Protecting Powers may, either at the invitation of one Party or on its own initiative, propose to the Parties to the conflict a meeting of their representatives, and in particular of the authorities responsible for protected persons, possibly on neutral territory suitably chosen. The Parties to the conflict shall be bound to give effect to the proposals made to them for this purpose. The Protecting Powers may, if necessary, propose for approval by the Parties to the conflict, a person belonging to a neutral Power or delegated by the International Committee of the Red Cross, who shall be invited to take part in such a meeting.

PART II – GENERAL PROTECTION OF POPULATIONS AGAINST CERTAIN CONSEQUENCES OF WAR

Article 13

The provisions of Part II cover the whole of the populations of the countries in conflict, without any adverse distinction based, in particular, on race, nationality, religion or political opinion, and are intended to alleviate the sufferings caused by war.

Article 14

In time of peace, the High Contracting Parties and, after the outbreak of hostilities, the Parties thereto, may establish in their own territory and, if the need arises, in occupied areas, hospital and safety zones and localities so organized as to protect from the effects of war, wounded, sick and aged persons, children under fifteen, expectant mothers and mothers of children under seven.

Upon the outbreak and during the course of hostilities, the Parties concerned may conclude agreements on mutual recognition of the zones and localities they have created. They may for this purpose implement the provisions of the Draft Agreement annexed to the present Convention, with such amendments as they may consider necessary.

The Protecting Powers and the International Committee of the Red Cross are invited to lend their good offices in order to facilitate the institution and recognition of these hospital and safety zones and localities.

Article 15
Any Party to the conflict may, either direct or through a neutral State or some humanitarian organization, propose to the adverse Party to establish, in the regions where fighting is taking place, neutralized zones intended to shelter from the effects of war the following persons, without distinction:
  (*a*) wounded and sick combatants or non-combatants;
  (*b*) civilian persons who take no part in hostilities, and who, while they reside in the zones, perform no work of a military character.
When the Parties concerned have agreed upon the geographical position, administration, food supply and supervision of the proposed neutralized zone, a written agreement shall be concluded and signed by the representatives of the Parties to the conflict. The agreement shall fix the beginning and the duration of the neutralization of the zone.

Article 16
The wounded and sick, as well as the infirm, and expectant mothers, shall be the object of particular protection and respect.

As far as military considerations allow, each Party to the conflict shall facilitate the steps taken to search for the killed and wounded, to assist the shipwrecked and other persons exposed to grave danger, and to protect them against pillage and ill-treatment.

Article 17
The Parties to the conflict shall endeavour to conclude local agreements for the removal from besieged or encircled areas, of wounded, sick, infirm, and aged persons, children and maternity cases, and for the passage of ministers of all religions, medical personnel and medical equipment on their way to such areas.

Article 18
Civilian hospitals organized to give care to the wounded and sick, the infirm and maternity cases, may in no circumstances be the object of attack, but shall at all times be respected and protected by the Parties to the conflict.

States which are Parties to a conflict shall provide all civilian hospitals with certificates showing that they are civilian hospitals and that the buildings which they occupy are not used for any purpose which would deprive these hospitals of protection in accordance with Article 19.

Civilian hospitals shall be marked by means of the emblem provided for in Article 38 of the Geneva Convention for the Amelioration of the Condition of the Wounded and Sick in Armed Forces in the Field of August 12, 1949, but only if so authorized by the State.

The Parties to the conflict shall, in so far as military considerations permit, take the necessary steps to make the distinctive emblems indicating civilian hospitals clearly visible to the enemy land, air and naval forces in order to obviate the possibility of any hostile action.

In view of the dangers to which hospitals may be exposed by being close to military objectives, it is recommended that such hospitals be situated as far as possible from such objectives.

Article 19
The protection to which civilian hospitals are entitled shall not cease unless they are used to commit, outside their humanitarian duties, acts harmful to the enemy. Protection may, however, cease only after due warning has been given, naming, in all appropriate cases, a reasonable time limit, and after such warning has remained unheeded.

The fact that sick or wounded members of the armed forces are nursed in these hospitals, or the presence of small arms and ammunition taken from such combatants and not yet handed to the proper service, shall not be considered to be acts harmful to the enemy.

Article 20
Persons regularly and solely engaged in the operation and administration of civilian hospitals, including the personnel engaged in the search for, removal and transporting of and caring for wounded and sick civilians, the infirm and maternity cases, shall be respected and protected.

In occupied territory and in zones of military operations, the above personnel shall be recognizable by means of an identity card certifying their status, bearing the photograph of the holder and embossed with the stamp of the responsible authority, and also by means of a stamped, water-resistant armlet which they shall wear on the left arm while carrying out their duties. This armlet shall be issued by the State and shall bear the emblem provided for in Article 38 of the Geneva Convention for the Amelioration of the Condition of the Wounded and Sick in Armed Forces in the Field of August 12, 1949.

Other personnel who are engaged in the operation and administration of civilian hospitals shall be entitled to respect and protection and to wear the armlet, as provided in and under the conditions prescribed in this Article, while they are employed on such duties. The identity card shall state the duties on which they are employed.

The management of each hospital shall at all times hold at the disposal of the competent national or occupying authorities an up-to-date list of such personnel.

Article 21

Convoys of vehicles or hospital trains on land or specially provided vessels on sea, conveying wounded and sick civilians, the infirm and maternity cases, shall be respected and protected in the same manner as the hospitals provided for in Article 18, and shall be marked, with the consent of the State, by the display of the distinctive emblem provided for in Article 38 of the Geneva Convention for the Amelioration of the Condition of the Wounded and Sick in Armed Forces in the Field of August 12, 1949.

Article 22

Aircraft exclusively employed for the removal of wounded and sick civilians, the infirm and maternity cases, or for the transport of medical personnel and equipment, shall not be attacked, but shall be respected while flying at heights, times and on routes specifically agreed upon between all the Parties to the conflict concerned.

They may be marked with the distinctive emblem provided for in Article 38 of the Geneva Convention for the Amelioration of the Condition of the Wounded and Sick in Armed Forces in the Field of August 12, 1949.

Unless agreed otherwise, flights over enemy or enemy-occupied territory are prohibited.

Such aircraft shall obey every summons to land. In the event of a landing thus imposed, the aircraft with its occupants may continue its flight after examination, if any.

Article 23

Each High Contracting Party shall allow the free passage of all consignments of medical and hospital stores and objects necessary for religious worship intended only for civilians of another High Contracting Party, even if the latter is its adversary. It shall likewise permit the free passage of all consignments of essential foodstuffs, clothing and tonics intended for children under fifteen, expectant mothers and maternity cases.

The obligation of a High Contracting Party to allow the free passage of the consignments indicated in the preceding paragraph

Civilians 281

is subject to the condition that this Party is satisfied that there are no serious reasons for fearing:

(a) that the consignments may be diverted from their destination,

(b) that the control may not be effective, or

(c) that a definite advantage may accrue to the military efforts or economy of the enemy through the substitution of the above-mentioned consignments for goods which would otherwise be provided or produced by the enemy or through the release of such material, services or facilities as would otherwise be required for the production of such goods.

The Power which allows the passage of the consignments indicated in the first paragraph of this Article may make such permission conditional on the distribution to the persons benefited thereby being made under the local supervision of the Protecting Powers.

Such consignments shall be forwarded as rapidly as possible, and the Power which permits their free passage shall have the right to prescribe the technical arrangements under which such passage is allowed.

Article 24

The Parties to the conflict shall take the necessary measures to ensure that children under fifteen, who are orphaned or are separated from their families as a result of the war, are not left to their own resources, and that their maintenance, the exercise of their religion and their education are facilitated in all circumstances. Their education shall, as far as possible, be entrusted to persons of a similar cultural tradition.

The Parties to the conflict shall facilitate the reception of such children in a neutral country for the duration of the conflict with the consent of the Protecting Power, if any, and under due safeguards for the observance of the principles stated in the first paragraph.

They shall, furthermore, endeavour to arrange for all children under twelve to be identified by the wearing of identity discs, or by some other means.

Article 25

All persons in the territory of a Party to the conflict, or in a territory occupied by it, shall be enabled to give news of a strictly personal nature to members of their families, wherever they may be, and to receive news from them. This correspondence shall be forwarded speedily and without undue delay.

If, as a result of circumstances, it becomes difficult or impossible to exchange family correspondence by the ordinary post, the Parties to the conflict concerned shall apply to a neutral intermediary, such as the Central Agency provided for in Article 140, and shall decide in consultation with it how to ensure the fulfilment of their obligations under the best possible conditions, in particular with the cooperation of the National Red Cross (Red Crescent, Red Lion and Sun) Societies.

If the Parties to the conflict deem it necessary to restrict family correspondence, such restrictions shall be confined to the compulsory use of standard forms containing twenty-five freely chosen words, and to the limitation of the number of these forms despatched to one each month.

Article 26

Each Party to the conflict shall facilitate enquiries made by members of families dispersed owing to the war, with the object of renewing contact with one another and of meeting, if possible. It shall encourage, in particular, the work of organizations engaged on this task provided they are acceptable to it and conform to its security regulations.

PART III — STATUS AND TREATMENT OF PROTECTED PERSONS

SECTION I — PROVISIONS COMMON TO THE TERRITORIES OF THE PARTIES TO THE CONFLICT AND TO OCCUPIED TERRITORIES

Article 27

Protected persons are entitled, in all circumstances, to respect for their persons, their honour, their family rights, their religious convictions and practices, and their manners and customs. They shall at all times be humanely treated, and shall be protected especially against all acts of violence or threats thereof and against insults and public curiosity.

Women shall be especially protected against any attack on their honour, in particular against rape, enforced prostitution, or any form of indecent assault.

Without prejudice to the provisions relating to their state of health, age and sex, all protected persons shall be treated with the same consideration by the Party to the conflict in whose power they are, without any adverse distinction based, in particular, on race, religion or political opinion.

However, the Parties to the conflict may take such measures of control and security in regard to protected persons as may be necessary as a result of the war.

Article 28

The presence of a protected person may not be used to render certain points or areas immune from military operations.

Article 29

The Party to the conflict in whose hands protected persons may be, is responsible for the treatment accorded to them by its agents, irrespective of any individual responsibility which may be incurred.

Article 30

Protected persons shall have every facility for making application to the Protecting Powers, the International Committee of the Red Cross, the National Red Cross (Red Crescent, Red Lion and Sun) Society of the country where they may be, as well as to any organization that might assist them.

These several organizations shall be granted all facilities for that purpose by the authorities, within the bounds set by military or security considerations.

Apart from the visits of the delegates of the Protecting Powers and of the International Committee of the Red Cross, provided for by Article 143, the Detaining or Occupying Powers shall facilitate as much as possible visits to protected persons by the representatives of other organizations whose object is to give spiritual aid or material relief to such persons.

Article 31

No physical or moral coercion shall be exercised against protected persons, in particular to obtain information from them or from third parties.

Article 32

The High Contracting Parties specifically agree that each of them is prohibited from taking any measure of such a character as to cause the physical suffering or extermination of protected persons in their hands. This prohibition applies not only to murder, torture, corporal punishment, mutilation and medical or scientific experiments not necessitated by the medical treatment of a protected person, but also to any other measures of brutality whether applied by civilian or military agents.

Article 33

No protected person may be punished for an offence he or she has not personally committed. Collective penalties and likewise all measures of intimidation or of terrorism are prohibited.

Pillage is prohibited.

Reprisals against protected persons and their property are prohibited.

Article 34

The taking of hostages is prohibited.

SECTION II — ALIENS IN THE TERRITORY OF A PARTY TO THE CONFLICT

Article 35

All protected persons who may desire to leave the territory at the outset of, or during a conflict, shall be entitled to do so, unless their departure is contrary to the national interests of the State. The applications of such persons to leave shall be decided in accordance with regularly established procedures and the decision shall be taken as rapidly as possible. Those persons permitted to leave may provide themselves with the necessary funds for their journey and take with them a reasonable amount of their effects and articles of personal use.

If any such person is refused permission to leave the territory, he shall be entitled to have such refusal reconsidered as soon as possible by an appropriate court or administrative board designated by the Detaining Power for that purpose.

Upon request, representatives of the Protecting Power shall, unless reasons of security prevent it, or the persons concerned object, be furnished with the reasons for refusal of any request for permission to leave the territory and be given, as expeditiously as possible, the names of all persons who have been denied permission to leave.

Article 36

Departures permitted under the foregoing Article shall be carried out in satisfactory conditions as regards safety, hygiene, sanitation and food. All costs in connection therewith, from the point of exit in the territory of the Detaining Power, shall be borne by the country of destination, or, in the case of accommodation in a neutral country, by the Power whose nationals are benefited. The practical details of such movements may, if necessary, be settled by special agreements between the Powers concerned.

The foregoing shall not prejudice such special agreements as may be concluded between Parties to the conflict concerning the exchange and repatriation of their nationals in enemy hands.

Article 37

Protected persons who are confined pending proceedings or serving a sentence involving loss of liberty, shall during their confinement be humanely treated.

As soon as they are released, they may ask to leave the territory in conformity with the foregoing Articles.

Article 38

With the exception of special measures authorized by the present Convention, in particular by Articles 27 and 41 thereof, the situation of protected persons shall continue to be regulated, in principle, by the provisions concerning aliens in time of peace. In any case, the following rights shall be granted to them:

(1) They shall be enabled to receive the individual or collective relief that may be sent to them.

(2) They shall, if their state of health so requires, receive medical attention and hospital treatment to the same extent as the nationals of the State concerned.

(3) They shall be allowed to practise their religion and to receive spiritual assitance from ministers of their faith.

(4) If they reside in an area particularly exposed to the dangers of war, they shall be authorized to move from that area to the same extent as the nationals of the State concerned.

(5) Children under fifteen years, pregnant women and mothers of children under seven years shall benefit by any preferential treatment to the same extent as the nationals of the State concerned.

Article 39

Protected persons who, as a result of the war, have lost their gainful employment, shall be granted the opportunity to find paid employment. That opportunity shall, subject to security considerations and to the provisions of Article 40, be equal to that enjoyed by the nationals of the Power in whose territory they are.

Where a Party to the conflict applies to a protected person methods of control which result in his being unable to support himself, and especially if such a person is prevented for reasons of security from finding paid employment on reasonable conditions, the said Party shall ensure his support and that of his dependants.

Protected persons may in any case receive allowances from their home country, the Protecting Power, or the relief societies referred to in Article 30.

Article 40

Protected persons may be compelled to work only to the same extent as nationals of the Party to the conflict in whose territory they are.

If protected persons are of enemy nationality, they may only be compelled to do work which is normally necessary to ensure the feeding, sheltering, clothing, transport and health of human beings and which is not directly related to the conduct of military operations.

In the cases mentioned in the two preceding paragraphs, protected persons compelled to work shall have the benefit of the same working conditions and of the same safeguards as national workers, in particular as regards wages, hours of labour, clothing and equipment, previous training and compensation for occupational accidents and diseases.

If the above provisions are infringed, protected persons shall be allowed to exercise their right of complaint in accordance with Article 30.

Article 41

Should the Power in whose hands protected persons may be consider the measures of control mentioned in the present Convention to be inadequate, it may not have recourse to any other measure of control more severe than that of assigned residence or internment, in accordance with the provisions of Articles 42 and 43.

In applying the provisions of Article 39, second paragraph, to the cases of persons required to leave their usual places of residence by virtue of a decision placing them in assigned residence elsewhere, the Detaining Power shall be guided as closely as possible by the standards of welfare set forth in Part III, Section IV of this Convention.

Article 42

The internment or placing in assigned residence of protected persons may be ordered only if the security of the Detaining Power makes it absolutely necessary.

If any person, acting through the representatives of the Protecting Power, voluntarily demands internment, and if his situation renders this step necessary, he shall be interned by the Power in whose hands he may be.

Article 43

Any protected person who has been interned or placed in assigned residence shall be entitled to have such action reconsidered as soon as possible by an appropriate court or administrative board designated by the Detaining Power for that purpose. If the internment or placing in assigned residence is maintained, the court or administrative board shall periodically, and at least twice yearly, give consideration to his or her case, with a view to the favourable amendment of the initial decision, if circumstances permit.

Unless the protected persons concerned object, the Detaining

Power shall, as rapidly as possible, give the Protecting Power the names of any protected persons who have been interned or subjected to assigned residence, or who have been released from internment or assigned residence. The decisions of the courts or boards mentioned in the first paragraph of the present Article shall also, subject to the same conditions, be notified as rapidly as possible to the Protecting Power.

Article 44

In applying the measures of control mentioned in the present Convention, the Detaining Power shall not treat as enemy aliens exclusively on the basis of their nationality *de jure* of an enemy State, refugees who do not, in fact, enjoy the protection of any government.

Article 45

Protected persons shall not be transferred to a Power which is not a party to the Convention.

This provision shall in no way constitute an obstacle to the repatriation of protected persons, or to their return to their country of residence after the cessation of hostilities.

Protected persons may be transferred by the Detaining Power only to a Power which is a party to the present Convention and after the Detaining Power has satisfied itself of the willingness and ability of such transferee Power to apply the present Convention. If protected persons are transferred under such circumstances, responsibility for the application of the present Convention rests on the Power accepting them, while they are in its custody. Nevertheless, if that Power fails to carry out the provisions of the present Convention in any important respect, the Power by which the protected persons were transferred shall, upon being so notified by the Protecting Power, take effective measures to correct the situation or shall request the return of the protected persons. Such request must be complied with.

In no circumstances shall a protected person be transferred to a country where he or she may have reason to fear persecution for his or her political opinions or religious beliefs.

The provisions of this Article do not constitute an obstacle to the extradition, in pursuance of extradition treaties concluded before the outbreak of hostilities, of protected persons accused of offences against ordinary criminal law.

Article 46

In so far as they have not been previously withdrawn, restrictive measures taken regarding protected persons shall be cancelled as soon as possible after the close of hostilities.

Restrictive measures affecting their property shall be cancelled, in accordance with the law of the Detaining Power, as soon as possible after the close of hostilities.

SECTION III — OCCUPIED TERRITORIES

Article 47

Protected persons who are in occupied territory shall not be deprived, in any case or in any manner whatsoever, of the benefits of the present Convention by any change introduced, as the result of the occupation of a territory, into the institutions or government of the said territory, nor by any agreement concluded between the authorities of the occupied territories and the Occupying Power, nor by any annexation by the latter of the whole or part of the occupied territory.

Article 48

Protected persons who are not nationals of the Power whose territory is occupied, may avail themselves of the right to leave the territory subject to the provisions of Article 35, and decisions thereon shall be taken according to the procedure which the Occupying Power shall establish in accordance with the said Article.

Article 49

Individual or mass forcible transfers, as well as deportations of protected persons from occupied territory to the territory of the Occupying Power or to that of any other country, occupied or not, are prohibited, regardless of their motive.

Nevertheless, the Occupying Power may undertake total or partial evacuation of a given area if the security of the population or imperative military reasons so demand. Such evacuations may not involve the displacement of protected persons outside the bounds of the occupied territory except when for material reasons it is impossible to avoid such displacement. Persons thus evacuated shall be transferred back to their homes as soon as hostilities in the area in question have ceased.

The Occupying Power undertaking such transfers or evacuations shall ensure, to the greatest practicable extent, that proper accommodation is provided to receive the protected persons, that the removals are effected in satisfactory conditions of hygiene, health, safety and nutrition, and that members of the same family are not separated.

The Protecting Power shall be informed of any transfers and evacuations as soon as they have taken place.

The Occupying Power shall not detain protected persons in an area particularly exposed to the dangers of war unless the security of the population or imperative military reasons so demand.

The Occupying Power shall not deport or transfer parts of its own civilian population into the territory it occupies.

Article 50

The Occupying Power shall, with the cooperation of the national and local authorities, facilitate the proper working of all institutions devoted to the care and education of children.

The Occupying Power shall take all necessary steps to facilitate the identification of children and the registration of their parentage. It may not, in any case, change their personal status, nor enlist them in formations or organizations subordinate to it.

Should the local institutions be inadequate for the purpose, the Occupying Power shall make arrangements for the maintenance and education, if possible by persons of their own nationality, language and religion, of children who are orphaned or separated from their parents as a result of the war and who cannot be adequately cared for by a near relative or friend.

A special section of the Bureau set up in accordance with Article 136 shall be responsible for taking all necessary steps to identify children whose identity is in doubt. Particulars of their parents or other near relatives should always be recorded if available.

The Occupying Power shall not hinder the application of any preferential measures in regard to food, medical care and protection against the effects of war, which may have been adopted prior to the occupation in favour of children under fifteen years, expectant mothers, and mothers of children under seven years.

Article 51

The Occupying Power may not compel protected persons to serve in its armed or auxiliary forces. No pressure or propaganda which aims at securing voluntary enlistment is permitted.

The Occupying Power may not compel protected persons to work unless they are over eighteen years of age, and then only on work which is necessary either for the needs of the army of occupation, or for the public utility services, or for the feeding, sheltering, clothing, transportation or health of the population of the occupied country. Protected persons may not be compelled to undertake any work which would involve them in the obligation of taking part in military operations. The Occupying Power may not compel protected persons to employ forcible means to ensure the security of the installations where they are performing compulsory labour.

The work shall be carried out only in the occupied territory where the persons whose services have been requisitioned are. Every such person shall, so far as possible, be kept in his usual place of employment. Workers shall be paid a fair wage and the work shall be proportionate to their physical and intellectual capacities. The legislation in force in the occupied country concerning working conditions, and safeguards as regards, in particular, such matters as wages, hours of work, equipment, preliminary training and compensation for occupational accidents and diseases, shall be applicable to the protected persons assigned to the work referred to in this Article.

In no case shall requisition of labour lead to a mobilization of workers in an organization of a military or semi-military character.

Article 52

No contract, agreement or regulation shall impair the right of any worker, whether voluntary or not and wherever he may be, to apply to the representatives of the Protecting Power in order to request the said Power's intervention.

All measures aiming at creating unemployment or at restricting the opportunities offered to workers in an occupied territory, in order to induce them to work for the Occupying Power, are prohibited.

Article 53

Any destruction by the Occupying Power of real or personal property belonging individually or collectively to private persons, or to the State, or to other public authorities, or to social or cooperative organizations, is prohibited, except where such destruction is rendered absolutely necessary by military operations.

Article 54

The Occupying Power may not alter the status of public officials or judges in the occupied territories, or in any way apply sanctions to or take any measures of coercion or discrimination against them, should they abstain from fulfilling their functions for reasons of conscience.

This prohibition does not prejudice the application of the second paragraph of Article 51. It does not affect the right of the Occupying Power to remove public officials from their posts.

Article 55

To the fullest extent of the means available to it, the Occupying Power has the duty of ensuring the food and medical supplies of the population; it should, in particular, bring in the necessary foodstuffs, medical stores and other articles if the resources of the occupied territory are inadequate.

The Occupying Power may not requisition foodstuffs, articles or medical supplies available in the occupied territory, except for use by the occupation forces and administration personnel, and then only if the requirements of the civilian population have been taken into account. Subject to the provisions of other international Conventions, the Occupying Power shall make arrangements to ensure that fair value is paid for any requisitioned goods.

The Protecting Power shall, at any time, be at liberty to verify the state of the food and medical supplies in occupied territories, except where temporary restrictions are made necessary by imperative military requirements.

Article 56

To the fullest extent of the means available to it, the Occupying Power has the duty of ensuring and maintaining, with the cooperation of national and local authorities, the medical and hospital establishments and services, public health and hygiene in the occupied territory, with particular reference to the adoption and application of the prophylactic and preventive measures necessary to combat the spread of contagious diseases and epidemics. Medical personnel of all categories shall be allowed to carry out their duties.

If new hospitals are set up in occupied territory and if the competent organs of the occupied State are not operating there, the occupying authorities shall, if necessary, grant them the recognition provided for in Article 18. In similar circumstances, the occupying authorities shall also grant recognition to hospital personnel and transport vehicles under the provisions of Articles 20 and 21.

In adopting measures of health and hygiene and in their implementation, the Occupying Power shall take into consideration the moral and ethical susceptibilities of the population of the occupied territory.

Article 57

The Occupying Power may requisition civilian hospitals only temporarily and only in cases of urgent necessity for the care of military wounded and sick, and then on condition that suitable arrangements are made in due time for the care and treatment of the patients and for the needs of the civilian population for hospital accommodation.

The material and stores of civilian hospitals cannot be requisitioned so long as they are necessary for the needs of the civilian population.

Article 58

The Occupying Power shall permit ministers of religion to give spiritual assistance to the members of their religious communities.

The Occupying Power shall also accept consignments of books and articles required for religious needs and shall facilitate their distribution in occupied territory.

Article 59

If the whole or part of the population of an occupied territory is inadequately supplied, the Occupying Power shall agree to relief schemes on behalf of the said population, and shall facilitate them by all the means at its disposal.

Such schemes, which may be undertaken either by States or by impartial humanitarian organizations such as the International Committee of the Red Cross, shall consist, in particular, of the provision of consignments of foodstuffs, medical supplies and clothing.

All Contracting Parties shall permit the free passage of these consignments and shall guarantee their protection.

A Power granting free passage to consignments on their way to territory occupied by an adverse Party to the conflict shall, however, have the right to search the consignments, to regulate their passage according to prescribed times and routes, and to be reasonably satisfied through the Protecting Power that these consignments are to be used for the relief of the needy population and are not to be used for the benefit of the Occupying Power.

Article 60

Relief consignments shall in no way relieve the Occupying Power of any of its responsibilities under Articles 55, 56 and 59. The Occupying Power shall in no way whatsoever divert relief consignments from the purpose for which they are intended, except in cases of urgent necessity, in the interests of the population of the occupied territory and with the consent of the Protecting Power.

Article 61

The distribution of the relief consignments referred to in the foregoing Articles shall be carried out with the cooperation and under the supervision of the Protecting Power. This duty may also be delegated, by agreement between the Occupying Power and the Protecting Power, to a neutral Power, to the International Committee of the Red Cross or to any other impartial humanitarian body.

Such consignments shall be exempt in occupied territory from all charges, taxes or customs duties unless these are necessary in the interests of the economy of the territory. The Occupying Power shall facilitate the rapid distribution of these consignments.

All Contracting Parties shall endeavour to permit the transit and transport, free of charge, of such relief consignments on their way to occupied territories.

Article 62
Subject to imperative reasons of security, protected persons in occupied territories shall be permitted to receive the individual relief consignments sent to them.

Article 63
Subject to temporary and exceptional measures imposed for urgent reasons of security by the Occupying Power:
(*a*) recognized National Red Cross (Red Crescent, Red Lion and Sun) Societies shall be able to pursue their activities in accordance with Red Cross principles, as defined by the International Red Cross Conferences. Other relief societies shall be permitted to continue their humanitarian activities under similar conditions;
(*b*) the Occupying Power may not require any changes in the personnel or structure of these societies, which would prejudice the aforesaid activities.
The same principles shall apply to the activities and personnel of special organizations of a non-military character, which already exist or which may be established, for the purpose of ensuring the living conditions of the civilian population by the maintenance of the essential public utility services, by the distribution of relief and by the organization of rescues.

Article 64
The penal laws of the occupied territory shall remain in force, with the exception that they may be repealed or suspended by the Occupying Power in cases where they constitute a threat to its security or an obstacle to the application of the present Convention. Subject to the latter consideration and to the necessity for ensuring the effective administration of justice, the tribunals of the occupied territory shall continue to function in respect of all offences covered by the said laws.
The Occupying Power may, however, subject the population of the occupied territory to provisions which are essential to enable the Occupying Power to fulfil its obligations under the present Convention, to maintain the orderly government of the territory, and to ensure the security of the Occupying Power, of the members and property of the occupying forces or administration, and likewise of the establishments and lines of communication used by them.

Article 65

The penal provisions enacted by the Occupying Power shall not come into force before they have been published and brought to the knowledge of the inhabitants in their own language. The effect of these penal provisions shall not be retroactive.

Article 66

In case of a breach of the penal provisions promulgated by it by virtue of the second paragraph of Article 64, the Occupying Power may hand over the accused to its properly constituted, non-political military courts, on condition that the said courts sit in the occupied country. Courts of appeal shall preferably sit in the occupied country.

Article 67

The courts shall apply only those provisions of law which were applicable prior to the offence, and which are in accordance with general principles of law, in particular the principle that the penalty shall be proportioned to the offence. They shall take into consideration the fact that the accused is not a national of the Occupying Power.

Article 68

Protected persons who commit an offence which is solely intended to harm the Occupying Power, but which does not constitute an attempt on the life or limb of members of the occupying forces or administration, nor a grave collective danger, nor seriously damage the property of the occupying forces or administration or the installations used by them, shall be liable to internment or simple imprisonment, provided the duration of such internment or imprisonment is proportionate to the offence committed. Furthermore, internment or imprisonment shall, for such offences, be the only measure adopted for depriving protected persons of liberty. The courts provided for under Article 66 of the present Convention may at their discretion convert a sentence of imprisonment to one of internment for the same period.

The penal provisions promulgated by the Occupying Power in accordance with Articles 64 and 65 may impose the death penalty on a protected person only in cases where the person is guilty of espionage, of serious acts of sabotage against the military installations of the Occupying Power or of intentional offences which have caused the death of one or more persons, provided that such offences were punishable by death under the law of the occupied territory in force before the occupation began.

The death penalty may not be pronounced against a protected

person unless the attention of the court has been particularly called to the fact that since the accused is not a national of the Occupying Power, he is not bound to it by any duty of allegiance.

In any case, the death penalty may not be pronounced against a protected person who was under eighteen years of age at the time of the offence.

Article 69

In all cases, the duration of the period during which a protected person accused of an offence is under arrest awaiting trial or punishment shall be deducted from any period of imprisonment awarded.

Article 70

Protected persons shall not be arrested, prosecuted or convicted by the Occupying Power for acts committed or for opinions expressed before the occupation, or during a temporary interruption thereof, with the exception of breaches of the laws and customs of war.

Nationals of the Occupying Power who, before the outbreak of hostilities, have sought refuge in the territory of the occupied State, shall not be arrested, prosecuted, convicted or deported from the occupied territory, except for offences committed after the outbreak of hostilities, or for offences under common law committed before the outbreak of hostilities which, according to the law of the occupied State, would have justified extradition in time of peace.

Article 71

No sentence shall be pronounced by the competent courts of the Occupying Power except after a regular trial.

Accused persons who are prosecuted by the Occupying Power shall be promptly informed, in writing, in a language which they understand, of the particulars of the charges preferred against them, and shall be brought to trial as rapidly as possible. The Protecting Power shall be informed of all proceedings instituted by the Occupying Power against protected persons in respect of charges involving the death penalty or imprisonment for two years or more; it shall be enabled, at any time, to obtain information regarding the state of such proceedings. Furthermore, the Protecting Power shall be entitled, on request, to be furnished with all particulars of these and of any other proceedings instituted by the Occupying Power against protected persons.

The notification to the Protecting Power, as provided for in the second paragraph above, shall be sent immediately, and shall in any case reach the Protecting Power three weeks before the date of the first hearing. Unless, at the opening of the trial, evidence is submitted that the provisions of this Article are fully complied with, the trial shall not proceed. The notification shall include the following particulars:

    (*a*) description of the accused;

    (*b*) place of residence or detention;

    (*c*) specification of the charge or charges (with mention of the penal provisions under which it is brought);

    (*d*) designation of the court which will hear the case;

    (*e*) place and date of the first hearing.

Article 72

Accused persons shall have the right to present evidence necessary to their defence and may, in particular, call witnesses. They shall have the right to be assisted by a qualified advocate or counsel of their own choice, who shall be able to visit them freely and shall enjoy the necessary facilities for preparing the defence.

Failing a choice by the accused, the Protecting Power may provide him with an advocate or counsel. When an accused person has to meet a serious charge and the Protecting Power is not functioning, the Occupying Power, subject to the consent of the accused, shall provide an advocate or counsel.

Accused persons shall, unless they freely waive such assistance, be aided by an interpreter, both during preliminary investigation and during the hearing in court. They shall have the right at any time to object to the interpreter and to ask for his replacement.

Article 73

A convicted person shall have the right of appeal provided for by the laws applied by the court. He shall be fully informed of his right to appeal or petition and of the time limit within which he may do so.

The penal procedure provided in the present Section shall apply, as far as it is applicable, to appeals. Where the laws applied by the Court make no provision for appeals, the convicted person shall have the right to petition against the finding and sentence to the competent authority of the Occupying Power.

Article 74

Representatives of the Protecting Power shall have the right to attend the trial of any protected person, unless the hearing has, as an exceptional measure, to be held *in camera* in the interests of the security of the Occupying Power, which shall then notify the Protecting Power. A notification in respect of the date and place of trial shall be sent to the Protecting Power.

Any judgment involving a sentence of death, or imprisonment for two years or more, shall be communicated, with the relevant grounds, as rapidly as possible to the Protecting Power. The notification shall contain a reference to the notification made under Article 71, and, in the case of sentences of imprisonment, the name of the place where the sentence is to be served. A record of judgments other than those referred to above shall be kept by the court and shall be open to inspection by representatives of the Protecting Power. Any period allowed for appeal in the case of sentences involving the death penalty, or imprisonment of two years or more, shall not run until notification of judgment has been received by the Protecting Power.

Article 75

In no case shall persons condemned to death be deprived of the right of petition for pardon or reprieve.

No death sentence shall be carried out before the expiration of a period of at least six months from the date of receipt by the Protecting Power of the notification of the final judgment confirming such death sentence, or of an order denying pardon or reprieve.

The six months period of suspension of the death sentence herein prescribed may be reduced in individual cases in circumstances of grave emergency involving an organized threat to the security of the Occupying Power or its forces, provided always that the Protecting Power is notified of such reduction and is given reasonable time and opportunity to make representations to the competent occupying authorities in respect of such death sentences.

Article 76

Protected persons accused of offences shall be detained in the occupied country, and if convicted they shall serve their sentences therein. They shall, if possible, be separated from other detainees and shall enjoy conditions of food and hygiene which will be sufficient to keep them in good health, and which will be at least equal to those obtaining in prisons in the occupied country.

They shall receive the medical attention required by their state of health.

They shall also have the right to receive any spiritual assistance which they may require.

Women shall be confined in separate quarters and shall be under the direct supervision of women.

Proper regard shall be paid to the special treatment due to minors.

Protected persons who are detained shall have the right to be visited by delegates of the Protecting Power and of the International Committee of the Red Cross, in accordance with the provisions of Article 143.

Such persons shall have the right to receive at least one relief parcel monthly.

Article 77

Protected persons who have been accused of offences or convicted by the courts in occupied territory, shall be handed over at the close of occupation, with the relevant records, to the authorities of the liberated territory.

Article 78

If the Occupying Power considers it necessary, for imperative reasons of security, to take safety measures concerning protected persons, it may, at the most, subject them to assigned residence or to internment.

Decisions regarding such assigned residence or internment shall be made according to a regular procedure to be prescribed by the Occupying Power in accordance with the provisions of the present Convention. This procedure shall include the right of appeal for the parties concerned. Appeals shall be decided with the least possible delay. In the event of the decision being upheld, it shall be subject to periodical review, if possible every six months, by a competent body set up by the said Power.

Protected persons made subject to assigned residence and thus required to leave their homes shall enjoy the full benefit of Article 39 of the present Convention.

SECTION IV — REGULATIONS FOR THE TREATMENT OF INTERNEES

CHAPTER I — *General Provisions*

Article 79

The Parties to the conflict shall not intern protected persons, except in accordance with the provisions of Articles 41, 42, 43, 68 and 78.

Article 80

Internees shall retain their full civil capacity and shall exercise such attendant rights as may be compatible with their status.

Article 81

Parties to the conflict who intern protected persons shall be bound to provide free of charge for their maintenance, and to grant them also the medical attention required by their state of health.

No deduction from the allowances, salaries or credits due to the internees shall be made for the repayment of these costs.

The Detaining Power shall provide for the support of those dependent on the internees, if such dependents are without adequate means of support or are unable to earn a living.

Article 82

The Detaining Power shall, as far as possible, accommodate the internees according to their nationality, language and customs. Internees who are nationals of the same country shall not be separated merely because they have different languages.

Throughout the duration of their internment, members of the same family, and in particular parents and children, shall be lodged together in the same place of internment, except when separation of a temporary nature is necessitated for reasons of employment or health or for the purposes of enforcement of the provisions of Chapter IX of the present Section. Internees may request that their children who are left at liberty without parental care shall be interned with them.

Wherever possible, interned members of the same family shall be housed in the same premises and given separate accommodation from other internees, together with facilities for leading a proper family life.

CHAPTER II — *Places of Internment*

Article 83

The Detaining Power shall not set up places of internment in areas particularly exposed to the dangers of war.

The Detaining Power shall give the enemy Powers, through the intermediary of the Protecting Powers, all useful information regarding the geographical location of places of internment.

Whenever military considerations permit, internment camps shall be indicated by the letters IC, placed so as to be clearly visible in the daytime from the air. The Powers concerned may, however, agree upon any other system of marking. No place other than an internment camp shall be marked as such.

Article 84

Internees shall be accommodated and administered separately from prisoners of war and from persons deprived of liberty for any other reason.

Article 85

The Detaining Power is bound to take all necessary and possible measures to ensure that protected persons shall, from the outset of their internment, be accommodated in buildings or quarters which afford every possible safeguard as regards hygiene and health, and provide efficient protection against the rigours of the climate and the effects of the war. In no case shall permanent places of internment be situated in unhealthy areas, or in districts the climate of which is injurious to the internees. In all cases where the district, in which a protected person is temporarily interned, is in an unhealthy area or has a climate which is harmful to his health, he shall be removed to a more suitable place of internment as rapidly as circumstances permit.

The premises shall be fully protected from dampness, adequately heated and lighted, in particular between dusk and lights out. The sleeping quarters shall be sufficiently spacious and well ventilated, and the internees shall have suitable bedding and sufficient blankets, account being taken of the climate, and the age, sex, and state of health of the internees.

Internees shall have for their use, day and night, sanitary conveniences which conform to the rules of hygiene and are constantly maintained in a state of cleanliness. They shall be provided with sufficient water and soap for their daily personal toilet and for washing their personal laundry; installations and facilities necessary for this purpose shall be granted to them. Showers or baths shall also be available. The necessary time shall be set aside for washing and for cleaning.

Whenever it is necessary, as an exceptional and temporary measure, to accommodate women internees who are not members of a family unit in the same place of internment as men, the provision of separate sleeping quarters and sanitary conveniences for the use of such women internees shall be obligatory.

Article 86

The Detaining Power shall place at the disposal of interned persons, of whatever denomination, premises suitable for the holding of their religious services.

Article 87

Canteens shall be installed in every place of internment, except where other suitable facilities are available. Their purpose shall be to enable internees to make purchases, at prices not higher than local market prices, of foodstuffs and articles of everyday use, including soap and tobacco, such as would increase their personal well-being and comfort.

Profits made by canteens shall be credited to a welfare fund to be set up for each place of internment, and administered for the benefit of the internees attached to such place of internment. The Internee Committee provided for in Article 102 shall have the right to check the management of the canteen and of the said fund.

When a place of internment is closed down, the balance of the welfare fund shall be transferred to the welfare fund of a place of internment for internees of the same nationality, or, if such a place does not exist, to a central welfare fund which shall be administered for the benefit of all internees remaining in the custody of the Detaining Power. In case of a general release, the said profits shall be kept by the Detaining Power, subject to any agreement to the contrary between the Powers concerned.

Article 88

In all places of internment exposed to air raids and other hazards of war, shelters adequate in number and structure to ensure the necessary protection shall be installed. In case of alarms, the internees shall be free to enter such shelters as quickly as possible, excepting those who remain for the protection of their quarters against the aforesaid hazards. Any protective measures taken in favour of the population shall also apply to them.

All due precautions must be taken in places of internment against the danger of fire.

CHAPTER III — *Food and Clothing*

Article 89

Daily food rations for internees shall be sufficient in quantity, quality and variety to keep internees in a good state of health and prevent the development of nutritional deficiencies. Account shall also be taken of the customary diet of the internees.

Internees shall also be given the means by which they can prepare for themselves any additional food in their possession.

Sufficient drinking water shall be supplied to internees. The use of tobacco shall be permitted.

Internees who work shall receive additional rations in proportion to the kind of labour which they perform.

Expectant and nursing mothers, and children under fifteen years of age, shall be given additional food, in proportion to their physiological needs.

Article 90

When taken into custody internees shall be given all facilities to provide themselves with the necessary clothing, footwear and change of underwear, and later on, to procure further supplies if required. Should any internees not have sufficient clothing, account being taken of the climate, and be unable to procure any, it shall be provided free of charge to them by the Detaining Power.

The clothing supplied by the Detaining Power to internees and the outward markings placed on their own clothes shall not be ignominious nor expose them to ridicule.

Workers shall receive suitable working outfits, including protective clothing, whenever the nature of their work so requires.

CHAPTER IV — *Hygiene and Medical Attention*

Article 91

Every place of internment shall have an adequate infirmary, under the direction of a qualified doctor, where internees may have the attention they require, as well as an appropriate diet. Isolation wards shall be set aside for cases of contagious or mental diseases.

Maternity cases and internees suffering from serious diseases, or whose condition requires special treatment, a surgical operation or hospital care, must be admitted to any institution where adequate treatment can be given and shall receive care not inferior to that provided for the general population.

Internees shall, for preference, have the attention of medical personnel of their own nationality.

Internees may not be prevented from presenting themselves to the medical authorities for examination. The medical authorities of the Detaining Power shall, upon request, issue to every internee who has undergone treatment an official certificate showing the nature of his illness or injury, and the duration and nature of the treatment given. A duplicate of this certificate shall be forwarded to the Central Agency provided for in Article 140.

Treatment, including the provision of any apparatus necessary for the maintenance of internees in good health, particularly dentures and other artificial appliances and spectacles, shall be free of charge to the internee.

Article 92

Medical inspections of internees shall be made at least once a month. Their purpose shall be, in particular, to supervise the general state of health, nutrition and cleanliness of internees, and to detect contagious diseases, especially tuberculosis, malaria, and venereal diseases. Such inspections shall include, in particular, the checking of weight of each internee and, at least once a year, radioscopic examination.

CHAPTER V — *Religious, Intellectual and Physical Activities*

Article 93

Internees shall enjoy complete latitude in the exercise of their religious duties, including attendance at the services of their faith, on condition that they comply with the disciplinary routine prescribed by the detaining authorities.

Ministers of religion who are interned shall be allowed to minister freely to the members of their community. For this purpose, the Detaining Power shall ensure their equitable allocation amongst the various places of internment in which there are internees speaking the same language and belonging to the same religion. Should such ministers be too few in number, the Detaining Power shall provide them with the necessary facilities, including means of transport, for moving from one place to another, and they shall be authorized to visit any internees who are in hospital. Ministers of religion shall be at liberty to correspond on matters concerning their ministry with the religious authorities in the country of detention and, as far as possible, with the international religious organizations of their faith. Such correspondence shall not be considered as forming a part of the quota mentioned in Article 107. It shall, however, be subject to the provisions of Article 112.

When internees do not have at their disposal the assistance of ministers of their faith, or should these latter be too few in number, the local religious authorities of the same faith may appoint, in agreement with the Detaining Power, a minister of the internees' faith or, if such a course is feasible from a denominational point of view, a minister of similar religion or a qualified layman. The latter shall enjoy the facilities granted to the ministry he has assumed. Persons so appointed shall comply with all regulations laid down by the Detaining Power in the interests of discipline and security.

Article 94

The Detaining Power shall encourage intellectual, educational and recreational pursuits, sports and games amongst internees, whilst leaving them free to take part in them or not. It shall take all practicable measures to ensure the exercise thereof, in particular by providing suitable premises.

All possible facilities shall be granted to internees to continue their studies or to take up new subjects. The education of children and young people shall be ensured; they shall be allowed to attend schools either within the place of internment or outside.

Internees shall be given opportunities for physical exercise, sports and outdoor games. For this purpose, sufficient open spaces shall be set aside in all places of internment. Special playgrounds shall be reserved for children and young people.

Article 95

The Detaining Power shall not employ internees as workers, unless they so desire. Employment which, if undertaken under compulsion by a protected person not in internment, would involve a breach of Articles 40 or 51 of the present Convention, and employment on work which is of a degrading or humiliating character are in any case prohibited.

After a working period of six weeks, internees shall be free to give up work at any moment, subject to eight days' notice.

These provisions constitute no obstacle to the right of the Detaining Power to employ interned doctors, dentists and other medical personnel in their professional capacity on behalf of their fellow internees, or to employ internees for administrative and maintenance work in places of internment and to detail such persons for work in the kitchens or for other domestic tasks, or to require such persons to undertake duties connected with the protection of internees against aerial bombardment or other war risks. No internee may, however, be required to perform tasks for which he is, in the opinion of a medical officer, physically unsuited.

The Detaining Power shall take entire responsibility for all working conditions, for medical attention, for the payment of wages, and for ensuring that all employed internees receive compensation for occupational accidents and diseases. The standards prescribed for the said working conditions and for compensation shall be in accordance with the national laws and regulations, and with the existing practice; they shall in no case be inferior to those obtaining for work of the same nature in the same district. Wages for work done shall be determined on an equitable basis by special agreements between the internees, the Detaining Power, and, if the case arises, employers other than the Detaining Power, due regard being paid to the obligation of the Detaining Power to provide for free maintenance of internees and for the medical attention which their state of health may require. Internees permanently detailed for categories of work mentioned in the third paragraph of this Article, shall be paid fair wages by the Detaining Power. The working conditions and the scale of compensation for occupational accidents and diseases to internees thus detailed, shall not be inferior to those applicable to work of the same nature in the same district.

Article 96

All labour detachments shall remain part of and dependent upon a place of internment. The competent authorities of the Detaining Power and the commandant of a place of internment shall be responsible for the observance in a labour detachment of the provisions of the present Convention. The commandant shall keep an up-to-date list of the labour detachments subordinate to him and shall communicate it to the delegates of the Protecting Power, of the International Committee of the Red Cross and of other humanitarian organizations who may visit the places of internment.

CHAPTER VI — *Personal Property and Financial Resources*

Article 97

Internees shall be permitted to retain articles of personal use. Monies, cheques, bonds, etc., and valuables in their possession may not be taken from them except in accordance with established procedure. Detailed receipts shall be given therefor.

The amounts shall be paid into the account of every internee as provided for in Article 98. Such amounts may not be converted into any other currency unless legislation in force in the territory in which the owner is interned so requires or the internee gives his consent.

Articles which have above all a personal or sentimental value may not be taken away.

A woman internee shall not be searched except by a woman.

On release or repatriation, internees shall be given all articles, monies or other valuables taken from them during internment and shall receive in currency the balance of any credit to their accounts kept in accordance with Article 98, with the exception of any articles or amounts withheld by the Detaining Power by virtue of its legislation in force. If the property of an internee is so withheld, the owner shall receive a detailed receipt.

Family or identity documents in the possession of internees may not be taken away without a receipt being given. At no time shall internees be left without identity documents. If they have none, they shall be issued with special documents drawn up by the detaining authorities, which will serve as their identity papers until the end of their internment.

Internees may keep on their persons a certain amount of money, in cash or in the shape of purchase coupons, to enable them to make purchases.

Article 98

All internees shall receive regular allowances, sufficient to enable them to purchase goods and articles, such as tobacco, toilet requisites, etc. Such allowances may take the form of credits or purchase coupons.

Furthermore, internees may receive allowances from the Power to which they owe allegiance, the Protecting Powers, the organizations which may assist them, or their families, as well as the income on their property in accordance with the law of the Detaining Power. The amount of allowances granted by the Power to which they owe allegiance shall be the same for each category of internees (infirm, sick, pregnant women, etc.), but may not be allocated by that Power or distributed by the Detaining Power on the basis of discriminations between internees which are prohibited by Article 27 of the present Convention.

The Detaining Power shall open a regular account for every internee, to which shall be credited the allowances named in the present Article, the wages earned and the remittances received, together with such sums taken from him as may be available under the legislation in force in the territory in which he is interned. Internees shall be granted all facilities consistent with the legislation in force in such territory to make remittances to their families and to other dependants. They may draw from their accounts the amounts necessary for their personal expenses, within the limits fixed by the Detaining Power. They shall at all times be afforded reasonable facilities for consulting and obtaining copies of their accounts. A statement of accounts shall be furnished to the Protecting Power on request, and shall accompany the internee in case of transfer.

CHAPTER VII — *Administration and Discipline*

Article 99

Every place of internment shall be put under the authority of a responsible officer, chosen from the regular military forces or the regular civil administration of the Detaining Power. The officer in charge of the place of internment must have in his possession a copy of the present Convention in the official language, or one of the official languages, of his country and shall be responsible for its application. The staff in control of internees shall be instructed in the provisions of the present Convention and of the administrative measures adopted to ensure its application.

The text of the present Convention and the texts of special agreements concluded under the said Convention shall be posted inside the place of internment, in a language which the internees understand, or shall be in the possession of the Internee Committee.

Regulations, orders, notices and publications of every kind shall be communicated to the internees and posted inside the places of internment, in a language which they understand.

Every order and command addressed to internees individually, must likewise be given in a language which they understand.

Article 100

The disciplinary regime in places of internment shall be consistent which humanitarian principles, and shall in no circumstances include regulations imposing on internees any physical exertion dangerous to their health or involving physical or moral victimization. Identification by tattooing or imprinting signs or markings on the body, is prohibited.

In particular, prolonged standing and roll-calls, punishment drill, military drill and manœuvres, or the reduction of food rations, are prohibited.

Article 101

Internees shall have the right to present to the authorities in whose power they are, any petition with regard to the conditions of internment to which they are subjected.

They shall also have the right to apply without restriction through the Internee Committee or, if they consider it necessary, direct to the representatives of the Protecting Power, in order to indicate to them any points on which they may have complaints to make with regard to the conditions of internment.

Such petitions and complaints shall be transmitted forthwith and without alteration, and even if the latter are recognized to be unfounded, they may not occasion any punishment.

Periodic reports on the situation in places of internment and as to the needs of the internees, may be sent by the Internee Committees to the representatives of the Protecting Powers.

Article 102

In every place of internment, the internees shall freely elect by secret ballot every six months, the members of a Committee empowered to represent them before the Detaining and the Protecting Powers, the International Committee of the Red Cross and any other organization which may assist them. The members of the Committee shall be eligible for re-election.

Internees so elected shall enter upon their duties after their election has been approved by the detaining authorities. The reasons for any refusals or dismissals shall be communicated to the Protecting Powers concerned.

Article 103

The Internee Committees shall further the physical, spiritual and intellectual well-being of the internees.

In case the internees decide, in particular, to organize a system of mutual assistance amongst themselves, this organization would be within the competence of the Committees in addition to the special duties entrusted to them under other provisions of the present Convention.

Article 104

Members of Internee Committees shall not be required to perform any other work, if the accomplishment of their duties is rendered more difficult thereby.

Members of Internee Committees may appoint from amongst the internees such assistants as they may require. All material facilities shall be granted to them, particularly a certain freedeom of movement necessary for the accomplishment of their duties (visits to labour detachments, receipt of supplies, etc.).

All facilities shall likewise be accorded to members of Internee Committees for communication by post and telegraph with the detaining authorities, the Protecting Powers, the International Committee of the Red Cross and their delegates, and with the organizations which give assistance to internees. Committee members in labour detachments shall enjoy similar facilities for communication with their Internee Committee in the principal place of internment. Such communications shall not be limited, nor considered as forming a part of the quota mentioned in Article 107.

Members of Internee Committees who are transferred shall be allowed a reasonable time to acquaint their successors with current affairs.

CHAPTER VIII — *Relations with the Exterior*

Article 105

Immediately upon interning protected persons, the Detaining Powers shall inform them, the Power to which they owe allegiance and their Protecting Power of the measures taken for executing the provisions of the present Chapter. The Detaining Powers shall likewise inform the Parties concerned of any subsequent modifications of such measures.

Article 106

As soon as he is interned, or at the latest not more than one week after his arrival in a place of internment, and likewise in cases of sickness or transfer to another place of internment or to a hospital, every internee shall be enabled to send direct to his family, on the one hand, and to the Central Agency provided for by Article 140, on the other, an internment card similar, if possible, to the model annexed to the present Convention, informing his relatives of his detention, address and state of health. The said cards shall be forwarded as rapidly as possible and may not be delayed in any way.

Article 107

Internees shall be allowed to send and receive letters and cards. If the Detaining Power deems it necessary to limit the number of letters and cards sent by each internee, the said number shall not be less than two letters and four cards monthly; these shall be drawn up so as to conform as closely as possible to the models annexed to the present Convention. If limitations must be placed on the correspondence addressed to internees, they may be ordered only by the Power to which such internees owe allegiance, possibly at the request of the Detaining Power. Such letters and cards must be conveyed with reasonable despatch; they may not be delayed or retained for disciplinary reasons.

Internees who have been a long time without news, or who find it impossible to receive news from their relatives, or to give them news by the ordinary postal route, as well as those who are at a considerable distance from their homes, shall be allowed to send telegrams, the charges being paid by them in the currency at their disposal. They shall likewise benefit by this provision in cases which are recognized to be urgent.

As a rule, internees' mail shall be written in their own language. The Parties to the conflict may authorize correspondence in other languages.

Article 108

Internees shall be allowed to receive, by post or by any other means, individual parcels or collective shipments containing in particular foodstuffs, clothing, medical supplies, as well as books and objects of a devotional, educational or recreational character which may meet their needs. Such shipments shall in no way free the Detaining Power from the obligations imposed upon it by virtue of the present Convention.

Should military necessity require the quantity of such shipments to be limited, due notice thereof shall be given to the Protecting Power and to the International Committee of the Red Cross, or to any other organization giving assistance to the internees and responsible for the forwarding of such shipments.

The conditions for the sending of individual parcels and collective shipments shall, if necessary, be the subject of special agreements between the Powers concerned, which may in no case delay the receipt by the internees of relief supplies. Parcels of clothing and foodstuffs may not include books. Medical relief supplies shall, as a rule, be sent in collective parcels.

Article 109

In the absence of special agreements between Parties to the conflict regarding the conditions for the receipt and distribution of collective relief shipments, the regulations concerning collective relief which are annexed to the present Convention shall be applied.

The special agreements provided for above shall in no case restrict the right of Internee Committees to take possession of collective relief shipments intended for internees, to undertake their distribution and to dispose of them in the interests of the recipients.

Nor shall such agreements restrict the right of representatives of the Protecting Powers, the International Committee of the Red Cross, or any other organization giving assistance to internees and responsible for the forwarding of collective shipments, to supervise their distribution to the recipients.

Article 110

All relief shipments for internees shall be exempt from import, customs and other dues.

All matter sent by mail, including relief parcels sent by parcel post and remittances of money, addressed from other countries to internees or despatched by them through the post office, either direct or through the Information Bureaux provided for in Article 136 and the Central Information Agency provided for in Article 140, shall be exempt from all postal dues both in the countries of origin and destination and in intermediate countries. To this end, in particular, the exemption provided by the Universal Postal Convention of 1947 and by the agreements of the Universal Postal Union in favour of civilians of enemy nationality detained in camps or civilian prisons, shall be extended to the other interned persons protected by the present Convention. The countries not signatory to the above-mentioned agreements shall be bound to grant freedom from charges in the same circumstances.

The cost of transporting relief shipments which are intended for internees and which, by reason of their weight or any other cause, cannot be sent through the post office, shall be borne by the Detaining Power in all the territories under its control. Other Powers which are Parties to the present Convention shall bear the cost of transport in their respective territories.

Costs connected with the transport of such shipments, which are not covered by the above paragraphs, shall be charged to the senders.

The High Contracting Parties shall endeavour to reduce, so far as possible, the charges for telegrams sent by internees, or addressed to them.

Article 111

Should military operations prevent the Powers concerned from fulfilling their obligation to ensure the conveyance of the mail and relief shipments provided for in Articles 106, 107, 108 and 113, the Protecting Powers concerned, the International Committee of the Red Cross or any other organization duly approved by the Parties to the conflict may undertake the conveyance of such shipments by suitable means (rail, motor vehicles, vessels or aircraft, etc.). For this purpose, the High Contracting Parties shall endeavour to supply them with such transport, and to allow its circulation, especially by granting the necessary safe-conducts.

Such transport may also be used to convey:

(*a*) correspondence, lists and reports exchange between the Central Information Agency referred to in Article 140 and the National Bureaux referred to in Article 136;

(*b*) correspondence and reports relating to internees which the Protecting Powers, the International Committee of the Red Cross or any other organization assisting the internees exchange either with their own delegates or with the Parties to the conflict.

These provisions in no way detract from the right of any Party to the conflict to arrange other means of transport if it should so prefer, nor preclude the granting of safe-conducts, under mutually agreed conditions, to such means of transport.

The costs occasioned by the use of such means of transport shall be borne, in proportion to the importance of the shipments, by the Parties to the conflict whose nationals are benefited thereby.

Article 112

The censoring of correspondence addressed to internees or despatched by them shall be done as quickly as possible.

The examination of consignments intended for internees shall not be carried out under conditions that will expose the goods contained in them to deterioration. It shall be done in the presence of the addressee, or of a fellow-internee duly delegated by him. The delivery to internees of individual or collective consignments shall not be delayed under the pretext of difficulties of censorship.

Any prohibition of correspondence ordered by the Parties to the conflict either for military or political reasons, shall be only temporary and its duration shall be as short as possible.

Article 113

The Detaining Powers shall provide all reasonable facilities for the transmission, through the Protecting Power or the Central Agency provided for in Article 140, or as otherwise required, of wills, powers of attorney, letters of authority, or any other documents intended for internees or despatched by them.

In all cases the Detaining Powers shall facilitate the execution and authentication in due legal form of such documents on behalf of internees, in particular by allowing them to consult a lawyer.

Article 114

The Detaining Power shall afford internees all facilities to enable them to manage their property, provided this is not incompatible with the conditions of internment and the law which is applicable. For this purpose, the said Power may give them permission to leave the place of internment in urgent cases and if circumstances allow.

Article 115

In all cases where an internee is a party to proceedings in any court, the Detaining Power shall, if he so requests, cause the court to be informed of his detention and shall, within legal limits, ensure that all necessary steps are taken to prevent him from being in any way prejudiced, by reason of his internment, as regards the preparation and conduct of his case or as regards the execution of any judgment of the court.

Article 116

Every internee shall be allowed to receive visitors, especially near relatives, at regular intervals and as frequently as possible.

As far as is possible, internees shall be permitted to visit their homes in urgent cases, particularly in cases of death or serious illness of relatives.

CHAPTER IX — *Penal and Disciplinary Sanctions*

Article 117

Subject to the provisions of the present Chapter, the laws in force in the territory in which they are detained will continue to apply to internees who commit offences during internment.

If general laws, regulations or orders declare acts committed by internees to be punishable, whereas the same acts are not punishable when committed by persons who are not internees, such acts shall entail disciplinary punishments only.

No internee may be punished more than once for the same act, or on the same count.

Article 118

The courts or authorities shall in passing sentence take as far as possible into account the fact that the defendant is not a national of the Detaining Power. They shall be free to reduce the penalty prescribed for the offence with which the internee is charged and shall not be obliged, to this end, to apply the minimum sentence prescribed.

Imprisonment in premises without daylight and, in general, all forms of cruelty without exception are forbidden.

Internees who have served disciplinary or judicial sentences shall not be treated differently from other internees.

The duration of preventive detention undergone by an internee shall be deducted from any disciplinary or judicial penalty involving confinement to which he may be sentenced.

Internee Committees shall be informed of all judicial proceedings instituted against internees whom they represent, and of their result.

Article 119

The disciplinary punishments applicable to internees shall be the following:

(1) A fine which shall not exceed 50 per cent of the wages which the internee would otherwise receive under the provisions of Article 95 during a period of not more than thirty days.
(2) Discontinuance of privileges granted over and above the treatment provided for by the present Convention.
(3) Fatigue duties, not exceeding two hours daily, in connection with the maintenance of the place of internment.
(4) Confinement.

In no case shall disciplinary penalties be inhuman, brutal or dangerous for the health of internees. Account shall be taken of the internee's age, sex and state of health.

The duration of any single punishment shall in no case exceed a maximum of thirty consecutive days, even if the internee is answerable for several breaches of discipline when his case is dealt with, whether such breaches are connected or not.

Article 120

Internees who are recaptured after having escaped or when attempting to escape, shall be liable only to disciplinary punishment in respect of this act, even if it is a repeated offence.

Article 118, paragraph 3, notwithstanding, internees punished as a result of escape or attempt to escape, may be subjected to special surveillance, on condition that such surveillance does not affect the state of their health, that it is exercised in a place of internment and that it does not entail the abolition of any of the safeguards granted by the present Convention.

Internees who aid and abet an escape or attempt to escape, shall be liable on this count to disciplinary punishment only.

Article 121

Escape, or attempt to escape, even if it is a repeated offence, shall not be deemed an aggravating circumstance in cases where an internee is prosecuted for offences committed during his escape.

The Parties to the conflict shall ensure that the competent authorities exercise leniency in deciding whether punishment inflicted for an offence shall be of a disciplinary or judicial nature, especially in respect of acts committed in connection with an escape, whether successful or not.

Article 122

Acts which constitute offences against discipline shall be investigated immediately. This rule shall be applied, in particular, in cases of escape or attempt to escape. Recaptured internees shall be handed over to the competent authorities as soon as possible.

In case of offences against discipline, confinement awaiting trial shall be reduced to an absolute minimum for all internees, and shall not exceed fourteen days. Its duration shall in any case be deducted from any sentence of confinement.

The provisions of Articles 124 and 125 shall apply to internees who are in confinement awaiting trial for offences against discipline.

Article 123

Without prejudice to the competence of courts and higher authorities, disciplinary punishment may be ordered only by the commandant of the place of internment, or by a responsible officer or official who replaces him, or to whom he has delegated his disciplinary powers.

Before any disciplinary punishment is awarded, the accused internee shall be given precise information regarding the offences of which he is accused, and given an opportunity of explaining his conduct and of defending himself. He shall be permitted, in particular, to call witnesses and to have recourse, if necessary, to the services of a qualified interpreter. The decision shall be announced in the presence of the accused and of a member of the Internee Committee.

The period elapsing between the time of award of a disciplinary punishment and its execution shall not exceed one month.

When an internee is awarded a further disciplinary punishment, a period of at least three days shall elapse between the execution of any two of the punishments, if the duration of one of these is ten days or more.

A record of disciplinary punishments shall be maintained by the commandant of the place of internment and shall be open to inspection by representatives of the Protecting Power.

Article 124
Internees shall not in any case be transferred to penitentiary establishments (prisons, penitentiaries, convict prisons, etc.) to undergo disciplinary punishment therein.

The premises in which disciplinary punishments are undergone shall conform to sanitary requirements; they shall in particular be provided with adequate bedding. Internees undergoing punishment shall be enabled to keep themselves in a state of cleanliness.

Women internees undergoing disciplinary punishment shall be confined in separate quarters from male internees and shall be under the immediate supervision of women.

Article 125
Internees awarded disciplinary punishment shall be allowed to exercise and to stay in the open air at least two hours daily.

They shall be allowed, if they so request, to be present at the daily medical inspections. They shall receive the attention which their state of health requires and, if necessary, shall be removed to the infirmary of the place of internment or to a hospital.

They shall have permission to read and write, likewise to send and receive letters. Parcels and remittances of money, however, may be withheld from them until the completion of their punishment; such consignments shall meanwhile be entrusted to the Internee Committee, who will hand over to the infirmary the perishable goods contained in the parcels.

No internee given a disciplinary punishment may be deprived of the benefit of the provisions of Articles 107 and 143 of the present Convention.

Article 126

The provisions of Articles 71 to 76 inclusive shall apply, by analogy, to proceedings against internees who are in the national territory of the Detaining Power.

CHAPTER X — *Transfers of Internees*

Article 127

The transfer of internees shall always be effected humanely. As a general rule, it shall be carried out by rail or other means of transport, and under conditions at least equal to those obtaining for the forces of the Detaining Power in their changes of station. If, as an exceptional measure, such removals have to be effected on foot, they may not take place unless the internees are in a fit state of health, and may not in any case expose them to excessive fatigue.

The Detaining Power shall supply internees during transfer with drinking water and food sufficient in quantity, quality and variety to maintain them in good health, and also with the necessary clothing, adequate shelter and the necessary medical attention. The Detaining Power shall take all suitable precautions to ensure their safety during transfer, and shall establish before their departure a complete list of all internees transferred.

Sick, wounded or infirm internees and maternity cases shall not be transferred if the journey would be seriously detrimental to them, unless their safety imperatively so demands.

If the combat zone draws close to a place of internment, the internees in the said place shall not be transferred unless their removal can be carried out in adequate conditions of safety, or unless they are exposed to greater risks by remaining on the spot than by being transferred.

When making decisions regarding the transfer of internees, the Detaining Power shall take their interests into account and, in particular, shall not do anything to increase the difficulties of repatriating them or returning them to their own homes.

Article 128

In the event of transfer, internees shall be officially advised of their departure and of their new postal address. Such notification shall be given in time for them to pack their luggage and inform their next of kin.

They shall be allowed to take with them their personal effects, and the correspondence and parcels which have arrived for them. The weight of such baggage may be limited if the conditions of transfer so require, but in no case to less than twenty-five kilograms per internee.

Mail and parcels addressed to their former place of internment shall be forwarded to them without delay.

The commandant of the place of internment shall take, in agreement with the Internee Committee, any measures needed to ensure the transport of the internees' community property and of the luggage the internees are unable to take with them in consequence of restrictions imposed by virtue of the second paragraph.

CHAPTER XI — *Deaths*

Article 129

The wills of internees shall be received for safe-keeping by the responsible authorities; and in the event of the death of an internee his will shall be transmitted without delay to a person whom he has previously designated.

Deaths of internees shall be certified in every case by a doctor, and a death certificate shall be made out, showing the causes of death and the conditions under which it occurred.

An official record of the death, duly registered, shall be drawn up in accordance with the procedure relating thereto in force in the territory where the place of internment is situated, and a duly certified copy of such record shall be transmitted without delay to the Protecting Power as well as to the Central Agency referred to in Article 140.

Article 130

The detaining authorities shall ensure that internees who die while interned are honourably buried, if possible according to the rites of the religion to which they belonged, and that their graves are respected, properly maintained, and marked in such a way that they can always be recognized.

Deceased internees shall be buried in individual graves unless unavoidable circumstances require the use of collective graves. Bodies may be cremated only for imperative reasons of hygiene, on account of the religion of the deceased or in accordance with his expressed wish to this effect. In case of cremation, the fact shall be stated and the reasons given in the death certificate of the deceased. The ashes shall be retained for safe-keeping by the detaining authorities and shall be transferred as soon as possible to the next of kin on their request.

As soon as circumstances permit, and not later than the close of hostilities, the Detaining Power shall forward lists of graves of deceased internees to the Powers on whom deceased internees depended, through the Information Bureaux provided for in Article 136. Such lists shall include all particulars necessary for the identification of the deceased internees, as well as the exact location of their graves.

Article 131

Every death or serious injury of an internee, caused or suspected to have been caused by a sentry, another internee or any other person, as well as any death the cause of which is unknown, shall be immediately followed by an official enquiry by the Detaining Power.

A communication on this subject shall be sent immediately to the Protecting Power. The evidence of any witnesses shall be taken, and a report including such evidence shall be prepared and forwarded to the said Protecting Power.

If the enquiry indicates the guilt of one or more persons, the Detaining Power shall take all necessary steps to ensure the prosecution of the person or persons responsible.

CHAPTER XII — *Release, Repatriation and
Accommodation in Neutral Countries*

Article 132

Each interned person shall be released by the Detaining Power as soon as the reasons which necessitated his internment no longer exist.

The Parties to the conflict shall, moreover, endeavour during the course of hostilities, to conclude agreements for the release, the repatriation, the return to places of residence or the accommodation in a neutral country of certain classes of internees, in particular children, pregnant women and mothers with infants and young children, wounded and sick, and internees who have been detained for a long time.

Article 133

Internment shall cease as soon as possible after the close of hostilities.

Internees in the territory or a Party to the conflict, against whom penal proceedings are pending for offences not exclusively subject to disciplinary penalties, may be detained until the close of such proceedings and, if circumstances require, until the completion of the penalty. The same shall apply to internees who have been previously sentenced to a punishment depriving them of liberty.

By agreement between the Detaining Power and the Powers

concerned, committees may be set up after the close of hostilities, or of the occupation of territories, to search for dispersed internees.

Article 134

The High Contracting Parties shall endeavour, upon the close of hostilities or occupation, to ensure the return of all internees to their last place of residence, or to facilitate their repatriation.

Article 135

The Detaining Power shall bear the expense of returning released internees to the places where they were residing when interned, or, if it took them into custody while they were in transit or on the high seas, the cost of completing their journey or of their return to their point of departure.

Where a Detaining Power refuses permission to reside in its territory to a released internee who previously had his permanent domicile therein, such Detaining Power shall pay the cost of the said internee's repatriation. If, however, the internee elects to return to his country on his own responsibility or in obedience to the Government of the Power to which he owes allegiance, the Detaining Power need not pay the expenses of his journey beyond the point of his departure from its territory. The Detaining Power need not pay the cost of repatriation of an internee who was interned at his own request.

If internees are transferred in accordance with Article 45, the transferring and receiving Powers shall agree on the portion of the above costs to be borne by each.

The foregoing shall not prejudice such special agreements as may be concluded between Parties to the conflict concerning the exchange and repatriation of their nationals in enemy hands.

SECTION V — INFORMATION BUREAUX AND CENTRAL AGENCY

Article 136

Upon the outbreak of a conflict and in all cases of occupation, each of the Parties to the conflict shall establish an official Information Bureau responsible for receiving and transmitting information in respect of the protected persons who are in its power.

Each of the Parties to the conflict shall, within the shortest possible period, give its Bureau information of any measure taken by it concerning any protected persons who are kept in custody for more than two weeks, who are subjected to assigned residence or who are interned. It shall, furthermore, require its various departments concerned with such matters to provide the aforesaid Bureau promptly with information concerning all changes pertaining to these protected persons, as, for example, transfers, releases, re-patriations, escapes, admittances to hospitals, births and deaths.

Article 137

Each national Bureau shall immediately forward information concerning protected persons by the most rapid means to the Powers of whom the aforesaid persons are nationals, or to Powers in whose territory they resided, through the intermediary of the Protecting Powers and likewise through the Central Agency provided for in Article 140. The Bureaux shall also reply to all enquiries which may be received regarding protected persons.

Information Bureaux shall transmit information concerning a protected person unless its transmission might be detrimental to the person concerned or to his or her relatives. Even in such a case, the information may not be withheld from the Central Agency which, upon being notified of the circumstances, will take the necessary precautions indicated in Article 140.

All communications in writing made by any Bureau shall be authenticated by a signature or a seal.

Article 138

The information received by the national Bureau and transmitted by it shall be of such a character as to make it possible to identify the protected person exactly and to advise his next of kin quickly. The information in respect of each person shall include at least his surname, first names, place and date of birth, nationality, last residence and distinguishing characteristics, the first name of the father and the maiden name of the mother, the date, place and nature of the action taken with regard to the individual, the address at which correspondence may be sent to him and the name and address of the person to be informed.

Likewise, information regarding the state of health of internees who are seriously ill or seriously wounded shall be supplied regularly and if possible every week.

Article 139

Each national Information Bureau shall, furthermore, be responsible for collecting all personal valuables left by protected persons mentioned in Article 136, in particular those who have been repatriated or released, or who have escaped or died; it shall forward the said valuables to those concerned, either direct, or, if necessary, through the Central Agency. Such articles shall be sent by the Bureau in sealed packets which shall be accompanied by statements giving clear and full identity particulars of the person to whom the articles belonged, and by a complete list of the contents of the parcel. Detailed records shall be maintained of the receipt and despatch of all such valuables.

Article 140

A Central Information Agency for protected persons, in particular for internees, shall be created in a neutral country. The International Committee of the Red Cross shall, if it deems necessary, propose to the Powers concerned the organization of such an Agency, which may be the same as that provided for in Article 123 of the Geneva Convention relative to the Treatment of Prisoners of War of August 12, 1949.

The function of the Agency shall be to collect all information of the type set forth in Article 136 which it may obtain through official or private channels and to transmit it as rapidly as possible to the countries of origin or of residence of the persons concerned, except in cases where such transmissions might be detrimental to the persons whom the said information concerns, or to their relatives. It shall receive from the Parties to the conflict all reasonable facilities for effecting such transmissions.

The High Contracting Parties, and in particular those whose nationals benefit by the services of the Central Agency, are requested to give the said Agency the financial aid it may require.

The foregoing provisions shall in no' way be interpreted as restricting the humanitarian activities of the International Committee of the Red Cross and of the relief Societies described in Article 142.

Article 141

The national Information Bureaux and the Central Information Agency shall enjoy free postage for all mail, likewise the exemptions provided for in Article 110, and further, so far as possible, exemption from telegraphic charges or, at least, greatly reduced rates.

PART IV — EXECUTION OF THE CONVENTION

SECTION I — GENERAL PROVISIONS

Article 142

Subject to the measures which the Detaining Powers may consider essential to ensure their security or to meet any other reasonable need, the representatives of religious organizations, relief societies, or any other organizations assisting the protected persons, shall receive from these Powers, for themselves or their duly accredited agents, all facilities for visiting the protected persons, for distributing relief supplies and material from any source, intended for educational, recreational or religious purposes, or for assisting them in organizing their leisure time within the places of internment. Such societies or organizations may be constituted in the territory of the Detaining Power, or in any other country, or they may have an international character.

The Detaining Power may limit the number of societies and organizations whose delegates are allowed to carry out their activities in its territory and under its supervision, on condition, however, that such limitation shall not hinder the supply of effective and adequate relief to all protected persons.

The special position of the International Committee of the Red Cross in this field shall be recognized and respected at all times.

Article 143

Representatives or delegates of the Protecting Powers shall have permission to go to all places where protected persons are, particularly to places of internment, detention and work.

They shall have access to all premises occupied by protected persons and shall be able to interview the latter without witnesses, personally or through an interpreter.

Such visits may not be prohibited except for reasons of imperative military necessity, and then only as an exceptional and temporary measure. Their duration and frequency shall not be restricted.

Such representatives and delegates shall have full liberty to select the places they wish to visit. The Detaining or Occupying Power, the Protecting Power and when occasion arises the Power of origin of the persons to be visited, may agree that compatriots of the internees shall be permitted to participate in the visits.

The delegates of the International Committee of the Red Cross shall also enjoy the above prerogatives. The appointment of such delegates shall be submitted to the approval of the Power governing the territories where they will carry out their duties.

Article 144

The High Contracting Parties undertake, in time of peace as in time of war, to disseminate the text of the present Convention as widely as possible in their respective countries, and, in particular, to include the study thereof in their programmes of military and, if possible, civil instruction, so that the principles thereof may become known to the entire population.

Any civilian, military, police or other authorities, who in time of war assume responsibilities in respect of protected persons, must possess the text of the Convention and be specially instructed as to its provisions.

Article 145

The High Contracting Parties shall communicate to one another through the Swiss Federal Council and, during hostilities, through the Protecting Powers, the official translations of the present Convention, as well as the laws and regulations which they may adopt to ensure the application thereof.

Article 146

The High Contracting Parties undertake to enact any legislation necessary to provide effective penal sanctions for persons committing, or ordering to be committed, any of the grave breaches of the present Convention defined in the following Article.

Each High Contracting Party shall be under the obligation to search for persons alleged to have committed, or to have ordered to be committed, such grave breaches, and shall bring such persons, regardless of their nationality, before its own courts. It may also, if it prefers, and in accordance with the provisions of its own legislation, hand such persons over for trial to another High Contracting Party concerned, provided such High Contracting Party has made out a *prima facie* case.

Each High Contracting Party shall take measures necessary for the suppression of all acts contrary to the provisions of the present Convention other than the grave breaches defined in the following Article.

In all circumstances, the accused persons shall benefit by safeguards of proper trial and defence, which shall not be less favourable than those provided by Article 105 and those following of the Geneva Convention relative to the Treatment of Prisoners of War of August 12, 1949.

Article 147

Grave breaches to which the preceding Article relates shall be those involving any of the following acts, if committed against persons or property protected by the present Convention: wilful killing, torture or inhuman treatment, including biological experiments, wilfully causing great suffering or serious injury to body or health, unlawful deportation or transfer or unlawful confinement of a protected person, compelling a protected person to serve in the forces of a hostile Power, or wilfully depriving a protected person of the rights of fair and regular trial prescribed in the present Convention, taking of hostages and extensive destruction and appropriation of property, not justified by military necessity and carried out unlawfully and wantonly.

Article 148

No High Contracting Party shall be allowed to absolve itself or any other High Contracting Party of any liability incurred by itself or by another High Contracting Party in respect of breaches referred to in the preceding Article.

Article 149

At the request of a Party to the conflict, an enquiry shall be instituted, in a manner to be decided between the interested Parties, concerning any alleged violation of the Convention.

If agreement has not been reached concerning the procedure for the enquiry, the Parties should agree on the choice of an umpire who will decide upon the procedure to be followed.

Once the violation has been established, the Parties to the conflict shall put an end to it and shall repress it with the least possible delay.

SECTION II — FINAL PROVISIONS

Article 150

The present Convention is established in English and in French. Both texts are equally authentic.

The Swiss Federal Council shall arrange for official translations of the Convention to be made in the Russian and Spanish languages.

Article 151

The present Convention, which bears the date of this day, is open to signature until February 12, 1950, in the name of the Powers represented at the Conference which opened at Geneva on April 21, 1949.

Article 152

The present Convention shall be ratified as soon as possible and the ratifications shall be deposited at Berne.

A record shall be drawn up of the deposit of each instrument of ratification and certified copies of this record shall be transmitted by the Swiss Federal Council to all the Powers in whose name the Convention has been signed, or whose accession has been notified.

Article 153

The present Convention shall come into force six months after not less than two instruments of ratification have been deposited.

Thereafter, it shall come into force for each High Contracting Party six months after the deposit of the instrument of ratification.

Article 154

In the relations between the Powers who are bound by the Hague Conventions respecting the Laws and Customs of War on Land, whether that of July 29, 1899, or that of October 18, 1907, and who are parties to the present Convention, this last Convention shall be supplementary to Sections II and III of the Regulations annexed to the above-mentioned Conventions of The Hague.

Article 155

From the date of its coming into force, it shall be open to any Power in whose name the present Convention has not been signed, to accede to this Convention.

Article 156

Accessions shall be notified in writing to the Swiss Federal Council, and shall take effect six months after the date on which they are received.

The Swiss Federal Council shall communicate the accessions to all the Powers in whose name the Convention has been signed, or whose accession has been notified.

Article 157

The situations provided for in Articles 2 and 3 shall give immediate effect to ratifications deposited and accessions notified by the Parties to the conflict before or after the beginning of hostilities or occupation. The Swiss Federal Council shall communicate by the quickest method any ratifications or accessions received from Parties to the conflict.

Article 158

Each of the High Contracting Parties shall be at liberty to denounce the present Convention.

The denunication shall be notified in writing to the Swiss Federal Council, which shall transmit it to the Governments of all the High Contracting Parties.

The denunciation shall take effect one year after the notification thereof has been made to the Swiss Federal Council. However, a denunciation of which notification has been made at a time when the denouncing Power is involved in a conflict shall not take effect until peace has been concluded, and until after operations connected with the release, repatriation and re-establishment of the persons protected by the present Convention have been terminated.

The denunciation shall have effect only in respect of the denouncing Power. It shall in no way impair the obligations which the Parties to the conflict shall remain bound to fulfil by virtue of the principles of the law of nations, as they result from the usages established among civilized peoples, from the laws of humanity and the dictates of the public conscience.

Article 159

The Swiss Federal Council shall register the present Convention with the Secretariat of the United Nations. The Swiss Federal Council shall also inform the Secretariat of the United Nations of all ratifications, accessions and denunciations received by it with respect to the present Convention.

IN WITNESS WHEREOF the undersigned, having deposited their respective full powers, have signed the present Convention.

DONE at Geneva this twelfth day of August 1949, in the English and French languages. The original shall be deposited in the Archives of the Swiss Confederation. The Swiss Federal Council shall transmit certified copies thereof to each of the signatory and acceding States.

[Annexes omitted]

CONCLUDING NOTES
relating to all four 1949 Geneva Conventions

Except where otherwise stated, all entries in this list apply to all four 1949 Geneva Conventions.

Signatures, Ratifications, Accessions, and Successions[1]

State (* denotes Reservation etc.: see below)	Date of Signature		Date of Ratification (r), Accession (a), or Succession (s)		
Afghanistan	8 December	1949	26 September	1956	r
*Albania	12 December	1949	27 May	1957	r
Algeria[2]			20 June	1960	a
*Argentina	8 December	1949	18 September	1956	r
*Australia	4 January	1950	14 October	1958	r
Austria (Convs. I, III, IV)	12 August	1949	27 August	1953	r
(Conv. II)	8 December	1949	27 August	1953	r
Bahamas			11 July	1975	s
Bahrain			30 November	1971	a
Bangladesh			4 April	1972	s
*Barbados			10 September	1968	s
Belgium[3]	8 December	1949	3 September	1952	r

[1] Information supplied in communications from the Swiss Federal Department for Foreign Affairs between January 1980 and March 1981, supplemented by various volumes of *UKTS* and *UNTS*.

[2] On 20 June 1960 the Provisional Government of the Algerian Republic deposited an instrument of accession to the four 1949 Geneva Conventions. Algeria became independent on 3 July 1962. The Depositary lists Algeria's accession as entering into force on 20 December 1960, but states that it is equally open to parties to the Conventions to consider that this accession took effect on 3 July 1962.

[3] At ratification, Belgium extended the application of the four Conventions to Belgian Congo and Ruanda-Urundi.

State (* denotes Reservation etc.: see below)	Date of Signature	Date of Ratification (r), Accession (a), or Succession (s)	
Bolivia	8 December 1949	10 December	1976 r
Botswana		29 March	1968 a
*Brazil	8 December 1949	29 June	1957 r
*Bulgaria	28 December 1949	22 July	1954 r
Burundi		27 December	1971 s
*Byelorussian SSR	12 December 1949	3 August	1954 r
Cambodia		8 December	1958 a
Cameroon		16 September	1963 s
*Canada	8 December 1949	14 May	1965 r
Central African Republic		1 August	1966 s
Ceylon (Convs. I, II, III)	8 December 1949	28 February	1959 r
(Conv. IV)		23 February	1959 a
Chad		5 August	1970 a
Chile	12 August 1949	12 October	1950 r
*China[4]	10 December 1949	28 December	1956 r
Colombia	12 August 1949	8 November	1961 r
Congo, Democratic Republic of (now Zaire)		20 February	1961 s
Congo, Republic of (now People's Republic of)		30 January	1967 s
Costa Rica		15 October	1969 a
Cuba	12 August 1949	15 April	1954 r
Cyprus		23 May	1962 a
*Czechoslovakia	8 December 1949	19 December	1950 r
Dahomey (now Benin)		14 December	1961 s
Denmark	12 August 1949	27 June	1951 r
Djibouti (Conv. I)		26 January	1978 s
(Convs. II, III, IV)		6 March	1978 s
Dominican Republic		22 January	1958 a
Ecuador	12 August 1949	11 August	1954 r
Egypt	8 December 1949	10 November	1952 r
El Salvador	8 December 1949	17 June	1953 r
Ethiopia	8 December 1949	2 October	1969 r
Fiji		9 August	1971 s
Finland	8 December 1949	22 February	1955 r
France	8 December 1949	28 June	1951 r
Gabon		20 February	1965 s
Gambia		11 October	1966 s
*German Democratic Republic		30 November	1956 a
*Germany, Federal Republic of[5]		3 September 1954	a

[4] The Conventions were signed on behalf of the Republic of China. However, it never ratified them. In 1952 the People's Republic of China announced that, subject to certain reservations, it recognized the Republic of China's signature of the four Geneva Conventions. In 1956 it ratified them, with reservations.

[5] At accession, the Federal Republic of Germany stated that the Conventions are also applicable to *Land Berlin*.

State (* denotes Reservation etc.: see below)	Date of Signature		Date of Ratification (r), Accession (a), or Succession (s)		
Ghana			2 August	1958	a
Greece	22 December	1949	5 June	1956	r
Guatemala	12 August	1949	14 May	1952	r
*Guinea-Bissau			21 February	1974	a
Guyana			22 July	1968	s
Haiti			11 April	1957	a
Holy See	8 December	1949	22 February	1951	r
Honduras			31 December	1965	a
*Hungary	8 December	1949	3 August	1954	r
Iceland			10 August	1965	a
India	16 December	1949	9 November	1950	r
Indonesia			30 September	1958	a
Iran	8 December	1949	20 February	1957	r
Iraq			14 February	1956	a
Ireland	19 December	1949	27 September	1962	r
*Israel	8 December	1949	6 July	1951	r
*Italy	8 December	1949	17 December	1951	r
Ivory Coast			28 December	1961	s
Jamaica			17 July	1964	s
Japan			21 April	1953	a
Jordan			29 May	1951	a
Kenya			20 September	1966	a
*Korea, Democratic People's Republic of (North)			27 August	1957	a
*Korea, Republic of (South)[6]			16 August	1966	a
*Kuwait			2 September	1967	a
Laos			29 October	1956	a
Lebanon	8 December	1949	10 April	1951	r
Lesotho			20 May	1968	s
Liberia			29 March	1954	a
Libya			22 May	1956	a
Liechtenstein	12 August	1949	21 September	1950	r
*Luxembourg	8 December	1949	1 July	1953	r
Madagascar			13 July	1963	s
Malawi			5 January	1968	a
Malaya, Federation of			24 August	1962	a
Mali			24 May	1965	a
Malta			22 August	1968	s
Mauritania			27 October	1962	s
Mauritius			18 August	1970	s
Mexico	8 December	1949	29 October	1952	r
Monaco	12 August	1949	5 July	1950	r
Mongolia			20 December	1958	a
Morocco			26 July	1956	a

[6] South Korea requested that, pursuant to Articles 62, 61, 141, and 157 respectively of the four Conventions, its accession should take effect immediately. The Depositary lists this accession as becoming effective on 23 September 1966.

State (* denotes Reservation etc.: see below)	Date of Signature		Date of Ratification (r), Accession (a), or Succession (s)		
Nepal			7 February	1964	a
*Netherlands	8 December	1949	3 August	1954	r
*New Zealand	11 February	1950	2 May	1959	r
Nicaragua	12 August	1949	17 December	1953	r
Niger			16 April	1964	s
Nigeria			9 June	1961	s
Norway	12 August	1949	3 August	1951	r
Oman			31 January	1974	a
*Pakistan	12 August	1949	12 June	1951	r
Panama			10 February	1956	a
Papua New Guinea			26 May	1976	s
Paraguay	10 December	1949	23 October	1961	r
Peru	12 August	1949	15 February	1956	r
Philippines (Conv. I)	8 December	1949	7 March	1951	r
(Convs. II, III, IV)	8 December	1949	6 October	1952	r
*Poland	8 December	1949	26 November	1954	r
*Portugal	11 February	1950	14 March	1961	r
Qatar			15 October	1975	a
*Romania	10 February	1950	1 June	1954	r
Rwanda			21 March	1964	s
San Marino			29 August	1953	a
Sao Tomé and Principe			21 May	1976	a
Saudi Arabia			18 May	1963	a
Senegal			23 April	1963	s
Sierra Leone			31 May	1965	s
Singapore			27 April	1973	a
Somalia			12 July	1962	a
South Africa			31 March	1952	a
*Spain	8 December	1949	4 August	1952	r
Sudan			23 September	1957	a
*Surinam			13 October	1976	s
Swaziland			28 June	1973	a
Sweden	8 December	1949	28 December	1953	r
Switzerland	12 August	1949	31 March	1950	r
Syria	12 August	1949	2 November	1953	r
Tanganyika			12 December	1962	s
Thailand			29 December	1954	a
Togo			6 January	1962	s
Tonga			13 April	1978	s
Trinidad and Tobago					
(Conv. I)			17 May	1963	a
(Convs. II, III, IV)			24 September	1963	a
Tunisia			4 May	1957	a
Turkey	12 August	1949	10 February	1954	r
Uganda			18 May	1964	a
*Ukrainian SSR	12 December	1949	3 August	1954	r
United Arab Emirates			10 May	1972	a

State (* denotes Reservation etc.: see below)	Date of Signature		Date of Ratification (*r*), Accession (*a*), or Succession (*s*)		
*United Kingdom[7]	8 December	1949	23 September	1957	r
Upper Volta			7 November	1961	s
*Uruguay	12 August	1949	5 March	1969	r
*USA (Convs. I, II, III)	12 August	1949	2 August	1955	r
(Conv. IV)	8 December	1949	2 August	1955	r
*USSR	12 December	1949	10 May	1954	r
Venezuela	10 February	1950	13 February	1956	r
*Vietnam, Democratic Republic of (North)[8]			28 December	1957	a
Vietnam, Republic of (South)[8]			14 November	1953	a
*Vietnam, Provisional Revolutionary Government of Republic of South[8]			3 December	1973	a
Yemen Arab Republic (North)			16 July	1970	a
*Yemen, People's Democratic Republic of (South)			25 May	1977	a
*Yugoslavia	10 February	1950	21 April	1950	r
Zambia			19 October	1966	a

Total Number of Parties Listed: 147 for each of Conventions I, II, III and IV.

Note on Entry into Force for States Parties

In accordance with a common article in all four Conventions (for example, in Convention I it is Article 58), the Conventions entered into force on 21 October 1950 for the states which had ratified them six months earlier. For each of the other ratifying states, and for each of the acceding states, the Conventions formally entered into force six months after the date indicated in the right-hand column above: however, the accessions of the Republic of Korea and of the Provisional Revolutionary Government of the Republic of South Vietnam became effective earlier, as noted in the list, in accord with another common article (in Convention I, Article 62).

Denunciations

None

[7] This ratification was also applicable in respect of Bahrain, Kuwait, Qatar, and the Trucial States to the extent of Her Majesty's powers in relation to those territories.

[8] On Vietnam, the Depositary states (1) that the accession of the Provisional Revolutionary Government of the Republic of South Vietnam became effective on the date of accession, 3 December 1973; and (2) that after the reunification of Vietnam, the foreign minister of the Socialist Republic of Vietnam declared on 4 July 1976 that it would continue the participation of the Democratic Republic of Vietnam and the Republic of South Vietnam in the four Conventions, with the same reservations.

Reservations etc.[9]

Except where otherwise stated, all of the following were (in the case of signatory states) made at signature and maintained at ratification; or (in the case of acceding states) made at accession.

Albania stated *re* common Articles 10 of Conventions I and II, and 11 of Convention IV, that it 'will not recognize a request by a Detaining Power to a humanitarian organization or to a neutral State to take the place of a Protecting Power, as being in order, unless the Power of which the protected persons are nationals has given its consent.'

On Convention III, *re* common Article 10 it made an identical statement to the above, but with the words 'prisoners of war' substituted for 'protected persons'. *Re* Article 12 it 'considers that in the case of prisoners of war being transferred to another Power by the Detaining Power, the responsibility for the application of the Convention to such prisoners of war will continue to rest with the Power which captured them.' *Re* Article 85 it 'considers that persons convicted under the law of the Detaining Power, in accordance with the principles of the Nuremberg trial, of war crimes and crimes against humanity, must be treated in the same manner as persons convicted in the country in question. Albania does not, therefore, consider herself bound by Article 85 so far as the category of persons mentioned in the present reservation is concerned.'

On Convention IV, *re* Article 45 it made an identical statement to that made *re* Convention III, Article 12, but with the words 'protected persons' substituted for 'prisoners of war'.

Argentina, at signature: 'With the reservation that Article 3, common to all four Conventions, shall be the only Article, to the exclusion of all others, which shall be applicable in the case of armed conflicts not of an international character. I shall likewise sign the Convention relative to the Protection of Civilian Persons with a reservation in respect of Article 68.' These reservations were not maintained at ratification.

Australia, at ratification only, stated *re* Convention IV that it 'reserves the right to impose the death penalty in accordance with the provisions of paragraph 2 of Article 68 of the said Convention without regard to whether the offences referred to therein are punishable by death under the law of the occupied territory at the time the occupation begins' and 'declares that it interprets the term "military installations" in paragraph 2 of Article 68 of the said Convention as meaning installations having an essential military interest for an Occupying Power.' On 21 February 1974 Australia withdrew its reservation to paragraph 2 of Article 68 of Convention IV.

At ratification, Australia also made a separate statement, which in its first part referred to some of the reservations to Conventions III and IV made by Albania and nine other states. Apart from the omission of China from the list of states, this part of Australia's statement was identical to the equivalent declaration which had been made by UK at ratification.

---

[9] This list is based on the sources referred to in footnote 1 above, and also (for texts of reservations at signature only) on *Final Record of the Diplomatic Conference of Geneva of 1949*, vol. 1, pp. 342–57. Reference may also be made to Claude Pilloud's authoritative survey, 'Reservations to the Geneva Conventions of 1949', *International Review of the Red Cross*, Geneva, March and April 1976, pp. 107–24 and 163–87. This was also made available by ICRC as a separate reprint, and page references below are to this edition.

The second part of the statement made by Australia at ratification referred to 'notifications concerning the "German Democratic Republic", the "Democratic People's Republic of Korea", the "Democratic Republic of Viet-Nam" and the "People's Republic of China". While the Government of the Commonwealth of Australia does not recognize any of the foregoing it has taken note of their acceptance of the provisions of the Conventions and their intention to apply them. The position of the Government of the Commonwealth of Australia towards the reservations referred to above applies equally in relation to the similar reservations attached to such acceptance.'

Barbados, at succession, made a declaration noting reservations *re* Article 85 of Convention III made by Albania, Byelorussia, Bulgaria, People's Republic of China, Czechoslovakia, Poland, Romania, Ukraine, and Soviet Union; and *re* Article 12 of Convention III and Article 45 of Convention IV made by Yugoslavia. While it regards all these states as being parties to the Conventions, it does not regard the above-mentioned reservations as valid.

Brazil, at signature, *re* Convention IV: 'Brazil wishes to make two express reservations — in regard to Article 44, because it is liable to hamper the action of the Detaining Power, and in regard to Article 46, because the matter dealt with in its second paragraph is outside the scope of the Convention, the essential and specific purpose of which is the protection of persons and not of their property.' These reservations were not maintained at ratification.

Bulgaria, Byelorussian SSR, China (at ratification by the People's Republic of China), *Czechoslovakia, German Democratic Republic, Democratic People's Republic of Korea, Poland, Ukrainian SSR, USSR,* and *Democratic Republic of Vietnam (North)* all made reservations to all four Conventions similar to those of Albania, although there are differences in wording.[10]

Canada, at signature, *re* Convention IV made an identical reservation to that of Netherlands, but it withdrew this reservation at ratification.

Germany, Federal Republic of, in a communication dated 3 March 1975, objected to the reservations made by Guinea-Bissau regarding sub-paragraph (2) of common Article 13 of Conventions I and II and of Article 4 of Convention III. It stated that its objections to these reservations will not affect the validity of the Conventions between the two states.

Guinea-Bissau made reservations to common Article 10 of Conventions I–III, and Articles 11 and 45 of Convention IV, which are similar to the reservations made by Albania to these particular Articles, although there are differences in wording. In addition, *re* sub-paragraph (2) of common Article 13 of Conventions I and II and of Article 4 of Convention III it made an identical reservation to that made (*re* Article 4 of Convention III alone) by the Provisional Revolutionary Government of the Republic of South Vietnam.

Hungary, after drawing attention to certain defects in Convention IV, referring particularly to Articles 4 and 5, made the following express reservations: (1) The provisions of common Articles 10 of Conventions I–III, and 11 of Convention IV, concerning the replacement of the Protecting Power, 'can

---

[10] In response to requests, the Depositary asked the USSR for an explanation of the exact interpretation to be placed on the reservation to Article 85 of Convention III. A note dated 26 May 1955 from the Soviet Union, received in reply and circulated by the Depositary, is reproduced in translation in Pilloud, 'Reservations to the Geneva Conventions of 1949', p. 29.

only be applied if the Government of the State of which the protected persons are nationals, no longer exists.' (2) Hungary cannot approve the provisions of common Article 11 of Conventions I–III, and 12 of Convention IV, 'according to which the competence of the Protecting Power extends to the interpretation of the Convention.' (3) *Re* Article 12 of Convention III, 'in the case of the transfer of prisoners of war from one Power to another, the responsibility for the application of the provisions of the Conventions must rest with both of these Powers.' (4) *Re* Article 85 of Convention III, Hungary made a reservation similar to that of Albania, although there are differences in wording. (5) *Re* Article 45 of Convention IV, 'in the case of the transfer of protected persons from one Power to another, the responsibility for the application of the Convention must rest with both of those Powers.'

Israel made reservations *re* Conventions I, II, and IV: while respecting the inviolability of the distinctive signs and emblems provided for in Article 38 of Convention I, 'Israel will use the Red Shield of David as the emblem and distinctive sign', for example on the flags, armlets, and on all equipment (including hospital ships), employed in the medical services of its armed forces.

In a communication to the Depositary dated 10 February 1978, Israel referred to the declaration made by People's Democratic Republic of Yemen: '. . . this is not the proper place for making such political pronouncements, which are, moreover, in flagrant contradiction to the principles, objects and purposes of the said Conventions. The said declaration cannot in any way affect whatever obligations are binding upon the Popular Democratic Republic of Yemen under general international law or under particular treaties.'

Italy, at signature, *re* Convention III 'makes a reservation in respect of the last paragraph of Article 66 . . .'. This reservation was not maintained at ratification.

Korea, Republic of (South) stated *re* Convention III that it 'interprets the provisions of Article 118, paragraph 1, as not binding upon a Power detaining prisoners of war to forcibly repatriate its prisoners against their openly and freely expressed will.' *Re* paragraph 2 of Article 68 of Convention IV, it made an identical reservation to that of Netherlands.

The instrument of accession to the four Conventions also contained a declaration: 'Furthermore, the Government of the Republic of Korea do hereby declare that it is the only lawful Government in Korea . . . and its accession shall not be constructed as recognizing any Contracting Party thereto which the Republic of Korea has not hitherto recognized.'

Kuwait: 'This Accession . . . does not imply recognition of Israel or entering with it into relations governed by the Conventions . . .'.

Luxembourg, at signature, *re* Convention III, with the reservation 'that its existing national law shall continue to be applied to cases now under consideration.' This reservation was withdrawn at ratification.

Netherlands stated *re* Convention IV that it 'reserves the right to impose the death penalty in accordance with the provisions of Article 68, paragraph 2, without regard to whether the offences referred to therein are punishable by death under the law of the occupied territory at the time the occupation begins.'

New Zealand, at signature, made two reservations with reference to Convention

IV: (1) *re* paragraph 2 of Article 68, a reservation identical to that of Netherlands; and (2) 'In view of the fact that the General Assembly of the United Nations, having approved the principles established by the Charter and judgement of the Nuremberg Tribunal, has directed the International Law Commission to include these principles in a general codification of offences against the peace and security of mankind. New Zealand reserves the right to take such action as may be necessary to ensure that such offences are punished, notwithstanding the provisions of Article 70, paragraph 1.'

At ratification, the first of these two reservations was maintained, but the second one was withdrawn. The first reservation was subsequently withdrawn in a communication received by the Depositary on 2 March 1976.

Also at ratification, New Zealand referred to some of the reservations to Conventions III and IV made by Albania and nine other states. Its statement, apart from the omission of China from the list of states, was virtually identical to the equivalent declaration which had been made by UK at ratification.

Pakistan, at ratification only, made two reservations with reference to Convention IV.

(1) *Re* Article 44: 'Every protected person who is national *de jure* of an enemy State, against whom action is taken or sought to be taken under Article 41 by assignment of residence or internment, or in accordance with any law, on the ground of his being an enemy alien, shall be entitled to submit proofs to the Detaining Power, or as the case may be, to any appropriate Court or administrative board which may review his case, that he does not enjoy the protection of any enemy State, and full weight shall be given to this circumstance, if it is established whether with or without further enquiry by the Detaining Power, in deciding appropriate action, by way of an initial order or, as the case may be, by amendment thereof.'

(2) *Re* paragraph 2 of Article 68, a reservation identical to that of the Netherlands.

Portugal, at signature, made four reservations. (1) *Re* common Article 3 in all four Conventions: 'As there is no actual definition of what is meant by a conflict not of an international character, and as, in case this term is intended to refer solely to civil war, it is not clearly laid down at what moment an armed rebellion within a country should be considered as having become a civil war, Portugal reserves the right not to apply the provisions of Article 3, in so far as they may be contrary to the provisions of Portuguese law, in all territories subject to her sovereignty in any part of the world.'

(2) Portugal made a reservation of Common Articles 10 of Conventions I–III, and 11 of Convention IV, similar to that of Albania, although there are differences in wording.

(3) *Re* Article 13 of Convention I and 4 of Convention III: 'The Portuguese Government makes a reservation regarding the application of the above Articles in all cases in which the legitimate Government has already asked for and agreed to an armistice or the suspension of military operations of no matter what character, even if the armed forces in the field have not yet capitulated.'

(4) Portugal accepts Article 60 of Convention III 'with the reservation that it in no case binds itself to grant prisoners a monthly rate of pay in excess of 50 per cent of the pay due to Portuguese soldiers of equivalent appointment or rank, on active service in the combat zone.'

At ratification, Portugal withdrew all the above, with the exception of the reservation listed under (2), which it maintained.

Romania made reservations to all four Conventions similar to those of Albania, although there are differences in wording.

In addition, in a note to the Depositary dated 18 January 1967 Romania made an objection to the reservations and the declaration made by the Republic of Korea in its instrument of accession: 'It regards those reservations as incompatible with the purposes of the aforementioned Conventions.' It also 'rejects the declaration of the South Korean authorities in which the latter claim to be the only lawful Government in Korea . . .'.

Spain, at signature, made a reservation to Convention III consisting of two parts: (1) 'In matters regarding procedural guarantees and penal and disciplinary sanctions, Spain will grant prisoners of war the same treatment as is provided by her legislation for members of her own national forces.' (2) 'Under "International law in force" (Article 99) Spain understands she only accepts that which arises from contractual sources or which has been previously elaborated by Organizations in which she participates.'

The first part was not maintained at ratification. The second part was maintained at ratification, but withdrawn in a communication received by the Depositary on 5 January 1979.

Surinam, at succession, made an identical reservation to Convention IV to that of Netherlands.

United Kingdom made an identical reservation to Convention IV to that of Netherlands. However, in a notification received by the Depositary on 15 December 1971 the UK withdrew this reservation.

In a declaration made at ratification, the UK referred to reservations to Article 85 of Convention III made by Albania, Byelorussian SSR, Bulgaria, People's Republic of China, Czechoslovakia, Hungary, Poland, Romania, Ukrainian SSR, and USSR, and also to reservations to Article 12 of Convention III and Article 45 of Convention IV made by all the above-mentioned and by Yugoslavia. 'I am instructed by Her Majesty's Government to state that whilst they regard all the above-mentioned states as being parties to the above-mentioned Conventions, they do not regard the above-mentioned reservations thereto made by those states as valid, and will therefore regard any application of any of those reservations as constituting a breach of the Convention to which the reservation relates.'[11]

In a communication to the Depositary dated 19 November 1975, the UK stated that it was 'unable to accept' the similar reservations made by the Provisional Revolutionary Government of the Republic of South Vietnam, the Republic of Guinea-Bissau, the German Democratic Republic, and the Democratic Republic of Vietnam: 'These reservations are not of the kind which intending parties to the Conventions are entitled to make.' The UK stated that it was likewise unable to accept the reservations to Article 4 of Convention III made by PRGRSVN and Guinea-Bissau, and to common Article 13 of Conventions I and II by Guinea-Bissau.

Uruguay, at ratification only, made a reservation to Articles 87, 100, and 101 of

---

[11] The USSR and other states contested the validity of this and of the similar statements made at ratification by Australia and New Zealand. See Pilloud, 'Reservations to the Geneva Conventions of 1949', pp. 9–11.

Convention III, and Article 68 of Convention IV, 'inasmuch as they involve the application of the death penalty'.

USA made a reservation to paragraph 2 of Article 68 of Convention IV identical to that of Netherlands. Also, at ratification only, *re* Convention I: '. . . with the reservation that irrespective of any provision or provisions in said convention to the contrary, nothing contained therein shall make unlawful . . . any use or right of use within the USA and its territories and possessions of the Red Cross emblem, sign, insignia or words as was lawful by reason of domestic law and a use begun prior to January 5, 1905, provided such use by pre-1905 users does not extend to the placing of the Red Cross emblem, sign or insignia upon aircraft, vessels, vehicles, buildings or other structures, or upon the ground.'

At ratification the USA also made a statement rejecting the reservations (other than those to paragraph 2 of Article 68 of Convention IV) which states had made with respect to the four Conventions, but stating that 'the United States accepts treaty relations with all parties' to the Conventions 'except as to the changes proposed by such reservations'.

In a note to the Depositary dated 31 December 1974 *re* the accession by the Provisional Revolutionary Government of the Republic of South Vietnam: 'The Government of the USA recognizes the Government of the Republic of Vietnam and does not recognize the "PRGRSVN" as a government. The US Government therefore does not recognize that the "PRGRSVN" is qualified to accede to the Geneva Conventions. Bearing in mind, however, that it is the purpose of the Geneva Conventions that their provisions should protect war victims in armed conflict, the Government of the USA notes that the "PRGRSVN" has indicated its willingness to apply them subject to certain reservations. The reservations expressed with respect to the Third Geneva Convention . . . go far beyond previous reservations, and are directed against the object and purpose of the Convention. Other reservations are similar to reservations expressed by others previously and concerning which the Government of the US has previously declared its views. The Government of the US rejects all the expressed reservations' and 'notes that the views expressed in this note should not be understood as implying any withdrawal from the policy heretofore pursued by its armed forces in according the treatment provided by the Conventions to hostile armed forces.'[12]

In a note to the Depositary dated 4 March 1975 the USA made the following declaration *re* the reservations made by Guinea-Bissau: 'The reservations are similar to reservations expressed by others previously with respect to the same or different conventions and concerning which the Government of the United States has previously declared its views. The attitude of the Government of the United States with respect to all the reservations by the Republic of Guinea-Bissau parallels its attitude toward such other reservations. The Government of the United States, while rejecting the reservations, accepts treaty relations with the Republic of Guinea-Bissau.'

Vietnam, Provisional Revolutionary Government of Republic of South made reservations to common Articles 10 of Convention I–III, and 11 of Convention IV, and to Articles 12 of Convention III and 45 of Convention IV,

---

[12] The full text is in US Department of State, *Treaties in Force: A List of Treaties and Other International Agreements of the United States in Force on January 1, 1976,* Washington, D. C., 1976, pp. 405-6. The original contains full titles, not initials as above.

which are similar to the reservations made by Albania to these particular Articles, although there are differences in wording. In addition, it made two further reservations *re* Convention III: (1) On Article 4, it 'does not recognise the "conditions" laid down in paragraph 2 concerning "members of other militias and members of other volunteer corps, including those of organized resistance movements", since those conditions are inappropriate to contemporary people's wars.' (2) On Article 85, it 'declares that prisoners of war prosecuted and convicted, in accordance with the principles laid down by the Nuremburg Court of Justice for crimes of aggression, crimes of genocide, war crimes or crimes against humanity shall not benefit from the provisions of this Convention.'

Yemen, People's Democratic Republic of (South): Declaration that this accession 'shall in no way imply recognition of Israel.'

Yugoslavia made reservations to all four Conventions similar to those of Albania, although there are differences in wording. But, unlike Albania, it did not make any reservation *re* Article 85 of Convention III.

22. 1954 Hague Convention for the Protection of Cultural Property in the Event of Armed Conflict

PREFATORY NOTE

The laws of war have long included some provision for the protection of cultural property in time of war or military occupation. For example, see Articles 27 and 56 of the Regulations annexed to both 1899 Hague Convention II and 1907 Hague Convention IV; Article 5 of 1907 Hague Convention IX; and Articles 25 and 26 of the 1923 Hague Draft Air Rules. In 1935 a regional agreement, the Washington Treaty on the Protection of Artistic and Scientific Institutions and Historic Monuments (known as the Roerich Pact) was signed by twenty-one American states. After its signature, attempts were made to codify a more comprehensive and widely accepted international agreement for the protection of cultural property in time of war. In 1939 the Netherlands presented to governments a draft convention on the protection of cultural property, but this effort was overtaken by the outbreak of the Second World War.

In fact, in the Second World War (as in the First World War) the existing provisions for the protection of cultural property proved to be inadequate, and such provisions were also extensively violated. On 3 September 1939 Great Britain and France jointly declared that every effort should be made to preserve 'those monuments of human achievement which are treasured in all civilized countries', but should the enemy fail to observe such restrictions, both reserved the right to take 'all such action as they may consider appropriate'. In reply, Hitler indicated his general agreement. However, Germany conducted a policy of systematic plunder in occupied territories in violation of Article 56 of the Hague Regulations, and this was one of the acts held to be criminal under Article 6(b) of the 1945 Charter of the International Military Tribunal at Nuremberg. Other belligerents also committed violations.

After the war, the Netherlands submitted a new proposal to the United Nations Educational, Scientific and Cultural Organization. In 1952, on the initiative of the General Conference of UNESCO, a committee of government experts was convened to draft a convention on the protection of cultural property. This committee submitted drafts to the General Conference of UNESCO.

From 21 April to 14 May 1954, representatives of fifty-six states met in The Hague at an Intergovernmental Conference to consider drafts prepared under the auspices of UNESCO. At the conclusion of the conference, the 1954 Hague Cultural Property Convention, together with its annexed Regulations, was adopted along with certain other acts. The Convention was the first comprehensive international agreement for the protection of cultural property. It provides both for preparations in peacetime for safeguarding cultural property against foreseeable effects of armed conflict, and also for respect for such property in time of war and/or military occupation. The Convention is also applicable in non-international armed conflicts.

In light of the long-established and general acceptance of the principle of special protection of cultural property (most recently affirmed in Article 53 of 1977 Geneva Protocol I and Article 16 of 1977 Geneva Protocol II), this special protection may be viewed as a part of customary international law.

However, the protection of cultural property is not absolute. If cultural property is used for military purposes, an opposing belligerent is released from the obligation to ensure immunity so long as the particular violation persists. In addition, exceptional cases of unavoidable military necessity may remove the special protection of cultural property only for such time as that necessity continues. In such circumstances, advance notice of the withdrawal of immunity is required.

Date of signature:	Signed on 14 May 1954, and open for signature (see Article 30) until 31 December 1954.
Entry into force:	7 August 1956
Depositary:	UNESCO
Authentic languages:	English, French, Russian, and Spanish
Text reprinted from:	249 *UNTS* 240–88
Also published in:	*UK Misc.* 6 (1956), Cmd. 9837 (Eng.); XLII *UKPP* (1955–1956) 763 (Eng.)

Convention for the Protection of Cultural Property in the Event of Armed Conflict

The High Contracting Parties,

Recognizing that cultural property has suffered grave damage during recent armed conflicts and that, by reason of the developments in the technique of warfare, it is in increasing danger of destruction;

Being convinced that damage to cultural property belonging to any people whatsoever means damage to the cultural heritage of all mankind, since each people makes its contribution to the culture of the world;

Considering that the preservation of the cultural heritage is of great importance for all peoples of the world and that it is important that this heritage should receive international protection;

Guided by the principles concerning the protection of cultural property during armed conflict, as established in the Conventions of The Hague of 1899 and of 1907 and in the Washington Pact of 15 April, 1935;

Being of the opinion that such protection cannot be effective unless both national and international measures have been taken to organize it in time of peace;

Being determined to take all possible steps to protect cultural property;

Have agreed upon the following provisions:

CHAPTER I — GENERAL PROVISIONS REGARDING PROTECTION

Article 1 — Definition of cultural property

For the purposes of the present Convention, the term 'cultural property' shall cover, irrespective of origin or ownership:

(*a*) movable or immovable property of great importance to the cultural heritage of every people, such as monuments of architecture, art or history, whether religious or secular; archaeological sites; groups of buildings which, as a whole, are of historical or artistic interest; works of art; manuscripts, books and other objects of artistic, historical or archaeological interest; as well as scientific collections and important collections of books or archives or of reproductions of the property defined above;

(*b*) buildings whose main and effective purpose is to preserve or exhibit the movable cultural property defined in sub-paragraph (*a*) such as museums, large libraries and depositories of archives, and refuges intended to shelter, in the event of armed conflict, the movable cultural property defined in sub-paragraph (*a*);

(*c*) centres containing a large amount of cultural property as defined in sub-paragraphs (*a*) and (*b*), to be known as 'centres containing monuments'.

Article 2 — Protection of cultural property

For the purposes of the present Convention, the protection of cultural property shall comprise the safeguarding of and respect for such property.

Article 3 — Safeguarding of cultural property

The High Contracting Parties undertake to prepare in time of peace for the safeguarding of cultural property situated within their own territory against the foreseeable effects of an armed conflict, by taking such measures as they consider appropriate.

Article 4 — Respect for cultural property

1. The High Contracting Parties undertake to respect cultural property situated within their own territory as well as within the territory of other High Contracting Parties by refraining from any use of the property and its immediate surroundings or of the appliances in use for its protection for purposes which are likely to expose it to destruction or damage in the event of armed conflict;

and by refraining from any act of hostility directed against such property.

2. The obligations mentioned in paragraph 1 of the present Article may be waived only in cases where military necessity imperatively requires such a waiver.

3. The High Contracting Parties further undertake to prohibit, prevent and, if necessary, put a stop to any form of theft, pillage or misappropriation of, and any acts of vandalism directed against, cultural property. They shall refrain from requisitioning movable cultural property situated in the territory of another High Contracting Party.

4. They shall refrain from any act directed by way of reprisals against cultural property.

5. No High Contracting Party may evade the obligations incumbent upon it under the present Article, in respect of another High Contracting Party, by reason of the fact that the latter has not applied the measures of safeguard referred to in Article 3.

Article 5 — Occupation

1. Any High Contracting Party in occupation of the whole or part of the territory of another High Contracting Party shall as far as possible support the competent national authorities of the occupied country in safeguarding and preserving its cultural property.

2. Should it prove necessary to take measures to preserve cultural property situated in occupied territory and damaged by military operations, and should the competent national authorities be unable to take such measures, the Occupying Power shall, as far as possible, and in close co-operation with such authorities, take the most necessary measures of preservation.

3. Any High Contracting Party whose government is considered their legitimate government by members of a resistance movement, shall, if possible, draw their attention to the obligation to comply with those provisions of the Convention dealing with respect for cultural property.

Article 6 — Distinctive marking of cultural property

In accordance with the provisions of Article 16, cultural property may bear a distinctive emblem so as to facilitate its recognition.

Article 7 — Military measures

1. The High Contracting Parties undertake to introduce in time of peace into their military regulations or instructions such provisions as may ensure observance of the present Convention, and to foster in the members of their armed forces a spirit of respect for the culture and cultural property of all peoples.

2. The High Contracting Parties undertake to plan or establish in peacetime, within their armed forces, services or specialist personnel whose purpose will be to secure respect for cultural property and to co-operate with the civilian authorities responsible for safeguarding it.

CHAPTER II — SPECIAL PROTECTION

Article 8 — Granting of special protection

1. There may be placed under special protection a limited number of refuges intended to shelter movable cultural property in the event of armed conflict, of centres containing monuments and other immovable cultural property of very great importance, provided that they:

(*a*) are situated at an adequate distance from any large industrial centre or from any important military objective constituting a vulnerable point, such as, for example, an aerodrome, broadcasting station, establishment engaged upon work of national defence, a port or railway station of relative importance or a main line of communication;

(*b*) are not used for military purposes.

2. A refuge for movable cultural property may also be placed under special protection, whatever its location, if it is so constructed that, in all probability, it will not be damaged by bombs.

3. A centre containing monuments shall be deemed to be used for military purposes whenever it is used for the movement of military personnel or material, even in transit. The same shall apply whenever activities directly connected with military operations, the stationing of military personnel, or the production of war material are carried on within the centre.

4. The guarding of cultural property mentioned in paragraph 1 above by armed custodians specially empowered to do so, or the presence, in the vicinity of such cultural property, of police forces normally responsible for the maintenance of public order shall not be deemed to be use for military purposes.

5. If any cultural property mentioned in paragraph 1 of the present Article is situated near an important military objective as defined in the said paragraph, it may nevertheless be placed under special protection if the High Contracting Party asking for that protection undertakes, in the event of armed conflict, to make no use of the objective and particularly, in the case of a port, railway station or aerodrome, to divert all traffic therefrom. In that event, such diversion shall be prepared in time of peace.

6. Special protection is granted to cultural property by its entry in the 'International Register of Cultural Property under Special Protection'. This entry shall only be made, in accordance with the provisions of the present Convention and under the conditions provided for in the Regulations for the execution of the Convention.

Article 9 — Immunity of cultural property under special protection

The High Contracting Parties undertake to ensure the immunity of cultural property under special protection by refraining, from the time of entry in the International Register, from any act of hostility directed against such property and, except for the cases provided for in paragraph 5 of Article 8, from any use of such property or its surroundings for military purposes.

Article 10 — Identification and control

During an armed conflict, cultural property under special protection shall be marked with the distinctive emblem described in Article 16, and shall be open to international control as provided for in the Regulations for the execution of the Convention.

Article 11 — Withdrawal of immunity

1. If one of the High Contracting Parties commits, in respect of any item of cultural property under special protection, a violation of the obligations under Article 9, the opposing Party shall, so long as this violation persists, be released from the obligation to ensure the immunity of the property concerned. Nevertheless, whenever possible, the latter Party shall first request the cessation of such violation within a reasonable time.

2. Apart from the case provided for in paragraph 1 of the present Article, immunity shall be withdrawn from cultural property under special protection only in exceptional cases of unavoidable military necessity, and only for such time as that necessity continues. Such necessity can be established only by the officer commanding a force the equivalent of a division in size or larger. Whenever circumstances permit, the opposing Party shall be notified, a reasonable time in advance, of the decision to withdraw immunity.

3. The Party withdrawing immunity shall, as soon as possible, so inform the Commissioner-General for cultural property provided for in the Regulations for the execution of the Convention, in writing, stating the reasons.

Chapter III — Transport of Cultural Property

Article 12 — Transport under special protection

1. Transport exclusively engaged in the transfer of cultural property, whether within a territory or to another territory, may, at the request of the High Contracting Party concerned, take place under special protection in accordance with the conditions specified in the Regulations for the execution of the Convention.

2. Transport under special protection shall take place under the international supervision provided for in the aforesaid Regulations and shall display the distinctive emblem described in Article 16.

3. The High Contracting Parties shall refrain from any act of hostility directed against transport under special protection.

Article 13 — Transport in urgent cases

1. If a High Contracting Party considers that the safety of certain cultural property requires its transfer and that the matter is of such urgency that the procedure laid down in Article 12 cannot be followed, especially at the beginning of an armed conflict, the transport may display the distinctive emblem described in Article 16, provided that an application for immunity referred to in Article 12 has not already been made and refused. As far as possible, notification of transfer should be made to the opposing Parties. Nevertheless, transport conveying cultural property to the territory of another country may not display the distinctive emblem unless immunity has been expressly granted to it.

2. The High Contracting Parties shall take, so far as possible, the necessary precautions to avoid acts of hostility directed against the transport described in paragraph 1 of the present Article and displaying the distinctive emblem.

Article 14 — Immunity from seizure, capture and prize

1. Immunity from seizure, placing in prize, or capture shall be granted to:

(*a*) cultural property enjoying the protection provided for in Article 12 or that provided for in Article 13;

(*b*) the means of transport exclusively engaged in the transfer of such cultural property.

2. Nothing in the present Article shall limit the right of visit and search.

CHAPTER IV — PERSONNEL

Article 15 — Personnel

As far as is consistent with the interests of security, personnel engaged in the protection of cultural property shall, in the interests of such property, be respected and, if they fall into the hands of the opposing Party, shall be allowed to continue to carry out their duties whenever the cultural property for which they are responsible has also fallen into the hands of the opposing Party.

CHAPTER V — THE DISTINCTIVE EMBLEM

Article 16 — Emblem of the Convention

1. The distinctive emblem of the Convention shall take the form of a shield, pointed below, per saltire blue and white (a shield consisting of a royal-blue square, one of the angles of which forms the point of the shield, and of a royal-blue triangle above the square, the space on either side being taken up by a white triangle).

2. The emblem shall be used alone, or repeated three times in a triangular formation (one shield below), under the conditions provided for in Article 17.

Article 17 — Use of the emblem

1. The distinctive emblem repeated three times may be used only as a means of identification of:

(a) immovable cultural property under special protection;

(b) the transport of cultural property under the conditions provided for in Articles 12 and 13;

(c) improvised refuges, under the conditions provided for in the Regulations for the execution of the Convention.

2. The distinctive emblem may be used alone only as a means of identification of:

(a) cultural property not under special protection;

(b) the persons responsible for the duties of control in accordance with the Regulations for the execution of the Convention;

(c) the personnel engaged in the protection of cultural property;

(d) the identity cards mentioned in the Regulations for the execution of the Convention.

3. During an armed conflict, the use of the distinctive emblem in any other cases than those mentioned in the preceding paragraphs of the present Article, and the use for any purpose whatever of a sign resembling the distinctive emblem, shall be forbidden.

4. The distinctive emblem may not be placed on any immovable cultural property unless at the same time there is displayed an authorization duly dated and signed by the competent authority of the High Contracting Party.

CHAPTER VI — SCOPE OF APPLICATION OF THE CONVENTION

Article 18 — *Application of the convention*

1. Apart from the provisions which shall take effect in time of peace, the present Convention shall apply in the event of declared war or of any other armed conflict which may arise between two or more of the High Contracting Parties, even if the state of war is not recognized by one or more of them.

2. The Convention shall also apply to all cases of partial or total occupation of the territory of a High Contracting Party, even if the said occupation meets with no armed resistance.

3. If one of the Powers in conflict is not a Party to the present Convention, the Powers which are Parties thereto shall nevertheless remain bound by it in their mutual relations. They shall furthermore be bound by the Convention, in relation to the said Power, if the latter has declared that it accepts the provisions thereof and so long as it applies them.

Article 19 — *Conflicts not of an international character*

1. In the event of an armed conflict not of an international character occurring within the territory of one of the High Contracting Parties, each party to the conflict shall be bound to apply, as a minimum, the provisions of the present Convention which relate to respect for cultural property.

2. The parties to the conflict shall endeavour to bring into force, by means of special agreements, all or part of the other provisions of the present Convention.

3. The United Nations Educational, Scientific and Cultural Organization may offer its services to the parties to the conflict.

4. The application of the preceding provisions shall not affect the legal status of the parties to the conflict.

CHAPTER VII — EXECUTION OF THE CONVENTION

Article 20 — *Regulations for the execution of the convention*

The procedure by which the present Convention is to be applied is defined in the Regulations for its execution, which constitute an integral part thereof.

Article 21 — *Protecting powers*

The present Convention and the Regulations for its execution shall be applied with the co-operation of the Protecting Powers responsible for safeguarding the interests of the Parties to the conflict.

Article 22 — *Conciliation procedure*

1. The Protecting Powers shall lend their good offices in all cases where they may deem it useful in the interests of cultural property, particularly if there is disagreement between the Parties to the conflict as to the application or interpretation of the provisions of the present Convention or the Regulations for its execution.

2. For this purpose, each of the Protecting Powers may, either at the invitation of one Party, of the Director-General of the United Nations Educational, Scientific and Cultural Organization, or on its own initiative, propose to the Parties to the conflict a meeting of their representatives, and in particular of the authorities responsible for the protection of cultural property, if considered appropriate on suitably chosen neutral territory. The Parties to the conflict shall be bound to give effect to the proposals for meeting made to them. The Protecting Powers shall propose for approval by the Parties to the conflict a person belonging to a neutral Power or a person presented by the Director-General of the United Nations Educational, Scientific and Cultural Organization, which person shall be invited to take part in such a meeting in the capacity of Chairman.

Article 23 — *Assistance of UNESCO*

1. The High Contracting Parties may call upon the United Nations Educational, Scientific and Cultural Organization for technical assistance in organizing the protection of their cultural property, or in connexion with any other problem arising out of the application of the present Convention or the Regulations for its execution. The Organization shall accord such assistance within the limits fixed by its programme and by its resources.

2. The Organization is authorized to make, on its own initiative, proposals on this matter to the High Contracting Parties.

Article 24 — *Special agreements*

1. The High Contracting Parties may conclude special agreements for all matters concerning which they deem it suitable to make separate provision.

2. No special agreement may be concluded which would diminish the protection afforded by the present Convention to cultural property and to the personnel engaged in its protection.

Article 25 — *Dissemination of the convention*

The High Contracting Parties undertake, in time of peace as in time of armed conflict, to disseminate the text of the present Convention and the Regulations for its execution as widely as possible in their respective countries. They undertake, in particular, to include the study thereof in their programmes of military and, if possible, civilian training, so that its principles are made known to the whole population, especially the armed forces and personnel engaged in the protection of cultural property.

Article 26 — *Translations, reports*

1. The High Contracting Parties shall communicate to one another, through the Director-General of the United Nations Educational, Scientific and Cultural Organization, the official translations of the present Convention and of the Regulations for its execution.

2. Furthermore, at least once every four years, they shall forward to the Director-General a report giving whatever information they think suitable concerning any measures being taken, prepared or contemplated by their respective administrations in fulfilment of the present Convention and of the Regulations for its execution.

Article 27 — *Meetings*

1. The Director-General of the United Nations Educational, Scientific and Cultural Organization may, with the approval of the Executive Board, convene meetings of representatives of the High Contracting Parties. He must convene such a meeting if at least one-fifth of the High Contracting Parties so request.

2. Without prejudice to any other functions which have been conferred on it by the present Convention or the Regulations for its execution, the purpose of the meeting will be to study problems concerning the application of the Convention and of the Regulations for its execution, and to formulate recommendations in respect thereof.

3. The meeting may further undertake a revision of the Convention or the Regulations for its execution if the majority of the High Contracting Parties are represented, and in accordance with the provisions of Article 39.

Article 28 — *Sanctions*

The High Contracting Parties undertake to take, within the framework of their ordinary criminal jurisdiction, all necessary steps to prosecute and impose penal or disciplinary sanctions upon those persons, of whatever nationality, who commit or order to be committed a breach of the present Convention.

FINAL PROVISIONS

Article 29 — *Languages*

1. The present Convention is drawn up in English, French, Russian and Spanish, the four texts being equally authoritative.

2. The United Nations Educational, Scientific and Cultural Organization shall arrange for translations of the Convention into the other official languages of its General Conference.

Article 30 — *Signature*

The present Convention shall bear the date of 14 May, 1954 and, until the date of 31 December, 1954, shall remain open for signature by all States invited to the Conference which met at The Hague from 21 April, 1954 to 14 May, 1954.

Article 31 — *Ratification*

1. The present Convention shall be subject to ratification by signatory States in accordance with their respective constitutional procedures.

2. The instruments of ratification shall be deposited with the Director-General of the United Nations Educational, Scientific and Cultural Organization.

Article 32 — *Accession*

From the date of its entry into force, the present Convention shall be open for accession by all States mentioned in Article 30 which have not signed it, as well as any other State invited to accede by the Executive Board of the United Nations Educational, Scientific and Cultural Organization. Accession shall be effected by the deposit of an instrument of accession with the Director-General of the United Nations Educational, Scientific and Cultural Organization.

Article 33 — *Entry into force*

1. The present Convention shall enter into force three months after five instruments of ratification have been deposited.

2. Thereafter, it shall enter into force, for each High Contracting Party, three months after the deposit of its instrument of ratification or accession.

3. The situations referred to in Articles 18 and 19 shall give immediate effect to ratifications or accessions deposited by the Parties to the conflict either before or after the beginning of hostilities or occupation. In such cases the Director-General of the United Nations Educational, Scientific and Cultural Organization shall transmit the communications referred to in Article 38 by the speediest method.

Article 34 — Effective application

1. Each State Party to the Convention on the date of its entry into force shall take all necessary measures to ensure its effective application within a period of six months after such entry into force.

2. This period shall be six months from the date of deposit of the instruments of ratification or accession for any State which deposits its instrument of ratification or accession after the date of the entry into force of the Convention.

Article 35 — Territorial extension of the convention

Any High Contracting Party may, at the time of ratification or accession, or at any time thereafter, declare by notification addressed to the Director-General of the United Nations Educational, Scientific and Cultural Organization, that the present Convention shall extend to all or any of the territories for whose international relations it is responsible. The said notification shall take effect three months after the date of its receipt.

Article 36 — Relation to previous conventions

1. In the relations between Powers which are bound by the Conventions of The Hague concerning the Laws and Customs of War on Land (IV) and concerning Naval Bombardment in Time of War (IX), whether those of 29 July, 1899 or those of 18 October, 1907, and which are Parties to the present Convention, this last Convention shall be supplementary to the aforementioned Convention (IX) and to the Regulations annexed to the aforementioned Convention (IV) and shall substitute for the emblem described in Article 5 of the aforementioned Convention (IX) the emblem described in Article 16 of the present Convention, in cases in which the present Convention and the Regulations for its execution provide for the use of this distinctive emblem.

2. In the relations between Powers which are bound by the Washington Pact of 15 April, 1935 for the Protection of Artistic and Scientific Institutions and of Historic Monuments (Roerich Pact) and which are Parties to the present Convention, the latter Convention shall be supplementary to the Roerich Pact and shall substitute for the distinguishing flag described in Article III of the Pact the emblem defined in Article 16 of the present Convention, in cases in which the present Convention and the Regulations for its execution provide for the use of this distinctive emblem.

Article 37 — Denunciation

1. Each High Contracting Party may denounce the present Convention, on its own behalf, or on behalf of any territory for whose international relations it is responsible.

2. The denunciation shall be notified by an instrument in writing, deposited with the Director-General of the United Nations Educational, Scientific and Cultural Organization.

3. The denunciation shall take effect one year after the receipt of the instrument of denunciation. However, if, on the expiry of this period, the denouncing Party is involved in an armed conflict, the denunciation shall not take effect until the end of hostilities, or until the operations of repatriating cultural property are completed, whichever is the later.

Article 38 — Notifications

The Director-General of the United Nations Educational, Scientific and Cultural Organization shall inform the States referred to in Articles 30 and 32, as well as the United Nations, of the deposit of all the instruments of ratification, accession or acceptance provided for in Articles 31, 32 and 39 and of the notifications and denunciations provided for respectively in Articles 35, 37 and 39.

Article 39 — Revision of the Convention and of the Regulations for its Execution

1. Any High Contracting Party may propose amendments to the present Convention or the Regulations for its execution. The text of any proposed amendment shall be communicated to the Director-General of the United Nations Educational, Scientific and Cultural Organization who shall transmit it to each High Contracting Party with the request that such Party reply within four months stating whether it:

(*a*) desires that a Conference be convened to consider the proposed amendment;

(*b*) favours the acceptance of the proposed amendment without a Conference; or

(*c*) favours the rejection of the proposed amendment without a Conference.

2. The Director-General shall transmit the replies, received under paragraph 1 of the present Article, to all High Contracting Parties.

3. If all the High Contracting Parties which have, within the prescribed time-limit, stated their views to the Director-General of the United Nations Educational, Scientific and Cultural Organization, pursuant to paragraph 1 (*b*) of this Article, inform him that they favour acceptance of the amendment without a Conference, notification of their decision shall be made by the Director-General in accordance with Article 38. The amendment shall become effective for all the High Contracting Parties on the expiry of ninety days from the date of such notification.

4. The Director-General shall convene a Conference of the High Contracting Parties to consider the proposed amendment if requested to do so by more than one-third of the High Contracting Parties.

5. Amendments to the Convention or to the Regulations for its execution, dealt with under the provisions of the preceding paragraph, shall enter into force only after they have been unanimously adopted by the High Contracting Parties represented at the Conference and accepted by each of the High Contracting Parties.

6. Acceptance by the High Contracting Parties of amendments to the Convention or to the Regulations for its execution, which have been adopted by the Conference mentioned in paragraphs 4 and 5, shall be effected by the deposit of a formal instrument with the Director-General of the United Nations Educational, Scientific and Cultural Organization.

7. After the entry into force of amendments to the present Convention or to the Regulations for its execution, only the text of the Convention or of the Regulations for its execution thus amended shall remain open for ratification or accession.

Article 40 — *Registration*

In accordance with Article 102 of the Charter of the United Nations, the present Convention shall be registered with the Secretariat of the United Nations at the request of the Director-General of the United Nations Educational, Scientific and Cultural Organization.

IN FAITH WHEREOF the undersigned, duly authorized, have signed the present Convention.

DONE at The Hague, this fourteenth day of May, 1954, in a single copy which shall be deposited in the archives of the United Nations Educational, Scientific and Cultural Organization, and certified true copies of which shall be delivered to all the States referred to in Articles 30 and 32 as well as to the United Nations.

Regulations for the Execution of the Convention for the Protection of Cultural Property in the Event of Armed Conflict

CHAPTER I — CONTROL

Article 1 — International list of persons

On the entry into force of the Convention, the Director-General of the United Nations Educational, Scientific and Cultural Organization shall compile an international list consisting of all persons nominated by the High Contracting Parties as qualified to carry out the functions of Commissioner-General for Cultural Property. On the initiative of the Director-General of the United Nations Educational, Scientific and Cultural Organization, this list shall be periodically revised on the basis of requests formulated by the High Contracting Parties.

Article 2 — Organization of control

As soon as any High Contracting Party is engaged in an armed conflict to which Article 18 of the Convention applies:

(*a*) It shall appoint a representative for cultural property situated in its territory; if it is in occupation of another territory, it shall appoint a special representative for cultural property situated in that territory;

(*b*) The Protecting Power acting for each of the Parties in conflict with such High Contracting Party shall appoint delegates accredited to the latter in conformity with Article 3 below;

(*c*) A Commissioner-General for Cultural Property shall be appointed to such High Contracting Party in accordance with Article 4.

Article 3 — Appointment of delegates of protecting powers

The Protecting Power shall appoint its delegates from among the members of its diplomatic or consular staff or, with the approval of the Party to which they will be accredited, from among other persons.

Article 4 — Appointment of Commissioner-General

1. The Commissioner-General for Cultural Property shall be chosen from the international list of persons by joint agreement between the Party to which he will be accredited and the Protecting Powers acting on behalf of the opposing Parties.

2. Should the Parties fail to reach agreement within three weeks

from the beginning of their discussions on this point, they shall request the President of the International Court of Justice to appoint the Commissioner-General, who shall not take up his duties until the Party to which he is accredited has approved his appointment.

Article 5 — Functions of delegates

The delegates of the Protecting Powers shall take note of violations of the Convention, investigate, with the approval of the Party to which they are accredited, the circumstances in which they have occurred, make representations locally to secure their cessation and, if necessary, notify the Commissioner-General of such violations. They shall keep him informed of their activities.

Article 6 — Functions of the Commissioner-General

1. The Commissioner-General for Cultural Property shall deal with all matters referred to him in connexion with the application of the Convention, in conjunction with the representative of the Party to which he is accredited and with the delegates concerned.

2. He shall have powers of decision and appointment in the cases specified in the present Regulations.

3. With the agreement of the Party to which he is accredited, he shall have the right to order an investigation or to conduct it himself.

4. He shall make any representations to the Parties to the conflict or to their Protecting Powers which he deems useful for the application of the Convention.

5. He shall draw up such reports as may be necessary on the application of the Convention and communicate them to the Parties concerned and to their Protecting Powers. He shall send copies to the Director-General of the United Nations Educational, Scientific and Cultural Organization, who may make use only of their technical contents.

6. If there is no Protecting Power, the Commissioner-General shall exercise the functions of the Protecting Power as laid down in Articles 21 and 22 of the Convention.

Article 7 — Inspectors and experts

1. Whenever the Commissioner-General for Cultural Property considers it necessary, either at the request of the delegates concerned or after consultation with them, he shall propose, for the approval of the Party to which he is accredited, an inspector of cultural property to be charged with a specific mission. An inspector shall be responsible only to the Commissioner-General.

2. The Commissioner-General, delegates and inspectors may have recourse to the services of experts, who will also be proposed for the approval of the Party mentioned in the preceding paragraph.

Article 8 — Discharge of the mission of control

The Commissioners-General for Cultural Property, delegates of the Protecting Powers, inspectors and experts shall in no case exceed their mandates. In particular, they shall take account of the security needs of the High Contracting Party to which they are accredited and shall in all circumstances act in accordance with the requirements of the military situation as communicated to them by that High Contracting Party.

Article 9 — Substitutes for protecting powers

If a Party to the conflict does not benefit or ceases to benefit from the activities of a Protecting Power, a neutral State may be asked to undertake those functions of a Protecting Power which concern the appointment of a Commissioner-General for Cultural Property in accordance with the procedure laid down in Article 4 above. The Commissioner-General thus appointed shall, if need be, entrust to inspectors the functions of delegates of Protecting Powers as specified in the present Regulations.

Article 10 — Expenses

The remuneration and expenses of the Commissioner-General for Cultural Property, inspectors and experts shall be met by the Party to which they are accredited. Remuneration and expenses of delegates of the Protecting Powers shall be subject to agreement between those Powers and the States whose interests they are safeguarding.

CHAPTER II — SPECIAL PROTECTION

Article 11 — Improvised refuges

1. If, during an armed conflict, any High Contracting Party is induced by unforeseen circumstances to set up an improvised refuge and desires that it should be placed under special protection, it shall communicate this fact forthwith to the Commissioner-General accredited to that Party.

2. If the Commissioner-General considers that such a measure is justified by the circumstances and by the importance of the cultural property sheltered in this improvised refuge, he may authorize the High Contracting Party to display on such refuge the distinctive emblem defined in Article 16 of the Convention. He shall communicate his decision without delay to the delegates of the Protecting Powers who are concerned, each of whom may, within a time-limit of 30 days, order the immediate withdrawal of the emblem.

3. As soon as such delegates have signified their agreement or if the time-limit of 30 days has passed without any of the delegates concerned having made an objection, and if, in the view of the Commissioner-General, the refuge fulfils the conditions laid down in Article 8 of the Convention, the Commissioner-General shall request the Director-General of the United Nations Educational, Scientific and Cultural Organization to enter the refuge in the Register of Cultural Property under Special Protection.

Article 12 — International register of cultural property under special protection

1. An 'International Register of Cultural Property under Special Protection' shall be prepared.

2. The Director-General of the United Nations Educational, Scientific and Cultural Organization shall maintain this Register. He shall furnish copies to the Secretary-General of the United Nations and to the High Contracting Parties.

3. The Register shall be divided into sections, each in the name of a High Contracting Party. Each section shall be sub-divided into three paragraphs, headed: Refuges, Centres containing Monuments, Other Immovable Cultural Property. The Director-General shall determine what details each section shall contain.

Article 13 — Requests for registration

1. Any High Contracting Party may submit to the Director-General of the United Nations Educational, Scientific and Cultural Organization an application for the entry in the Register of certain refuges, centres containing monuments or other immovable cultural property situated within its territory. Such application shall contain a description of the location of such property and shall certify that the property complies with the provisions of Article 8 of the Convention.

2. In the event of occupation, the Occupying Power shall be competent to make such application.

3. The Director-General of the United Nations Educational, Scientific and Cultural Organization shall, without delay, send copies of applications for registration to each of the High Contracting Parties.

Article 14 — Objections

1. Any High Contracting Party may, by letter addressed to the Director-General of the United Nations Educational, Scientific and Cultural Organization, lodge an objection to the registration of cultural property. This letter must be received by him within four months of the day on which he sent a copy of the application for registration.

2. Such objection shall state the reasons giving rise to it, the only valid grounds being that:

(*a*) the property is not cultural property;

(*b*) the property does not comply with the conditions mentioned in Article 8 of the Convention.

3. The Director-General shall send a copy of the letter of objection to the High Contracting Parties without delay. He shall, if necessary, seek the advice of the International Committee on Monuments, Artistic and Historical Sites and Archæological Excavations and also, if he thinks fit, of any other competent organization or person.

4. The Director-General, or the High Contracting Party requesting registration, may make whatever representations they deem necessary to the High Contracting Parties which lodged the objection, with a view to causing the objection to be withdrawn.

5. If a High Contracting Party which has made an application for registration in time of peace becomes involved in an armed conflict before the entry has been made, the cultural property concerned shall at once be provisionally entered in the Register, by the Director-General, pending the confirmation, withdrawal or cancellation of any objection that may be, or may have been, made.

6. If, within a period of six months from the date of receipt of the letter of objection, the Director-General has not received from the High Contracting Party lodging the objection a communication stating that it has been withdrawn, the High Contracting Party applying for registration may request arbitration in accordance with the procedure in the following paragraph.

7. The request for arbitration shall not be made more than one year after the date of receipt by the Director-General of the letter of objection. Each of the two Parties to the dispute shall appoint an arbitrator. When more than one objection has been lodged against an application for registration, the High Contracting Parties which have lodged the objections shall, by common consent, appoint a single arbitrator. These two arbitrators shall select a chief arbitrator from the international list mentioned in Article 1 of the present Regulations. If such arbitrators cannot agree upon their choice, they shall ask the President of the International Court of Justice to appoint a chief arbitrator who need not necessarily be chosen from the international list. The arbitral tribunal thus constituted shall fix its own procedure. There shall be no appeal from its decisions.

8. Each of the High Contracting Parties may declare, whenever a dispute to which it is a Party arises, that it does not wish to apply

Cultural Property 359

the arbitration procedure provided for in the preceding paragraph. In such cases, the objection to an application for registration shall be submitted by the Director-General to the High Contracting Parties. The objection will be confirmed only if the High Contracting Parties so decide by a two-third majority of the High Contracting Parties voting. The vote shall be taken by correspondence, unless the Director-General of the United Nations Educational, Scientific and Cultural Organization deems it essential to convene a meeting under the powers conferred upon him by Article 27 of the Convention. If the Director-General decides to proceed with the vote by correspondence, he shall invite the High Contracting Parties to transmit their votes by sealed letter within six months from the day on which they were invited to do so.

Article 15 — *Registration*

1. The Director-General of the United Nations Educational, Scientific and Cultural Organization shall cause to be entered in the Register, under a serial number, each item of property for which application for registration is made, provided that he has not received an objection within the time-limit prescribed in paragraph 1 of Article 14.

2. If an objection has been lodged, and without prejudice to the provision of paragraph 5 of Article 14, the Director-General shall enter property in the Register only if the objection has been withdrawn or has failed to be confirmed following the procedures laid down in either paragraph 7 or paragraph 8 of Article 14.

3. Whenever paragraph 3 of Article 11 applies, the Director-General shall enter property in the Register if so requested by the Commissioner-General for Cultural Property.

4. The Director-General shall send without delay to the Secretary-General of the United Nations, to the High Contracting Parties, and, at the request of the Party applying for registration, to all other States referred to in Articles 30 and 32 of the Convention, a certified copy of each entry in the Register. Entries shall become effective thirty days after despatch of such copies.

Article 16 — *Cancellation*

1. The Director-General of the United Nations Educational, Scientific and Cultural Organization shall cause the registration of any property to be cancelled:

(*a*) at the request of the High Contracting Party within whose territory the cultural property is situated;

(*b*) if the High Contracting Party which requested registration has denounced the Convention, and when that denunciation has taken effect;

(*c*) in the special case provided for in Article 14, paragraph 5, when an objection has been confirmed following the procedures mentioned either in paragraph 7 or in paragraph 8 of Article 14.

2. The Director-General shall send without delay, to the Secretary-General of the United Nations and to all States which received a copy of the entry in the Register, a certified copy of its cancellation. Cancellation shall take effect thirty days after the despatch of such copies.

CHAPTER III — TRANSPORT OF CULTURAL PROPERTY

Article 17 — Procedure to obtain immunity

1. The request mentioned in paragraph 1 of Article 12 of the Convention shall be addressed to the Commissioner-General for Cultural Property. It shall mention the reasons on which it is based and specify the approximate number and the importance of the objects to be transferred, their present location, the location now envisaged, the means of transport to be used, the route to be followed, the date proposed for the transfer, and any other relevant information.

2. If the Commissioner-General, after taking such opinions as he deems fit, considers that such transfer is justified, he shall consult those delegates of the Protecting Powers who are concerned, on the measures proposed for carrying it out. Following such consultation, he shall notify the Parties to the conflict concerned of the transfer, including in such notification all useful information.

3. The Commissioner-General shall appoint one or more inspectors, who shall satisfy themselves that only the property stated in the request is to be transferred and that the transport is to be by the approved methods and bears the distinctive emblem. The inspector or inspectors shall accompany the property to its destination.

Article 18 — Transport abroad

Where the transfer under special protection is to the territory of another country, it shall be governed not only by Article 12 of the Convention and by Article 17 of the present Regulations, but by the following further provisions:

(*a*) while the cultural property remains on the territory of another State, that State shall be its depositary and shall extend to it as great a measure of care as that which it bestows upon its own cultural property of comparable importance;

(*b*) the depositary State shall return the property only on the cessation of the conflict; such return shall be effected within six months from the date on which it was requested;

(*c*) during the various transfer operations, and while it remains on the territory of another State, the cultural property shall be exempt from confiscation and may not be disposed of either by the depositor or by the depositary. Nevertheless, when the safety of the property requires it, the depositary may, with the assent of the depositor, have the property transported to the territory of a third country, under the conditions laid down in the present article;

(*d*) the request for special protection shall indicate that the State to whose territory the property is to be transferred accepts the provisions of the present Article.

Article 19 — Occupied territory

Whenever a High Contracting Party occupying territory of another High Contracting Party transfers cultural property to a refuge situated elsewhere in that territory, without being able to follow the procedure provided for in Article 17 of the Regulations, the transfer in question shall not be regarded as misappropriation within the meaning of Article 4 of the Convention, provided that the Commissioner-General for Cultural Property certifies in writing, after having consulted the usual custodians, that such transfer was rendered necessary by circumstances.

CHAPTER IV — THE DISTINCTIVE EMBLEM

Article 20 — Affixing of the emblem

1. The placing of the distinctive emblem and its degree of visibility shall be left to the discretion of the competent authorities of each High Contracting Party. It may be displayed on flags or armlets; it may be painted on an object or represented in any other appropriate form.

2. However, without prejudice to any possible fuller markings, the emblem shall, in the event of armed conflict and in the cases mentioned in Articles 12 and 13 of the Convention, be placed on the vehicles of transport so as to be clearly visible in daylight from the air as well as from the ground.

The emblem shall be visible from the ground:

(*a*) at regular intervals sufficient to indicate clearly the perimeter of a centre containing monuments under special protection;

(*b*) at the entrance to other immovable cultural property under special protection.

Article 21 — Identification of persons

1. The persons mentioned in Article 17, paragraph 2 (*b*) and (*c*)

of the Convention may wear an armlet bearing the distinctive emblem, issued and stamped by the competent authorities.

2. Such persons shall carry a special identity card bearing the distinctive emblem. This card shall mention at least the surname and first names, the date of birth, the title or rank, and the function of the holder. The card shall bear the photograph of the holder as well as his signature or his fingerprints, or both. It shall bear the embossed stamp of the competent authorities.

3. Each High Contracting Party shall make out its own type of identity card, guided by the model annexed, by way of example, to the present Regulations. The High Contracting Parties shall transmit to each other a specimen of the model they are using. Identity cards shall be made out, if possible, at least in duplicate, one copy being kept by the issuing Power.

4. The said persons may not, without legitimate reason, be deprived of their identity card or of the right to wear the armlet.

[Annex omitted]

CONCLUDING NOTES

The concluding notes for the 1954 Hague Cultural Property Convention are combined with those for the 1954 Hague Cultural Property Protocol and are to be found at the end of the latter document, below, p. 366.

23. 1954 Hague Protocol for the Protection of Cultural Property in the Event of Armed Conflict

PREFATORY NOTE

At the conclusion of the 1954 Hague Intergovernmental Conference which adopted the Cultural Property Convention and annexed Regulations, certain other acts were also adopted, including a Protocol to the Cultural Property Convention. Regarding the events leading to the adoption of the 1954 Convention and Protocol, see the prefatory note to the 1954 Hague Cultural Property Convention.

The Protocol sets forth in some detail provisions on the prevention of the export of cultural property from occupied territory, and on the safeguarding and return of any such property which has been exported. In addition, in cases where cultural property has been deposited in third states to protect it from the dangers of an armed conflict, the Protocol provides for the return of such property.

Date of signature: Signed on 14 May 1954, and open for signature (see paragraph 6) until 31 December 1954.
Entry into force: 7 August 1956
Depositary: UNESCO
Authentic languages: English, French, Russian, and Spanish
Text reprinted from: 249 *UNTS* 358–64
Also published in: *UK Misc.* 6 (1956), Cmd. 9837 (Eng.);
XLII *UKPP* (1955–1956) 763 (Eng.)

Protocol

The High Contracting Parties are agreed as follows:

I

1. Each High Contracting Party undertakes to prevent the exportation, from a territory occupied by it during an armed conflict, of cultural property as defined in Article 1 of the Convention for the Protection of Cultural Property in the Event of Armed Conflict, signed at The Hague on 14 May, 1954.

2. Each High Contracting Party undertakes to take into its custody cultural property imported into its territory either directly or indirectly from any occupied territory. This shall either be effected automatically upon the importation of the property or, failing this, at the request of the authorities of that territory.

3. Each High Contracting Party undertakes to return, at the close of hostilities, to the competent authorities of the territory previously occupied, cultural property which is in its territory, if such property has been exported in contravention of the principle laid down in the first paragraph. Such property shall never be retained as war reparations.

4. The High Contracting Party whose obligation it was to prevent the exportation of cultural property from the territory occupied by it, shall pay an indemnity to the holders in good faith of any cultural property which has to be returned in accordance with the preceding paragraph.

II

5. Cultural property coming from the territory of a High Contracting Party and deposited by it in the territory of another High Contracting Party for the purpose of protecting such property against the dangers of an armed conflict, shall be returned by the latter, at the end of hostilities, to the competent authorities of the territory from which it came.

III

6. The present Protocol shall bear the date of 14 May, 1954 and, until the date of 31 December, 1954, shall remain open for signature by all States invited to the Conference which met at The Hague from 21 April, 1954 to 14 May, 1954.

7. (*a*) The present Protocol shall be subject to ratification by signatory States in accordance with their respective constitutional procedures.

(*b*) The instruments of ratification shall be deposited with the Director-General of the United Nations Educational, Scientific and Cultural Organization.

8. From the date of its entry into force, the present Protocol shall be open for accession by all States mentioned in paragraph 6 which have not signed it as well as any other State invited to accede by the Executive Board of the United Nations Educational, Scientific and Cultural Organization. Accession shall be effected by the deposit of an instrument of accession with the Director-General of the United Nations Educational, Scientific and Cultural Organization.

9. The States referred to in paragraphs 6 and 8 may declare, at the time of signature, ratification or accession, that they will not be bound by the provisions of Section I or by those of Section II of the present Protocol.

10. (*a*) The present Protocol shall enter into force three months after five instruments of ratification have been deposited.

(*b*) Thereafter, it shall enter into force, for each High Contracting Party, three months after the deposit of its instrument of ratification or accession.

(*c*) The situations referred to in Articles 18 and 19 of the Convention for the Protection of Cultural Property in the Event of Armed Conflict, signed at The Hague on 14 May, 1954, shall give immediate effect to ratifications and accessions deposited by the Parties to the conflict either before or after the beginning of hostilities or occupation. In such cases, the Director-General of the United Nations Educational, Scientific and Cultural Organization shall transmit the communications referred to in paragraph 14 by the speediest method.

11. (*a*) Each State Party to the Protocol on the date of its entry into force shall take all necessary measures to ensure its effective application within a period of six months after such entry into force.

(*b*) This period shall be six months from the date of deposit of the instruments of ratification or accession for any State which deposits its instrument of ratification or accession after the date of the entry into force of the Protocol.

12. Any High Contracting Party may, at the time of ratification or accession, or at any time thereafter, declare by notification addressed to the Director-General of the United Nations Educational, Scientific and Cultural Organization, that the present Protocol shall extend to all or any of the territories for whose international relations it is responsible. The said notification shall take effect three months after the date of its receipt.

13. (*a*) Each High Contracting Party may denounce the present Protocol, on its own behalf, or on behalf of any territory for whose international relations it is responsible.

(*b*) The denunciation shall be notified by an instrument in writing, deposited with the Director-General of the United Nations Educational, Scientific and Cultural Organization.

(*c*) The denunciation shall take effect one year after receipt of the instrument of denunciation. However, if, on the expiry of this period, the denouncing Party is involved in an armed conflict, the denunciation shall not take effect until the end of hostilities, or until the operations of repatriating cultural property are completed, whichever is the later.

14. The Director-General of the United Nations Educational, Scientific and Cultural Organization shall inform the States referred to in paragraphs 6 and 8, as well as the United Nations, of the deposit of all the instruments of ratification, accession or acceptance

provided for in paragraphs 7, 8 and 15 and the notifications and denunciations provided for respectively in paragraphs 12 and 13.

15. (*a*) The present Protocol may be revised if revision is requested by more than one-third of the High Contracting Parties.

(*b*) The Director-General of the United Nations Educational, Scientific and Cultural Organization shall convene a Conference for this purpose.

(*c*) Amendments to the present Protocol shall enter into force only after they have been unanimously adopted by the High Contracting Parties represented at the Conference and accepted by each of the High Contracting Parties.

(*d*) Acceptance by the High Contracting Parties of amendments to the present Protocol, which have been adopted by the Conference mentioned in subparagraphs (*b*) and (*c*), shall be effected by the deposit of a formal instrument with the Director-General of the United Nations Educational, Scientific and Cultural Organization.

(*e*) After the entry into force of amendments to the present Protocol, only the text of the said Protocol thus amended shall remain open for ratification or accession.

In accordance with Article 102 of the Charter of the United Nations, the present Protocol shall be registered with the Secretariat of the United Nations at the request of the Director-General of the United Nations Educational, Scientific and Cultural Organization.

IN FAITH WHEREOF the undersigned, duly authorized, have signed the present Protocol.

DONE at The Hague, this fourteenth day of May, 1954, in English, French, Russian and Spanish, the four texts being equally authoritative, in a single copy which shall be deposited in the archives of the United Nations Educational, Scientific and Cultural Organization, and certified true copies of which shall be delivered to all the States referred to in paragraphs 6 and 8 as well as to the United Nations.

CONCLUDING NOTES
relating both to the 1954 Hague
Convention and to the Protocol

Except where otherwise stated, all entries in this list apply *both* to the 1954 Hague Cultural Property Convention *and* to the 1954 Hague Cultural Property Protocol. In cases where information applies only to one of these agreements, it is prefaced by (Conv.) or (Prot.) as appropriate. *Re* the Protocol, no states have indicated (as they could have in accord with paragraph 9) that they will not be bound by the provisions of Section I or those of Section II.

Signatures, Ratifications, and Accessions[1]

State (* denotes Reservation etc.: see below)	Date of Signature		Date of Ratification (r), or Accession (a)[2]		
Albania			20 December	1960	a
Andorra[3] (Conv.)	14 May	1954	—		
Australia (Conv.)	14 May	1954	—		
Austria	31 December	1954	25 March	1964	r
Belgium	14 May	1954	16 September	1960	r
Brazil	31 December	1954	12 September	1958	r
Bulgaria (Conv.)			7 August	1956	a
(Prot.)			9 October	1958	a
Burma	31 December	1954	10 February	1956	r
*Byelorussian SSR (Conv.)	14 May	1954	7 May	1957	r
(Prot.)	30 December	1954	7 May	1957	r
Cambodia	17 December	1954	4 April	1962	r
Cameroon			12 October	1961	a
China, Republic of (i.e. Taiwan)	14 May	1954	—		
Congo, Democratic Republic of (now Zaire)			18 April	1961	a
Cuba (Conv.)	14 May	1954	26 November	1957	r
(Prot.)	10 December	1954	26 November	1957	r
Cyprus[4]			9 September	1964	a
Czechoslovakia (Conv.)	14 May	1954	6 December	1957	r
(Prot.)	30 December	1954	6 December	1957	r
Denmark	18 October	1954	—		
Dominican Republic (Conv.)			5 January	1960	a
Ecuador (Conv.)	14 May	1954	2 October	1956	r
(Prot.)	14 May	1954	8 February	1961	r
Egypt	30 December	1954	17 August	1955	r
El Salvador	14 May	1954	—		
France	14 May	1954	7 June	1957	r
Gabon			4 December	1961	a
German Democratic Republic			16 January	1974	a

[1] Information in communications from the Office of International Standards and Legal Affairs of UNESCO between January 1980 and February 1981.

[2] There have been no declarations of succession in respect of these two agreements.

[3] Signature was by the head of the delegation of Spain to the Intergovernmental Conference at The Hague. He signed in the name of His Excellency the Bishop of Urgel, co-Prince of Andorra. In a letter to the Depositary dated 5 August 1954 the French Ministry of Foreign Affairs reported the objections of the President of France, co-Prince of Andorra, regarding this signature. A letter to the Depositary from the Bishop of Urgel, dated 6 December 1954, was also conveyed to states.

[4] Entered into force immediately, in conformity with paragraph 3 of Article 33 of the Convention, and paragraph 10(c) of the Protocol.

State (* denotes Reservation etc.: see below)	Date of Signature		Date of Ratification (r), or Accession (a)		
Germany, Federal Republic of[5]	14 May	1954	11 August	1967	r
Ghana			25 July	1960	a
Greece	14 May	1954	—		
Guinea (Conv.)			20 September	1960	a
(Prot.)			11 December	1961	a
Holy See			24 February	1958	a
Hungary (Conv.)	14 May	1954	17 May	1956	r
(Prot.)			16 August	1956	a
India	14 May	1954	16 June	1958	r
Indonesia (Conv.)	24 December	1954	10 January	1967	r
(Prot.)	24 December	1954	26 July	1967	r
Iran	14 May	1954	22 June	1959	r
Iraq	14 May	1954	21 December	1967	r
Ireland	14 May	1954	—		
Israel (Conv.)	14 May	1954	3 October	1957	r
(Prot.)			1 April	1958	a
Italy	14 May	1954	9 May	1958	r
Ivory Coast (Conv.)			24 January	1980	a
Japan	6 September	1954	—		
Jordan	22 December	1954	2 October	1957	r
Kuwait (Conv.)			6 June	1969	a
(Prot.)			11 February	1970	a
Lebanon	25 May	1954	1 June	1960	r
Libya	14 May	1954	19 November	1957	r
Liechtenstein			28 April	1960	a
Luxembourg	14 May	1954	29 September	1961	r
Madagascar			3 November	1961	a
Malaya, Federation of			12 December	1960	a
Mali			18 May	1961	a
Mexico	29 December	1954	7 May	1956	r
Monaco	14 May	1954	10 December	1957	r
Mongolia (Conv.)			4 November	1964	a

[5] Two separate points should be noted. (a) In a communication received by the Depositary on 12 January 1962 the Federal Republic of Germany stated that, in accordance with paragraph 3 of Article 18 of the Convention, it 'accepts and applies the provisions of the said Convention.' (b) At ratification in 1967, the Federal Republic of Germany stated that the Convention and Protocol would also apply to *Land Berlin*; and, in a further communication, dated 4 April 1968, it added the supplementary phrase, ' . . . account being taken of the rights and responsibilities of the Allied Authorities . . .' The USSR, Ukrainian SSR, Byelorussian SSR, and other states objected to these statements regarding West Berlin. Subsequent communications were received from all of these and also from others, including France, United Kingdom, and USA. In 1974–5, in connection with the German Democratic Republic's accession to the Convention and Protocol, there were further notes to the Depositary about West Berlin, from the German Democratic Republic, Ukrainian SSR, Byelorussian SSR, France, United Kingdom, and USA.

State (* denotes Reservation etc.: see below)	Date of Signature		Date of Ratification (r), or Accession (a)		
Morocco			30 August	1968	a
Netherlands	14 May	1954	14 October	1958	r
New Zealand (Conv.)	20 December	1954	—		
Nicaragua	14 May	1954	25 November	1959	r
Niger			6 December	1976	a
Nigeria			5 June	1961	a
*Norway	14 May	1954	19 September	1961	r
Oman (Conv.)			26 October	1977	a
Pakistan			27 March	1959	a
Panama (Conv.)			17 July	1962	a
Philippines	14 May	1954	—		
Poland (Conv.)	14 May	1954	6 August	1956	r
(Prot.)	31 December	1954	6 August	1956	r
Portugal (Conv.)	14 May	1954	—		
Qatar (Conv.)			31 July	1973	a
Romania (Conv.)	14 May	1954	21 March	1958	r
(Prot.)			21 March	1958	a
San Marino	14 May	1954	9 February	1956	r
Saudi Arabia (Conv.)			20 January	1971	a
Spain (Conv.)	14 May	1954	7 July	1960	r
(Prot.)	30 December	1954	—		
*Sudan (Conv.)			23 July	1970	a
Switzerland			15 May	1962	u
Syria	14 May	1954	6 March	1958	r
Tanzania (Conv.)			23 September	1971	a
Thailand			2 May	1958	a
Turkey			15 December	1965	a
*Ukrainian SSR (Conv.)	14 May	1954	6 February	1957	r
(Prot.)	30 December	1954	6 February	1957	r
United Kingdom (Conv.)	30 December	1954	—		
Upper Volta (Conv.)			18 December	1969	a
Uruguay	14 May	1954	—		
USA (Conv.)	14 May	1954			
*USSR (Conv.)	14 May	1954	4 January	1957	r
(Prot.)	30 December	1954	4 January	1957	r
Yemen, South			6 February	1970	a
Yugoslavia	14 May	1954	13 February	1956	r

Total Number of Parties Listed: 69 for the Convention; 58 for the Protocol.

Note on Entry into Force for States Parties

In accordance with Article 33 of the Convention, and paragraph 10 of the Protocol, both the Convention and the Protocol entered into force on 7 August 1956 for the five states which had ratified them three months earlier. For each of the other ratifying states, and for each of the acceding states, the

Convention and the Protocol formally entered into force three months after date indicated in the right-hand column above: however, as noted in the list, the accession of Cyprus to the Convention and Protocol became effective immediately, and the Federal Republic of Germany stated before ratification that it accepts and applies the provisions of the Convention.

Denunciations

None

Reservations etc.[6]

Byelorussian SSR, at signature of the Convention, noted that 'various provisions included in the Convention and Regulations weaken these agreements with regard to the conservation and defence of cultural property in the event of armed conflict and that, for that reason, he could not express his satisfaction.'

Norway, at ratification of the Convention and Protocol, made the reservation that 'the return of cultural property in accord with the provisions of Sections I and II of the Protocol cannot be demanded after the end of a period of twenty years, starting from the date when the property concerned came into the possession of a holder in good faith.' Sixteen states made observations to the Depositary about this reservation. In a note to the Depositary dated 3 October 1979 Norway withdrew the reservation.

Sudan, in a communication dated 25 August 1972, *re* an application by the Khmer Republic for an entry in the International Register of Cultural Property under Special Protection, stated that it 'considers that the Royal Government of the National Union of Cambodia, of Samdeck Norodom Sihanouk is the only Government empowered to represent the Kingdom of Cambodia' and therefore it 'does not recognize the right of the Phnom-Penh régime to enter into international obligations on behalf of the Kingdom of Cambodia.'

Ukrainian SSR and *USSR*, at signature of the Convention, noted similar comments to those of Byelorussian SSR.

---

[6] This list is based on information supplied by UNESCO. The Depositary does not have an English translation of the reservation made by Norway. The translation from the French original text is ours, and has been confirmed as accurate by the Depositary.

24. 1971 Zagreb Resolution of the Institute of International Law on Conditions of Application of Humanitarian Rules of Armed Conflict to Hostilities in which United Nations Forces May Be Engaged

PREFATORY NOTE

The United Nations itself is not a party to any international agreements on the laws of war. Moreover, these agreements do not expressly provide for the application of the laws of war by UN forces. However, it is widely held that the laws of war remain directly relevant to such forces.

Various international bodies have addressed the application of the laws of war to UN forces. The 1954 Hague Intergovernmental Conference, which adopted the 1954 Hague Cultural Property Convention, also approved a resolution recommending that the UN ensure the application of that Convention by UN forces involved in military action. The International Committee of the Red Cross has frequently raised with the UN the issue of the application of the laws of war to UN forces. In 1971 the Institute of International Law adopted a resolution which is one of the best-known formulations of principles relating to this issue. The resolution is set forth below.

Founded in 1873, the Institute of International Law is an unofficial body consisting of sixty members and approximately sixty associates, all of whom are distinguished international lawyers from various states throughout the world. According to its Statute, the objective of the Institute is to assist the progressive development of international law by, *inter alia*, contributing to the maintenance of peace and the observance of the laws of war. Since its founding, the Institute has adopted many resolutions relating to the laws of war.

In 1965 the Institute conferred upon its First Commission the task of studying the conditions of the application of the laws of war to military operations of the United Nations and regional organizations. In 1967 the Commission decided to restrict its enquiry to UN forces. The Commission attempted to take a practical rather than dogmatic approach by avoiding controversial questions relating to the character of UN forces or their conformity with the UN Charter. The Commission assumed both the existence of UN forces (whatever their particular mission), and the possibility that such forces might became involved in armed hostilities. The Commission's preparatory study was considered by the Institute of International Law at the Institute's 55th Session, held in Zagreb from 26 August to 4 September 1971. On 3 September 1971 the Institute adopted the resolution. (On 13 August 1975 the Institute adopted a further, complementary, resolution on this issue.)

In addition to such unofficial formulations as this resolution, the actual directives relating to the laws of war issued by the UN to its forces should be noted. In late 1950, during the Korean War, the UN Command in Korea specifically instructed all the forces under its command to observe all the provisions of 1949 Geneva Convention III on prisoners of war. The UN Emergency Force in Egypt was subject to Regulations (drawn up by the Secretary-General and dated 20 February 1957) of which Article 44 stated: 'The Force shall observe the principles and spirit of the general international Conventions applicable to the conduct of military personnel.' The UN Operation in the Congo was subject to an identical Article in its Regulations dated 15 July 1963. In a letter to the ICRC, published in *International Review of the Red Cross* in January 1962, UN Secretary-General U Thant confirmed that the 'UNO insists on its armed forces in the field applying the principles of these 1949 Geneva Conventions as scrupulously as possible.'

The application of the laws of war to UN forces may not depend exclusively on the position taken by the UN. National contingents in the service of the UN remain bound, to the same extent and the same degree, by the laws of war which would apply if the same forces were engaged in international armed conflict for their own states; states retain a responsibility for their contingents.

However, the fact that national contingents remain bound by the laws of war does not remove the need to address issues relating to UN forces. While all national contingents of a UN force are equally bound by customary law, they may not be equally bound by such other parts of the laws of war as do not have the status of customary law. Also, despite the measure of international personality possessed by the UN, it does not have the same attributes as a state, and this may make the application of certain specific provisions of the international agreements on the laws of war (as opposed to their 'principles and spirit') less practicable. Such difficulties highlight the importance of efforts aimed at clarifying the particular manner in which the laws of war apply to UN forces. In this connection, note also the references to UN forces in the 1981 UN Weapons Convention and its Protocol II.

Text reprinted from: *Annuaire de l'Institut de Droit International*, vol. 54, II, (1971), pp. 465–70. (This is the Institute's authoritative English version of the authentic French text, which is on pp. 449–54.)

Also published in: 66 *AJIL* (1972) 465–8 (Eng.)

Conditions of Application of Humanitarian Rules of Armed Conflict to Hostilities in which United Nations Forces May Be Engaged

The Institute of International Law,

Recalling its Resolution on 'Equality of application of the rules of the law of war to parties to an armed conflict' (Brussels Session, 1963);

Recalling its Resolutions on 'The distinction between military objectives and non-military objects in general and particularly the problems associated with weapons of mass destruction' (Edinburgh Session, 1969);

Noting that the United Nations on various occasions has made use of armed Forces and that such Forces, whatever their mission, might become involved in actual hostilities;

Considering that pending the elaboration of a comprehensive set of rules governing the status of United Nations Forces, it is necessary to determine the conditions under which the humanitarian rules of armed conflict apply to such Forces;

Reserving the study of the general problem of the effects which the outlawry of war and of the use of force may have upon the principle of non-discrimination in the application of the other rules relating to armed conflict;

Declaring, in addition, that the present Resolution is without prejudice to the solution which may be given to the problems connected with the competence of United Nations organs to create or to direct United Nations Forces;

Has adopted the following Articles:

Article 1

For the purposes of the present Articles, the term 'United Nations Forces' shall apply to all armed units under the control of the United Nations.

Article 2

The humanitarian rules of the law of armed conflict apply to the United Nations as of right, and they must be complied with in all circumstances by United Nations Forces which are engaged in hostilities.

The rules referred to in the preceding paragraph include in particular:

(*a*) the rules pertaining to the conduct of hostilities in general and especially those prohibiting the use or some uses of certain weapons, those concerning the means of injuring the other party, and those relating to the distinction between military and non-military objectives;

(*b*) the rules contained in the Geneva Conventions of August 12, 1949;

(*c*) the rules which aim at protecting civilian persons and property.

Article 3

A.If United Nations Forces are formed through individual recruitment, the United Nations shall issue regulations defining the rights and duties of the members of such Forces.

In the event of these Forces becoming involved in hostilities, these regulations shall name the international authorities which, in regard to said Forces, shall be vested with the regulatory, executive and judicial powers necessary to secure effective compliance with the humanitarian rules of armed conflict.

B. If United Nations Forces are composed of national contingents with regard to which the United Nations has not issued any regulations such as those mentioned in the preceding paragraph, effective compliance with the humanitarian rules of armed conflict must be secured through agreements concluded between the Organisation and the several States which contribute contingents.

These agreements shall at least confer upon the United Nations the right to receive all information pertaining to, and the right to supervise at any time and at any place, the effective compliance with the humanitarian rules of armed conflict by each contingent.

Article 4

In order to secure effective compliance with the humanitarian rules of armed conflict by United Nations Forces, it is necessary that the individuals who may be called upon to participate in such Forces receive adequate and previous instruction on the law of armed conflict in its entirety, and especially on the meaning and the scope of the Geneva Conventions of August 12, 1949.

It is desirable that the United Nations, as well as those of its specialised agencies which are concerned with furthering education and health, take all steps within their power in order to coordinate the measures which the States parties to the Geneva Conventions have been invited to take in this field by the International Conferences of the Red Cross.

Article 5

In order to secure effective compliance with the humanitarian rules of armed conflict during hostilities in which United Nations Forces are engaged, it is necessary that the Organisation should ensure that there are, within its Forces, health services composed of competent personnel in sufficient numbers and provided with means of action that are proportionate to the foreseeable needs.

If the direction of such services is entrusted to the States which have contributed contingents, the Organisation shall take all measures in its power to coordinate the activities of these services.

Article 6

In order to ensure effective compliance with the humanitarian rules of armed conflict during hostilities in which United Nations Forces may become involved, it is desirable, if there is no Protecting Power, that an impartial body be empowered to assume the duties entrusted to the Protecting Power by the Geneva Conventions of August 12, 1949.

The body referred to in the present article as well as its members should enjoy the facilities necessary to carry out their functions effectively.

Article 7

Without prejudice to the individual or collective responsibility which derives from the very fact that the party opposing the United Nations Forces has committed aggression, that party shall make reparation for injuries caused in violation of the humanitarian rules of armed conflict. The United Nations is entitled to demand compliance with these rules for the benefit of its Forces and to claim damages for injuries suffered by its Forces in violation of these rules.

Article 8

The United Nations is liable for damage which may be caused by its Forces in violation of the humanitarian rules of armed conflict, without prejudice to any possible recourse against the State whose contingent has caused the damage.

It is desirable that claims presented by persons thus injured be submitted to bodies composed of independent and impartial persons. Such bodies should be designated or set up either by the regulations issued by the United Nations or by the agreements concluded by the Organisation with the States which put contingents at its disposal and, possibly, with any other interested State.

It is equally desirable that if such bodies have been designated or set up by a binding decision of the United Nations, or if the jurisdiction of similar bodies has been accepted by the State of which the injured person is a national, no claims may be presented to the United Nations by that State unless the injured person has exhausted the remedy thus made available to it.

25. 1977 United Nations Convention on the Prohibition of Military or Any Other Hostile Use of Environmental Modification Techniques

PREFATORY NOTE

This international agreement was negotiated at a time of growing international concern about the environment generally, and about the possible future development of environmental modification techniques. The USA's widespread use of various methods of forest and crop destruction in Vietnam had been much criticized. Then in early July 1972 US newspapers carried detailed reports (later confirmed before the US Senate) stating that the USA had been attempting to manipulate weather in Indo-China with a view *inter alia* to muddying or flooding land routes from North Vietnam. On 26 July 1972 the US Senate Subcommittee on Oceans and International Environment opened its hearings on a resolution that the USA should seek the agreement of other governments to a proposed treaty prohibiting the use of any environmental or geophysical modification activity as a weapon of war. On 11 July 1973 the US Senate passed a resolution to that effect.

International negotiations followed. At the Moscow summit meeting on 3 July 1974, the USA and USSR agreed to hold discussions to consider the dangers of environmental warfare. On 21 August 1975 the USA and USSR tabled identical drafts of a convention at the Conference of the Committee on Disarmament in Geneva. After negotiations under the auspices of the CCD, in which all thirty CCD participating member states took part, on 2 September 1976 the CCD transmitted a revised text to the UN General Assembly, together with a set of Understandings relating to Articles I, II, III, and VIII of the Convention. On 10 December 1976 the General Assembly adopted a resolution referring the Convention to all states for signature and ratification.

Of the four 1976 CCD Understandings, the first two (relating to Articles I and II of the Environmental Convention respectively) are the most important.

Article I of the Environmental Convention limits the application of the Convention to techniques which have 'widespread, long-lasting or severe' effects, and the first Understanding interpreted these three words:

> It is the understanding of the Committee that, for the purposes of this Convention, the terms, 'widespread', 'long-lasting' and 'severe' shall be interpreted as follows:
> (a) 'widespread': encompassing an area on the scale of several hundred square kilometres;
> (b) 'long-lasting': lasting for a period of months, or approximately a season;
> (c) 'severe': involving serious or significant disruption or harm to human life, natural and economic resources or other assets.

It is further understood that the interpretation set forth above is intended exclusively for this Convention and is not intended to prejudice the interpretation of the same or similar terms if used in connexion with any other international agreement.

This last point was made because three virtually identical words were employed in 1977 Geneva Protocol I; as adopted, Article 35(3) of 1977 Geneva Protocol I prohibits the employment of methods or means of warfare which cause 'widespread, long-term and severe damage to the natural environment'. This latter provision is worded slightly differently from the Environmental Convention (note the 'and' as against 'or'), and has a different purpose: it is concerned with damage *to* the environment, whatever the weapons used. This is distinct from the manipulation of the forces of the environment as weapons, which is the central concern of the Environmental Convention. None the less, the two areas of concern could overlap in practice.

The second 1976 CCD Understanding related to Article II of the Environmental Convention, and included a non-exhaustive list of phenomena which could be caused by the environmental modification techniques: 'earthquakes; tsunamis; an upset in the ecological balance of a region; changes in weather patterns (clouds, precipitation, cyclones of various types, and tornadic storms); changes in climate patterns; changes in ocean currents; changes in the state of the ozone layer; and changes in the state of the ionosphere.'

There has been criticism of the Convention on three main grounds. First, the terms 'widespread, long-lasting or severe' are so broad and vague as to place few limits on actual activities. Second, although most such techniques have yet to be developed, it is a prohibition exclusively on use, rather than on testing and development. Third, its provisions for investigation and settlement of disputes are weak, because of the possible use of the veto in the UN Security Council. (An Annex to the Convention, not included here, provides for the work of a Consultative Committee of Experts.)

Although this Convention is the only international agreement which exclusively addresses environmental modification techniques, existing customary and conventional law relating to armed conflicts and occupations could be regarded as applicable, including Articles 22, 23(*a*) and (*e*) and 55 of the Regulations annexed to 1899 Hague Convention II and 1907 Hague Convention IV; the 1925 Geneva Protocol; and Article 53 of 1949 Geneva Convention IV.

Date of signature:	Signed on 18 May 1977, and open for signature (see Article IX) thereafter.
Entry into force:	5 October 1978
Depositary:	United Nations
Authentic languages:	Arabic, Chinese, English, French, Russian, and Spanish
Text reprinted from:	UKTS 24 (1979), Cmnd. 7469 (Eng.)
Also published in:	UK Misc. 21 (1977), Cmnd. 6985 (Eng.)

Convention on the Prohibition of Military or Any Other Hostile Use of Environmental Modification Techniques

The States Parties to this Convention,

Guided by the interest of consolidating peace, and wishing to contribute to the cause of halting the arms race, and of bringing about general and complete disarmament under strict and effective international control, and of saving mankind from the danger of using new means of warfare,

Determined to continue negotiations with a view to achieving effective progress towards further measures in the field of disarmament,

Recognizing that scientific and technical advances may open new possibilities with respect to modification of the environment,

Recalling the Declaration of the United Nations Conference on the Human Environment, adopted at Stockholm on 16 June 1972,

Realizing that the use of environmental modification techniques for peaceful purposes could improve the interrelationship of man and nature and contribute to the preservation and improvement of the environment for the benefit of present and future generations,

Recognizing, however, that military or any other hostile use of such techniques could have effects extremely harmful to human welfare,

Desiring to prohibit effectively military or any other hostile use of environmental modification techniques in order to eliminate the dangers to mankind from such use, and affirming their willingness to work towards the achievement of this objective,

Desiring also to contribute to the strengthening of trust among nations and to the further improvement of the international situation in accordance with the purposes and principles of the Charter of the United Nations,

Have agreed as follows:

Article I

1. Each State Party to this Convention undertakes not to engage in military or any other hostile use of environmental modification techniques having widespread, long-lasting or severe effects as the means of destruction, damage or injury to any other State Party.

2. Each State Party to this Convention undertakes not to assist, encourage or induce any State, group of States or international

organization to engage in activities contrary to the provisions of paragraph 1 of this article.

Article II

As used in article I, the term 'environmental modification techniques' refers to any technique for changing — through the deliberate manipulation of natural processes — the dynamics, composition or structure of the Earth, including its biota, lithosphere, hydrosphere and atmosphere, or of outer space.

Article III

1. The provisions of this Convention shall not hinder the use of environmental modification techniques for peaceful purposes and shall be without prejudice to the generally recognized principles and applicable rules of international law concerning such use.

2. The States Parties to this Convention undertake to facilitate, and have the right to participate in, the fullest possible exchange of scientific and technological information on the use of environmental modification techniques for peaceful purposes. States Parties in a position to do so shall contribute, alone or together with other States or international organizations, to international economic and scientific co-operation in the preservation, improvement and peaceful utilization of the environment, with due consideration for the needs of the developing areas of the world.

Article IV

Each State Party to this Convention undertakes to take any measures it considers necessary in accordance with its constitutional processes to prohibit and prevent any activity in violation of the provisions of the Convention anywhere under its jurisdiction or control.

Article V

1. The States Parties to this Convention undertake to consult one another and to co-operate in solving any problems which may arise in relation to the objectives of, or in the application of the provisions of, the Convention. Consultation and co-operation pursuant to this article may also be undertaken through appropriate international procedures within the framework of the United Nations and in accordance with its Charter. These international procedures may include the services of appropriate international organizations, as well as of a Consultative Committee of Experts as provided for in paragraph 2 of this article.

2. For the purposes set forth in paragraph 1 of this article, the Depositary shall, within one month of the receipt of a request

from any State Party to this Convention, convene a Consultative Committee of Experts. Any State Party may appoint an expert to the Committee whose functions and rules of procedure are set out in the annex, which constitutes an integral part of this Convention. The Committee shall transmit to the Depositary a summary of its findings of fact, incorporating all views and information presented to the Committee during its proceedings. The Depositary shall distribute the summary to all States Parties.

3. Any State Party to this Convention which has reason to believe that any other State Party is acting in breach of obligations deriving from the provisions of the Convention may lodge a complaint with the Security Council of the United Nations. Such a complaint should include all relevant information as well as all possible evidence supporting its validity.

4. Each State Party to this Convention undertakes to co-operate in carrying out any investigation which the Security Council may initiate, in accordance with the provisions of the Charter of the United Nations, on the basis of the complaint received by the Council. The Security Council shall inform the State Parties of the results of the investigation.

5. Each State Party to this Convention undertakes to provide or support assistance, in accordance with the provisions of the Charter of the United Nations, to any State Party which so requests, if the Security Council decides that such Party has been harmed or is likely to be harmed as a result of violation of the Convention.

Article VI

1. Any State Party to this Convention may propose amendments to the Convention. The text of any proposed amendment shall be submitted to the Depositary, who shall promptly circulate it to all States Parties.

2. An amendment shall enter into force for all States Parties to this Convention which have accepted it, upon the deposit with the Depositary of instruments of acceptance by a majority of States Parties. Thereafter it shall enter into force for any remaining State Party on the date of deposit of its instrument of acceptance.

Article VII

This Convention shall be of unlimited duration.

Article VIII

1. Five years after the entry into force of this Convention, a conference of the States Parties to the Convention shall be convened by the Depositary at Geneva, Switzerland. The conference shall review the operation of the Convention with a view to ensuring

that its purposes and provisions are being realized, and shall in particular examine the effectiveness of the provisions of paragraph 1 of article I in eliminating the dangers of military or any other hostile use of environmental modification techniques.

2. At intervals of not less than five years thereafter, a majority of the States Parties to this Convention may obtain, by submitting a proposal to this effect to the Depositary, the convening of a conference with the same objectives.

3. If no conference has been convened pursuant to paragraph 2 of this article within ten years following the conclusion of a previous conference, the Depositary shall solicit the views of all States Parties to this Convention concerning the convening of such a conference. If one third or ten of the States Parties, whichever number is less, respond affirmatively, the Depositary shall take immediate steps to convene the conference.

Article IX

1. This Convention shall be open to all States for signature. Any State which does not sign the Convention before its entry into force in accordance with paragraph 3 of this article may accede to it at any time.

2. This Convention shall be subject to ratification by signatory States. Instruments of ratification or accession shall be deposited with the Secretary-General of the United Nations.

3. This Convention shall enter into force upon the deposit of instruments of ratification by twenty Governments in accordance with paragraph 2 of this article.

4. For those States whose instruments of ratification or accession are deposited after the entry into force of this Convention, it shall enter into force on the date of the deposit of their instruments of ratification or accession.

5. The Depositary shall promptly inform all signatory and acceding States of the date of each signature, the date of deposit of each instrument of ratification or accession and the date of the entry into force of this Convention and of any amendments thereto, as well as of the receipt of other notices.

6. This Convention shall be registered by the Depositary in accordance with Article 102 of the Charter of the United Nations.

Article X

This Convention of which the English, Arabic, Chinese, French, Russian and Spanish texts are equally authentic, shall be deposited with the Secretary-General of the United Nations, who shall send duly certified copies thereof to the Governments of the signatory and acceding States.

In witness whereof, the undersigned, being duly authorized thereto by their respective Governments, have signed this Convention, opened for signature at Geneva on the eighteenth day of May, one thousand nine hundred and seventy-seven.

[Annex omitted]

CONCLUDING NOTES

Signatures, Ratifications, and Accessions[1]

State (* denotes Reservation etc.: see below)	Date of Signature		Date of Ratification (*r*), or Accession (*a*)[2]		
Australia	31 May	1978	—		
Bangladesh			3 October	1979	*a*
Belgium	18 May	1977	—		
Benin	10 June	1977	—		
Bolivia	18 May	1977	—		
Brazil	9 November	1977			
Bulgaria	18 May	1977	31 May	1978	*r*
Byelorussian SSR	18 May	1977	7 June	1978	*r*
Canada	18 May	1977	—		
Cape Verde			3 October	1979	*a*
Cuba	23 September	1977	10 April	1978	*r*
Cyprus	7 October	1977	12 April	1978	*r*
Czechoslovakia	18 May	1977	12 May	1978	*r*
Denmark	18 May	1977	19 April	1978	*r*
Ethiopia	18 May	1977	—		
Finland	18 May	1977	12 May	1978	*r*
German Democratic Republic	18 May	1977	25 May	1978	*r*
Germany, Federal Republic of	18 May	1977	—		
Ghana	21 March	1978	22 June	1978	*r*
Holy See	27 May	1977	—		
Hungary	18 May	1977	19 April	1978	*r*
Iceland	18 May	1977	—		
India	15 December	1977	15 December	1978	*r*
Iran	18 May	1977	—		
Iraq	15 August	1977			
Ireland	18 May	1977	—		
Italy	18 May	1977	—		

[1] Information supplied in communications from the Treaty Section of the United Nations between January 1980 and February 1981.
[2] There have been no declarations of succession.

State (* denotes Reservation etc.: see below)	Date of Signature		Date of Ratification (*r*), or Accession (*a*)		
*Kuwait			2 January	1980	*a*
Laos	13 April	1978	5 October	1978	*r*
Lebanon	18 May	1977	—		
Liberia	18 May	1977	—		
Luxembourg	18 May	1977	—		
Malawi			5 October	1978	*a*
Mongolia	18 May	1977	19 May	1978	*r*
Morocco	18 May	1977	—		
Netherlands	18 May	1977	—		
Nicaragua	11 August	1977	—		
Norway	18 May	1977	15 February	1979	*r*
Papua New Guinea			28 October	1980	*a*
Poland	18 May	1977	8 June	1978	*r*
Portugal	18 May	1977	—		
Romania	18 May	1977	—		
Sao Tomé and Principe			5 October	1979	*a*
Sierra Leone	12 April	1978	—		
Spain	18 May	1977	19 July	1978	*r*
Sri Lanka	8 June	1977	25 April	1978	*r*
Syria	4 August	1977	—		
Tunisia	11 May	1978	11 May	1978	*r*
*Turkey	18 May	1977	—		
Uganda	18 May	1977	—		
Ukrainian SSR	18 May	1977	13 June	1978	*r*
United Kingdom[3]	18 May	1977	16 May	1978	*r*
USA	18 May	1977	17 January	1980	*r*
USSR	18 May	1977	30 May	1978	*r*
Vietnam			26 August	1980	*a*
Yemen Arab Republic (North)	18 May	1977	20 July	1977	*r*
Yemen, People's Democratic Republic of (South)			12 June	1979	*a*
Zaire	28 February	1978	—		

Total Number of Parties Listed: 31

Note on Entry into Force for States Parties

In accordance with Article IX, the Convention entered into force on 5 October 1978 for the twenty states which ratified it by that date. For each of the other ratifying and acceding states, the Convention entered into force on the date of deposit of its instrument of ratification or accession, as indicated in the right-hand column above.

[3] The instrument of ratification specifies that the Convention is also ratified in respect of various territories outside the UK.

Denunciations
None

Reservations etc.

Kuwait, at accession: (1) 'Reservation: This Convention binds the State of Kuwait only towards States Parties thereto. Its obligatory character shall *ipso facto* terminate with respect to any hostile state which does not abide by the prohibition contained therein.' (2) 'Understanding: It is understood that accession to the Convention . . . does not mean in any way recognition of Israel by the State of Kuwait. Furthermore, no treaty relation will arise between the State of Kuwait and Israel.'[4]

Turkey, at signature, made an interpretative statement: 'In the opinion of the Turkish Government the terms "widespread", "long-lasting" and "severe effects" contained in the Convention need to be more clearly defined. So long as this clarification is not made the Government of Turkey will be compelled to interpret itself the terms in question and consequently it reserves the right to do so as and when required. Furthermore the Government of Turkey believes that the differences between "military or any other hostile purposes" and "peaceful purposes" should be more clearly defined so as to prevent subjective evaluations.

[4] In a communication received by the Depositary on 23 June 1980 Israel stated: 'The Government of Israel has noted the political character of the statement made by the Government of Kuwait . . . This Convention is not the proper place for making such political pronouncements. Moreover, the said declaration cannot in any way affect whatever obligations are binding upon Kuwait, under general international law or under particular conventions. Insofar as concerns the substance of the matter, the Government of Israel will adopt towards the Government of Kuwait an attitude of complete reciprocity.'

26. 1977 Geneva Protocol I Additional to the Geneva Conventions of 12 August 1949, and Relating to the Protection of Victims of International Armed Conflicts

PREFATORY NOTE

The Two 1977 Geneva Protocols: General

After the adoption of the four 1949 Geneva Conventions, developments in the character of warfare led to the growing realization that the laws of war required further adaptation to the conditions of contemporary hostilities. For example, many armed conflicts occurring since the Second World War have been regarded, at least by some, as non-international in character, and hence the need arose to further clarify the application of the law in such conflicts. Moreover, the widespread resort to guerrilla warfare raised questions concerning the application of the law, because in most cases the activities of guerrillas challenged the existing legal conditions for combatant status. Also, events in armed conflicts and occupations demonstrated the need for further protection to be given to victims.

By the late 1960s, efforts to reaffirm and develop the rules applicable in armed conflict had gathered momentum. The 21st International Conference of the Red Cross, held in Istanbul in 1969, adopted a resolution requesting the International Committee of the Red Cross to propose supplementary rules of humanitarian law and to invite government experts to consider them. In 1971 and 1972 a conference of government experts met in Geneva under the auspices of the ICRC to consider two draft protocols prepared by the ICRC. The purpose of these drafts was not to revise the 1949 Geneva Conventions, but to reaffirm and develop the law.

In 1974 the Swiss government convened in Geneva the Diplomatic Conference on the Reaffirmation and Development of International Humanitarian Law Applicable in Armed Conflicts. The Conference held four sessions: from 20 February to 29 March 1974, from 3 February to 18 April 1975, from 21 April to 11 June 1976, and from 17 March to 10 June 1977. 124 states were represented at the first session, 120 at the second session, 107 at the third session, and 109 at the final session. In order to ensure broad participation, the Conference invited certain national liberation movements to participate fully in the deliberations, although only states were to be entitled to vote. In fact, in recognition of the particular importance of achieving universality of acceptance in addressing the laws of war, for most of the time the Conference used the procedure of making decisions by consensus. Various international organizations were represented in an observer status and the ICRC participated in an expert capacity.

On 8 June 1977 the Conference formally adopted the two Protocols Additional to the Geneva Conventions of 12 August 1949, which were opened for signature in Berne on 12 December 1977.

A notable feature of both Protocols is the way in which their content has been influenced by the law relating to human rights. From their inception, the law relating to human rights and the laws of war evolved along different lines, the former being primarily concerned with the relationship between states and their own nationals in time of peace, and the latter being primarily concerned with the treatment of enemy persons in time of war. However, the distinction between the two areas began to be blurred. On the one hand, the provisions of the 1949 Geneva Conventions came to be seen as embodying individual rights of protected persons; and on the other hand, certain human rights conventions included provisions for at least their partial application in time of war. Certain provisions of the two 1977 Geneva Protocols (for example, Article 75 of Protocol I and Article 6 of Protocol II) are directly derived from the 1966 International Covenant on Civil and Political Rights.

1977 Geneva Protocol I

This Protocol relates to the protection of victims of international armed conflicts. According to its title as well as its terms, the Protocol supplements rather than replaces the 1949 Geneva Conventions. Certain controversial innovations embodied in the Protocol merit particular attention.

First, while Article 1 states that the Protocol applies in situations described in common Article 2 of the 1949 Geneva Conventions, it also states in paragraph 4 that this includes 'armed conflicts in which people are fighting against colonial domination and alien occupation and against racist regimes in the exercise of their right of self-determination'. Moreover, Article 96(3) states that an authority representing a people engaged in such an armed conflict against a state party to the Protocol may undertake to apply the 1949 Geneva Conventions and 1977 Geneva Protocol I by means of a unilateral declaration. These provisions represent an attempt to bring certain armed conflicts within the ambit of the more fully developed regime governing international armed conflicts. If such armed conflicts were only deemed to be internal conflicts, they would be governed by the more elementary regime relating to non-international armed conflicts, as embodied in common Article 3 of the 1949 Geneva Conventions, and 1977 Geneva Protocol II.

Second, the category of 'lawful belligerents' (that is, those combatants entitled to the protection afforded combatants by the laws of war) has been enlarged in several significant ways. Article 1 of the Regulations annexed to 1907 Hague Convention IV defined lawful belligerents as those fulfilling certain conditions. 1949 Geneva Conventions I, II, and III reiterate these conditions, making express reference to resistance movements as well. However, by their very nature, guerrilla movements would more often than not fail to conform to these conditions. Article 44 of 1977 Geneva Protocol I attempts to afford legal recognition to certain types of guerrilla activity by modifying the requirements of distinctive emblems and carrying arms openly. The provisions relating to guerrillas are an important development in the law governing military occupation as well as armed conflict generally.

Third, Geneva Protocol I states that mercenaries shall not have the right to be considered as lawful combatants or prisoners of war, and it attempts to provide a definition of mercenaries. None the less, a capturing state may choose to accord such status to captured mercenaries who, in any case, remain under the protection of the fundamental guarantees, applicable to all persons, as set forth in Article 75. (On 4 December 1980 the UN General Assembly created a committee to draft an international agreement to prohibit employment of mercenaries.)

Although such controversial innovations in Geneva Protocol I have attracted considerable attention, the Protocol also incorporates other important developments, including provisions regarding the identification and protection of medical aircraft, and provisions regarding the protection of civilians from indiscriminate attacks. In addition, the Protocol contains the first explicit reference to civil defence in a binding international agreement on the laws of war.

Date of signature:	Signed on 12 December 1977, and open for signature (see Article 92) for twelve months thereafter.
Entry into force:	7 December 1978
Depositary:	Switzerland
Authentic languages:	Arabic, Chinese, English, French, Russian, and Spanish
Text reprinted from:	International Committee of the Red Cross, *Protocols Additional to the Geneva Conventions of 12 August 1949*, Geneva, 1977, pp. 3–73.
Also published in:	*UK Misc.* 19 (1977), Cmnd. 6927 (Eng.); XVI *UKPP* (1976–1977) 471 (Eng.)

Protocol Additional to the Geneva Conventions of 12 August 1949, and Relating to the Protection of Victims of International Armed Conflicts (Protocol I)

PREAMBLE

The High Contracting Parties,

Proclaiming their earnest wish to see peace prevail among peoples,

Recalling that every State has the duty, in conformity with the Charter of the United Nations, to refrain in its international relations from the threat or use of force against the sovereignty, territorial integrity or political independence of any State, or in any other manner inconsistent with the purposes of the United Nations,

Believing it necessary nevertheless to reaffirm and develop the provisions protecting the victims of armed conflicts and to supplement measures intended to reinforce their application,

Expressing their conviction that nothing in this Protocol or in the Geneva Conventions of 12 August 1949 can by construed as legitimizing or authorizing any act of aggression or any other use of force inconsistent with the Charter of the United Nations,

Reaffirming further that the provisions of the Geneva Conventions of 12 August 1949 and of this Protocol must be fully applied in all circumstances to all persons who are protected by those instruments, without any adverse distinction based on the nature or origin of the armed conflict or on the causes espoused by or attributed to the Parties to the conflict,

Have agreed on the following:

PART I – GENERAL PROVISIONS

Article 1 – General principles and scope of application

1. The High Contracting Parties undertake to respect and to ensure respect for this Protocol in all circumstances.

2. In cases not covered by this Protocol or by other international agreements, civilians and combatants remain under the protection and authority of the principles of international law derived from established custom, from the principles of humanity and from the dictates of public conscience.

3. This Protocol, which supplements the Geneva Conventions of 12 August 1949 for the protection of war victims, shall apply in the situations referred to in Article 2 common to those Conventions.

4. The situations referred to in the preceding paragraph include armed conflicts in which peoples are fighting against colonial domination and alien occupation and against racist régimes in the exercise of their right of self-determination, as enshrined in the Charter of the United Nations and the Declaration on Principles of International Law concerning Friendly Relations and Co-operation among States in accordance with the Charter of the United Nations.

Article 2 – Definitions

For the purposes of this Protocol:

(a) 'First Convention', 'Second Convention', 'Third Convention' and 'Fourth Convention' mean, respectively, the Geneva Convention for the Amelioration of the Condition of the Wounded and Sick in Armed Forces in the Field of 12 August 1949; the Geneva Convention for the Amelioration of the Condition of Wounded, Sick and Shipwrecked Members of Armed Forces at Sea of 12 August 1949; the Geneva Convention relative to the Treatment of Prisoners of War of 12 August 1949; the Geneva Convention relative to the Protection of Civilian Persons in Time of War of 12 August 1949; 'the Conventions' means the four Geneva Conventions of 12 August 1949 for the protection of war victims;

(b) 'rules of international law applicable in armed conflict' means the rules applicable in armed conflict set forth in international agreements to which the Parties to the conflict are Parties and the generally recognized principles and rules of international law which are applicable to armed conflict;

(*c*) 'Protecting Power' means a neutral or other State not a Party to the conflict which has been designated by a Party to the conflict and accepted by the adverse Party and has agreed to carry out the functions assigned to a Protecting Power under the Conventions and this Protocol;

(*d*) 'substitute' means an organization acting in place of a Protecting Power in accordance with Article 5.

Article 3 — Beginning and end of application

Without prejudice to the provisions which are applicable at all times:

(*a*) the Conventions and this Protocol shall apply from the beginning of any situation referred to in Article 1 of this Protocol;

(*b*) the application of the Conventions and of this Protocol shall cease, in the territory of Parties to the conflict, on the general close of military operations and, in the case of occupied territories, on the termination of the occupation, except, in either circumstance, for those persons whose final release, repatriation or re-establishment takes place thereafter. These persons shall continue to benefit from the relevant provisions of the Conventions and of this Protocol until their final release, repatriation or re-establishment.

Article 4 — Legal status of the Parties to the conflict

The application of the Conventions and of this Protocol, as well as the conclusion of the agreements provided for therein, shall not affect the legal status of the Parties to the conflict. Neither the occupation of a territory nor the application of the Conventions and this Protocol shall affect the legal status of the territory in question.

Article 5 — Appointment of Protecting Powers and of their substitute

1. It is the duty of the Parties to a conflict from the beginning of that conflict to secure the supervision and implementation of the Conventions and of this Protocol by the application of the system of Protecting Powers, including *inter alia* the designation and acceptance of those Powers, in accordance with the following paragraphs. Protecting Powers shall have the duty of safeguarding the interests of the Parties to the conflict.

2. From the beginning of a situation referred to in Article 1, each Party to the conflict shall without delay designate a Protecting Power for the purpose of applying the Conventions and this Protocol and shall, likewise without delay and for the same purpose, permit the activities of a Protecting Power which has been accepted by it as such after designation by the adverse Party.

3. If a Protecting Power has not been designated or accepted from the beginning of a situation referred to in Article 1, the International Committee of the Red Cross, without prejudice to the right of any other impartial humanitarian organization to do likewise, shall offer its good offices to the Parties to the conflict with a view to the designation without delay of a Protecting Power to which the Parties to the conflict consent. For that purpose it may, *inter alia*, ask each Party to provide it with a list of at least five States which that Party considers acceptable to act as Protecting Power on its behalf in relation to an adverse Party, and ask each adverse Party to provide a list of at least five States which it would accept as the Protecting Power of the first Party; these lists shall be communicated to the Committee within two weeks after the receipt of the request; it shall compare them and seek the agreement of any proposed State named on both lists.

4. If, despite the foregoing, there is no Protecting Power, the Parties to the conflict shall accept without delay an offer which may be made by the International Committee of the Red Cross or by any other organization which offers all guarantees of impartiality and efficacy, after due consultations with the said Parties and taking into account the result of these consultations, to act as a substitute. The functioning of such a substitute is subject to ·the consent of the Parties to the conflict; every effort shall be made by the Parties to the conflict to facilitate the operations of the substitute in the performance of its tasks under the Conventions and this Protocol.

5. In accordance with Article 4, the designation and acceptance of Protecting Powers for the purpose of applying the Conventions and this Protocol shall not affect the legal status of the Parties to the conflict or of any territory, including occupied territory.

6. The maintenance of diplomatic relations between Parties to the conflict or the entrusting of the protection of a Party's interests and those of its nationals to a third State in accordance with the rules of international law relating to diplomatic relations is no obstacle to the designation of Protecting Powers for the purpose of applying the Conventions and this Protocol.

7. Any subsequent mention in this Protocol of a Protecting Power includes also a substitute.

Article 6 — Qualified persons
1. The High Contracting Parties shall, also in peacetime, endeavour, with the assistance of the national Red Cross (Red Crescent, Red Lion and Sun) Societies, to train qualified personnel to facilitate the application of the Conventions and of this Protocol, and in

particular the activities of the Protecting Powers.

2. The recruitment and training of such personnel are within domestic jurisdiction.

3. The International Committee of the Red Cross shall hold at the disposal of the High Contracting Parties the lists of persons so trained which the High Contracting Parties may have established and may have transmitted to it for that purpose.

4. The conditions governing the employment of such personnel outside the national territory shall, in each case, be the subject of special agreements between the Parties concerned.

Article 7 — Meetings

The depositary of this Protocol shall convene a meeting of the High Contracting Parties, at the request of one or more of the said Parties and upon the approval of the majority of the said Parties, to consider general problems concerning the application of the Conventions and of the Protocol.

PART II — WOUNDED, SICK AND SHIPWRECKED

SECTION I — GENERAL PROTECTION

Article 8 — Terminology

For the purposes of this Protocol:

(a) 'wounded' and 'sick' mean persons, whether military or civilian, who, because of trauma, disease or other physical or mental disorder or disability, are in need of medical assistance or care and who refrain from any act of hostility. These terms also cover maternity cases, new-born babies and other persons who may be in need of immediate medical assistance or care, such as the infirm or expectant mothers, and who refrain from any act of hostility;

(b) 'shipwrecked' means persons, whether military or civilian, who are in peril at sea or in other waters as a result of misfortune affecting them or the vessel or aircraft carrying them and who refrain from any act of hostility. These persons, provided that they continue to refrain from any act of hostility, shall continue to be considered shipwrecked during their rescue until they acquire another status under the Conventions or this Protocol;

(c) 'medical personnel' means those persons assigned, by a Party to the conflict, exclusively to the medical purposes enumerated under sub-paragraph (e) or to the administration of medical units or to the operation or administration of medical transports. Such assignments may be either permanent or temporary. The term includes:

  (i) medical personnel of a Party to the conflict, whether military or civilian, including those described in the First and Second Conventions, and those assigned to civil defence organizations;

 (ii) medical personnel of national Red Cross (Red Crescent, Red Lion and Sun) Societies and other national voluntary aid societies duly recognized and authorized by a Party to the conflict;

(iii) medical personnel of medical units or medical transports described in Article 9, paragraph 2;

(*d*) 'religious personnel' means military or civilian persons, such as chaplains, who are exclusively engaged in the work of their ministry and attached:

  (i) to the armed forces of a Party to the conflict;

 (ii) to medical units or medical transports of a Party to the conflict;

(iii) to medical units or medical transports described in Article 9, paragraph 2; or

(iv) to civil defence organizations of a Party to the conflict.

The attachment of religious personnel may be either permanent or temporary, and the relevant provisions mentioned under sub-paragraph (*k*) apply to them;

(*e*) 'medical units' means establishments and other units, whether military or civilian, organized for medical purposes, namely the search for, collection, transportation, diagnosis or treatment — including first-aid treatment — of the wounded, sick and shipwrecked, or for the prevention of disease. The term includes, for example, hospitals and other similar units, blood transfusion centres, preventive medicine centres and institutes, medical depots and the medical and pharmaceutical stores of such units. Medical units may be fixed or mobile, permanent or temporary;

(*f*) 'medical transportation' means the conveyance by land, water or air of the wounded, sick, shipwrecked, medical personnel, religious personnel, medical equipment or medical supplies protected by the Conventions and by this Protocol;

(*g*) 'medical transports' means any means of transportation, whether military or civilian, permanent or temporary, assigned exclusively to medical transportation and under the control of a competent authority of a Party to the conflict;

(*h*) 'medical vehicles' means any medical transports by land;

(*i*) 'medical ships and craft' means any medical transports by water;

(*j*) 'medical aircraft' means any medical transports by air;

(*k*) 'permanent medical personnel', 'permanent medical units' and 'permanent medical transports' mean those assigned exclusively to medical purposes for an indeterminate period. 'Temporary medical personnel', 'temporary medical units' and 'temporary medical transports' mean those devoted exclusively to medical purposes for limited periods during the whole of such periods. Unless otherwise specified, the terms 'medical personnel', 'medical units' and 'medical transports' cover both permanent and temporary categories;

(*l*) 'distinctive emblem' means the distinctive emblem of the red cross, red crescent or red lion and sun on a white ground when used for the protection of medical units and transports, or medical and religious personnel, equipment or supplies;

(*m*) 'distinctive signal' means any signal or message specified for the identification exclusively of medical units or transports in Chapter III of Annex I to this Protocol.

Article 9 — Field of application

1. This Part, the provisions of which are intended to ameliorate the condition of the wounded, sick and shipwrecked, shall apply to all those affected by a situation referred to in Article 1, without any adverse distinction founded on race, colour, sex, language, religion or belief, political or other opinion, national or social origin, wealth, birth or other status, or on any other similar criteria.

2. The relevant provisions of Articles 27 and 32 of the First Convention shall apply to permanent medical units and transports (other than hospital ships, to which Article 25 of the Second Convention applies) and their personnel made available to a Party to the conflict for humanitarian purposes:

(*a*) by a neutral or other State which is not a Party to that conflict;

(*b*) by a recognized and authorized aid society of such a State;

(*c*) by an impartial international humanitarian organization.

Article 10 — Protection and care

1. All the wounded, sick and shipwrecked, to whichever Party they belong, shall be respected and protected.

2. In all circumstances they shall be treated humanely and shall receive, to the fullest extent practicable and with the least possible delay, the medical care and attention required by their condition. There shall be no distinction among them founded on any grounds other than medical ones.

Article 11 — *Protection of persons*

1. The physical or mental health and integrity of persons who are in the power of the adverse Party or who are interned, detained or otherwise deprived of liberty as a result of a situation referred to in Article 1 shall not be endangered by any unjustified act or omission. Accordingly, it is prohibited to subject the persons described in this Article to any medical procedure which is not indicated by the state of health of the person concerned and which is not consistent with generally accepted medical standards which would be applied under similar medical circumstances to persons who are nationals of the Party conducting the procedure and who are in no way deprived of liberty.

2. It is, in particular, prohibited to carry out on such persons, even with their consent:

(*a*) physical mutilations;

(*b*) medical or scientific experiments;

(*c*) removal of tissue organs for transplation,

except where these acts are justified in conformity with the conditions provided for in paragraph 1.

3. Exceptions to the prohibition in paragraph 2 (*c*) may be made only in the case of donations of blood for transfusion or of skin for grafting, provided that they are given voluntarily and without any coercion or inducement, and then only for therapeutic purposes, under conditions consistent with generally accepted medical standards and controls designed for the benefit of both the donor and the recipient.

4. Any wilful act or omission which seriously endangers the physical or mental health or integrity of any person who is in the power of a Party other than the one on which he depends and which either violates any of the prohibitions in paragraphs 1 and 2 or fails to comply with the requirements of paragraph 3 shall be a grave breach of this Protocol.

5. The persons described in paragraph 1 have the right to refuse any surgical operation. In case of refusal, medical personnel shall endeavour to obtain a written statement to that effect, signed or acknowledged by the patient.

6. Each Party to the conflict shall keep a medical record for every donation of blood for transfusion or skin for grafting by persons referred to in paragraph 1, if that donation is made under the responsibility of that Party. In addition, each Party to the conflict shall endeavour to keep a record of all medical procedures undertaken with respect to any person who is interned, detained or otherwise deprived of liberty as a result of a situation referred to in Article 1. These records shall be available at all times for inspection by the Protecting Power.

Article 12 — *Protection of medical units*

1. Medical units shall be respected and protected at all times and shall not be the object of attack.

2. Paragraph 1 shall apply to civilian medical units, provided that they:

  (*a*) belong to one of the Parties to the conflict;

  (*b*) are recognized and authorized by the competent authority of one of the Parties to the conflict; or

  (*c*) are authorized in conformity with Article 9, paragraph 2, of this Protocol or Article 27 of the First Convention.

3. The Parties to the conflict are invited to notify each other of the location of their fixed medical units. The absence of such notification shall not exempt any of the Parties from the obligation to comply with the provisions of paragraph 1.

4. Under no circumstances shall medical units be used in an attempt to shield military objectives from attack. Whenever possible, the Parties to the conflict shall ensure that medical units are so sited that attacks against military objectives do not imperil their safety.

Article 13 — *Discontinuance of protection of civilian medical units*

1. The protection to which civilian medical units are entitled shall not cease unless they are used to commit, outside their humanitarian function, acts harmful to the enemy. Protection may, however, cease only after a warning has been given setting, whenever appropriate, a reasonable time-limit, and after such warning has remained unheeded.

2. The following shall not be considered as acts harmful to the enemy:

  (*a*) that the personnel of the unit are equipped with light individual weapons for their own defence or for that of the wounded and sick in their charge;

  (*b*) that the unit is guarded by a picket or by sentries or by an escort;

  (*c*) that small arms and ammunition taken from the wounded and sick, and not yet handed to the proper service, are found in the units;

  (*d*) that members of the armed forces or other combatants are in the unit for medical reasons.

Article 14 — *Limitations on requisition of civilian medical units*

1. The Occupying Power has the duty to ensure that the medical needs of the civilian population in occupied territory continue to be satisfied.

2. The Occupying Power shall not, therefore, requisition civilian

medical units, their equipment, their *matériel* or the services of their personnel, so long as these resources are necessary for the provision of adequate medical services for the civilian population and for the continuing medical care of any wounded and sick already under treatment.

3. Provided that the general rule in paragraph 2 continues to be observed, the Occupying Power may requisition the said resources, subject to the following particular conditions:

    (*a*) that the resources are necessary for the adequate and immediate medical treatment of the wounded and sick members of the armed forces of the Occupying Power or of prisoners of war;

    (*b*) that the requisition continues only while such necessity exists; and

    (*c*) that immediate arrangements are made to ensure that the medical needs of the civilian population, as well as those of any wounded and sick under treatment who are affected by the requisition, continue to be satisfied.

Article 15 — *Protection of civilian medical and religious personnel*

1. Civilian medical personnel shall be respected and protected.

2. If needed, all available help shall be afforded to civilian medical personnel in an area where civilian medical services are disrupted by reason of combat activity.

3. The Occupying Power shall afford civilian medical personnel in occupied territories every assistance to enable them to perform, to the best of their ability, their humanitarian functions. The Occupying Power may not require that, in the performance of those functions, such personnel shall give priority to the treatment of any person except on medical grounds. They shall not be compelled to carry out tasks which are not compatible with their humanitarian mission.

4. Civilian medical personnel shall have access to any place where their services are essential, subject to such supervisory and safety measures as the relevant Party to the conflict may deem necessary.

5. Civilian religious personnel shall be respected and protected. The provisions of the Conventions and of this Protocol concerning the protection and identification of medical personnel shall apply equally to such persons.

Article 16 — *General protection of medical duties*

1. Under no circumstances shall any person be punished for carrying out medical activities compatible with medical ethics, regardless of the person benefiting therefrom.

2. Persons engaged in medical activities shall not be compelled

to perform acts or to carry out work contrary to the rules of medical ethics or to other medical rules designed for the benefit of the wounded and sick or to the provisions of the Conventions or of this Protocol, or to refrain from performing acts or from carrying out work required by those rules and provisions.

3. No person engaged in medical activities shall be compelled to give to anyone belonging either to an adverse Party, or to his own Party except as required by the law of the latter Party, any information concerning the wounded and sick who are, or who have been, under his care, if such information would, in his opinion, prove harmful to the patients concerned or to their families. Regulations for the compulsory notification of communicable diseases shall, however, be respected.

Article 17 — *Role of the civilian population and of aid societies*

1. The civilian population shall respect the wounded, sick and shipwrecked, even if they belong to the adverse Party, and shall commit no act of violence against them. The civilian population and aid societies, such as national Red Cross (Red Crescent, Red Lion and Sun) Societies, shall be permitted, even on their own initiative, to collect and care for the wounded, sick and shipwrecked, even in invaded or occupied areas. No one shall be harmed, prosecuted, convicted or punished for such humanitarian acts.

2. The Parties to the conflict may appeal to the civilian population and the aid societies referred to in paragraph 1 to collect and care for the wounded, sick and shipwrecked, and to search for the dead and report their location; they shall grant both protection and the necessary facilities to those who respond to this appeal. If the adverse Party gains or regains control of the area, that Party also shall afford the same protection and facilities for so long as they are needed.

Article 18 — *Identification*

1. Each Party to the conflict shall endeavour to ensure that medical and religious personnel and medical units and transports are identifiable.

2. Each Party to the conflict shall also endeavour to adopt and to implement methods and procedures which will make it possible to recognize medical units and transports which use the distinctive emblem and distinctive signals.

3. In occupied territory and in areas where fighting is taking place or is likely to take place, civilian medical personnel and civilian religious personnel should be recognizable by the distinctive emblem and an identity card certifying their status.

4. With the consent of the competent authority, medical units and transports shall be marked by the distinctive emblem. The ships and craft referred to in Article 22 of this Protocol shall be marked in accordance with the provisions of the Second Convention.

5. In addition to the distinctive emblem, a Party to the conflict may, as provided in Chapter III of Annex I to this Protocol, authorize the use of distinctive signals to identify medical units and transports. Exceptionally, in the special cases covered in that Chapter, medical transports may use distinctive signals without displaying the distinctive emblem.

6. The application of the provisions of paragraphs 1 to 5 of this Article is governed by Chapters I to III of Annex I to this Protocol. Signals designated in Chapter III of the Annex for the exclusive use of medical units and transports shall not, except as provided therein, be used for any purpose other than to identify the medical units and transports specified in that Chapter.

7. This Article does not authorize any wider use of the distinctive emblem in peacetime than is prescribed in Article 44 of the First Convention.

8. The provisions of the Conventions and of this Protocol relating to supervision of the use of the distinctive emblem and to the prevention and repression of any misuse thereof shall be applicable to distinctive signals.

Article 19 — *Neutral and other States not Parties to the conflict*

Neutral and other States not Parties to the conflict shall apply the relevant provisions of this Protocol to persons protected by this Part who may be received or interned within their territory, and to any dead of the Parties to that conflict whom they may find.

Article 20 — *Prohibition of reprisals*

Reprisals against the persons and objects protected by this Part are prohibited.

Section II — Medical Transportation

Article 21 — *Medical vehicles*

Medical vehicles shall be respected and protected in the same way as mobile medical units under the Conventions and this Protocol.

Article 22 — *Hospitals ships and coastal rescue craft*

1. The provisions of the Conventions relating to:
    (*a*) vessels described in Articles 22, 24, 25 and 27 of the Second Convention,
    (*b*) their lifeboats and small craft,

(*c*) their personnel and crews, and

(*d*) the wounded, sick and shipwrecked on board,

shall also apply where these vessels carry civilian wounded, sick and shipwrecked who do not belong to any of the categories mentioned in Article 13 of the Second Convention. Such civilians shall not, however, be subject to surrender to any Party which is not their own, or to capture at sea. If they find themselves in the power of a Party to the conflict other than their own they shall be covered by the Fourth Convention and by this Protocol.

2. The protection provided by the Conventions to vessels described in Article 25 of the Second Convention shall extend to hospital ships made available for humanitarian purposes to a Party to the conflict:

(*a*) by a neutral or other State which is not a Party to that conflict; or

(*b*) by an impartial international humanitarian organization,

provided that, in either case, the requirements set out in that Article are complied with.

3. Small craft described in Article 27 of the Second Convention shall be protected even if the notification envisaged by that Article has not been made. The Parties to the conflict are, nevertheless, invited to inform each other of any details of such craft which will facilitate their identification and recognition.

Article 23 — Other medical ships and craft

1. Medical ships and craft other than those referred to in Article 22 of this Protocol and Article 38 of the Second Convention shall, whether at sea or in other waters, be respected and protected in the same way as mobile medical units under the Conventions and this Protocol. Since this protection can only be effective if they can be identified and recognized as medical ships or craft, such vessels should be marked with the distinctive emblem and as far as possible comply with the second paragraph of Article 43 of the Second Convention.

2. The ships and craft referred to in paragraph 1 shall remain subject to the laws of war. Any warship on the surface able immediately to enforce its command may order them to stop, order them off, or make them take a certain course, and they shall obey every such command. Such ships and craft may not in any other way be diverted from their medical mission so long as they are needed for the wounded, sick and shipwrecked on board.

3. The protection provided in paragraph 1 shall cease only under the conditions set out in Articles 34 and 35 of the Second

Convention. A clear refusal to obey a command given in accordance with paragraph 2 shall be an act harmful to the enemy under Article 34 of the Second Convention.

4. A Party to the conflict may notify any adverse Party as far in advance of sailing as possible of the name, description, expected time of sailing, course and estimated speed of the medical ship or craft, particularly in the case of ships of over 2,000 gross tons, and may provide any other information which would facilitate identification and recognition. The adverse Party shall acknowledge receipt of such information.

5. The provisions of Article 37 of the Second Convention shall apply to medical and religious personnel in such ships and craft.

6. The provisions of the Second Convention shall apply to the wounded, sick and shipwrecked belonging to the categories referred to in Article 13 of the Second Convention and in Article 44 of this Protocol who may be on board such medical ships and craft. Wounded, sick and shipwrecked civilians who do not belong to any of the categories mentioned in Article 13 of the Second Convention shall not be subject, at sea, either to surrender to any Party which is not their own, or to removal from such ships or craft; if they find themselves in the power of a Party to the conflict other than their own, they shall be covered by the Fourth Convention and by this Protocol.

Article 24 — Protection of medical aircraft
Medical aircraft shall be respected and protected, subject to the provisions of this Part.

Article 25 — Medical aircraft in areas not controlled by an
    adverse Party
In and over land areas physically controlled by friendly forces, or in and over sea areas not physically controlled by an adverse Party, the respect and protection of medical aircraft of a Party to the conflict is not dependent on any agreement with an adverse Party. For greater safety, however, a Party to the conflict operating its medical aircraft in these areas may notify the adverse Party, as provided in Article 29, in particular when such aircraft are making flights bringing them within range of surface-to-air weapons systems of the adverse Party.

Article 26 — Medical aircraft in contact or similar zones
1. In and over those parts of the contact zone which are physically controlled by friendly forces and in and over those areas the physical control of which is not clearly established, protection for medical aircraft can be fully effective only by prior agreement

between the competent military authorities of the Parties to the conflict, as provided for in Article 29. Although, in the absence of such an agreement, medical aircraft operate at their own risk, they shall nevertheless be respected after they have been recognized as such.

2. 'Contact zone' means any area on land where the forward elements of opposing forces are in contact with each other, especially where they are exposed to direct fire from the ground.

Article 27 — Medical aircraft in areas controlled by an adverse Party

1. The medical aircraft of a Party to the conflict shall continue to be protected while flying over land or sea areas physically controlled by an adverse Party, provided that prior agreement to such flights has been obtained from the competent authority of that adverse Party.

2. A medical aircraft which flies over an area physically controlled by an adverse Party without, or in deviation from the terms of, an agreement provided for in paragraph 1, either through navigational error or because of an emergency affecting the safety of the flight, shall make every effort to identify itself and to inform the adverse Party of the circumstances. As soon as such medical aircraft has been recognized by the adverse Party, that Party shall make all reasonable efforts to give the order to land or to alight on water, referred to in Article 30, paragraph 1, or to take other measures to safeguard its own interests, and, in either case, to allow the aircraft time for compliance, before resorting to an attack against the aircraft.

Article 28 — Restrictions on operations of medical aircraft

1. The Parties to the conflict are prohibited from using their medical aircraft to attempt to acquire any military advantage over an adverse Party. The presence of medical aircraft shall not be used in an attempt to render military objectives immune from attack.

2. Medical aircraft shall not be used to collect or transmit intelligence data and shall not carry any equipment intended for such purposes. They are prohibited from carrying any persons or cargo not included within the definition in Article 8, sub-paragraph (f). The carrying on board of the personal effects of the occupants or of equipment intended solely to facilitate navigation, communication or identification shall not be considered as prohibited.

3. Medical aircraft shall not carry any armament except small arms and ammunition taken from the wounded, sick and shipwrecked

on board and not yet handed to the proper service, and such light individual weapons as may be necessary to enable the medical personnel on board to defend themselves and the wounded, sick and shipwrecked in their charge.

4.   While carrying out the flights referred to in Articles 26 and 27, medical aircraft shall not, except by prior agreement with the adverse Party, be used to search for the wounded, sick and shipwrecked.

Article 29 — *Notifications and agreements concerning medical aircraft*

1.   Notifications under Article 25, or requests for prior agreement under Articles 26, 27, 28 (paragraph 4), or 31 shall state the proposed number of medical aircraft, their flight plans and means of identification, and shall be understood to mean that every flight will be carried out in compliance with Article 28.

2.   A Party which receives a notification given under Article 25 shall at once acknowledge receipt of such notification.

3.   A Party which receives a request for prior agreement under Articles 26, 27, 28 (paragraph 4), or 31 shall, as rapidly as possible, notify the requesting Party:

(*a*)   that the request is agreed to;

(*b*)   that the request is denied; or

(*c*)   of reasonable alternative proposals to the request. It may also propose a prohibition or restriction of other flights in the area during the time involved. If the Party which submitted the request accepts the alternative proposals, it shall notify the other Party of such acceptance.

4.   The Parties shall take the necessary measures to ensure that notifications and agreements can be made rapidly.

5.   The Parties shall also take the necessary measures to disseminate rapidly the substance of any such notifications and agreements to the military units concerned and shall instruct those units regarding the means of identification that will be used by the medical aircraft in question.

Article 30 — *Landing and inspection of medical aircraft*

1.   Medical aircraft flying over areas which are physically controlled by an adverse Party, or over areas the physical control of which is not clearly established, may be ordered to land or to alight on water, as appropriate, to permit inspection in accordance with the following paragraphs. Medical aircraft shall obey any such order.

2.   If such an aircraft lands or alights on water, whether ordered to do so or for other reasons, it may be subjected to inspection

solely to determine the matters referred to in paragraphs 3 and 4. Any such inspection shall be commenced without delay and shall be conducted expeditiously. The inspecting Party shall not require the wounded and sick to be removed from the aircraft unless their removal is essential for the inspection. That Party shall in any event ensure that the condition of the wounded and sick is not adversely affected by the inspection or by the removal.

    3. If the inspection discloses that the aircraft:

        (*a*) is a medical aircraft within the meaning of Article 8, sub-paragraph (*j*),

        (*b*) is not in violation of the conditions prescribed in Article 28, and

        (*c*) has not flown without or in breach of a prior agreement where such agreement is required,

the aircraft and those of its occupants who belong to the adverse Party or to a neutral or other State not a Party to the conflict shall be authorized to continue the flight without delay.

    4. If the inspection discloses that the aircraft:

        (*a*) is not a medical aircraft within the meaning of Article 8, sub-paragraph (*j*),

        (*b*) is in violation of the conditions prescribed in Article 28, or

        (*c*) has flown without or in breach of a prior agreement where such agreement is required,

the aircraft may be seized. Its occupants shall be treated in conformity with the relevant provisions of the Conventions and of this Protocol. Any aircraft seized which had been assigned as a permanent medical aircraft may be used thereafter only as a medical aircraft.

Article 31 — *Neutral or other States not Parties to the conflict*

    1. Except by prior agreement, medical aircraft shall not fly over or land in the territory of a neutral or other State not a Party to the conflict. However, with such an agreement, they shall be respected throughout their flight and also for the duration of any calls in the territory. Nevertheless they shall obey any summons to land or to alight on water, as appropriate.

    2. Should a medical aircraft, in the absence of an agreement or in deviation from the terms of an agreement, fly over the territory of a neutral or other State not a Party to the conflict, either through navigational error or because of an emergency affecting the safety of the flight, it shall make every effort to give notice of the flight and to identify itself. As soon as such medical aircraft is recognized,

that State shall make all reasonable efforts to give the order to land or to alight on water referred to in Article 30, paragraph 1, or to take other measures to safeguard its own interests, and, in either case, to allow the aircraft time for compliance, before resorting to an attack against the aircraft.

3. If a medical aircraft, either by agreement or in the circumstances mentioned in paragraph 2, lands or alights on water in the territory of a neutral or other State not Party to the conflict, whether ordered to do so or for other reasons, the aircraft shall be subject to inspection for the purposes of determining whether it is in fact a medical aircraft. The inspection shall be commenced without delay and shall be conducted expeditiously. The inspecting Party shall not require the wounded and sick of the Party operating the aircraft to be removed from it unless their removal is essential for the inspection. The inspecting Party shall in any event ensure that the condition of the wounded and sick is not adversely affected by the inspection or the removal. If the inspection discloses that the aircraft is in fact a medical aircraft, the aircraft with its occupants, other than those who must be detained in accordance with the rules of international law applicable in armed conflict, shall be allowed to resume its flight, and reasonable facilities shall be given for the continuation of the flight. If the inspection discloses that the aircraft is not a medical aircraft, it shall be seized and the occupants treated in accordance with paragraph 4.

4. The wounded, sick and shipwrecked disembarked, otherwise than temporarily, from a medical aircraft with the consent of the local authorities in the territory of a neutral or other State not a Party to the conflict shall, unless agreed otherwise between that State and the Parties to the conflict, be detained by that State where so required by the rules of international law applicable in armed conflict, in such a manner that they cannot again take part in the hostilities. The cost of hospital treatment and internment shall be borne by the State to which those persons belong.

5. Neutral or other States not Parties to the conflict shall apply any conditions and restrictions on the passage of medical aircraft over, or on the landing of medical aircraft in, their territory equally to all Parties to the conflict.

SECTION III — MISSING AND DEAD PERSONS

Article 32 — General principle

In the implementation of this Section, the activities of the High Contracting Parties, of the Parties to the conflict and of the international humanitarian organizations mentioned in the Conventions and in this Protocol shall be prompted mainly by the right of families to know the fate of their relatives.

Article 33 — Missing persons

1. As soon as circumstances permit, and at the latest from the end of active hostilities, each Party to the conflict shall search for the persons who have been reported missing by an adverse Party. Such adverse Party shall transmit all relevant information concerning such persons in order to facilitate such searches.

2. In order to facilitate the gathering of information pursuant to the preceding paragraph, each Party to the conflict shall, with respect to persons who would not receive more favourable consideration under the Conventions and this Protocol:

(*a*) record the information specified in Article 138 of the Fourth Convention in respect of such persons who have been detained, imprisoned or otherwise held in captivity for more than two weeks as a result of hostilities or occupation, or who have died during any period of detention;

(*b*) to the fullest extent possible, facilitate and, if need be, carry out the search for and the recording of information concerning such persons if they have died in other circumstances as a result of hostilities or occupation.

3. Information concerning persons reported missing pursuant to paragraph 1 and requests for such information shall be transmitted either directly or through the Protecting Power or the Central Tracing Agency of the International Committee of the Red Cross or national Red Cross (Red Crescent, Red Lion and Sun) Societies. Where the information is not transmitted through the International Committee of the Red Cross and its Central Tracing Agency, each Party to the conflict shall ensure that such information is also supplied to the Central Tracing Agency.

4. The Parties to the conflict shall endeavour to agree on arrangements for teams to search for, identify and recover the dead from battlefied areas, including arrangements, if appropriate, for such teams to be accompanied by personnel of the adverse Party while carrying out these missions in areas controlled by the adverse Party. Personnel of such teams shall be respected and protected while exclusively carrying out these duties.

Article 34 — Remains of deceased

1. The remains of persons who have died for reasons related to occupation or in detention resulting from occupation or hostilities

and those of persons not nationals of the country in which they have died as a result of hostilities shall be respected, and the gravesites of all such persons shall be respected, maintained and marked as provided for in Article 130 of the Fourth Convention, where their remains or gravesites would not receive more favourable consideration under the Conventions and this Protocol.

2. As soon as circumstances and the relations between the adverse Parties permit, the High Contracting Parties in whose territories graves and, as the case may be, other locations of the remains of persons who have died as a result of hostilities or during occupation or in detention are situated, shall conclude agreements in order:

  (*a*) to facilitate access to the gravesites by relatives of the deceased and by representatives of official graves registration services and to regulate the practical arrangements for such access;

  (*b*) to protect and maintain such gravesites permanently;

  (*c*) to facilitate the return of the remains of the deceased and of personal effects to the home country upon its request or, unless that country objects, upon the request of the next of kin.

3. In the absence of the agreements provided for in paragraph 2 (*b*) or (*c*) and if the home country of such deceased is not willing to arrange at its expense for the maintenance of such gravesites, the High Contracting Party in whose territory the gravesites are situated may offer to facilitate the return of the remains of the deceased to the home country. Where such an offer has not been accepted the High Contracting Party may, after the expiry of five years from the date of the offer and upon due notice to the home country, adopt the arrangements laid down in its own laws relating to cemeteries and graves.

4. A High Contracting Party in whose territory the gravesites referred to in this Article are situated shall be permitted to exhume the remains only:

  (*a*) in accordance with paragraphs 2 (*c*) and 3, or

  (*b*) where exhumation is a matter of overriding public necessity, including cases of medical and investigative necessity, in which case the High Contracting Party shall at all times respect the remains, and shall give notice to the home country of its intention to exhume the remains together with details of the intended place of reinterment.

PART III — METHODS AND MEANS OF WARFARE, COMBATANT AND PRISONER-OF-WAR STATUS

Section I — Methods and Means of Warfare

Article 35 — Basic rules

1. In any armed conflict, the right of the Parties to the conflict to choose methods or means of warfare is not unlimited.

2. It is prohibited to employ weapons, projectiles and material and methods of warfare of a nature to cause superfluous injury or unnecessary suffering.

3. It is prohibited to employ methods or means of warfare which are intended, or may be expected, to cause widespread, long-term and severe damage to the natural environment.

Article 36 — New weapons

In the study, development, acquisition or adoption of a new weapon, means or method of warfare, a High Contracting Party is under an obligation to determine whether its employment would, in some or all circumstances, be prohibited by this Protocol or by any other rule of international law applicable to the High Contracting Party.

Article 37 — Prohibition of perfidy

1. It is prohibited to kill, injure or capture an adversary by resort to perfidy. Acts inviting the confidence of an adversary to lead him to believe that he is entitled to, or is obliged to accord, protection under the rules of international law applicable in armed conflict, with intent to betray that confidence, shall constitute perfidy. The following acts are examples of perfidy:

    (*a*) the feigning of an intent to negotiate under a flag of truce or of a surrender;

    (*b*) the feigning of an incapacitation by wounds or sickness;

    (*c*) the feigning of civilian, non-combatant status; and

    (*d*) the feigning of protected status by the use of signs, emblems or uniforms of the United Nations or of neutral or other States not Parties to the conflict.

2. Ruses of war are not prohibited. Such ruses are acts which are intended to mislead an adversary or to induce him to act recklessly but which infringe no rule of international law applicable in armed conflict and which are not perfidious because they do not invite the confidence of an adversary with respect to protection under the law. The following are examples of such ruses: the use of camouflage, decoys, mock operations and misinformation.

Article 38 — *Recognized emblems*

1. It is prohibited to make improper use of the distinctive emblem of the red cross, red crescent or red lion and sun or of other emblems, signs or signals provided for by the Conventions or by this Protocol. It is also prohibited to misuse deliberately in an armed conflict other internationally recognized protective emblems, signs or signals, including the flag of truce, and the protective emblem of cultural property.

2. It is prohibited to make use of the distinctive emblem of the United Nations, except as authorized by that Organization.

Article 39 — *Emblems of nationality*

1. It is prohibited to make use in an armed conflict of the flags or military emblems, insignia or uniforms of neutral or other States not Parties to the conflict.

2. It is prohibited to make use of the flags or military emblems, insignia or uniforms of adverse Parties while engaging in attacks or in order to shield, favour, protect or impede military operations.

3. Nothing in this Article or in Article 37, paragraph 1 (*d*), shall affect the existing generally recognized rules of international law applicable to espionage or to the use of flags in the conduct of armed conflict at sea.

Article 40 — *Quarter*

It is prohibited to order that there shall be no survivors, to threaten an adversary therewith or to conduct hostilities on this basis.

Article 41 — *Safeguard of an enemy hors de combat*

1. A person who is recognized or who, in the circumstances, should be recognized to be *hors de combat* shall not be made the object of attack.

2. A person is *hors de combat* if:
   (*a*) he is in the power of an adverse Party;
   (*b*) he clearly expresses an intention to surrender; or
   (*c*) he has been rendered unconscious or is otherwise incapacitated by wounds or sickness, and therefore is incapable of defending himself;

provided that in any of these cases he abstains from any hostile act and does not attempt to escape.

3. When persons entitled to protection as prisoners of war have fallen into the power of an adverse Party under unusual conditions of combat which prevent their evacuation as provided for in Part III, Section I, of the Third Convention, they shall be released and all feasible precautions shall be taken to ensure their safety.

Article 42 — Occupants of aircraft

1. No person parachuting from an aircraft in distress shall be made the object of attack during his descent.

2. Upon reaching the ground in territory controlled by an adverse Party, a person who has parachuted from an aircraft in distress shall be given an opportunity to surrender before being made the object of attack, unless it is apparent that he is engaging in a hostile act.

3. Airborne troops are not protected by this Article.

SECTION II — COMBATANT AND PRISONER-OF-WAR STATUS

Article 43 — Armed forces

1. The armed forces of a Party to a conflict consist of all organized armed forces, groups and units which are under a command responsible to that Party for the conduct of its subordinates, even if that Party is represented by a government or an authority not recognized by an adverse Party. Such armed forces shall be subject to an internal disciplinary system which, *inter alia*, shall enforce compliance with the rules of international law applicable in armed conflict.

2. Members of the armed forces of a Party to a conflict (other than medical personnel and chaplains covered by Article 33 of the Third Convention) are combatants, that is to say, they have the right to participate directly in hostilities.

3. Whenever a Party to a conflict incorporates a paramilitary or armed law enforcement agency into its armed forces it shall so notify the other Parties to the conflict.

Article 44 — Combatants and prisoners of war

1. Any combatant, as defined in Article 43, who falls into the power of an adverse Party shall be a prisoner of war.

2. While all combatants are obliged to comply with the rules of international law applicable in armed conflict, violations of these rules shall not deprive a combatant of his right to be a combatant or, if he falls into the power of an adverse Party, of his right to be a prisoner of war, except as provided in paragraphs 3 and 4.

3. In order to promote the protection of the civilian population from the effects of hostilities, combatants are obliged to distinguish themselves from the civilian population while they are engaged in an attack or in a military operation preparatory to an attack. Recognizing, however, that there are situations in armed conflicts where, owing to the nature of the hostilities an armed combatant cannot so distinguish himself, he shall retain his status as a combatant,

provided that, in such situations, he carries his arms openly:

(*a*) during each military engagement, and

(*b*) during such time as he is visible to the adversary while he is engaged in a military deployment preceding the launching of an attack in which he is to participate.

Acts which comply with the requirements of this paragraph shall not be considered as perfidious within the meaning of Article 37, paragraph 1 (*c*).

4. A combatant who falls into the power of an adverse Party while failing to meet the requirements set forth in the second sentence of paragraph 3 shall forfeit his right to be a prisoner of war, but he shall, nevertheless, be given protections equivalent in all respects to those accorded to prisoners of war by the Third Convention and by this Protocol. This protection includes protections equivalent to those accorded to prisoners of war by the Third Convention in the case where such a person is tried and punished for any offences he has committed.

5. Any combatant who falls into the power of an adverse Party while not engaged in an attack or in a military operation preparatory to an attack shall not forfeit his rights to be a combatant and a prisoner of war by virtue of his prior activities.

6. This Article is without prejudice to the right of any person to be a prisoner of war pursuant to Article 4 of the Third Convention.

7. This Article is not intended to change the generally accepted practice of States with respect to the wearing of the uniform by combatants assigned to the regular, uniformed armed units of a Party to the conflict.

8. In addition to the categories of persons mentioned in Article 13 of the First and Second Conventions, all members of the armed forces of a Party to the conflict, as defined in Article 43 of this Protocol, shall be entitled to protection under those Conventions if they are wounded or sick or, in the case of the Second Convention, shipwrecked at sea or in other waters.

Article 45 — *Protection of persons who have taken part in hostilities*

1. A person who takes part in hostilities and falls into the power of an adverse Party shall be presumed to be a prisoner of war, and therefore shall be protected by the Third Convention, if he claims the status of prisoner of war, or if he appears to be entitled to such status, or if the Party on which he depends claims such status on his behalf by notification to the detaining Power or to the Protecting

Power. Should any doubt arise as to whether any such person is entitled to the status of prisoner of war, he shall continue to have such status and, therefore, to be protected by the Third Convention and this Protocol until such time as his status has been determined by a competent tribunal.

2. If a person who has fallen into the power of an adverse Party is not held as a prisoner of war and is to be tried by that Party for an offence arising out of the hostilities, he shall have the right to assert his entitlement to prisoner-of-war status before a judicial tribunal and to have that question adjudicated. Whenever possible under the applicable procedure, this adjudication shall occur before the trial for the offence. The representatives of the Protecting Power shall be entitled to attend the proceedings in which that question is adjudicated, unless, exceptionally, the proceedings are held *in camera* in the interest of State security. In such a case the detaining Power shall advise the Protecting Power accordingly.

3. Any person who has taken part in hostilities, who is not entitled to prisoner-of-war status and who does not benefit from more favourable treatment in accordance with the Fourth Convention shall have the right at all times to the protection of Article 75 of this Protocol. In occupied territory, any such person, unless he is held as a spy, shall also be entitled, notwithstanding Article 5 of the Fourth Convention, to his rights of communication under that Convention.

Article 46 — Spies

1. Notwithstanding any other provision of the Conventions or of this Protocol, any member of the armed forces of a Party to the conflict who falls into the power of an adverse Party while engaging in espionage shall not have the right to the status of prisoner of war and may be treated as a spy.

2. A member of the armed forces of a Party to the conflict who, on behalf of that Party and in territory controlled by an adverse Party, gathers or attempts to gather information shall not be considered as engaging in espionage if, while so acting, he is in the uniform of his armed forces.

3. A member of the armed forces of a Party to the conflict who is a resident of territory occupied by an adverse Party and who, on behalf of the Party on which he depends, gathers or attempts to gather information of military value within that territory shall not be considered as engaging in espionage unless he does so through an act of false pretences or deliberately in a clandestine manner. Moreover, such a resident shall not lose his right to the status of prisoner of war and may not be treated as a spy unless he is captured while engaging in espionage.

4. A member of the armed forces of a Party to the conflict who is not a resident of territory occupied by an adverse Party and who has engaged in espionage in that territory shall not lose his right to the status of prisoner of war and may not be treated as a spy unless he is captured before he has rejoined the armed forces to which he belongs.

Article 47 — Mercenaries

1. A mercenary shall not have the right to be a combatant or a prisoner of war.

2. A mercenary is any person who:

(*a*) is specially recruited locally or abroad in order to fight in an armed conflict;

(*b*) does, in fact, take a direct part in the hostilities;

(*c*) is motivated to take part in the hostilities essentially by the desire for private gain and, in fact, is promised, by or on behalf of a Party to the conflict, material compensation substantially in excess of that promised or paid to combatants of similar ranks and functions in the armed forces of that Party;

(*d*) is neither a national of a Party to the conflict nor a resident of territory controlled by a Party to the conflict;

(*e*) is not a member of the armed forces of a Party to the conflict; and

(*f*) has not been sent by a State which is not a Party to the conflict on official duty as a member of its armed forces.

PART IV — CIVILIAN POPULATION

SECTION I — GENERAL PROTECTION AGAINST EFFECTS OF HOSTILITIES

CHAPTER I — *Basic Rule and Field of Application*

Article 48 — Basic Rule

In order to ensure respect for and protection of the civilian population and civilian objects, the Parties to the conflict shall at all times distinguish between the civilian population and combatants and between civilian objects and military objectives and accordingly shall direct their operations only against military objectives.

Article 49 — Definition of attacks and scope of application

1. 'Attacks' means acts of violence against the adversary, whether in offence or in defence.

2. The provisions of this Protocol with respect to attacks apply

to all attacks in whatever territory conducted, including the national territory belonging to a Party to the conflict but under the control of an adverse Party.

3. The provisions of this Section apply to any land, air or sea warfare which may affect the civilian population, individual civilians or civilian objects on land. They further apply to all attacks from the sea or from the air against objectives on land but do not otherwise affect the rules of international law applicable in armed conflict at sea or in the air.

4. The provisions of this Section are additional to the rules concerning humanitarian protection contained in the Fourth Convention, particularly in Part II thereof, and in other international agreements binding upon the High Contracting Parties, as well as to other rules of international law relating to the protection of civilians and civilian objects on land, at sea or in the air against the effects of hostilities.

CHAPTER II — *Civilians and Civilian Population*

Article 50 — Definition of civilians and civilian population

1. A civilian is any person who does not belong to one of the categories of persons referred to in Article 4 A (1), (2), (3) and (6) of the Third Convention and in Article 43 of this Protocol. In case of doubt whether a person is a civilian, that person shall be considered to be a civilian.

2. The civilian population comprises all persons who are civilians.

3. The presence within the civilian population of individuals who do not come within the definition of civilians does not deprive the population of its civilian character.

Article 51 — Protection of the civilian population

1. The civilian population and individual civilians shall enjoy general protection against dangers arising from military operations. To give effect to this protection, the following rules, which are additional to other applicable rules of international law, shall be observed in all circumstances.

2. The civilian population as such, as well as individual civilians, shall not be the object of attack. Acts or threats of violence the primary purpose of which is to spread terror among the civilian population are prohibited.

3. Civilians shall enjoy the protection afforded by this Section, unless and for such time as they take a direct part in hostilities.

4. Indiscriminate attacks are prohibited. Indiscriminate attacks are:

(*a*) those which are not directed at a specific military objective;

(*b*) those which employ a method or means of combat which cannot be directed at a specific military objective; or

(*c*) those which employ a method or means of combat the effects of which cannot be limited as required by this Protocol;

and consequently, in each such case, are of a nature to strike military objectives and civilians or civilian objects without distinction.

5. Among others, the following types of attacks are to be considered as indiscriminate:

(*a*) an attack by bombardment by any methods or means which treats as a single military objective a number of clearly separated and distinct military objectives located in a city, town, village or other area containing a similar concentration of civilians or civilian objects; and

(*b*) an attack which may be expected to cause incidental loss of civilian life, injury to civilians, damage to civilian objects, or a combination thereof, which would be excessive in relation to the concrete and direct military advantage anticipated.

6. Attacks against the civilian population or civilians by way of reprisals are prohibited.

7. The presence or movements of the civilian population or individual civilians shall not be used to render certain points or areas immune from military operations, in particular in attempts to shield military objectives from attacks or to shield, favour or impede military operations. The Parties to the conflict shall not direct the movement of the civilian population or individual civilians in order to attempt to shield military objectives from attacks or to shield military operations.

8. Any violation of these prohibitions shall not release the Parties to the conflict from their legal obligations with respect to the civilian population and civilians, including the obligation to take the precautionary measures provided for in Article 57.

CHAPTER III — *Civilian Objects*

Article 52 — General protection of civilian objects

1. Civilian objects shall not be the object of attack or of reprisals. Civilian objects are all objects which are not military objectives as defined in paragraph 2.

2. Attacks shall be limited strictly to military objectives. In so far as objects are concerned, military objectives are limited to those objects which by their nature, location, purpose or use make an effective contribution to military action and whose total or partial destruction, capture or neutralization, in the circumstances ruling at the time, offers a definite military advantage.

3. In case of doubt whether an object which is normally dedicated to civilian purposes, such as a place of worship, a house or other dwelling or a school, is being used to make an effective contribution to military action, it shall be presumed not to be so used.

Article 53 — Protection of cultural objects and of places of worship
Without prejudice to the provisions of the Hague Convention for the Protection of Cultural Property in the Event of Armed Conflict of 14 May 1954, and of other relevant international instruments, it is prohibited:
  (*a*) to commit any acts of hostility directed against the historic monuments, works of art or places of worship which constitute the cultural or spiritual heritage of peoples;
  (*b*) to use such objects in support of the military effort;
  (*c*) to make such objects the object of reprisals.

Article 54 — Protection of objects indispensable to the survival of the civilian population
1. Starvation of civilians as a method of warfare is prohibited.

2. It is prohibited to attack, destroy, remove or render useless objects indispensable to the survival of the civilian population, such as foodstuffs, agricultural areas for the production of foodstuffs, crops, livestock, drinking water installations and supplies and irrigation works, for the specific purpose of denying them for their sustenance value to the civilian population or to the adverse Party, whatever the motive, whether in order to starve out civilians, to cause them to move away, or for any other motive.

3. The prohibitions in paragraph 2 shall not apply to such of the objects covered by it as are used by an adverse Party:
  (*a*) as sustenance solely for the members of its armed forces; or
  (*b*) if not as sustenance, then in direct support of military action, provided, however, that in no event shall actions against these objects be taken which may be expected to leave the civilian population with such inadequate food or water as to cause its starvation or force its movement.

4. These objects shall not be made the object of reprisals.

5. In recognition of the vital requirements of any Party to the conflict in the defence of its national territory against invasion,

derogation from the prohibitions contained in paragraph 2 may be made by a Party to the conflict within such territory under its own control where required by imperative military necessity.

Article 55 — Protection of the natural environment

1. Care shall be taken in warfare to protect the natural environment against widespread, long-term and severe damage. This protection includes a prohibition of the use of methods or means of warfare which are intended or may be expected to cause such damage to the natural environment and thereby to prejudice the health or survival of the population.

2. Attacks against the natural environment by way of reprisals are prohibited.

Article 56 — Protection of works and installations containing dangerous forces

1. Works or installations containing dangerous forces, namely dams, dykes and nuclear electrical generating stations, shall not be made the object of attack, even where these objects are military objectives, if such attack may cause the release of dangerous forces and consequent severe losses among the civilian population. Other military objectives located at or in the vicinity of these works or installations shall not be made the object of attack if such attack may cause the release of dangerous forces from the works or installations and consequent severe losses among the civilian population.

2. The special protection against attack provided by paragraph 1 shall cease:

   (*a*) for a dam or a dyke only if it is used for other than its normal function and in regular, significant and direct support of military operations and if such attack is the only feasible way to terminate such support;

   (*b*) for a nuclear electrical generating station only if it provides electric power in regular, significant and direct support of military operations and if such attack is the only feasible way to terminate such support;

   (*c*) for other military objectives located at or in the vicinity of these works or installations only if they are used in regular, significant and direct support of military operations and if such attack is the only feasible way to terminate such support.

3. In all cases, the civilian population and individual civilians shall remain entitled to all the protection accorded them by international law, including the protection of the precautionary measures provided

for in Article 57. If the protection ceases and any of the works, installations or military objectives mentioned in paragraph 1 is attacked, all practical precautions shall be taken to avoid the release of the dangerous forces.

4. It is prohibited to make any of the works, installations or military objectives mentioned in paragraph 1 the object of reprisals.

5. The Parties to the conflict shall endeavour to avoid locating any military objectives in the vicinity of the works or installations mentioned in paragraph 1. Nevertheless, installations erected for the sole purpose of defending the protected works or installations from attack are permissible and shall not themselves be made the object of attack, provided that they are not used in hostilities except for defensive actions necessary to respond to attacks against the protected works or installations and that their armament is limited to weapons capable only of repelling hostile action against the protected works or installations.

6. The High Contracting Parties and the Parties to the conflict are urged to conclude further agreements among themselves to provide additional protection for objects containing dangerous forces.

7. In order to facilitate the identification of the objects protected by this article, the Parties to the conflict may mark them with a special sign consisting of a group of three bright orange circles placed on the same axis, as specified in Article 16 of Annex I to this Protocol. The absence of such marking in no way relieves any Party to the conflict of its obligations under this Article.

CHAPTER IV — *Precautionary Measures*

Article 57 — *Precautions in attack*

1. In the conduct of military operations, constant care shall be taken to spare the civilian population, civilians and civilian objects.

2. With respect to attacks, the following precautions shall be taken:

    (*a*) those who plan or decide upon an attack shall:

        (i) do everything feasible to verify that the objectives to be attacked are neither civilians nor civilian objects and are not subject to special protection but are military objectives within the meaning of paragraph 2 of Article 52 and that it is not prohibited by the provisions of this Protocol to attack them;

       (ii) take all feasible precautions in the choice of means

and methods of attack with a view to avoiding, and in any event to minimizing, incidental loss of civilian life, injury to civilians and damage to civilian objects;

(iii) refrain from deciding to launch any attack which may be expected to cause incidental loss of civilian life, injury to civilians, damage to civilian objects, or a combination thereof, which would be excessive in relation to the concrete and direct military advantage anticipated;

(b) an attack shall be cancelled or suspended if it becomes apparent that the objective is not a military one or is subject to special protection or that the attack may be expected to cause incidental loss of civilian life, injury to civilians, damage to civilian objects, or a combination thereof, which would be excessive in relation to the concrete and direct military advantage anticipated;

(c) effective advance warning shall be given of attacks which may affect the civilian population, unless circumstances do not permit.

3.   When a choice is possible between several military objectives for obtaining a similar military advantage, the objective to be selected shall be that the attack on which may be expected to cause the least danger to civilian lives and to civilian objects.

4.   In the conduct of military operations at sea or in the air, each Party to the conflict shall, in conformity with its rights and duties under the rules of international law applicable in armed conflict, take all reasonable precautions to avoid losses of civilian lives and damage to civilian objects.

5.   No provision of this Article may be construed as authorizing any attacks against the civilian population, civilians or civilian objects.

Article 58 — Precautions against the effects of attacks

The Parties to the conflict shall, to the maximum extent feasible:

(a) without prejudice to Article 49 of the Fourth Convention, endeavour to remove the civilian population, individual civilians and civilian objects under their control from the vicinity of military objectives;

(b) avoid locating military objectives within or near densely populated areas;

(c) take the other necessary precautions to protect the civilian population, individual civilians and civilian objects under their control against the dangers resulting from military operations.

CHAPTER V — *Localities and Zones under Special Protection*

Article 59 — Non-defended localities

1. It is prohibited for the Parties to the conflict to attack, by any means whatsoever, non-defended localities.

2. The appropriate authorities of a Party to the conflict may declare as a non-defended locality any inhabited place near or in a zone where armed forces are in contact which is open for occupation by an adverse Party. Such a locality shall fulfil the following conditions:

   (*a*) all combatants, as well as mobile weapons and mobile military equipment must have been evacuated;

   (*b*) no hostile use shall be made of fixed military installations or establishments;

   (*c*) no acts of hostility shall be committed by the authorities or by the population; and

   (*d*) no activities in support of military operations shall be undertaken.

3. The presence, in this locality, of persons specially protected under the Conventions and this Protocol, and of police forces retained for the sole purpose of maintaining law and order, is not contrary to the conditions laid down in paragraph 2.

4. The declaration made under paragraph 2 shall be addressed to the adverse Party and shall define and describe, as precisely as possible, the limits of the non-defended locality. The Party to the conflict to which the declaration is addressed shall acknowledge its receipt and shall treat the locality as a non-defended locality unless the conditions laid down in paragraph 2 are not in fact fulfilled, in which event it shall immediately so inform the Party making the declaration. Even if the conditions laid down in paragraph 2 are not fulfilled, the locality shall continue to enjoy the protection provided by the other provisions of this Protocol and the other rules of international law applicable in armed conflict.

5. The Parties to the conflict may agree on the establishment of non-defended localities even if such localities do not fulfil the conditions laid down in paragraph 2. The agreement should define and describe, as precisely as possible, the limits of the non-defended locality; if necessary, it may lay down the methods of supervision.

6. The Party which is in control of a locality governed by such an agreement shall mark it, so far as possible, by such signs as may be agreed upon with the other Party, which shall be displayed where they are clearly visible, especially on its perimeter and limits and on highways.

7. A locality loses its status as a non-defended locality when it

ceases to fulfil the conditions laid down in paragraph 2 or in the agreement referred to in paragraph 5. In such an eventuality, the locality shall continue to enjoy the protection provided by the other provisions of this Protocol and the other rules of international law applicable in armed conflict.

Article 60 — *Demilitarized zones*

1. It is prohibited for the Parties to the conflict to extend their military operations to zones on which they have conferred by agreement the status of demilitarized zone, if such extension is contrary to the terms of this agreement.

2. The agreement shall be an express agreement, may be concluded verbally or in writing, either directly or through a Protecting Power or any impartial humanitarian organization, and may consist of reciprocal and concordant declarations. The agreement may be concluded in peacetime, as well as after the outbreak of hostilities, and should define and describe, as precisely as possible, the limits of the demilitarized zone and, if necessary, lay down the methods of supervision.

3. The subject of such an agreement shall normally be any zone which fulfils the following conditions:

   (*a*) all combatants, as well as mobile weapons and mobile military equipment, must have been evacuated;

   (*b*) no hostile use shall be made of fixed military installations or establishments;

   (*c*) no acts of hostility shall be committed by the authorities or by the population; and

   (*d*) any activity linked to the military effort must have ceased.

The Parties to the conflict shall agree upon the interpretation to be given to the condition laid down in sub-paragraph (*d*) and upon persons to be admitted to the demilitarized zone other than those mentioned in paragraph 4.

4. The presence, in this zone, of persons specially protected under the Conventions and this Protocol, and of police forces retained for the sole purpose of maintaining law and order, is not contrary to the conditions laid down in paragraph 3.

5. The Party which is in control of such a zone shall mark it, so far as possible, by such signs as may be agreed upon with the other Party, which shall be displayed where they are clearly visible, especially on its perimeter and limits and on highways.

6. If the fighting draws near to a demilitarized zone, and if the Parties to the conflict have so agreed, none of them may use the zone for purposes related to the conduct of military operations

or unilaterally revoke its status.

7. If one of the Parties to the conflict commits a material breach of the provisions of paragraphs 3 or 6, the other Party shall be released from its obligations under the agreement conferring upon the zone the status of demilitarized zone. In such an eventuality, the zone loses its status but shall continue to enjoy the protection provided by the other provisions of this Protocol and the other rules of international law applicable in armed conflict.

CHAPTER VI — *Civil Defence*

Article 61 — Definitions and scope

For the purposes of this Protocol:

(*a*) 'civil defence' means the performance of some or all of the undermentioned humanitarian tasks intended to protect the civilian population against the dangers, and to help it to recover from the immediate effects, of hostilities or disasters and also to provide the conditions necessary for its survival. These tasks are:

   (i) warning;
   (ii) evacuation;
   (iii) management of shelters;
   (iv) management of blackout measures;
   (v) rescue;
   (vi) medical services, including first aid, and religious assistance;
   (vii) fire-fighting;
   (viii) detection and marking of danger areas;
   (ix) decontamination and similar protective measures;
   (x) provision of emergency accommodation and supplies;
   (xi) emergency assistance in the restoration and maintenance of order in distressed areas;
   (xii) emergency repair of indispensable public utilities;
   (xiii) emergency disposal of the dead;
   (xiv) assistance in the preservation of objects essential for survival;
   (xv) complementary activities necessary to carry out any of the tasks mentioned above, including, but not limited to, planning and organization;

(*b*) 'civil defence organizations' means those establishments and other units which are organized or authorized by the competent authorities of a Party to the conflict to perform any of the tasks mentioned under sub-paragraph (*a*), and which are assigned and devoted exclusively to such tasks;

(c) 'personnel' of civil defence organizations means those persons assigned by a Party to the conflict exclusively to the performance of the tasks mentioned under sub-paragraph (a), including personnel assigned by the competent authority of that Party exclusively to the administration of these organizations;

(d) '*matériel*' of civil defence organizations means equipment, supplies and transports used by these organizations for the performance of the tasks mentioned under sub-paragraph (a).

Article 62 — General protection

1. Civilian civil defence organizations and their personnel shall be respected and protected, subject to the provisions of this Protocol, particularly the provisions of this Section. They shall be entitled to perform their civil defence tasks except in case of imperative military necessity.

2. The provisions of paragraph 1 shall also apply to civilians who, although not members of civilian civil defence organizations, respond to an appeal from the competent authorities and perform civil defence tasks under their control.

3. Buildings and *matériel* used for civil defence purposes and shelters provided for the civilian population are covered by Article 52. Objects used for civil defence purposes may not be destroyed or diverted from their proper use except by the Party to which they belong.

Article 63 — Civil defence in occupied territories

1. In occupied territories, civilian civil defence organizations shall receive from the authorities the facilities necessary for the performance of their tasks. In no circumstances shall their personnel be compelled to perform activities which would interfere with the proper performance of these tasks. The Occupying Power shall not change the structure or personnel of such organizations in any way which might jeopardize the efficient performance of their mission. These organizations shall not be required to give priority to the nationals or interests of that Power.

2. The Occupying Power shall not compel, coerce or induce civilian civil defence organizations to perform their tasks in any manner prejudicial to the interests of the civilian population.

3. The Occupying Power may disarm civil defence personnel for reasons of security.

4. The Occupying Power shall neither divert from their proper use nor requisition buildings or *matériel* belonging to or used by

civil defence organizations if such diversion or requisition would be harmful to the civilian population.

5. Provided that the general rule in paragraph 4 continues to be observed, the Occupying Power may requisition or divert these resources, subject to the following particular conditions:

(*a*) that the buildings or *matériel* are necessary for other needs of the civilian population; and

(*b*) that the requisition or diversion continues only while such necessity exists.

6. The Occupying Power shall neither divert nor requisition shelters provided for the use of the civilian population or needed by such population.

Article 64 — Civilian civil defence organizations of neutral or other States not Parties to the conflict and international co-ordinating organizations

1. Articles 62, 63, 65 and 66 shall also apply to the personnel and *matériel* of civilian civil defence organizations of neutral or other States not Parties to the conflict which perform civil defence tasks mentioned in Article 61 in the territory of a Party to the conflict, with the consent and under the control of that Party. Notification of such assistance shall be given as soon as possible to any adverse Party concerned. In no circumstances shall this activity be deemed to be an interference in the conflict. This activity should, however, be performed with due regard to the security interests of the Parties to the conflict concerned.

2. The Parties to the conflict receiving the assistance referred to in paragraph 1 and the High Contracting Parties granting it should facilitate international co-ordination of such civil defence actions when appropriate. In such cases the relevant international organizations are covered by the provisions of this Chapter.

3. In occupied territories, the Occupying Power may only exclude or restrict the activities of civilian civil defence organizations of neutral or other States not Parties to the conflict and of international co-ordinating organizations if it can ensure the adequate performance of civil defence tasks from its own resources or those of the occupied territory.

Article 65 — Cessation of protection

1. The protection to which civilian civil defence organizations, their personnel, buildings, shelters and *matériel* are entitled shall not cease unless they commit or are used to commit, outside their proper tasks, acts harmful to the enemy. Protection may, however, cease only after a warning has been given setting, whenever appropriate,

a reasonable time-limit, and after such warning has remained unheeded.

2. The following shall not be considered as acts harmful to the
enemy:

(a) that civil defence tasks are carried out under the direction
or control of military authorities;

(b) that civilian civil defence personnel co-operate with
military personnel in the performance of civil defence
tasks, or that some military personnel are attached to
civilian civil defence organizations;

(c) that the performance of civil defence tasks may incident-
ally benefit military victims, particularly those who are
hors de combat.

3. It shall also not be considered as an act harmful to the enemy
that civilian civil defence personnel bear light individual weapons
for the purpose of maintaining order of for self-defence. However,
in areas where land fighting is taking place or is likely to take place,
the Parties to the conflict shall undertake the appropriate measures
to limit these weapons to handguns, such as pistols or revolvers,
in order to assist in distinguishing between civil defence personnel
and combatants. Although civil defence personnel bear other light
individual weapons in such areas, they shall nevertheless be respected
and protected as soon as they have been recognized as such.

4. The formation of civilian civil defence organizations along
military lines, and compulsory service in them, shall also not deprive
them of the protection conferred by this Chapter.

Article 66 — *Identification*

1. Each Party to the conflict shall endeavour to ensure that its
civil defence organizations, their personnel, buildings and *matériel*,
are identifiable while they are exclusively devoted to the performance of civil defence tasks. Shelters provided for the civilian population should be similarly identifiable.

2. Each Party to the conflict shall also endeavour to adopt and
implement methods and procedures which will make it possible
to recognize civilian shelters as well as civil defence personnel,
buildings and *matériel* on which the international distinctive sign
of civil defence is displayed.

3. In occupied territories and in areas where fighting is taking
place or is likely to take place, civilian civil defence personnel should
be recognizable by the international distinctive sign of civil defence
and by an identity card certifying their status.

4. The International distinctive sign of civil defence is an

equilateral blue triangle on an orange ground when used for the protection of civil defence organizations, their personnel, buildings and *matériel* and for civilian shelters.

5. In addition to the distinctive sign, Parties to the conflict may agree upon the use of distinctive signals for civil defence identification purposes.

6. The application of the provisions of paragraphs 1 to 4 is governed by Chapter V of Annex I to this Protocol.

7. In time of peace, the sign described in paragraph 4 may, with the consent of the competent national authorities, be used for civil defence identification purposes.

8. The High Contracting Parties and the Parties to the conflict shall take the measures necessary to supervise the display of the international distinctive sign of civil defence and to prevent and repress any misuse thereof.

9. The identification of civil defence medical and religious personnel, medical units and medical transports is also governed by Article 18.

Article 67 — Members of the armed forces and military units assigned to civil defence organizations

1. Members of the armed forces and military units assigned to civil defence organizations shall be respected and protected, provided that:

   (*a*) such personnel and such units are permanently assigned and exclusively devoted to the performance of any of the tasks mentioned in Article 61;

   (*b*) if so assigned, such personnel do not perform any other military duties during the conflict;

   (*c*) such personnel are clearly distinguishable from the other members of the armed forces by prominently displaying the international distinctive sign of civil defence, which shall be as large as appropriate, and such personnel are provided with the identity card referred to in Chapter V of Annex I to this Protocol certifying their status;

   (*d*) such personnel and such units are equipped only with light individual weapons for the purpose of maintaining order or for self-defence. The provisions of Article 65, paragraph 3 shall also apply in this case;

   (*e*) such personnel do not participate directly in hostilities, and do not commit, or are not used to commit, outside their civil defence tasks, acts harmful to the adverse Party;

   (*f*) such personnel and such units perform their civil defence tasks only within the national territory of their Party.

The non-observance of the conditions stated in (*e*) above by any member of the armed forces who is bound by the conditions prescribed in (*a*) and (*b*) above is prohibited.

2. Military personnel serving within civil defence organizations shall, if they fall into the power of an adverse Party, be prisoners of war. In occupied territory they may, but only in the interest of the civilian population of that territory, be employed on civil defence tasks in so far as the need arises, provided however that, if such work is dangerous, they volunteer for such tasks.

3. The buildings and major items of equipment and transports of military units assigned to civil defence organizations shall be clearly marked with the international distinctive sign of civil defence. This distinctive sign shall be as large as appropriate.

4. The *matériel* and buildings of military units permanently assigned to civil defence organizations and exclusively devoted to the performance of civil defence tasks shall, if they fall into the hands of an adverse Party, remain subject to the laws of war. They may not be diverted from their civil defence purpose so long as they are required for the performance of civil defence tasks, except in case of imperative military necessity, unless previous arrangements have been made for adequate provision for the needs of the civilian population.

SECTION II — RELIEF IN FAVOUR OF THE CIVILIAN POPULATION

Article 68 — Field of application

The provisions of this Section apply to the civilian population as defined in this Protocol and are supplementary to Articles 23, 55, 59, 60, 61 and 62 and other relevant provisions of the Fourth Convention.

Article 69 — Basic needs in occupied territories

1. In addition to the duties specified in Article 55 of the Fourth Convention concerning food and medical supplies, the Occupying Power shall, to the fullest extent of the means available to it and without any adverse distinction, also ensure the provision of clothing, bedding, means of shelter, other supplies essential to the survival of the civilian population of the occupied territory and objects necessary for religious worship.

2. Relief actions for the benefit of the civilian population of occupied territories are governed by Articles 59, 60, 61, 62, 108, 109, 110 and 111 of the Fourth Convention, and by Article 71 of this Protocol, and shall be implemented without delay.

Article 70 — *Relief actions*

1. If the civilian population of any territory under the control of a Party to the conflict, other than occupied territory, is not adequately provided with the supplies mentioned in Article 69, relief actions which are humanitarian and impartial in character and conducted without any adverse distinction shall be undertaken, subject to the agreement of the Parties concerned in such relief actions. Offers of such relief shall not be regarded as interference in the armed conflict or as unfriendly acts. In the distribution of relief consignments, priority shall be given to those persons, such as children, expectant mothers, maternity cases and nursing mothers, who, under the Fourth Convention or under this Protocol, are to be accorded privileged treatment or special protection.

2. The Parties to the conflict and each High Contracting Party shall allow and facilitate rapid and unimpeded passage of all relief consignments, equipment and personnel provided in accordance with this Section, even if such assistance is destined for the civilian population of the adverse Party.

3. The Parties to the conflict and each High Contracting Party which allow the passage of relief consignments, equipment and personnel in accordance with paragraph 2:

   (*a*) shall have the right to prescribe the technical arrangements, including search, under which such passage is permitted;

   (*b*) may make such permission conditional on the distribution of this assistance being made under the local supervision of a Protecting Power;

   (*c*) shall, in no way whatsoever, divert relief consignments from the purpose for which they are intended nor delay their forwarding, except in cases of urgent necessity in the interest of the civilian population concerned.

4. The Parties to the conflict shall protect relief consignments and facilitate their rapid distribution.

5. The Parties to the conflict and each High Contracting Party concerned shall encourage and facilitate effective international co-ordination of the relief actions referred to in paragraph 1.

Article 71 — *Personnel participating in relief actions*

1. Where necessary, relief personnel may form part of the assistance provided in any relief action, in particular for the transportation and distribution of relief consignments; the participation of such personnel shall be subject to the approval of the Party in whose territory they will carry out their duties.

2. Such personnel shall be respected and protected.

3. Each Party in receipt of relief consignments shall, to the fullest extent practicable, assist the relief personnel referred to in paragraph 1 in carrying out their relief mission. Only in case of imperative military necessity may the activities of the relief personnel be limited or their movements temporarily restricted.

4. Under no circumstances may relief personnel exceed the terms of their mission under this Protocol. In particular they shall take account of the security requirements of the Party in whose territory they are carrying out their duties. The mission of any of the personnel who do not respect these conditions may be terminated.

SECTION III — TREATMENT OF PERSONS IN THE POWER OF A PARTY TO THE CONFLICT

CHAPTER I — *Field of Application and Protection of Persons and Objects*

Article 72 — Field of application

The provisions of this Section are additional to the rules concerning humanitarian protection of civilians and civilian objects in the power of a Party to the conflict contained in the Fourth Convention, particularly Parts I and III thereof, as well as to other applicable rules of international law relating to the protection of fundamental human rights during international armed conflict.

Article 73 — Refugees and stateless persons

Persons who, before the beginning of hostilities, were considered as stateless persons or refugees under the relevant international instruments accepted by the Parties concerned or under the national legislation of the State of refuge or State of residence shall be protected persons within the meaning of Parts I and III of the Fourth Convention, in all circumstances and without any adverse distinction.

Article 74 — Reunion of dispersed families

The High Contracting Parties and the Parties to the conflict shall facilitate in every possible way the reunion of families dispersed as a result of armed conflicts and shall encourage in particular the work of the humanitarian organizations engaged in this task in accordance with the provisions of the Conventions and of this Protocol and in conformity with their respective security regulations.

Article 75 — Fundamental guarantees

1. In so far as they are affected by a situation referred to in

Article 1 of this Protocol, persons who are in the power of a Party
to the conflict and who do not benefit from more favourable treatment under the Conventions or under this Protocol shall be treated
humanely in all circumstances and shall enjoy, as a minimum, the
protection provided by this Article without any adverse distinction
based upon race, colour, sex, language, religion or belief, political
or other opinion, national or social origin, wealth, birth or other
status, or on any other similar criteria. Each Party shall respect
the person, honour, convictions and religious practices of all such
persons.

2. The following acts are and shall remain prohibited at any
time and in any place whatsoever, whether committed by civilian
or by military agents:

(*a*) violence to the life, health, or physical or mental well-
being of persons, in particular:
(i) murder;
(ii) torture of all kinds, whether physical or mental;
(iii) corporal punishment; and
(iv) mutilation;
(*b*) outrages upon personal dignity, in particular humiliating
and degrading treatment, enforced prostitution and any
form of indecent assault;
(*c*) the taking of hostages;
(*d*) collective punishments; and
(*e*) threats to commit any of the foregoing acts.

3. Any person arrested, detained or interned for actions related
to the armed conflict shall be informed promptly, in a language he
understands, of the reasons why these measures have been taken.
Except in cases of arrest or detention for penal offences, such
persons shall be released with the minimum delay possible and
in any event as soon as the circumstances justifying the arrest,
detention or internment have ceased to exist.

4. No sentence may be passed and no penalty may be executed
on a person found guilty of a penal offence related to the armed
conflict except pursuant to a conviction pronounced by an impartial
and regularly constituted court respecting the generally recognized
principles of regular judicial procedure, which include the following:

(*a*) the procedure shall provide for an accused to be informed
without delay of the particulars of the offence alleged
against him and shall afford the accused before and during
his trial all necessary rights and means of defence;
(*b*) no one shall be convicted of an offence except on the
basis of individual penal responsibility;

(*c*) no one shall be accused or convicted of a criminal offence on account of any act or omission which did not constitute a criminal offence under the national or international law to which he was subject at the time when it was committed; nor shall a heavier penalty be imposed than that which was applicable at the time when the criminal offence was committed; if, after the commission of the offence, provision is made by law for the imposition of a lighter penalty, the offender shall benefit thereby;

(*d*) anyone charged with an offence is presumed innocent until proved guilty according to law;

(*e*) anyone charged with an offence shall have the right to tried in his presence;

(*f*) no one shall be compelled to testify against himself or to confess guilt;

(*g*) anyone charged with an offence shall have the right to examine, or have examined, the witnesses against him and to obtain the attendance and examination of witnesses on his behalf under the same conditions as witnesses against him;

(*h*) no one shall be prosecuted or punished by the same Party for an offence in respect of which a final judgement acquitting or convicting that person has been previously pronounced under the same law and judicial procedure;

(*i*) anyone prosecuted for an offence shall have the right to have the judgement pronounced publicly; and

(*j*) a convicted person shall be advised on conviction of his judicial and other remedies and of the time-limits within which they may be exercised.

5. Women whose liberty has been restricted for reasons related to the armed conflict shall be held in quarters separated from men's quarters. They shall be under the immediate supervision of women. Nevertheless, in cases where families are detained or interned, they shall, whenever possible, be held in the same place and accommodated as family units.

6. Persons who are arrested, detained or interned for reasons related to the armed conflict shall enjoy the protection provided by this Article until their final release, repatriation or re-establishment, even after the end of the armed conflict.

7. In order to avoid any doubt concerning the prosecution and trial of persons accused of war crimes or crimes against humanity, the following principles shall apply:

(*a*) persons who are accused of such crimes should be submitted for the purpose of prosecution and trial in accordance with the applicable rules of international law; and

(*b*) any such persons who do not benefit from more favourable treatment under the Conventions or this Protocol shall be accorded the treatment provided by this Article, whether or not the crimes of which they are accused constitute grave breaches of the Conventions or of this Protocol.

8. No provision of this Article may be construed as limiting or infringing any other more favourable provision granting greater protection, under any applicable rules of international law, to persons covered by paragraph 1.

CHAPTER II — *Measures in Favour of Women and Children*

Article 76 — Protection of women

1. Women shall be the object of special respect and shall be protected in particular against rape, forced prostitution and any other form of indecent assault.

2. Pregnant women and mothers having dependent infants who are arrested, detained or interned for reasons related to the armed conflict, shall have their cases considered with the utmost priority.

3. To the maximum extent feasible, the Parties to the conflict shall endeavour to avoid the pronouncement of the death penalty on pregnant women or mothers having dependent infants, for an offence related to the armed conflict. The death penalty for such offences shall not be executed on such women.

Article 77 — Protection of children

1. Children shall be the object of special respect and shall be protected against any form of indecent assault. The Parties to the conflict shall provide them with the care and aid they require, whether because of their age or for any other reason.

2. The Parties to the conflict shall take all feasible measures in order that children who have not attained the age of fifteen years do not take a direct part in hostilities and, in particular, they shall refrain from recruiting them into their armed forces. In recruiting among those persons who have attained the age of fifteen years but who have not attained the age of eighteen years, the Parties to the conflict shall endeavour to give priority to those who are oldest.

3. If, in exceptional cases, despite the provisions of paragraph 2, children who have not attained the age of fifteen years take a direct

part in hostilities and fall into the power of an adverse Party, they shall continue to benefit from the special protection accorded by this Article, whether or not they are prisoners of war.

4. If arrested, detained or interned for reasons related to the armed conflict, children shall be held in quarters separate from the quarters of adults, except where families are accommodated as family units as provided in Article 75, paragraph 5.

5. The death penalty for an offence related to the armed conflict shall not be executed on persons who had not attained the age of eighteen years at the time the offence was committed.

Article 78 — Evacuation of children

1. No Party to the conflict shall arrange for the evacuation of children, other than its own nationals, to a foreign country except for a temporary evacuation where compelling reasons of the health or medical treatment of the children or, except in occupied territory, their safety, so require. Where the parents or legal guardians can be found, their written consent to such evacuation is required. If these persons cannot be found, the written consent to such evacuation of the persons who by law or custom are primarily responsible for the care of the children is required. Any such evacuation shall be supervised by the Protecting Power in agreement with the Parties concerned, namely, the Party arranging for the evacuation, the Party receiving the children and any Parties whose nationals are being evacuated. In each case, all Parties to the conflict shall take all feasible precautions to avoid endangering the evacuation.

2. Whenever an evacuation occurs pursuant to paragraph 1, each child's education, including his religious and moral education as his parents desire, shall be provided while he is away with the greatest possible continuity.

3. With a view to facilitating the return to their families and country of children evacuated pursuant to this Article, the authorities of the Party arranging for the evacuation and, as appropriate, the authorities of the receiving country shall establish for each child a card with photographs, which they shall send to the Central Tracing Agency of the International Committee of the Red Cross. Each card shall bear, whenever possible, and whenever it involves no risk of harm to the child, the following information:

(*a*) surname(s) of the child;

(*b*) the child's first name(s);

(*c*) the child's sex;

(*d*) the place and date of birth (or, if that date is not known, the approximate age);

(*e*)   the father's full name;
(*f*)   the mother's full name and her maiden name;
(*g*)   the child's next-of-kin;
(*h*)   the child's nationality;
(*i*)   the child's native language, and any other languages he speaks;
(*j*)   the address of the child's family;
(*k*)   any identification number for the child;
(*l*)   the child's state of health;
(*m*)   the child's blood group;
(*n*)   any distinguishing features;
(*o*)   the date on which and the place where the child was found;
(*p*)   the date on which and the place from which the child left the country;
(*q*)   the child's religion, if any;
(*r*)   the child's present address in the receiving country;
(*s*)   should the child die before his return, the date, place and circumstances of death and place of interment.

CHAPTER III — *Journalists*

Article 79 — Measures of protection for journalists

1. Journalists engaged in dangerous professional missions in areas of armed conflict shall be considered as civilians within the meaning of Article 50, paragraph 1.

2. They shall be protected as such under the Conventions and this Protocol, provided that they take no action adversely affecting their status as civilians, and without prejudice to the right of war correspondents accredited to the armed forces to the status provided for in Article 4A (4) of the Third Convention.

3. They may obtain an identity card similar to the model in Annex II of this Protocol. This card, which shall be issued by the government of the State of which the journalist is a national or in whose territory he resides or in which the news medium employing him is located, shall attest to his status as a journalist.

PART V — EXECUTION OF THE CONVENTIONS AND OF THIS PROTOCOL

SECTION I — GENERAL PROVISIONS

Article 80 — Measures for execution

1. The High Contracting Parties and the Parties to the conflict

shall without delay take all necessary measures for the execution of their obligations under the Conventions and this Protocol.

2. The High Contracting Parties and the Parties to the conflict shall give orders and instructions to ensure observance of the Conventions and this Protocol, and shall supervise their execution.

Article 81 — Activities of the Red Cross and other humanitarian organizations

1. The Parties to the conflict shall grant to the International Committee of the Red Cross all facilities within their power so as to enable it to carry out the humanitarian functions assigned to it by the Conventions and this Protocol in order to ensure protection and assistance to the victims of conflicts; the International Committee of the Red Cross may also carry out any other humanitarian activities in favour of these victims, subject to the consent of the Parties to the conflict concerned.

2. The Parties to the conflict shall grant to their respective Red Cross (Red Crescent, Red Lion and Sun) organizations the facilities necessary for carrying out their humanitarian activities in favour of the victims of the conflict, in accordance with the provisions of the Conventions and this Protocol and the fundamental principles of the Red Cross as formulated by the International Conferences of the Red Cross.

3. The High Contracting Parties and the Parties to the conflict shall facilitate in every possible way the assistance which Red Cross, (Red Crescent, Red Lion and Sun) organizations and the League of Red Cross Societies extend to the victims of conflicts in accordance with the provisions of the Conventions and this Protocol and with the fundamental principles of the Red Cross as formulated by the International Conferences of the Red Cross.

4. The High Contracting Parties and the Parties to the conflict shall, as far as possible, make facilities similar to those mentioned in paragraphs 2 and 3 available to the other humanitarian organizations referred to in the Conventions and this Protocol which are duly authorized by the respective Parties to the conflict and which perform their humanitarian activities in accordance with the provisions of the Conventions and this Protocol.

Article 82 — Legal advisers in armed forces

The High Contracting Parties at all times, and the Parties to the conflict in time of armed conflict, shall ensure that legal advisers are available, when necessary, to advise military commanders at the appropriate level on the application of the Conventions and this Protocol and on the appropriate instruction to be given to the armed forces on this subject.

Article 83 — *Dissemination*

1. The High Contracting Parties undertake, in time of peace as in time of armed conflict, to disseminate the Conventions and this Protocol as widely as possible in their respective countries and, in particular, to include the study thereof in their programmes of military instruction and to encourage the study thereof by the civilian population, so that those instruments may become known to the armed forces and to the civilian population.

2. Any military or civilian authorities who, in time of armed conflict, assume responsibilities in respect of the application of the Conventions and this Protocol shall be fully acquainted with the text thereof.

Article 84 — *Rules of application*

The High Contracting Parties shall communicate to one another, as soon as possible, through the depositary and, as appropriate, through the Protecting Powers, their official translations of this Protocol, as well as the laws and regulations which they may adopt to ensure its application.

SECTION II — REPRESSION OF BREACHES OF THE
CONVENTIONS AND OF THIS PROTOCOL

Article 85 — *Repression of breaches of this Protocol*

1. The provisions of the Conventions relating to the repression of breaches and grave breaches, supplemented by this Section, shall apply to the repression of breaches and grave breaches of this Protocol.

2. Acts described as grave breaches in the Conventions are grave breaches of this Protocol if committed against persons in the power of an adverse Party protected by Articles 44, 45 and 73 of this Protocol, or against the wounded, sick and shipwrecked of the adverse Party who are protected by this Protocol, or against those medical or religious personnel, medical units or medical transports which are under the control of the adverse Party and are protected by this Protocol.

3. In addition to the grave breaches defined in Article 11, the following acts shall be regarded as grave breaches of this Protocol, when committed wilfully, in violation of the relevant provisions of this Protocol, and causing death or serious injury to body or health:

    (*a*) making the civilian population or individual civilians the object of attack;

    (*b*) launching an indiscriminate attack affecting the civilian population or civilian objects in the knowledge that such attack will cause excessive loss of life, injury to civilians or damage to civilian objects, as defined in Article 57, paragraph 2(*a*) (iii);

(*c*) launching an attack against works or installations containing dangerous forces in the knowledge that such attack will cause excessive loss of life, injury to civilians or damage to civilian objects, as defined in Article 57, paragraph 2(*a*) (iii);

(*d*) making non-defended localities and demilitarized zones the object of attack;

(*e*) making a person the object of attack in the knowledge that he is *hors de combat*;

(*f*) the perfidious use, in violation of Article 37, of the distinctive emblem of the red cross, red crescent or red lion and sun or of other protective signs recognized by the Conventions or this Protocol.

4. In addition to the grave breaches defined in the preceding paragraphs and in the Conventions, the following shall be regarded as grave breaches of this Protocol, when committed wilfully and in violation of the Conventions or the Protocol:

(*a*) the transfer by the Occupying Power of parts of its own civilian population into the territory it occupies, or the deportation or transfer of all or parts of the population of the occupied territory within or outside this territory, in violation of Article 49 of the Fourth Convention;

(*b*) unjustifiable delay in the repatriation of prisoners of war or civilians;

(*c*) practices of *apartheid* and other inhuman and degrading practices involving outrages upon personal dignity, based on racial discrimination;

(*d*) making the clearly-recognized historic monuments, works of art or places of worship which constitute the cultural or spiritual heritage of peoples and to which special protection has been given by special arrangement, for example, within the framework of a competent international organization, the object of attack, causing as a result extensive destruction thereof, where there is no evidence of the violation by the adverse Party of Article 53, sub-paragraph (*b*), and when such historic monuments, works of art and places of worship are not located in the immediate proximity of military objectives;

(*e*) depriving a person protected by the Conventions or referred to in paragraph 2 of this Article of the rights of fair and regular trial.

5. Without prejudice to the application of the Conventions and of this Protocol, grave breaches of these instruments shall be regarded as war crimes.

Article 86 — *Failure to act*

1. The High Contracting Parties and the Parties to the conflict shall repress grave breaches, and take measures necessary to suppress all other breaches, of the Conventions or of this Protocol which result from a failure to act when under a duty to do so.

2. The fact that a breach of the Conventions or of this Protocol was committed by a subordinate does not absolve his superiors from penal or disciplinary responsibility, as the case may be, if they knew, or had information which should have enabled them to conclude in the circumstances at the time, that he was committing or was going to commit such a breach and if they did not take all feasible measures within their power to prevent or repress the breach.

Article 87 — *Duty of commanders*

1. The High Contracting Parties and the Parties to the conflict shall require military commanders, with respect to members of the armed forces under their command and other persons under their control, to prevent and, where necessary, to suppress and to report to competent authorities breaches of the Conventions and of this Protocol.

2. In order to prevent and suppress breaches, High Contracting Parties and Parties to the conflict shall require that, commensurate with their level of responsibility, commanders ensure that members of the armed forces under their command are aware of their obligations under the Conventions and this Protocol.

3. The High Contracting Parties and Parties to the conflict shall require any commander who is aware that subordinates or other persons under his control are going to commit or have committed a breach of the Conventions or of this Protocol, to initiate such steps as are necessary to prevent such violations of the Conventions or this Protocol, and, where appropriate, to initiate disciplinary or penal action against violators thereof.

Article 88 — *Mutual assistance in criminal matters*

1. The High Contracting Parties shall afford one another the greatest measure of assistance in connexion with criminal proceedings brought in respect of grave breaches of the Conventions or of this Protocol.

2. Subject to the rights and obligations established in the Conventions and in Article 85, paragraph 1, of this Protocol, and when circumstances permit, the High Contracting Parties shall co-operate in the matter of extradition. They shall give due consideration to the request of the State in whose territory the alleged offence has occurred.

3. The law of the High Contracting Party requested shall apply in all cases. The provisions of the preceding paragraphs shall not, however, affect the obligations arising from the provisions of any other treaty of a bilateral or multilateral nature which governs or will govern the whole or part of the subject of mutual assistance in criminal matters.

Article 89 — *Co-operation*

In situations of serious violations of the Conventions or of this Protocol, the High Contracting Parties undertake to act, jointly or individually, in co-operation with the United Nations and in conformity with the United Nations Charter.

Article 90 — *International Fact-Finding Commission*

1. (*a*) An International Fact-Finding Commission (hereinafter referred to as 'the Commission') consisting of fifteen members of high moral standing and acknowledged impartiality shall be established.

    (*b*) When not less than twenty High Contracting Parties have agreed to accept the competence of the Commission pursuant to paragraph 2, the depositary shall then, and at intervals of five years thereafter, convene a meeting of representatives of those High Contracting Parties for the purpose of electing the members of the Commission. At the meeting, the representatives shall elect the members of the Commission by secret ballot from a list of persons to which each of those High Contracting Parties may nominate one person.

    (*c*) The members of the Commission shall serve in their personal capacity and shall hold office until the election of new members at the ensuing meeting.

    (*d*) At the election, the High Contracting Parties shall ensure that the persons to be elected to the Commission individually possess the qualifications required and that, in the Commission as a whole, equitable geographical representation is assured.

    (*e*) In the case of a casual vacancy, the Commission itself shall fill the vacancy, having due regard to the provisions of the preceding sub-paragraphs.

(*f*) The depositary shall make available to the Commission the necessary administrative facilities for the performance of its functions.

2. (*a*) The High Contracting Parties may at the time of signing, ratifying or acceding to the Protocol, or at any other subsequent time, declare that they recognize *ipso facto* and without special agreement, in relation to any other High Contracting Party accepting the same obligation, the competence of the Commission to enquire into allegations by such other Party, as authorized by this Article.

(*b*) The declarations referred to above shall be deposited with the depositary, which shall transmit copies thereof to the High Contracting Parties.

(*c*) The Commission shall be competent to:
   (i) enquire into any facts alleged to be a grave breach as defined in the Conventions and this Protocol or other serious violation of the Conventions or of this Protocol;
   (ii) facilitate, through its good offices, the restoration of an attitude of respect for the Conventions and this Protocol.

(*d*) In other situations, the Commission shall institute an enquiry at the request of a Party to the conflict only with the consent of the other Party or Parties concerned.

(*e*) Subject to the foregoing provisions of this paragraph, the provisions of Article 52 of the First Convention, Article 53 of the Second Convention, Article 132 of the Third Convention and Article 149 of the Fourth Convention shall continue to apply to any alleged violation of the Conventions and shall extend to any alleged violation of this Protocol.

3. (*a*) Unless otherwise agreed by the Parties concerned, all enquiries shall be undertaken by a Chamber consisting of seven members appointed as follows:
   (i) five members of the Commission, not nationals of any Party to the conflict, appointed by the President of the Commission on the basis of equitable representation of the geographical areas, after consultation with the Parties to the conflict;
   (ii) two *ad hoc* members, not nationals of any Party to the conflict, one to be appointed by each side.

(*b*) Upon receipt of the request for an enquiry, the President of the Commission shall specify an appropriate time limit for setting up a Chamber. If any *ad hoc* member has not been appointed within the time limit, the President shall immediately appoint such additional member or members of the Commission as may be necessary to complete the membership of the Chamber.

4. (*a*) The Chamber set up under paragraph 3 to undertake an enquiry shall invite the Parties to the conflict to assist it and to present evidence. The Chamber may also seek such other evidence as it deems appropriate and may carry out an investigation of the situation *in loco*.

(*b*) All evidence shall be fully disclosed to the Parties, which shall have the right to comment on it to the Commission.

(*c*) Each Party shall have the right to challenge such evidence.

5. (*a*) The Commission shall submit to the Parties a report on the findings of fact of the Chamber, with such recommendations as it may deem appropriate.

(*b*) If the Chamber is unable to secure sufficient evidence for factual and impartial findings, the Commission shall state the reasons for that inability.

(*c*) The Commission shall not report its findings publicly, unless all the Parties to the conflict have requested the Commission to do so.

6. The Commission shall establish its own rules, including rules for the presidency of the Commission and the presidency of the Chamber. Those rules shall ensure that the functions of the President of the Commission are exercised at all times and that, in the case of an enquiry, they are exercised by a person who is not a national of a Party to the conflict.

7. The administrative expenses of the Commission shall be met by contributions from the High Contracting Parties which made declarations under paragraph 2, and by voluntary contributions. The Party or Parties to the conflict requesting an enquiry shall advance the necessary funds for expenses incurred by a Chamber and shall be reimbursed by the Party or Parties against which the allegations are made to the extent of fifty per cent of the costs of the Chamber. Where there are counter-allegations before the Chamber each side shall advance fifty per cent of the necessary funds.

Article 91 — *Responsibility*

A Party to the conflict which violates the provisions of the Conventions or of this Protocol shall, if the case demands, be liable to pay compensation. It shall be responsible for all acts committed by persons forming part of its armed forces.

PART VI — FINAL PROVISIONS

Article 92 — Signature

This Protocol shall be open for signature by the Parties to the Conventions six months after the signing of the Final Act and will remain open for a period of twelve months.

Article 93 — Ratification

This Protocol shall be ratified as soon as possible. The instruments of ratification shall be deposited with the Swiss Federal Council, depositary of the Conventions.

Article 94 — Accession

This Protocol shall be open for accession by any Party to the Conventions which has not signed it. The instruments of accession shall be deposited with the depositary.

Article 95 — Entry into force

1. This Protocol shall enter into force six months after two instruments of ratification or accession have been deposited.

2. For each Party to the Conventions thereafter ratifying or acceding to this Protocol, it shall enter into force six months after the deposit by such Party of its instrument of ratification or accession.

Article 96 — Treaty relations upon entry into force of this Protocol

1. When the Parties to the Conventions are also Parties to this Protocol, the Conventions shall apply as supplemented by this Protocol.

2. When one of the Parties to the conflict is not bound by this Protocol, the Parties to the Protocol shall remain bound by it in their mutual relations. They shall futhermore be bound by this Protocol in relation to each of the Parties which are not bound by it, if the latter accepts and applies the provisions thereof.

3. The authority representing a people engaged against a High Contracting Party in an armed conflict of the type referred to in Article 1, paragraph 4, may undertake to apply the Conventions and this Protocol in relation to that conflict by means of a unilateral declaration addressed to the depositary. Such declaration shall, upon its receipt by the depositary, have in relation to that conflict the following effects:

    (*a*) the Conventions and this Protocol are brought into force for the said authority as a Party to the conflict with immediate effect;

    (*b*) the said authority assumes the same rights and obligations as those which have been assumed by a High Contracting Party to the Conventions and this Protocol; and

(c) the Conventions and this Protocol are equally binding upon all Parties to the conflict.

Article 97 — Amendment

1. Any High Contracting Party may propose amendments to this Protocol. The text of any proposed amendment shall be communicated to the depositary, which shall decide, after consultation with all the High Contracting Parties and the International Committee of the Red Cross, whether a conference should be convened to consider the proposed amendment.

2. The depositary shall invite to that conference all the High Contracting Parties as well as the Parties to the Conventions, whether or not they are signatories of this Protocol.

Article 98 — Revision of Annex I[1]

1. Not later than four years after the entry into force of this Protocol and thereafter at intervals of not less than four years, the International Committee of the Red Cross shall consult the High Contracting Parties concerning Annex I to this Protocol and, if it considers it necessary, may propose a meeting of technical experts to review Annex I and to propose such amendments to it as may appear to be desirable. Unless, within six months of the communication of a proposal for such a meeting to the High Contracting Parties, one third of them object, the International Committee of the Red Cross shall convene the meeting, inviting also observers of appropriate international organizations. Such a meeting shall also be convened by the International Committee of the Red Cross at any time at the request of one third of the High Contracting Parties.

2. The depositary shall convene a conference of the High Contracting Parties and the Parties to the Conventions to consider amendments proposed by the meeting of technical experts if, after that meeting, the International Committee of the Red Cross or one third of the High Contracting Parties so request.

3. Amendments to Annex I may be adopted at such a conference by a two-thirds majority of the High Contracting Parties present and voting.

4. The depositary shall communicate any amendment so adopted to the High Contracting Parties and to the Parties to the Conventions. The amendment shall be considered to have been accepted

[1] Annex I contains regulations concerning identification.

at the end of a period of one year after it has been so communicated, unless within that period a declaration of non-acceptance of the amendment has been communicated to the depositary by not less than one third of the High Contracting Parties.

5. An amendment considered to have been accepted in accordance with paragraph 4 shall enter into force three months after its acceptance for all High Contracting Parties other than those which have made a declaration of non-acceptance in accordance with that paragraph. Any Party making such a declaration may at any time withdraw it and the amendment shall then enter into force for that Party three months thereafter.

6. The depositary shall notify the High Contracting Parties and the Parties to the Conventions of the entry into force of any amendment, of the Parties bound thereby, of the date of its entry into force in relation to each Party, of declarations of non-acceptance made in accordance with paragraph 4, and of withdrawals of such declarations.

Article 99 — *Denunciation*
1. In case a High Contracting Party should denounce this Protocol, the denunciation shall only take effect one year after receipt of the instrument of denunciation. If, however, on the expiry of that year the denouncing Party is engaged in one of the situations referred to in Article 1, the denunciation shall not take effect before the end of the armed conflict or occupation and not, in any case, before operations connected with the final release, repatriation or re-establishment of the persons protected by the Conventions or this Protocol have been terminated.

2. The denunciation shall be notified in writing to the depositary, which shall transmit it to all the High Contracting Parties.

3. The denunciation shall have effect only in respect of the denouncing Party.

4. Any denunciation under paragraph 1 shall not affect the obligations already incurred, by reason of the armed conflict, under this Protocol by such denouncing Party in respect of any act committed before this denunciation becomes effective.

Article 100 — *Notifications*
The depositary shall inform the High Contracting Parties as well as the Parties to the Conventions, whether or not they are signatories of this Protocol, of:
  (*a*) signatures affixed to this Protocol and the deposit of instruments of ratification and accession under Articles 93 and 94;

(*b*) the date of entry into force of this Protocol under Article 95;

(*c*) communications and declarations received under Articles 84, 90 and 97;

(*d*) declarations received under Article 96, paragraph 3, which shall be communicated by the quickest methods; and

(*e*) denunciations under Article 99.

Article 101 — *Registration*

1. After its entry into force, this Protocol shall be transmitted by the depositary to the Secretariat of the United Nations for registration and publication, in accordance with Article 102 of the Charter of the United Nations.

2. The depositary shall also inform the Secretariat of the United Nations of all ratifications, accessions and denunciations received by it with respect to this Protocol.

Article 102 — *Authentic texts*

The original of this Protocol, of which the Arabic, Chinese, English, French, Russian and Spanish texts are equally authentic, shall be deposited with the depositary, which shall transmit certified true copies thereof to all the Parties to the Conventions.

[Annexes omitted]

CONCLUDING NOTES

The concluding notes for 1977 Geneva Protocol I are combined with those for 1977 Geneva Protocol II and are to be found after the end of the latter document, below, p. 459.

27. 1977 Geneva Protocol II Additional to the Geneva Conventions of 12 August 1949, and Relating to the Protection of Victims of Non-International Armed Conflicts

PREFATORY NOTE

1977 Geneva Protocol II relates to the protection of victims of non-international armed conflicts. Such conflicts are by no means a new phenomenon. However, before 1949, international agreements on the laws of war applied (according to their specific terms) to wars between states, and had no formal bearing on non-international armed conflicts. The laws of war, as embodied in customary international law, were only regarded as applicable in a civil war if the government of the state in which the insurrection existed, or a third state, chose to recognize the belligerent status of the insurgent group and thereby acknowledge the law's application.

At an International Conference of the Red Cross in 1912, the American Red Cross Society proposed that an international agreement be adopted to permit aid to victims of internal conflicts. This proposal was opposed by the Russian representative, who contended that Red Cross Societies should have no duty towards insurgents regarded under domestic law as criminals. However, beginning with the Russian Revolution, the Red Cross did assist victims of a number of internal conflicts. In 1921, the 10th International Conference of the Red Cross adopted the principle that all victims of civil wars, social disputes and revolutions are entitled to humanitarian assistance. The Conference further appealed for the laws of war to be respected even in time of civil war. In 1937 a commission of government experts convened by the International Committee of the Red Cross unanimously recognized that the Red Cross principles should be respected in all circumstances (even when the Geneva Conventions were not formally applicable). This view was reaffirmed in 1938 at the 16th International Conference of the Red Cross.

The four draft conventions, prepared by the ICRC after the Second World War and approved by the 17th International Conference of the Red Cross in Stockholm in 1948, contained a common article under which the provisions of the conventions would be applicable in non-international armed conflicts. During the 1949 Geneva diplomatic conference, at which these drafts were the sole negotiating texts, there was substantial debate over the inclusion of any provision relating to internal conflicts. The conference rejected the notion that all of the laws of war should apply to internal conflicts. However, negotiation resulted in the adoption of common Article 3 of the four 1949 Geneva Conventions, which binds parties to observe a limited number of fundamental humanitarian principles in 'armed conflict not of an international character'.

Following the adoption of common Article 3 of the 1949 Geneva Conventions, the ICRC attempted to secure application of its provisions to a number of non-international armed conflicts. However, experience demonstrated the inadequacy of the common article. Useful as common Article 3 is, its provisions do little more than extend certain fundamental humanitarian protections to non-combatants. They do not provide any definitive codification of the laws of war for non-international armed conflicts. Moreover, the provisions are so general and incomplete that they cannot be regarded as an adequate guide for the conduct of belligerents in such conflicts. Consequently, under the auspices of the ICRC, commissions of experts were convened in Geneva to examine certain questions relating to non-international armed conflicts.

The question of non-international armed conflicts was also taken up at the 1954 Hague Intergovernmental Conference. Article 19 of the 1954 Hague Cultural Property Convention provides for the application of the Convention to non-international conflicts.

At the 21st International Conference of the Red Cross, held in Istanbul in 1969, the ICRC submitted a special report on the protection of victims of non-international armed conflicts. The Conference adopted several resolutions that common Article 3 be developed. The conclusions of the ICRC on non-international armed conflicts were endorsed in the 1969 and 1970 reports of the UN Secretary-General on respect for human rights in time of armed conflict. The latter report suggested that additional rules relating to non-international armed conflicts be adopted in the form of a protocol or a separate additional convention.

As indicated in the general prefatory note to the two 1977 Geneva Protocols, the ICRC submitted a draft protocol (which had been considered by a conference of government experts in 1971-2) to a diplomatic conference convened by the Swiss government in Geneva in 1974. On 8 June 1977 the conference finally adopted Geneva Protocol II.

In general, it is evident that the provisions of Geneva Protocol II are much fewer and far less restrictive than those of Geneva Protocol I. According to its terms, Geneva Protocol II develops and supplements common Article 3 of the 1949 Geneva Conventions without modifying its existing conditions of application; it applies to all armed conflicts which are not covered by Article 1 of 1977 Geneva Protocol I, and which take place within a state's territory between its armed forces and organized armed groups in sufficient control of part of the territory to enable such groups to carry out sustained and concerted military operations and to implement Protocol II. Like common Article 3 of the 1949 Geneva Conventions and Article 19 of the 1954 Hague Cultural Property Convention, Protocol II does not apply to situations of internal disturbances and tensions, such as riots, isolated and sporadic acts of violence and other acts of a similar nature (which are not deemed to be 'armed conflicts'). At lower levels of violence, the distinction between 'armed conflicts' and internal disturbances may not be free from difficulty, and yet it is also open to abuse. In the past, governments have often denied the application of common Article 3 of the 1949 Geneva Conventions, and this may raise questions regarding the extent to which 1977 Geneva Protocol II will be applied in practice.

Date of signature:	Signed on 12 December 1977, and open for signature (see Article 20) for twelve months thereafter.
Entry into force:	7 December 1978
Depositary:	Switzerland
Authentic languages:	Arabic, Chinese, English, French, Russian, and Spanish

Text reprinted from: International Committee of the Red Cross, *Protocols Additional to the Geneva Conventions of 12 August 1949*, Geneva, 1977, pp. 89–101.
Also published in: *UK Misc*. 19 (1977), Cmnd. 6927 (Eng.);
XVI *UKPP* (1976–1977) 471 (Eng.)

Protocol Additional to the Geneva Conventions of 12 August 1949, and Relating to the Protection of Victims of Non-International Armed Conflicts (Protocol II)

PREAMBLE

The High Contracting Parties,

Recalling that the humanitarian principles enshrined in Article 3 common to the Geneva Conventions of 12 August 1949, constitute the foundation of respect for the human person in cases of armed conflict not of an international character,

Recalling furthermore that international instruments relating to human rights offer a basic protection to the human person,

Emphasizing the need to ensure a better protection for the victims of those armed conflicts,

Recalling that, in cases not covered by the law in force, the human person remains under the protection of the principles of humanity and the dictates of the public conscience,

Have agreed on the following:

PART I – SCOPE OF THIS PROTOCOL

Article 1 – Material field of application

1. This Protocol, which develops and supplements Article 3 common to the Geneva Conventions of 12 August 1949 without modifying its existing conditions of application, shall apply to all armed conflicts which are not covered by Article 1 of the Protocol Additional to the Geneva Conventions of 12 August 1949, and relating to the Protection of Victims of International Armed Conflicts (Protocol I) and which take place in the territory of a High Contracting Party between its armed forces and dissident armed forces or other organized armed groups which, under responsible command, exercise such control over a part of its territory as to

enable them to carry out sustained and concerted military operations and to implement this Protocol.

2. This Protocol shall not apply to situations of internal disturbances and tensions, such as riots, isolated and sporadic acts of violence and other acts of a similar nature, as not being armed conflicts.

Article 2 — *Personal field of application*

1. This Protocol shall be applied without any adverse distinction founded on race, colour, sex, language, religion or belief, political or other opinion, national or social origin, wealth, birth or other status, or on any other similar criteria (hereinafter referred to as 'adverse distinction') to all persons affected by an armed conflict as defined in Article 1.

2. At the end of the armed conflict, all the persons who have been deprived of their liberty or whose liberty has been restricted for reasons related to such conflict, as well as those deprived of their liberty or whose liberty is restricted after the conflict for the same reasons, shall enjoy the protection of Articles 5 and 6 until the end of such deprivation or restriction of liberty.

Article 3 — *Non-intervention*

1. Nothing in this Protocol shall be invoked for the purpose of affecting the sovereignty of a State or the responsibility of the government, by all legitimate means, to maintain or re-establish law and order in the State or to defend the national unity and territorial integrity of the State.

2. Nothing in this Protocol shall be invoked as a justification for intervening, directly or indirectly, for any reason whatever, in the armed conflict or in the internal or external affairs of the High Contracting Party in the territory of which that conflict occurs.

PART II — HUMANE TREATMENT

Article 4 — *Fundamental guarantees*

1. All persons who do not take a direct part or who have ceased to take part in hostilities, whether or not their liberty has been restricted, are entitled to respect for their person, honour and convictions and religious practices. They shall in all circumstances be treated humanely, without any adverse distinction. It is prohibited to order that there shall be no survivors.

2. Without prejudice to the generality of the foregoing, the following acts against the persons referred to in paragraph 1 are and shall remain prohibited at any time and in any place whatsoever:

(a) violence to the life, health and physical or mental well-being of persons, in particular murder as well as cruel treatment such as torture, mutilation or any form of corporal punishment;
(b) collective punishments;
(c) taking of hostages;
(d) acts of terrorism;
(e) outrages upon personal dignity, in particular humiliating and degrading treatment, rape, enforced prostitution and any form of indecent assault;
(f) slavery and the slave trade in all their forms;
(g) pillage;
(h) threats to commit any of the foregoing acts.

3. Children shall be provided with the care and aid they require, and in particular:

(a) they shall receive an education, including religious and moral education, in keeping with the wishes of their parents, or in the absence of parents, of those responsible for their care;
(b) all appropriate steps shall be taken to facilitate the re-union of families temporarily separated;
(c) children who have not attained the age of fifteen years shall neither be recruited in the armed forces or groups nor allowed to take part in hostilities;
(d) the special protection provided by this Article to children who have not attained the age of fifteen years shall remain applicable to them if they take a direct part in hostilities despite the provisions of sub-paragraph (c) and are captured;
(e) measures shall be taken, if necessary, and whenever possible with the consent of their parents or persons who by law or custom are primarily responsible for their care, to remove children temporarily from the area in which hostilities are taking place to a safer area within the country and ensure that they are accompanied by persons responsible for their safety and well-being.

Article 5 — Persons whose liberty has been restricted

1. In addition to the provisions of Article 4, the following provisions shall be respected as a minimum with regard to persons deprived of their liberty for reasons related to the armed conflict, whether they are interned or detained:

(a) the wounded and the sick shall be treated in accordance with Article 7;

(b) the persons referred to in this paragraph shall, to the same extent as the local civilian population, be provided with food and drinking water and be afforded safeguards as regards health and hygiene and protection against the rigours of the climate and the dangers of the armed conflict;

(c) they shall be allowed to receive individual or collective relief;

(d) they shall be allowed to practise their religion and, if requested and appropriate, to receive spiritual assistance from persons, such as chaplains, performing religious functions;

(e) they shall, if made to work, have the benefit of working conditions and safeguards similar to those enjoyed by the local civilian population.

2. Those who are responsible for the internment or detention of the persons referred to in paragraph 1 shall also, within the limits of their capabilities, respect the following provisions relating to such persons:

(a) except when men and women of a family are accommodated together, women shall be held in quarters separated from those of men and shall be under the immediate supervision of women;

(b) they shall be allowed to send and receive letters and cards, the number of which may be limited by competent authority if it deems necessary;

(c) places of internment and detention shall not be located close to the combat zone. The persons referred to in paragraph 1 shall be evacuated when the places where they are interned or detained become particularly exposed to danger arising out of the armed conflict, if their evacuation can be carried out under adequate conditions of safety;

(d) they shall have the benefit of medical examinations;

(e) their physical or mental health and integrity shall not be endangered by any unjustified act or omission. Accordingly, it is prohibited to subject the persons described in this Article to any medical procedure which is not indicated by the state of health of the person concerned, and which is not consistent with the generally accepted medical standards applied to free persons under similar medical circumstances.

3. Persons who are not covered by paragraph 1 but whose liberty

has been restricted in any way whatsoever for reasons related to the armed conflict shall be treated humanely in accordance with Article 4 and with paragraphs 1(*a*), (*c*) and (*d*), and 2(*b*) of this Article.

4. If it is decided to release persons deprived of their liberty, necessary measures to ensure their safety shall be taken by those so deciding.

Article 6 — *Penal prosecutions*

1. This Article applies to the prosecution and punishment of criminal offences related to the armed conflict.

2. No sentence shall be passed and no penalty shall be executed on a person found guilty of an offence except pursuant to a conviction pronounced by a court offering the essential guarantees of independence and impartiality. In particular:

    (*a*) the procedure shall provide for an accused to be informed without delay of the particulars of the offence alleged against him and shall afford the accused before and during his trial all necessary rights and means of defence;

    (*b*) no one shall be convicted of an offence except on the basis of individual penal responsibility;

    (*c*) no one shall be held guilty of any criminal offence on account of any act or omission which did not constitute a criminal offence, under the law, at the time when it was committed; nor shall a heavier penalty be imposed than that which was applicable at the time when the criminal offence was committed; if, after the commission of the offence, provision is made by law for the imposition of a lighter penalty, the offender shall benefit thereby;

    (*d*) anyone charged with an offence is presumed innocent until proved guilty according to law;

    (*e*) anyone charged with an offence shall have the right to be tried in his presence;

    (*f*) no one shall be compelled to testify against himself or to confess guilt.

3. A convicted person shall be advised on conviction of his judicial and other remedies and of the time-limits within which they may be exercised.

4. The death penalty shall not be pronounced on persons who were under the age of eighteen years at the time of the offence and shall not be carried out on pregnant women or mothers of young children.

5. At the end of hostilities, the authorities in power shall

endeavour to grant the broadest possible amnesty to persons who have participated in the armed conflict, or those deprived of their liberty for reasons related to the armed conflict, whether they are interned or detained.

PART III – WOUNDED, SICK AND SHIPWRECKED

Article 7 – Protection and care

1. All the wounded, sick and shipwrecked, whether or not they have taken part in the armed conflict, shall be respected and protected.

2. In all circumstances they shall be treated humanely and shall receive, to the fullest extent practicable and with the least possible delay, the medical care and attention required by their condition. There shall be no distinction among them founded on any grounds other than medical ones.

Article 8 – Search

Whenever circumstances permit, and particularly after an engagement, all possible measure shall be taken, without delay, to search for and collect the wounded, sick and shipwrecked, to protect them against pillage and ill-treatment, to ensure their adequate care, and to search for the dead, prevent their being despoiled, and decently dispose of them.

Article 9 – Protection of medical and religious personnel

1. Medical and religious personnel shall be respected and protected and shall be granted all available help for the performance of their duties. They shall not be compelled to carry out tasks which are not compatible with their humanitarian mission.

2. In the performance of their duties medical personnel may not be required to give priority to any person except on medical grounds.

Article 10 – General protection of medical duties

1. Under no circumstances shall any person be punished for having carried out medical activities compatible with medical ethics, regardless of the person benefiting therefrom.

2. Persons engaged in medical activities shall neither be compelled to perform acts or to carry out work contrary to, nor be compelled to refrain from acts required by, the rules of medical ethics or other rules designed for the benefit of the wounded and sick, or this Protocol.

3. The professional obligations of persons engaged in medical

activities regarding information which they may acquire concerning the wounded and sick under their care shall, subject to national law, be respected.

4. Subject to national law, no person engaged in medical activities may be penalized in any way for refusing or failing to give information concerning the wounded and sick who are, or who have been, under his care.

Article 11 — *Protection of medical units and transports*

1. Medical units and transports shall be respected and protected at all times and shall not be the object of attack.

2. The protection to which medical units and transports are entitled shall not cease unless they are used to commit hostile acts, outside their humanitarian function. Protection may, however, cease only after a warning has been given setting, whenever appropriate, a reasonable time-limit, and after such warning has remained unheeded.

Article 12 — *The distinctive emblem*

Under the direction of the competent authority concerned, the distinctive emblem of the red cross, red crescent or red lion and sun on a white ground shall be displayed by medical and religious personnel and medical units, and on medical transports. It shall be respected in all circumstances. It shall not be used improperly.

PART IV — CIVILIAN POPULATION

Article 13 — *Protection of the civilian population*

1. The civilian population and individual civilians shall enjoy general protection against the dangers arising from military operations. To give effect to this protection, the following rules shall be observed in all circumstances.

2. The civilian population as such, as well as individual civilians, shall not be the object of attack. Acts or threats of violence the primary purpose of which is to spread terror among the civilian population are prohibited.

3. Civilians shall enjoy the protection afforded by this Part, unless and for such time as they take a direct part in hostilities.

Article 14 — *Protection of objects indispensable to the survival*
of the civilian population

Starvation of civilians as a method of combat is prohibited. It is therefore prohibited to attack, destroy, remove or render useless, for that purpose, objects indispensable to the survival of the civilian population, such as foodstuffs, agricultural areas for the production of foodstuffs, crops, livestock, drinking water installations and supplies and irrigation works.

Article 15 — *Protection of works and installations containing dangerous forces*

Works or installations containing dangerous forces, namely dams, dykes and nuclear electrical generating stations, shall not be made the object of attack, even where these objects are military objectives, if such attack may cause the release of dangerous forces and consequent severe losses among the civilian population.

Article 16 — *Protection of cultural objects and of places of worship*

Without prejudice to the provisions of the Hague Convention for the Protection of Cultural Property in the Event of Armed Conflict of 14 May 1954, it is prohibited to commit any acts of hostility directed against historic monuments, works of art or places of worship which constitute the cultural or spiritual heritage of peoples, and to use them in support of the military effort.

Article 17 — *Prohibition of forced movement of civilians*

1. The displacement of the civilian population shall not be ordered for reasons related to the conflict unless the security of the civilians involved or imperative military reasons so demand. Should such displacements have to be carried out, all possible measures shall be taken in order that the civilian population may be received under satisfactory conditions of shelter, hygiene, health, safety and nutrition.

2. Civilians shall not be compelled to leave their own territory for reasons connected with the conflict.

Article 18 — *Relief societies and relief actions*

1. Relief societies located in the territory of the High Contracting Party, such as Red Cross (Red Crescent, Red Lion and Sun) organizations, may offer their services for the performance of their traditional functions in relation to the victims of the armed conflict. The civilian population may, even on its own initiative, offer to collect and care for the wounded, sick and shipwrecked.

2. If the civilian population is suffering undue hardship owing to a lack of the supplies essential for its survival, such as foodstuffs and medical supplies, relief actions for the civilian population which are of an exclusively humanitarian and impartial nature and which are conducted without any adverse distinction shall be undertaken subject to the consent of the High Contracting Party concerned.

PART V — FINAL PROVISIONS

Article 19 — *Dissemination*
This Protocol shall be disseminated as widely as possible.

Article 20 — *Signature*
This Protocol shall be open for signature by the Parties to the Conventions six months after the signing of the Final Act and will remain open for a period of twelve months.

Article 21 — *Ratification*
This Protocol shall be ratified as soon as possible. The instruments of ratification shall be deposited with the Swiss Federal Council, depositary of the Conventions.

Article 22 — *Accession*
This Protocol shall be open for accession by any Party to the Conventions which has not signed it. The instruments of accession shall be deposited with the depositary.

Article 23 — *Entry into force*
1. This Protocol shall enter into force six months after two instruments of ratification or accession have been deposited.
2. For each Party to the Conventions thereafter ratifying or acceding to this Protocol, it shall enter into force six months after the deposit by such Party of its instrument of ratification or accession.

Article 24 — *Amendment*
1. Any High Contracting Party may propose amendments to this Protocol. The text of any proposed amendment shall be communicated to the depositary which shall decide, after consultation with all the High Contracting Parties and the International Committee of the Red Cross, whether a conference should be convened to consider the proposed amendment.
2. The depositary shall invite to that conference all the High Contracting Parties as well as the Parties to the Conventions, whether or not they are signatories of this Protocol.

Article 25 — *Denunciation*
1. In case a High Contracting Party should denounce this Protocol, the denunciation shall only take effect six months after receipt of the instrument of denunciation. If, however, on the expiry of six months, the denouncing Party is engaged in the situation referred to in Article 1, the denunciation shall not take effect before the end of the armed conflict. Persons who have been deprived of liberty,

or whose liberty has been restricted, for reasons related to the conflict shall nevertheless continue to benefit from the provisions of this Protocol until their final release.

2.   The denunciation shall be notified in writing to the depositary, which shall transmit it to all the High Contracting Parties.

Article 26 — *Notifications*

The depositary shall inform the High Contracting Parties as well as the Parties to the Conventions, whether or not they are signatories of this Protocol, of:

(*a*) signatures affixed to this Protocol and the deposit of instruments of ratification and accession under Articles 21 and 22;

(*b*) the date of entry into force of this Protocol under Article 23; and

(*c*) communications and declarations received under Article 24.

Article 27 — *Registration*

1.   After its entry into force, this Protocol shall be transmitted by the depositary to the Secretariat of the United Nations for registration and publication, in accordance with Article 102 of the Charter of the United Nations.

2.   The depositary shall also inform the Secretariat of the United Nations of all ratifications and accessions received by it with respect to this Protocol.

Article 28 — *Authentic texts*

The original of this Protocol, of which the Arabic, Chinese, English, French, Russian and Spanish texts are equally authentic shall be deposited with the depositary, which shall transmit certified true copies thereof to all the Parties to the Conventions.

[Annexes omitted]

CONCLUDING NOTES
relating to the 1977 Geneva Protocols I and II

Except where otherwise stated, all entries in this list apply *both* to the 1977 Geneva Protocol I *and* to the 1977 Geneva Protocol II.

Signatures, Ratifications and Accessions[1]

State (* denotes Reservation etc.: see below)	Date of Signature	Date of Ratification (*r*), or Accession (*a*)[2]
*Australia	7 December 1978	—
Austria	12 December 1977	—
Bahamas		10 April 1980 *a*
Bangladesh		8 September 1980 *a*
Belgium	12 December 1977	—
Botswana		23 May 1979 *a*
Bulgaria	11 December 1978	—
Byelorussian SSR	12 December 1977	—
*Canada	12 December 1977	—
Chile	12 December 1977	—
Cyprus (Prot. I)	12 July 1978	1 June 1979 *r*
Czechoslovakia	6 December 1978	—
Denmark	12 December 1977	—
Ecuador	12 December 1977	10 April 1979 *r*
Egypt	12 December 1977	—
El Salvador	12 December 1977	23 November 1978 *r*
*Finland	12 December 1977	7 August 1980 *r*
Gabon		8 April 1980 *a*
German Democratic Republic	12 December 1977	
*Germany, Federal Republic of	23 December 1977	—
Ghana	12 December 1977	28 February 1978 *r*
*Greece (Prot. I)	22 March 1978	
Guatemala	12 December 1977	—
Holy See	12 December 1977	—
Honduras	12 December 1977	—
Hungary	12 December 1977	—
Iceland	12 December 1977	—
Iran	12 December 1977	—
Ireland	12 December 1977	—
*Italy	12 December 1977	—
Ivory Coast	12 December 1977	—
Jordan	12 December 1977	1 May 1979 *r*
Korea, Republic of (South)	7 December 1978	—
Laos	18 April 1978	18 November 1980 *r*

[1] Information supplied in communications from the Swiss Federal Department for Foreign Affairs between January 1980 and March 1981.

[2] There have been no declarations of succession in respect of these two agreements.

State (* denotes Reservation etc.: see below)	Date of Signature		Date of Ratification (*r*), or Accession (*a*)		
Libya			7 June	1978	*a*
Liechtenstein	12 December	1977	—		
Luxembourg	12 December	1977	—		
Madagascar	13 October	1978	—		
Mauritania			14 March	1980	*a*
Mongolia	12 December	1977	—		
Morocco	12 December	1977	—		
Netherlands	12 December	1977	—		
New Zealand	27 November	1978	—		
Nicaragua	12 December	1977	—		
Niger	16 June	1978	8 June	1979	*r*
Norway	12 December	1977	—		
Pakistan	12 December	1977	—		
Panama	12 December	1977	—		
Peru	12 December	1977	—		
Philippines (Prot. I)	12 December	1977	—		
Poland	12 December	1977	—		
*Portugal	12 December	1977	—		
Romania	28 March	1978	—		
San Marino	22 June	1978	—		
Senegal	12 December	1977	—		
*Spain	7 November	1978	—		
*Sweden	12 December	1977	31 August	1979	*r*
*Switzerland	12 December	1977	—		
Togo	12 December	1977	—		
Tunisia	12 December	1977	9 August	1979	*r*
Ukrainian SSR	12 December	1977	—		
*United Kingdom	12 December	1977	—		
Upper Volta	11 January	1978	—		
*USA	12 December	1977	—		
USSR	12 December	1977	—		
Vietnam (Prot. I)	12 December	1977	—		
Yemen Arab Republic (North)	14 February	1978	—		
*Yugoslavia	12 December	1977	11 June	1979	*r*

Total Number of Parties Listed: 17 for Protocol I; 16 for Protocol II.

Note on Entry into Force for States Parties

In accordance with Articles 95 in Protocol I and 23 in Protocol II, each Protocol entered into force on 7 December 1978 for the two states which had ratified or acceded six months earlier. For each of the other ratifying and acceding states, the Protocols formally entered into force six months after the date indicated in the right-hand column above.

Denunciations

None

Reservations etc.

Australia, Canada, Federal Republic of Germany, Greece, Italy, Portugal, and *Spain* all, at signature, in separate statements of varying content, length, and degree of detail, indicated that they were reserving the right to make declarations and/or reservations upon ratification. Of these seven states, the first three indicated specifically that such declarations or reservations would be likely to relate to Protocol I; and the fourth state, Greece, signed only Protocol I.

Finland, at ratification, *re* Protocol I made the following reservation: 'With regard to Article 75, paragraph 4(i), Finland enters a reservation to the effect that under Finnish law a judgment can be declared secret if its publication could be an affront to morals or endanger national security.'

Also at ratification, Finland made the following declaration: 'With reference to Articles 75 and 85 of the Protocol, the Finnish Government declare their understanding that, under Article 72, the field of application of Article 75 shall be interpreted to include also the nationals of the Contracting Party applying the provisions of that Article, as well as the nationals of neutral or other States not Parties to the conflict, and that the provisions of Article 85 shall be interpreted to apply to nationals of neutral or other States not Parties to the conflict as they apply to those mentioned in paragraph 2 of that Article. With reference to Article 75, paragraph 4(h), of the Protocol, the Finnish Government wish to clarify that under Finnish law a judgment shall not be considered final until the time-limit for exercising any extra-ordinary legal remedies has expired.' In addition, *re* paragraph 2 of Article 90, Finland made an identical declaration to that made by Sweden *re* the same paragraph.

Sweden, at ratification, made the following declaration *re* Protocol I: '. . . subject to the reservation that Article 75, paragraph 4, sub-paragraph (*h*) shall be applied only to the extent that it is not in conflict with legal provisions which allow, in exceptional circumstances, the reopening of proceedings which have resulted in a final conviction or acquittal. I furthermore declare, pursuant to Article 90, paragraph 2 of the Protocol, that Sweden recognizes *ipso facto* and without special agreement, in relation to any other High Contracting Party accepting the same obligation, the competence of the International Fact-Finding Commission.'

Switzerland, at signature: '*Re* Article 57 Protocol I: The provisions of number 2 of this article do not create obligations except for commanding officers at batallion or unit level upwards and at higher echelons. *Re* Article 58 Protocol I: Bearing in mind that this article contains the words "to the maximum extent feasible", paragraphs (*a*) and (*b*) will be applied under reservation of the requirements of the defence of the national territory.'[3]

United Kingdom, at signature, declared that it had signed Protocol I on the basis of the following understandings:

'(*a*) in relation to Article 1, that the term "armed conflict" of itself and in its context implies a certain level of intensity of military operations which must be present before the Conventions or the Protocol are to apply to

---

[3] The Depositary does not have an English translation of the reservation made by Switzerland. The translation from the French original text is ours, and has been confirmed as accurate by the Depositary.

any given situation, and that this level of intensity cannot be less than that required for the application of Protocol II, by virtue of Article 1 of that Protocol, to internal conflicts;

(*b*) in relation to Articles 41, 57 and 58, that the word "feasible" means that which is practicable or practically possible, taking into account all circumstances at the time including those relevant to the success of military operations;

(*c*) in relation to Article 44, that the situation described in the second sentence of paragraph 3 of the Article can exist only in occupied territory or in armed conflicts covered by paragraph 4 of Article 1, and that the Government of the United Kingdom will interpret the word "deployment" in paragraph 3(*b*) of the Article as meaning "any movement towards a place from which an attack is to be launched";

(*d*) in relation to Articles 51 to 58 inclusive, that military commanders and others responsible for planning, deciding upon or executing attacks necessarily have to reach decisions on the basis of their assessment of the information from all sources which is available to them at the relevant time;

(*e*) in relation to paragraph 5(*b*) of Article 51 and paragraph (2) (*a*) (iii) of Article 57, that the military advantage anticipated from an attack is intended to refer to the advantage anticipated from the attack considered as a whole and not only from isolated or particular parts of the attack;

(*f*) in relation to Article 52, that a specific area of land may be a military objective if, because of its location or other reasons specified in the Article, its total or partial destruction, capture or neutralisation in the circumstances ruling at the time offers definite military advantage;

(*g*) in relation to Article 53, that if the objects protected by the Article are unlawfully used for military purposes they will thereby lose protection from attacks directed against such unlawful military uses;

(*h*) in relation to paragraph 3 of Article 96, that only a declaration made by an authority which genuinely fulfils the criteria of paragraph 4 of Article 1 can have the effects stated in paragraph 3 of Article 96, and that, in the light of the negotiating history, it is to be regarded as necessary also that the authority concerned be recognised as such by the appropriate regional inter-governmental organisation;

(*i*) that the new rules introduced by the Protocol are not intended to have any effect on and do not regulate or prohibit the use of nuclear weapons; and

(*j*) that the provisions of the Protocol shall not apply to Southern Rhodesia unless and until the Government of the United Kingdom inform the depositary that they are in a position to ensure that the obligations imposed by the Protocol in respect of that territory can be fully implemented.'

In addition, the UK declared that it had signed Protocol II on the same understanding as in (*j*) above.

USA, at signature, stated that its signature is subject to the following understandings:

'A) Protocol I. 1. It is the understanding of the United States of America that the rules established by this protocol were not intended to have any effect on and do not regulate or prohibit the use of nuclear weapons. 2. It is the understanding of the United States of America that the phrase "military deployment preceding the launching of an attack" in Article 44, Paragraph 3, means any movement towards a place from which an attack is to be launched.

B) Protocol II. It is the understanding of the United States of America that the terms used in Part III of this protocol which are the same as the terms defined in Article 8 of Protocol I shall so far as relevant be construed in the same sense as those definitions.'

Yugoslavia, at ratification, stated that the provisions of Protocol I relating to occupation 'shall be applied in keeping with Article 238 of the Constitution of the Socialist Federal Republic of Yugoslavia according to which no one shall have the right to acknowledge or sign an act of capitulation, nor to accept or recognize the occupation of the Socialist Federal Republic of Yugoslavia or any of its individual parts.'

28. 1978 Red Cross Fundamental Rules of International Humanitarian Law Applicable in Armed Conflicts

PREFATORY NOTE

Because the laws of war are numerous and complex, short informal summaries of their main principles and provisions play an important role. In October 1975, at a meeting in Geneva of the Council of Delegates of the National Red Cross Societies, it was proposed that a declaration should be drawn up, setting out in condensed and easily understandable form the fundamental rules of humanitarian law applicable in armed conflicts. This suggestion was based on a concern that the two Geneva Protocols (at that time in an advanced stage of negotiation) plus the four 1949 Geneva Conventions which they supplement, would result in a large body of law, many of the provisions of which were complex. In fact there is a total of over 550 articles in the four 1949 Conventions and the two 1977 Protocols.

The suggestion for such a declaration was supported by several national Red Cross delegations. A small working group of experts from the International Committee of the Red Cross, the League of Red Cross Societies, and national Red Cross Societies produced a draft of fundamental rules. This draft was discussed at the Round Table of the San Remo International Institute of Humanitarian Law in 1977. The text was first published, under the title 'Fundamental Rules of Humanitarian Law Applicable in Armed Conflicts', in *International Review of the Red Cross*, Geneva, September–October 1978. In 1979 the ICRC and the League of Red Cross Societies made it available as an offprint, with the word 'international' included in the title. It is reprinted here by kind permission of the ICRC and the League.

This text is based not only on the four 1949 Geneva Conventions and the two 1977 Geneva Protocols, but also on the 'law of the Hague' and on customary law. Wherever possible, the exact wording of existing international agreements has been used.

The informal character of this text should be emphasized. As the ICRC and the League clearly stated on publishing this document: 'This text does not possess the authority of an international legal instrument, nor is it in any way intended to take the place of existing treaties. Its only purpose is to facilitate the dissemination of knowledge of international humanitarian law.' The text has never been submitted to the International Conference of the Red Cross or to any other official body for approval, because the ICRC and the League did not want these seven rules to be considered as an official statement of the law, and thus as a substitute for the four 1949 Geneva Conventions and the two 1977 Geneva Protocols.

Informal and unofficial as this text is, it does express in a useful condensed form some of the most fundamental principles of international humanitarian law governing armed conflicts.

Text reprinted from: Fundamental Rules of International Humanitarian
                          Law Applicable in Armed Conflicts, ICRC and League
                          of Red Cross Societies, Geneva, 1979.
Also published in: *International Review of the Red Cross*, Geneva,
                          September–October 1978, pp. 248–9.

Fundamental Rules of International Humanitarian Law Applicable in Armed Conflicts

1. Persons *hors de combat* and those who do not take a direct part in hostilities are entitled to respect for their lives and physical and moral integrity. They shall in all circumstances be protected and treated humanely without any adverse distinction.

2. It is forbidden to kill or injure an enemy who surrenders or who is *hors de combat*.

3. The wounded and sick shall be collected and cared for by the party to the conflict which has them in its power. Protection also covers medical personnel, establishments, transports and *matériel*. The emblem of the red cross (red crescent, red lion and sun) is the sign of such protection and must be respected.

4. Captured combatants and civilians under the authority of an adverse party are entitled to respect for their lives, dignity, personal rights and convictions. They shall be protected against all acts of violence and reprisals. They shall have the right to correspond with their families and to receive relief.

5. Everyone shall be entitled to benefit from fundamental judicial guarantees. No one shall be held responsible for an act he has not committed. No one shall be subjected to physical or mental torture, corporal punishment or cruel or degrading treatment.

6. Parties to a conflict and members of their armed forces do not have an unlimited choice of methods and means of warfare. It is prohibited to employ weapons or methods of warfare of a nature to cause unnecessary losses or excessive suffering.

7. Parties to a conflict shall at all times distinguish between the civilian population and combatants in order to spare civilian population and property. Neither the civilian population as such nor civilian persons shall be the object of attack. Attacks shall be directed solely against military objectives.

29. 1981 United Nations Convention on Prohibitions or Restrictions on the Use of Certain Conventional Weapons Which May be Deemed to be Excessively Injurious or to Have Indiscriminate Effects

PREFATORY NOTE

When the Diplomatic Conference of the Reaffirmation and Development of International Humanitarian Law Applicable in Armed Conflicts was convened in Geneva in 1974 to consider two draft protocols to the four 1949 Geneva Conventions (eventually to emerge as 1977 Geneva Protocols I and II), it was expected that the question of the use of specific conventional weapons would also be addressed by the Conference. During all four sessions of the Conference, from 1974 to 1977, the issue of prohibitions or restrictions of the use of specific conventional weapons was discussed in the Conference's *Ad Hoc* Committee on Conventional Weapons. In addition, the issue of restricting the use of specific conventional weapons was the subject of substantive discussion at the ICRC Conference of Government Experts on the Use of Certain Conventional Weapons, which met in Lucerne in 1974 and in Lugano in 1976. At the conclusion of the Geneva Diplomatic Conference in 1977, the Conference's *Ad Hoc* Committee had not reached agreement on specific conventional weapons, and 1977 Geneva Protocol I only contains some provisions of a rather general character relating to such weapons. However, on 9 June 1977 the Geneva Conference adopted Resolution 22(IV) which recommended that a separate conference be convened not later than 1979 with a view to reaching agreements on prohibitions or restrictions of the use of specific conventional weapons.

On 19 December 1977 the UN General Assembly resolved that a UN conference on specific conventional weapons be convened in 1979. The preparatory sessions for such a conference were held in Geneva in August–September 1978 and March–April 1979, attended by representatives of eighty-five states. On 10 September 1979 the United Nations Conference on Prohibitions or Restrictions of Use of Certain Conventional Weapons Which May be Deemed to be Excessively Injurious or to Have Indiscriminate Effects was convened in Geneva and held its first session from 10–28 September 1979, attended by representatives of eighty-two states. The second session of the Conference was held from 15 September to 10 October 1980, attended by representatives of seventy-six states.

On 10 October 1980 agreement was reached on a convention and three annexed protocols: Protocol I relating to fragments not detectable by X-rays; Protocol II relating to mines, booby traps, and other devices; and Protocol III relating to incendiary weapons. No agreement was reached on small-calibre weapons, which was the fourth principal subject of deliberation at the Conference, but a resolution was adopted on the subject. In addition, no agreement was reached on the use of incendiary weapons against combatants, or on the use of many other types of weapon, including fuel-air explosives and fragments other than those addressed by Protocol I (such as metallic fléchettes discharged at high velocity from rockets or canister shell). Some delegations expressed the hope that a review conference would address these points.

The Convention and its Protocols were sent to the UN General Assembly, and on 12 December 1980 the General Assembly adopted a resolution commending them to all states 'with a view to achieving the widest possible adherence to these instruments'. As the General Assembly resolution noted, there is provision in Article 8 for the review of the Convention at subsequent conferences during which amendments may be agreed upon, and additional protocols may be adopted to be annexed to the Convention.

The Convention is derived from two fundamental customary principles of the laws of war: the right of belligerents to adopt means of warfare is not unlimited; and the use of weapons, projectiles or material calculated to cause unnecessary suffering is prohibited. Both customary principles had been codified in Articles 22 and 23(e) of the Regulations annexed to 1899 Hague Convention II and 1907 Hague Convention IV. These customary principles had also been applied to particular weapons in such international agreements as the 1868 St. Petersburg Declaration, the three 1899 Hague Declarations, the 1907 Hague Declaration, some of the 1907 Hague Conventions, and the 1925 Geneva Protocol.

The 1981 UN Weapons Convention differs from previous agreements on specific conventional weapons in that the Protocols as a whole primarily afford protection to civilians. Although the attempt was made during the 1979–80 Conference to formulate limitations on specific conventional weapons which would apply to combatants as well as non-combatants, such efforts were largely unsuccessful. Protocol I does completely prohibit the use of certain weapons, but major military powers declined to consider such a comprehensive prohibition in respect of the other two Protocols. Protocols II and III only prohibit the use of certain weapons against civilians, and their use in some other contexts, but do not absolutely proscribe their use against military objectives.

Date of signature:	Signed on 10 April 1981, and open for signature (see Article 3) for twelve months from that date.
Entry into force:	
Depositary:	United Nations
Authentic languages:	Arabic, Chinese, English, French, Russian, and Spanish
Text reprinted from:	United Nations General Assembly document A/CONF. 95/15 dated 27 October 1980.
Also published in:	*UK Misc.* 23 (1981), Cmnd. 8370 (Eng.)

Convention on Prohibitions or Restrictions on the Use of Certain Conventional Weapons Which May be Deemed to be Excessively Injurious or to Have Indiscriminate Effects

The High Contracting Parties,

Recalling that every State has the duty, in conformity with the Charter of the United Nations, to refrain in its international relations from the threat or use of force against the sovereignty, territorial integrity or political independence of any State, or in any other manner inconsistent with the purposes of the United Nations,

Further recalling the general principle of the protection of the civilian population against the effects of hostilities,

Basing themselves on the principle of international law that the right of the parties to an armed conflict to choose methods or means of warfare is not unlimited, and on the principle that prohibits the employment in armed conflicts of weapons, projectiles and material and methods of warfare of a nature to cause superfluous injury or unnecessary suffering,

Also recalling that it is prohibited to employ methods or means of warfare which are intended, or may be expected, to cause widespread, long-term and severe damage to the natural environment,

Confirming their determination that in cases not covered by this Convention and its annexed Protocols or by other international agreements, the civilian population and the combatants shall at all times remain under the protection and authority of the principles of international law derived from established custom, from the principles of humanity and from the dictates of public conscience,

Desiring to contribute to international détente, the ending of the arms race and the building of confidence among States, and hence to the realization of the aspiration of all peoples to live in peace,

Recognizing the importance of pursuing every effort which may contribute to progress towards general and complete disarmament under strict and effective international control,

Reaffirming the need to continue the codification and progressive development of the rules of international law applicable in armed conflict,

Wishing to prohibit or restrict further the use of certain conventional weapons and believing that the positive results achieved in this area may facilitate the main talks on disarmament with a view to putting an end to the production, stockpiling and proliferation of such weapons,

Emphasizing the desirability that all States become parties to this Convention and its annexed Protocols, especially the military significant States,

Bearing in mind that the General Assembly of the United Nations and the United Nations Disarmament Commission may decide to examine the question of a possible broadening of the scope of the prohibitions and restrictions contained in this Convention and its annexed Protocols,

Further bearing in mind that the Committee on Disarmament may decide to consider the question of adopting further measures to prohibit or restrict the use of certain conventional weapons,

Have agreed as follows:

Article 1 — Scope of application

This Convention and its annexed Protocols shall apply in the situations referred to in Article 2 common to the Geneva Coventions of 12 August 1949 for the Protection of War Victims, including any situation described in paragraph 4 of Article 1 of Additional Protocol I to these Conventions.

Article 2 — Relations with other international agreements

Nothing in this Convention or its annexed Protocols shall be interpreted as detracting from other obligations imposed upon the High Contracting Parties by international humanitarian law applicable in armed conflict.

Article 3 — Signature

This Convention shall be open for signature by all States at United Nations Headquarters in New York for a period of twelve months from 10 April 1981.

Article 4 — Ratification, acceptance, approval or accession

1. This Convention is subject to ratification, acceptance or approval by the Signatories. Any State which has not signed this Convention may accede to it.

2. The instruments of ratification, acceptance, approval or accession shall be deposited with the Depositary.

3. Expressions of consent to be bound by any of the Protocols annexed to this Convention shall be optional for each State, provided that at the time of the deposit of its instrument of ratification, acceptance or approval of this Convention or of accession thereto, that State shall notify the Depositary of its consent to be bound by any two or more of these Protocols.

4. At any time after the deposit of its instrument of ratification, acceptance or approval of this Convention or of accession thereto,

a State may notify the Depositary of its consent to be bound by any annexed Protocol by which it is not already bound.

5. Any Protocol by which a High Contracting Party is bound shall for that Party form an integral part of this Convention.

Article 5 — Entry into force

1. This Convention shall enter into force six months after the date of deposit of the twentieth instrument of ratification, acceptance, approval or accession.

2. For any State which deposits its instrument of ratification, acceptance, approval or accession after the date of the deposit of the twentieth instrument of ratification, acceptance, approval or accession, this Convention shall enter into force six months after the date on which that State has deposited its instrument of ratification, acceptance, approval or accession.

3. Each of the Protocols annexed to this Convention shall enter into force six months after the date by which twenty States have notified their consent to be bound by it in accordance with paragraph 3 or 4 of Article 4 of this Convention.

4. For any State which notifies its consent to be bound by a Protocol annexed to this Convention after the date by which twenty States have notified their consent to be bound by it, the Protocol shall enter into force six months after the date on which that State has notified its consent so to be bound.

Article 6 — Dissemination

The High Contracting Parties undertake, in time of peace as in time of armed conflict, to disseminate this Convention and those of its annexed Protocols by which they are bound as widely as possible in their respective countries and, in particular, to include the study thereof in their programmes of military instruction, so that those instruments may become known to their armed forces.

Article 7 — Treaty relations upon entry into force of this Convention

1. When one of the parties to a conflict is not bound by an annexed Protocol, the parties bound by this Convention and that annexed Protocol shall remain bound by them in their mutual relations.

2. Any High Contracting Party shall be bound by this Convention and any Protocol annexed thereto which is in force for it, in any situation contemplated by Article 1, in relation to any State which is not a party to this Convention or bound by the relevant annexed Protocol, if the latter accepts and applies this Convention or the relevant Protocol, and so notifies the Depositary.

3. The Depositary shall immediately inform the High Contracting Parties concerned of any notification received under paragraph 2 of this Article.

4. This Convention, and the annexed Protocols by which a High Contracting Party is bound, shall apply with respect to an armed conflict against that High Contracting Party of the type referred to in Article 1, paragraph 4, of Additional Protocol I to the Geneva Conventions of 12 August 1949 for the Protection of War Victims:

> (*a*) where the High Contracting Party is also a party to Additional Protocol I and an authority referred to in Article 96, paragraph 3, of that Protocol has undertaken to apply the Geneva Conventions and Additional Protocol I in accordance with Article 96, paragraph 3, of the said Protocol, and undertakes to apply this Convention and the relevant annexed Protocols in relation to that conflict; or

> (*b*) where the High Contracting Party is not a party to Additional Protocol I and an authority of the type referred to in subparagraph (*a*) above accepts and applies the obligations of the Geneva Conventions and of this Convention and the relevant annexed Protocols in relation to that conflict. Such an acceptance and application shall have in relation to that conflict the following effects:
>
> > (i) the Geneva Conventions and this Convention and its relevant annexed Protocols are brought into force for the parties to the conflict with immediate effect;
> >
> > (ii) the said authority assumes the same rights and obligations as those which have been assumed by a High Contracting Party to the Geneva Conventions, this Convention and its relevant annexed Protocols; and
> >
> > (iii) the Geneva Conventions, this Convention and its relevant annexed Protocols are equally binding upon all parties to the conflict.

The High Contracting Party and the authority may also agree to accept and apply the obligations of Additional Protocol I to the Geneva Conventions on a reciprocal basis.

Article 8 — Review and amendments

> 1. (*a*) At any time after the entry into force of this Convention any High Contracting Party may propose amendments to this Convention or any annexed Protocol by which it is bound. Any proposal for an amendment shall be communicated to the Depositary, who shall notify it to all the High

Contracting Parties and shall seek their views on whether a conference should be convened to consider the proposal. If a majority, that shall not be less than eighteen of the High Contracting Parties so agree, he shall promptly convene a conference to which all High Contracting Parties shall be invited. States not parties to this Convention shall be invited to the conference as observers.

(b) Such a conference may agree upon amendments which shall be adopted and shall enter into force in the same manner as this Convention and the annexed Protocols, provided that amendments to this Convention may be adopted only by the High Contracting Parties and that amendments to a specific annexed Protocol may be adopted only by the High Contracting Parties which are bound by that Protocol.

2. (a) At any time after the entry into force of this Convention any High Contracting Party may propose additional protocols relating to other categories of conventional weapons not covered by the existing annexed Protocols. Any such proposal for an additional protocol shall be communicated to the Depositary, who shall notify it to all the High Contracting Parties in accordance with subparagraph 1 (a) of this Article. If a majority, that shall not be less than eighteen of the High Contracting Parties so agree, the Depositary shall promptly convene a conference to which all States shall be invited.

(b) Such a conference may agree, with the full participation of all States represented at the conference, upon additional protocols which shall be adopted in the same manner as this Convention, shall be annexed thereto and shall enter into force as provided in paragraphs 3 and 4 of Article 5 of this Convention.

3. (a) If, after a period of ten years following the entry into force of this Convention, no conference has been convened in accordance with subparagraph 1 (a) or 2 (a) of this Article, any High Contracting Party may request the Depositary to convene a conference to which all High Contracting Parties shall be invited to review the scope and operation of this Convention and the Protocols annexed thereto and to consider any proposal for amendments of this Convention or of the existing Protocols. States not parties to this Convention shall be invited as observers to the conference. The conference may agree upon amend-

ments which shall be adopted and enter into force in accordance with subparagraph 1 (*b*) above.

(*b*) At such conference consideration may also be given to any proposal for additional protocols relating to other categories of conventional weapons not covered by the existing annexed Protocols. All States represented at the conference may participate fully in such consideration. Any additional protocols shall be adopted in the same manner as this Convention, shall be annexed thereto and shall enter into force as provided in paragraphs 3 and 4 of Article 5 of this Convention.

(*c*) Such a conference may consider whether provision should be made for the convening of a further conference at the request of any High Contracting Party if, after a similar period to that referred to in subparagraph 3 (*a*) of this Article, no conference has been convened in accordance with subparagraph 1 (*a*) or 2 (*a*) of this Article.

Article 9 — Denunciation

1. Any High Contracting Party may denounce this Convention or any of its annexed Protocols by so notifying the Depositary.

2. Any such denunciation shall only take effect one year after receipt by the Depositary of the notification of denunciation. If, however, on the expiry of that year the denouncing High Contracting Party is engaged in one of the situations referred to in Article 1, the Party shall continue to be bound by the obligations of this Convention and of the relevant annexed Protocols until the end of the armed conflict or occupation and, in any case, until the termination of operations connected with the final release, repatriation or re-establishment of the persons protected by the rules of international law applicable in armed conflict, and in the case of any annexed Protocol containing provisions concerning situations in which peace-keeping, observation or similar functions are performed by United Nations forces or missions in the area concerned, until the termination of those functions.

3. Any denunciation of this Convention shall be considered as also applying to all annexed Protocols by which the denouncing High Contracting Party is bound.

4. Any denunciation shall have effect only in respect of the denouncing High Contracting Party.

5. Any denunciation shall not affect the obligations already incurred, by reason of an armed conflict, under this Convention and its annexed Protocols by such denouncing High Contracting

Party in respect of any act committed before this denunciation becomes effective.

Article 10 — *Depositary*
1. The Secretary-General of the United Nations shall be the Depositary of this Convention and of its annexed Protocols.
2. In addition to his usual functions, the Depositary shall inform all States of:
  (*a*) signatures affixed to this Convention under Article 3;
  (*b*) deposits of instruments of ratification, acceptance or approval of or accession to this Convention deposited under Article 4;
  (*c*) notifications of consent to be bound by annexed Protocols under Article 4;
  (*d*) the dates of entry into force of this Convention and of each of its annexed Protocols under Article 5; and
  (*e*) notifications of denunciation received under Article 9, and their effective date.

Article 11 — *Authentic texts*
The original of this Convention with the annexed Protocols, of which the Arabic, Chinese, English, French, Russian and Spanish texts are equally authentic, shall be deposited with the Depositary, who shall transmit certified true copies thereof to all States.

* * *

Protocol on Non-Detectable Fragments (Protocol I)

It is prohibited to use any weapon the primary effect of which is to injure by fragments which in the human body escape detection by X-rays.

* * *

Protocol on Prohibitions or Restrictions on the Use of Mines, Booby Traps and Other Devices (Protocol II)

Article 1 — *Material scope of application*
This Protocol relates to the use on land of the mines, booby-traps and other devices defined herein, including mines laid to interdict

beaches, waterway crossings or river crossings, but does not apply to the use of anti-ship mines at sea or in inland waterways.

Article 2 — Definitions

For the purpose of this Protocol:

1. 'Mine' means any munition placed under, on or near the ground or other surface area and designed to be detonated or exploded by the presence, proximity or contact of a person or vehicle, and 'remotely delivered mine' means any mine so defined delivered by artillery, rocket, mortar or similar means or dropped from an aircraft.

2. 'Booby-trap' means any device or material which is designed, constructed or adapted to kill or injure and which functions unexpectedly when a person disturbs or approaches an apparently harmless object or performs an apparently safe act.

3. 'Other devices' means manually-emplaced munitions and devices designed to kill, injure or damage and which are actuated by remote control or automatically after a lapse of time.

4. 'Military objective' means, so far as objects are concerned, any object which by its nature, location, purpose or use makes an effective contribution to military action and whose total or partial destruction, capture or neutralization, in the circumstances ruling at the time, offers a definite military advantage.

5. 'Civilian objects' are all objects which are not military objectives as defined in paragraph 4.

6. 'Recording' means a physical, administrative and technical operation designed to obtain, for the purpose of registration in the official records, all available information facilitating the location of minefields, mines and booby-traps.

Article 3 — General restrictions of the use of mines, booby-traps and other devices

1. This Article applies to:
   (a) mines;
   (b) booby-traps; and
   (c) other devices.

2. It is prohibited in all circumstances to direct weapons to which this Article applies, either in offence, defence or by way of reprisals, against the civilian population as such or against individual civilians.

3. The indiscriminate use of weapons to which this Article applies is prohibited. Indiscriminate use is any placement of such weapons:
   (a) which is not on, or directed at, a military objective; or

(*b*) which employs a method or means of delivery which cannot be directed at a specific military objective; or
(*c*) which may be expected to cause incidental loss of civilian life, injury to civilians, damage to civilian objects, or a combination thereof, which would be excessive in relation to the concrete and direct military advantage anticipated.

4. All feasible precautions shall be taken to protect civilians from the effects of weapons to which this Article applies. Feasible precautions are those precautions which are practicable or practically possible taking into account all circumstances ruling at the time, including humanitarian and military considerations.

Article 4 — Restrictions on the use of mines other than remotely delivered mines, booby-traps and other devices in populated areas

1. This Article applies to:
(*a*) mines other than remotely delivered mines;
(*b*) booby-traps; and
(*c*) other devices.

2. It is prohibited to use weapons to which this Article applies in any city, town, village or other area containing a similar concentration of civilians in which combat between ground forces is not taking place or does not appear to be imminent, unless either:
(*a*) they are placed on or in the close vicinity of a military objective belonging to or under the control of an adverse party; or
(*b*) measures are taken to protect civilians from their effects, for example, the posting of warning signs, the posting of sentries, the issue of warnings or the provision of fences.

Article 5 — Restrictions on the use of remotely delivered mines

1. The use of remotely delivered mines is prohibited unless such mines are only used within an area which is itself a military objective or which contains military objectives, and unless:
(*a*) their location can be accurately recorded in accordance with Article 7(1)(*à*); or
(*b*) an effective neutralizing mechanism is used on each such mine, that is to say, a self-actuating mechanism which is designed to render a mine harmless or cause it to destroy itself when it is anticipated that the mine will no longer serve the military purpose for which it was placed in position, or a remotely-controlled mechanism which is designed to render harmless or destroy a mine when the

mine no longer serves the military purpose for which it was placed in position.

2.   Effective advance warning shall be given of any delivery or dropping of remotely delivered mines which may affect the civilian population, unless circumstances do not permit.

Article 6 — *Prohibition on the use of certain booby-traps*

1.   Without prejudice to the rules of international law applicable in armed conflict relating to treachery and perfidy, it is prohibited in all circumstances to use:

(*a*)   any booby-trap in the form of an apparently harmless portable object which is specifically designed and con-constructed to contain explosive material and to detonate when it is disturbed or approached, or

(*b*)   booby-traps which are in any way attached to or associated with:

(i)   internationally recognized protective emblems, signs or signals;

(ii)   sick, wounded or dead persons;

(iii)   burial or cremation sites or graves;

(iv)   medical facilities, medical equipment, medical supplies or medical transportation;

(v)   children's toys or other portable objects or products specially designed for the feeding, health, hygiene, clothing or education of children;

(vi)   food or drink;

(vii)   kitchen utensils or appliances except in military establishments, military locations or military supply depots;

(viii)   objects clearly of a religious nature;

(ix)   historic monuments, works of art or places or worship which constitute the cultural or spiritual heritage of peoples;

(x)   animals or their carcasses.

2.   It is prohibited in all circumstances to use any booby-trap which is designed to cause superfluous injury or unnecessary suffering.

Article 7 — *Recording and publication of the location of minefields, mines and booby-traps*

1.   The parties to a conflict shall record the location of:

(*a*)   all pre-planned minefields laid by them; and

(*b*)   all areas in which they have made large-scale and pre-planned use of booby-traps.

2. The parties shall endeavour to ensure the recording of the location of all other minefields, mines and booby-traps which they have laid or placed in position.

3. All such records shall be retained by the parties who shall:

    (*a*) immediately after the cessation of active hostilities:

        (i) take all necessary and appropriate measures, including the use of such records, to protect civilians from the effects of minefields, mines and booby-traps; and either

        (ii) in cases where the forces of neither party are in the territory of the adverse party, make available to each other and to the Secretary-General of the United Nations all information in their possession concerning the location of minefields, mines and booby-traps in the territory of the adverse party; or

        (iii) once complete withdrawl of the forces of the parties from the territory of the adverse party has taken place, make available to the adverse party and to the Secretary-General of the United Nations all information in their possession concerning the location of minefields, mines and booby-traps in the territory of the adverse party;

    (*b*) when a United Nations force or mission performs functions in any area, make available to the authority mentioned in Article 8 such information as is required by that Article;

    (*c*) whenever possible, by mutual agreement, provide for the release of information concerning the location of minefields, mines and booby-traps, particularly in agreements governing the cessation of hostilities.

Article 8 — Protection of United Nations forces and missions from the effects of minefields, mines and booby-traps

1. When a United Nations force or mission performs functions of peacekeeping, observation or similar functions in any area, each party to the conflict shall, if requested by the head of the United Nations force or mission in that area, as far as it is able:

    (*a*) remove or render harmless all mines or booby-traps in that area;

    (*b*) take such measures as may be necessary to protect the force or mission from the effects of minefields, mines and booby-traps while carrying out its duties; and

    (*c*) make available to the head of the United Nations force or mission in that area, all information in the party's possession concerning the location of minefields, mines and booby-traps in that area.

2. When a United Nations fact-finding mission performs functions in any area, any party to the conflict concerned shall provide protection to that mission except where, because of the size of such mission, it cannot adequately provide such protection. In that case it shall make available to the head of the mission the information in its possession concerning the location of minefields, mines and booby-traps in that area.

Article 9 — *International co-operation in the removal of minefields, mines and booby-traps*

After the cessation of active hostilities, the parties shall endeavour to reach agreement, both among themselves and, where appropriate, with other States and with international organizations, on the provision of information and technical and material assistance — including, in appropriate circumstances, joint operations — necessary to remove or otherwise render ineffective minefields, mines and booby-traps placed in position during the conflict.

[Technical annex omitted]

* * *

Protocol on Prohibitions or Restrictions on the Use of Incendiary Weapons (Protocol III)

Article 1 — *Definitions*

For the purpose of this Protocol:

1. 'Incendiary weapon' means any weapon or munition which is primarily designed to set fire to objects or to cause burn injury to persons through the action of flame, heat, or a combination thereof, produced by a chemical reaction of a substance delivered on the target.

> (*a*) Incendiary weapons can take the form of, for example, flame throwers, fougasses, shells, rockets, grenades, mines, bombs and other containers of incendiary substances.
>
> (*b*) Incendiary weapons do not include:
>
> > (i) Munitions which may have incidental incendiary effects, such as illuminants, tracers, smoke or signalling systems;

(ii) Munitions designed to combine penetration, blast or fragmentation effects with an additional incendiary effect, such as armour-piercing projectiles, fragmentation shells, explosive bombs and similar combined-effects munitions in which the incendiary effect is not specifically designed to cause burn injury to persons, but to be used against military objectives, such as armoured vehicles, aircraft and installations or facilities.

2. 'Concentration of civilians' means any concentration of civilians, be it permanent or temporary, such as in inhabited parts of cities, or inhabited towns or villages, or as in camps or columns of refugees or evacuees, or groups of nomads.

3. 'Military objective' means, so far as objects are concerned, any object which by its nature, location, purpose or use makes an effective contribution to military action and whose total or partial destruction, capture or neutralization, in the circumstances ruling at the time, offers a definite military advantage.

4. 'Civilian objects' are all objects which are not military objectives as defined in paragraph 3.

5. 'Feasible precautions' are those precautions which are practicable or practically possible taking into account all circumstances ruling at the time, including humanitarian and military considerations.

Article 2 — Protection of civilians and civilian objects

1. It is prohibited in all circumstances to make the civilian population as such, individual civilians or civilian objects the object of attack by incendiary weapons.

2. It is prohibited in all circumstances to make any military objective located within a concentration of civilians the object of attack by air-delivered incendiary weapons.

3. It is further prohibited to make any military objective located within a concentration of civilians the object of attack by means of incendiary weapons other than air-delivered incendiary weapons, except when such military objective is clearly separated from the concentration of civilians and all feasible precautions are taken with a view to limiting the incendiary effects to the military objective and to avoiding, and in any event to minimizing, incidental loss of civilian life, injury to civilians and damage to civilian objects.

4. It is prohibited to make forests or other kinds of plant cover the object of attack by incendiary weapons except when such natural elements are used to cover, conceal or camouflage combatants or other military objectives, or are themselves military objectives.

CONCLUDING NOTES

Note on Entry into Force for States Parties

In accordance with Article 5, the Convention will enter into force six months after the date of deposit of the twentieth ratification or accession; and for each state ratifying or acceding thereafter, it will enter into force six months after the deposit of the relevant instrument.

Each of the Protocols will enter into force six months after the date by which twenty states have consented to be bound to the particular Protocol; and for each state consenting to be bound to the particular Protocol thereafter, it will enter into force six months after the date of notification.

Select Bibliography on the Laws of War

This brief list is indicative rather than comprehensive in character, and does not contain all the works mentioned in this book. It is confined to the modern laws of war in the period since 1856; to works in the English language, or containing substantial materials in English; and primarily to general works, rather than those dealing with particular conflicts. It is divided into five parts:

1. Collections of the Laws of War;
2. Records of Conferences;
3. Reports of Cases;
4. Journals and Annuals;
5. Works.

The reader seeking a more complete bibliography is referred particularly to the *General Bibliography of International Humanitarian Law*, compiled under the direction of Dr Jiri Toman and being published in 1981 jointly by the International Committee of the Red Cross and the Institut Henry-Dunant, Geneva.

1. COLLECTIONS OF THE LAWS OF WAR

This part does not list official sources such as treaty series, many of which have been set forth at the end of the prefatory notes to each individual document.

Deltenre, Marcel, *Recueil Général des Lois et Coutumes de la Guerre — terrestre, maritime, sous-marine et aérienne — d'après les Actes élaborés par les Conférences Internationales depuis 1856*, Editions Ferd. Wellens-Pay, Brussels, 1943. Contains texts in four langagues: French, Dutch, German, and English.

Friedman, Leon (ed.), *The Laws of War: A Documentary History*, 2 vols., Random House, New York, [1972]. Contains documents without information on sources, on entry into force, or on ratifications, accessions, etc.

Schindler, Dietrich, and Toman, Jiri (eds.), *The Laws of Armed Conflicts: A Collection of Conventions, Resolutions and Other Documents*, Sijthoff, Leyden, 1973. A comprehensive collection, with over 800 pages of materials. Revised and completed edition published by Sijthoff & Noordhoff, 1981.

Scott, James Brown (ed.), *The Hague Conventions and Declarations of 1899 and 1907*, 3rd edn., Oxford University Press, New York, 1918. There are also editions of this book in the French and Spanish languages.

LEVIE, Howard

2. RECORDS OF CONFERENCES

The following contain records of some of the major conferences at which some of the international agreements contained in this volume were concluded.

Final Record of the Diplomatic Conference of Geneva of 1949, 3 vols., Federal Political Department, Berne, n.d.

Official Records of the Diplomatic Conference on the Reaffirmation and Development of International Humanitarian Law Applicable in Armed

Conflicts, Geneva (1974–1977), 17 vols., Federal Political Department, Berne, 1978.

The Proceedings of the Hague Peace Conferences: Translation of the Official Texts, ed. James Brown Scott, 4 vols. plus index vol., Oxford University Press, New York, 1920-1.

Records of the Conference Convened by the United Nations Educational, Scientific and Cultural Organization held at The Hague from 21 April to 14 May 1954, Government of the Netherlands, The Hague, 1961.

3. REPORTS OF CASES

This part lists only a general digest of cases since 1919; and reports of some trials following the Second World War. Many other cases, including some before 1919, are referred to in works listed in the final part.

Annual Digest and Reports of Public International Law Cases (vols. 1–16 covering the years 1919–49); later entitled *International Law Reports* (vols. 17– covering the years 1950-). Early volumes published by Longmans Green, London, and subsequent volumes by Butterworths, London. See Part XI, 'War and Neutrality', of each volume.

International Military Tribunal for the Far East: Judgment, duplicated, Tokyo, November 1948.

The Trial of German Major War Criminals: Proceedings of the International Military Tribunal Sitting at Nuremberg Germany, 23 vols., HMSO, London, 1946-51.

Trial of the Major War Criminals before the International Military Tribunal, Nuremberg, 14 November 1945 - 1 October 1946, 42 vols., IMT Secretariat, Nuremberg, 1947-9.

Trials of War Criminals Before the Nuernberg Military Tribunals Under Control Council Law No. 10, Nuernberg October 1946 - April 1949, 15 vols., US Government Printing Office, Washington, D.C., [1949–53]. The record of those cases which were dealt with by US Military Tribunals at Nuremberg. They are quite separate from the trial of major war criminals by the International Military Tribunal.

United Nations War Crimes Commission: Law Reports of Trials of War Criminals, 15 vols., HMSO for UNWCC, London, 1947-9. Accounts of proceedings before Allied courts against persons accused of committing war crimes in the Second World War, apart from the major war criminals tried by the Nuremburg and Tokyo International Military Tribunals.

4. JOURNALS AND ANNUALS

Articles in various law journals and annuals frequently contain the most detailed treatment of particular aspects of the laws of war. Rather than listing such articles at length, this part contains the titles of some of the main journals and annuals of international law in which such articles in the English language may be found.

American Journal of International Law
Annuaire de l'Institut de Droit International
British Year Book of International Law

Canadian Yearbook of International Law
Columbia Journal of Transnational Law
Harvard International Law Journal
Indian Journal of International Law
International and Comparative Law Quarterly
International Lawyer
International Review of the Red Cross
Israel Yearbook on Human Rights
Military Law Review
Netherlands Yearbook of International Law
New York University Journal of International Law and Politics
Nordisk Tidsskrift for International Ret
Proceedings of the American Society of International Law
Recueil des Cours: Collected Courses of the Hague Academy of International Law
Revue de Droit Pénal Militaire et de Droit de la Guerre
US Naval War College International Law Studies
Virginia Journal of International Law

5. WORKS

This part contains a selection of some of the major works on the laws of war, including some military manuals.

Bailey, Sydney, *Prohibitions and Restraints in War*, Oxford University Press, London, 1972.

Bassiouni, M. Cherif, and Nanda, Ved P. (eds.), *A Treatise on International Criminal Law*, 2 vols., Charles C. Thomas, Springfield, Illinois, [1973].

Benton, Wilbourn E., and Grimm, Georg (eds.), *Nuremberg: German Views of the War Trials*, Southern Methodist University Press, Dallas, Texas, 1955.

Best, Geoffrey, *Humanity in Warfare: The Modern History of the International Law of Armed Conflicts*, Weidenfeld and Nicolson, London, 1980.

Bond, James E., *The Rules of Riot: Internal Conflict and the Law of War*, Princeton University Press, Princeton, New Jersey, [1974].

Bordwell, Percy, *The Law of War Between Belligerents: A History and Commentary*, Callaghan, Chicago, Illinois, 1908.

Bowett, Derek W., *United Nations Forces: A Legal Study of United Nations Practice*, Stevens, London, 1964.

Cassese, Antonio (ed.), *The New Humanitarian Law of Armed Conflict*, 2 vols., Editoriale Scientifica, Naples, [1979-80].

Castrén, Erik, *Civil War*, Suomalainen Tiedeakatemia, Helsinki, 1966.

Castrén, Erik, *The Present Law of War and Neutrality*, Suomalaisen Tiedeakatemian Toimituksia, Helsinki, 1954.

Cohen, Jerome, and Chiu, Hungdah (eds.), *People's China and International Law: A Documentary Study*, 2 vols., Princeton University Press, Princeton, New Jersey, [1974]. See chapters 43-5 on legal regulation of conflict, prisoners of war, and war criminals.

Colombos, C. John, *The International Law of the Sea*, 6th rev. edn., Longmans, London, 1967. See Part II on war.

Davis, Calvin De Armond, *The United States and the Second Hague Peace Conference: American Diplomacy and International Organization 1899-1914*, Duke University Press, Durham, N. Carolina, 1975.

Delessert, Christiane Shields, *Release and Repatriation of Prisoners of War at the End of Active Hostilities: A Study of Article 118, Paragraph 1 of the Third Geneva Convention Relative to the Treatment of Prisoners of War*, Schulthess Polygraphischer Verlag, Zurich, [1977].

Dinstein, Yoram, *The Defence of 'Obedience to Superior Orders' in International Law*, Sijthoff, Leyden, 1965.

Draper, G. I. A. D., *The Red Cross Conventions*, Stevens, London, 1958.

Feilchenfeld, Ernst H., *The International Economic Law of Belligerent Occupation*, Carnegie Endowment for International Peace, Washington, D.C., 1942.

Fessler, E. Anthony, *Directed-Energy Weapons: A Juridical Analysis*, Praeger, New York, 1979.

Forsythe, David P., *Humanitarian Politics: The International Committee of the Red Cross*, Johns Hopkins University Press, Baltimore, Maryland, 1977.

Garner, James Wilford, *International Law and the World War*, 2 vols., Longmans Green, London, 1920.

Glahn, Gerhard von, *Law Among Nations: An Introduction to Public International Law*, 3rd edn., Macmillan, New York, 1976. See Part VI, 'War'.

Glahn, Gerhard von, *The Occupation of Enemy Territory: A Commentary on the Law and Practice of Belligerent Occupation*, University of Minnesota Press, Minneapolis, [1957].

Graber, Doris Appel, *The Development of the Law of Belligerent Occupation 1863–1914: A Historical Survey*, Columbia University Press, New York, 1949.

Green, L. C., *Superior Orders in National and International Law*, Sijthoff, Leyden, 1976.

Greenspan, Morris, *The Modern Law of Land Warfare*, University of California Press, Berkeley, 1959.

Hall, William Edward, *A Treatise on International Law*, 8th edn., edited by A. Pearce Higgins, Clarendon Press, Oxford, 1924. See Parts III and IV on war and neutrality.

Howard, Michael (ed.), *Restraints on War: Studies in the Limitation of Armed Conflict*, Oxford University Press, Oxford, 1979.

Jessup, P. C., Deak, F., Philips, W. A., Reede, A. H., and Turlington, E., *Neutrality: Its History, Economics and Law*, 4 vols., Columbia University Press, New York, 1935–6.

Kalshoven, Frits, *Belligerent Reprisals*, Sijthoff, Leyden, 1971.

Kalshoven, Frits, *The Law of Warfare: A Summary of its Recent History and Trends in Development*, Sijthoff, Leyden, 1973.

Karsten, Peter, *Law, Soldiers, and Combat*, Greenwood Press, Westport, Connecticut, 1978.

Keijer, Nico, *Military Obedience*, Sijthoff and Noordhoff, Alphen aan den Rijn, 1978.

Kossoy, Edward, *Living with Guerrilla: Guerrilla as a Legal Problem and a Political Fact*, Droz, Geneva, 1976.

Kotzsch, Lothar, *The Concept of War in Contemporary History and International Law*, Droz, Geneva, 1956.

Kozhevnikov, F. I. (ed.), *International Law: A Textbook for Use in Law Schools*, trans. Dennis Ogden, Foreign Languages Publishing House, Moscow, [1961]. See Chapter X, 'Laws and Customs of War'.

Levie, Howard S., *Prisoners of War in International Armed Conflict*, US Naval War College International Law Studies vol. 59, Naval War College Press, Newport, Rhode Island, [1978].

McDougal, Myres S., and Feliciano, Florentino P., *Law and Minimum World Public Order: The Legal Regulation of International Coercion*, Yale University Press, New Haven, Connecticut, 1961.

Miller, Richard I. (ed.), *The Law of War*, D.C. Heath, Lexington, Mass., [1975].

Moore, John Norton (ed.), *Law and Civil War in the Modern World*, Johns Hopkins University Press, Baltimore, Maryland, [1974].

Oglesby, Roscoe Ralph, *Internal War and the Search for Normative Order*, Martinus Nijhoff, The Hague, 1971.

Ogley, Roderick, *The Theory and Practice of Neutrality in the Twentieth Century*, Routledge and Kegan Paul, London, 1970.

Oppenheim, L., *International Law: A Treatise*, vol. 2, *Disputes, War and Neutrality*, 7th edn., edited by H. Lauterpacht, Longmans Green, London, 1952.

Ørvik, Nils, *The Decline of Neutrality 1914-1941: with special reference to the United States and the Northern Neutrals*, 2nd edn., Frank Cass, London, 1971.

Pictet, Jean S. (ed.), *The Geneva Conventions of 12 August 1949: Commentary*, 4 vols., International Committee of the Red Cross, Geneva, 1952-60.

Pictet, Jean S., *Humanitarian Law and the Protection of War Victims*, Sijthoff, Leyden, 1975.

Piggott, Francis, *The Declaration of Paris 1856*, University of London Press, London, 1919.

Roberts, Adam, *Occupation, Resistance and Law: International Law on Military Occupations and on Resistance (both Guerrilla and Non-violent)*, Oxford University Press, forthcoming.

Rosas, Allan, *The Legal Status of Prisoners of War: A Study in International Humanitarian Law Applicable in Armed Conflicts*, Suomalainen Tiedeakatemia, Helsinki, 1976.

Schwarzenberger, Georg, *International Law as Applied by International Courts and Tribunals*, vol. 2, *The Law of Armed Conflict*, Stevens, London, 1968.

Schwarzenberger, Georg, *The Legality of Nuclear Weapons*, Stevens, London, 1958.

Seyersted, F., *United Nations Forces in the Law of Peace and War*, Sijthoff, Leyden, 1966.

Singh, Nagendra, *Nuclear Weapons and International Law*, Stevens, London, 1959.

Smith, Bradley F., *Reaching Judgment at Nuremberg*, Andre Deutsch, London, 1977.

Spaight, J. M., *Air Power and War Rights*, 3rd edn., Longmans Green, London, 1947.

Stockholm International Peace Research Institute, *The Law of War and Dubious Weapons*, Almqvist and Wiksell, Stockholm, [1976].

Stockholm International Peace Research Institute, *The Problem of Chemical and Biological Warfare*, vol. III, *CBW and the Law of War*, Almqvist and Wiksell, Stockholm, [1973].

Stone, Julius, *Legal Controls of International Conflict: A Treatise on the Dynamics of Disputes- and War-Law*, 2nd edn., Stevens, London, 1959.

Thomas, Ann Van Wynen, and Thomas, A. J., *Legal Limits on the Use of Chemical and Biological Weapons*, Southern Methodist University Press, Dallas, Texas, [1970].

Tucker, Robert W., *The Law of War and Neutrality at Sea*, US Naval War College International Law Studies 1955, US Government Printing Office, Washington, D.C., 1957.

United Kingdom War Office, *Manual of Military Law*, Part III, *The Law of War on Land*, HMSO, London, 1958. Currently being revised. The intention is to replace it with a tri-service manual on the law of armed conflict.

United Nations War Crimes Commission, *History of the United Nations War Crimes Commission and the Development of the Laws of War*, HMSO for UNWCC, London, 1948.

United States, Department of the Air Force, Judge Advocate General Activities, *International Law: The Conduct of Armed Conflict and Air Operations*, AF Pamphlet 110–31, Washington, D.C., 19 November 1976.

United States, Department of the Army, *The Law of Land Warfare*, Field Manual No. 27–10, Washington, D.C., 18 July 1956. Currently being revised.

United States, Department of the Navy, Chief of Naval Operations, *Law of Naval Warfare*, NWIP 10–2, Washington, D.C., July 1959.

Verzijl, J. H. W., *International Law in Historical Perspective*, vol. IX, *The Laws of War*, Sijthoff and Noordhoff, Alphen aan den Rijn, 1978.

Walzer, Michael, *Just and Unjust Wars: A Moral Argument with Historical Illustrations*, Allen Lane, London, 1978.

Whiteman, Marjorie M. (ed.), *Digest of International Law*, vols. 10 and 11, US Government Printing Office, Washington, D.C., 1968.

Williams, Sharon A., *The International and National Protection of Movable Cultural Property: A Comparative Study*, Oceana, Dobbs Ferry, N.Y., 1978.

Woetzel, Robert K., *The Nuremberg Trials in International Law, with a Postlude on the Eichmann Case*, Stevens, London, 1962.

Index

This index refers mainly to international agreements; organizations; major subject headings of the laws of war; and particular wars.

It does not list titles of conferences; states adhering to agreements; names of individuals; nor does it refer to the bibliography.

A detailed breakdown by subject headings, dealing only with the 1949 Geneva Conventions, is Jiri Toman, *Index of the Geneva Conventions for the Protection of War Victims of 12 August 1949*, Sijthoff, Leyden, 1973.

Geneva Conventions, 15; (I), 174, 175, 180; (II), 197, 198; (III), 220–1, 237, 244–8 *pass.*, 265–7 *pass.*; (IV), 276–9 *pass.*, 283, 292, 298, 305–11 *pass.*, 321–2
functions of, in international armed conflicts, as provided for in 1977 Geneva Protocol I, 392–3, 407, 434, 436, 444
functions of, in non-international armed conflicts, 172, 195, 217, 273
role in preparing texts, conferences, etc., 2n., 8, 169–71, 193, 215, 271, 387, 447–8, 457, 465, 467
and UN forces, 371–2

Identity cards, certificates, discs etc.
of children under twelve, 281
of civil defence personnel, 426–7
of journalists etc., 50, 218, 435
of personnel protecting cultural property, 362
of persons liable to become prisoners of war, 223
of religious and medical personnel and agents of relief societies, 51, 181, 186, 207–8, 399
of wounded, sick, shipwrecked, or dead persons, 177–8, 201–2
See also Emblems

Incendiary weapons, 29–31, 125, 467–8, 480–1

Indiscriminate attacks, wanton destruction, 122, 126, 155, 389, 415–6, 437, 466, 476–7

Individuals, application of laws of war to, 10–12, 154, 159, 222, 283, 439
See also Repression of breaches; War crimes

Information bureaux
re civilians, 289, 310–11, 318, 319–21
re prisoners of war, 50–1, 177, 178, 201, 244, 245, 262, 264–5
See also Central Information Agency; Central Prisoners of War Agency; Central Tracing Agency; Deaths; Missing persons

Inspection of medical aircraft, 280, 404–6
See also Medical transport; Visit and search

Institute of International Law, 8, 93, 121, 371, 372

Instruction, military and civil, in laws of war, 188, 209–10, 267, 322, 342–3, 349, 374, 436–7, 471

Intelligence data, gathering and transmission of, 125, 403, 410
See also Spies

International Court of Justice, 157, 160, 165–7, 355, 358
International Covenant on Civil and Political Rights (1966), 18, 388
International Fact-Finding Commission, 440–2
declarations *re*, 461
International Institute of Humanitarian Law, 8
International Law Association, 8
International Law Commission, 9, 154, 157, 334
International Military Tribunals
at Nuremberg, 6, 9, 11–12, 18–19, 44, 148, 153–6, 331–7 *pass.*, 339
at Tokyo, 6, 11–12, 153
Internment, 218–19, 396
of civilians, 102, 286–7, 294, 298–322, 334, 431–3
by a neutral power, 64, 65, 131, 173, 185, 196, 219, 258–9, 400, 406
in non-international armed conflicts, 450–4
of prisoners of war, 49, 51, 218–19, 225–35, 266
See also Prisoners of war

Journalists, war correspondents, 50, 176, 199, 218, 435
Judicial proceedings, 189, 210, 274, 323, 431–2, 439, 466
and internees, 313
in non-international armed conflicts, 172, 195, 217, 273, 453–4
in occupied territory, 295–7
and prisoners of war, 249–50, 254–8, 268
See also Repression of breaches

Kellogg-Briand Pact (1928), 14, 18, 61
Korean War (1950–3), 216, 371–2

Land war, 29–69, 137–45, 153–92, 215–481
See also Bombardment; Civilians; Combatant status; Emblems; Gas; Medical units; Military objectives; Mines; Occupation; Wounded and sick; etc.
League of Nations, 8–9, 122, 137
Covenant (1919), 18, 61
League of Red Cross Societies, 436, 465
See also ICRC; National Red Cross Societies
Legal advisers in armed forces, 436
See also Instruction, military and civil
Levée en masse, 48, 176, 200, 218
Lieber Code (1863), 7